*Beyond Patriotic Phobias*

# *Beyond Patriotic Phobias*

CONNECTIONS, COOPERATION, AND SOLIDARITY
IN THE PERUVIAN-CHILEAN PACIFIC WORLD

*Joshua Savala*

UNIVERSITY OF CALIFORNIA PRESS

University of California Press
Oakland, California

© 2022 by Joshua Savala

Library of Congress Cataloging-in-Publication Data

Names: Savala, Joshua, 1984– author.
Title: Beyond patriotic phobias : connections, cooperation, and solidarity in the Peruvian-Chilean Pacific world / Joshua Savala.
Description: Oakland, California : University of California Press, [2022] | Includes bibliographical references and index.
Identifiers: LCCN 2021061566 (print) | LCCN 2021061567 (ebook) | ISBN 9780520385887 (cloth) | ISBN 9780520385894 (paperback) | ISBN 9780520385917 (epub)
Subjects: LCSH: Borderlands—Social aspects—Peru. | Borderlands—Social aspects—Chile. | War of the Pacific, 1879–1884. | BISAC: HISTORY / Latin America / South America | HISTORY / General
Classification: LCC JC323 .S29 2022 (print) | LCC JC323 (ebook) | DDC 320.12—dc23/eng/20220213
LC record available at https://lccn.loc.gov/2021061566
LC ebook record available at https://lccn.loc.gov/2021061567

31  30  29  28  27  26  25  24  23  22
10  9  8  7  6  5  4  3  2  1

*To my grandparents,
Sylvia Sanchez, Robert Gilbert Sanchez,
Jovita Savala, and Amado Savala*

CONTENTS

List of Illustrations   ix
Acknowledgments   xi

Introduction   1

1 · A South American Pacific   16

2 · Gender and Sexuality in the Pacific   40

3 · Transnational Cholera   59

4 · Comparisons and Connections in Pacific Anarchism   86

5 · Pacific Policing   111

Epilogue: Of Parallels   137

Notes   145
Bibliography   201
Index   225

ILLUSTRATIONS

TABLES

1. Workers Picked up in Callao by the *Amazonas*, 1863   *19*
2. Workers Picked up in Valparaíso and Iquique by the *Amazonas*, 1863   *20*
3. Origins of Peruvians Picked up in Callao by the *Amazonas*, 1863   *20*
4. Foreigners in Callao, 1905 and 1920   *22*
5. Origin of Peruvians in Callao, 1905 and 1920   *23*

FIGURES

1. Patente de sanidad for the British steamship *Peru*, 27 April 1906   *64*
2. Patente de sanidad for the British steamship *Peru*, 16 May 1906   *65*
3. Portrait of David Matto, 1888   *73*
4. Spirillum *Cholerae Asiáticae* in hard gelatin, at a magnification of 500, after forty-eight hours at an average room temperature of 26°C   *79*
5. Mollendo, Peru, date unknown   *89*
6. *La Voz del Mar* (Valparaíso, Chile) masthead, 1st half of November 1924   *105*
7. *La Voz del Mar* (Valparaíso, Chile) masthead, 1 May 1926   *105*
8. Profiles of the nose   *119*

9. Measurements of the head  *119*
10. Tattoos on a prisoner  *125*
11. General view of Valparaíso, Chile, date unknown  *127*
12. Lima Police filiación form, based on the form created in Callao  *129*

ACKNOWLEDGMENTS

When I finally found a home in history after a brief stint in chemical engineering during my time as an undergraduate, I used to pick up books and immediately flip to the endnotes and the acknowledgments sections. The endnotes showed me some of the material the author had used in the book. And the acknowledgments helped me get a sense of the people who had influenced the author and the book. I did not know back then that I would be in a place to write the acknowledgments to my own book, but now that the time has come, it is humbling to run through the number of people, institutions, and financial funders who have all played a part in this process.

When I was an undergraduate at the University of California, Davis, Chuck Walker welcomed me to the world of Latin American history. Chuck sparked my interest in disasters (which later became the inspiration for an MA thesis and my first journal article), encouraged my desire to study abroad, taught me how to do research, and spoke to my worried mother when I forgot to call her after arriving in Cuzco. He has also spent entirely too much time talking to me about graduate school and looking out for me in multiple ways. A number of other people at UC Davis read my rambling papers and were willing to continue chatting about history and politics outside of the classroom, including Louis Segal, Omnia El Shakry, Sunaina Maira, Neil Larsen, and Vera Candiani. While at Davis I also had the good fortune to take Spanish with Claudia Darrigrandi, who tried her best to bring me up to speed on Chilean Spanish. Claudia also kindly let me stay with her years later as I conducted research in Santiago during my MA program, helped me with plenty of things in Santiago at various times, and is a wonderful friend.

At Tufts University I had the pleasure of working with Peter Winn. Much of what I know about Chile, and about labor and working-class history, is a direct result of those late-night seminars with Peter and Romina Akemi Green Rioja. Beginning and finishing the MA with Romina as a cohort member, intellectual interlocutor, and political partner made Tufts all the more enjoyable. Kris Manjapra taught me much about South Asia, urban history, spatial theory and history, and comparative analysis. Kris also brought compassion to the field. Many thanks. David Ekbladh, too, opened up new avenues of research.

While applying to PhD programs, I wrote to Ray Craib about the possibility of studying with him at Cornell. We scheduled a phone call, and I came prepared with a long list of questions; Ray must have thought to himself: "What in the world did I get myself into here?" Ryan Edwards told me how happy he was to have chosen Cornell to work with Ray. And when he told me, I could not possibly have imagined all that it came with. Ray has read every paper I wrote as a graduate student, given comments on my work that would add up to a book-length treatment, and taught me the field and academic culture, with his own twist, of course. This book owes quite a bit to Ray, and I will forever be thankful. Ernesto Bassi arrived at Cornell the same year as I did and brought with him a joy for history and the oceanic perspective. Readings with Ernesto and his questions have left their mark on my work. Eric Tagliacozzo, similarly, has always asked me comparative and methodological questions throughout this process. Ray, Ernesto, and Eric formed a committee who get along socially and intellectually, and I really could not have asked for a better group. I initially met Paulo Drinot early in my PhD years, and though he joined my committee late in the process, I owe thanks to Paulo for reading and commenting on my work, saving me from my own interpretations, and thinking about me when it came to book reviews. I also want to thank Kyle Harvey, the other Latin Americanist in my cohort. We read one another's work time and time again, discussed books and articles in the numerous classes we took together, and drank a few too many beers on more than one occasion. Kyle is one of the closest and most careful readers I have met over these years, and I am excited for the world to read his work. My cohort at Cornell is also an example of cooperative intellectual environment. When many of us were applying for the same grants, we read and critiqued one another's proposals to make them better; it was never about competition, but rather improving the proposals as a whole. To Nick Bujalski, Osama Sidiqui, Matt Minarchek, Ai Baba, Margaret Moline,

Matts Fidiger, Shiau-Yun Chen, Kaitlin Pontzer, and Jason Kelly, you all proved what a collaborative graduate program could be. A number of other people at Cornell have made my time in Ithaca much better, socially and intellectually, including Ryan Edwards, Max McComb, Al Milian, Jackie Reynoso, Nick Meyers, Daniela Samur, Laura Menchaca, Elena Guzman, Jane Glaubman, Susana Romero Sánchez, Omar Manky, Paulo Marzionna, and Joe Bazler. And a shout out to the folks involved with organizing in Cornell Graduate Students United. We may not have won the union vote, and although some of those meetings were frustrating, I would do it all over again (but in a slightly different form).

I initially arrived at Rollins College as a visiting assistant professor in fall 2019 and have since become an assistant professor. The people at Rollins have offered a welcoming home despite a hurricane threat in my first semester and COVID-19 beginning in the second semester. Claire Strom has gone above and beyond in every way, from looking for housing with me, teaching suggestions, navigating the professorial life, and conversations over a drink or bike rides. Hannah Ewing is probably exhausted after talking with me about teaching. Susan Montgomery purchased new books for the library for my classes, stepped in to do library sessions with my students, and has been a great colleague through LACS.

The research for the dissertation was conducted mostly in Peru and Chile. In the summer of 2013 I wrote to Chuck Walker about archives in Peru, and he immediately put me in touch with José Ragas. José, without having ever met me or even heard of me, talked to me over lunch about archives in Peru and helped me sort through the pedido process at the Archivo General de la Nación in Lima. In later years, José opened his home to me, talked with me about Peruvian and Latin American history, and put me in contact with a number of other people. Paty Palma brought me to the Archivo de la Facultad de Medicina, shared coffee with me, and patiently listened to me as I began to learn about the history of medicine. I am also appreciative of other historians in Lima who made my time there much more enjoyable: Agnes Telamarinera, Mark Dries, Matthew Casey, and Victor Arrambide. Friends like Tilsa Ponce, Omar Manky, and Jacqui Aliaga made life in Lima all the better with movies, food, and, of course, drinks. In Arequipa, Andrea Ocampo showed me around town, took me to my first chichería, and advised me on the archive.

A number of people in Chile made my time in Santiago a wonderful experience. Marianne González Le Saux, Brandi Townsend, Alfonso Salgado,

Javier Puente, Ignacio Mujica Torres, Denisa Jashari, Roberto Velázquez, and Mara Freilich all overlapped with me in the archive, in restaurants and bars, and in the streets. The Taller Team also read the cholera chapter and have formed an active, transnational support network ever since. Jesse Zarley has nerded out with me since we first met in 2014 during a cold lunch break while working at the archive. Tamara Alicia Araya Fuentes and I shared many lunches, dinners, and beers and talked about our research, and I look forward to the day we can continue these conversations in person. Amie Campos, who joined the Taller Team a bit later, and who never overlapped with me in Chile, has been a particularly close friend over the years; we have read one another's work at various stages and enjoyed the bicoastal laughs of It's Always Sunny. I also am thankful to Pablo Whipple for supporting my visit. Marcelo López Campillay and Javier Puente offered comments and suggestions on an earlier draft of chapter 3.

Of course, none of the research could have been done without archivists. At the AGN in Lima, thank you to Diana Vidal Flores and Lucy Valdez; at the Archivo Histórico de Marina in Callao, thanks to Elia Chávez Mejía, Micaela Ascord, Giuliana Reyes Segura, Thania, and William Eduardo Chamorro; and to the archivists at the Archivo de la Facultad de Medicina, Archivo del Ministerio de Relaciones Exteriores in Lima, librarians at the Biblioteca Nacional in Lima, and archivists at the Archivo Regional de Arequipa in Arequipa. In Chile, thank you to José Huenupi H. and Pedro González Cancino at the Archivo Nacional Histórico and to the archivists at the Archivo Nacional de la Administración, Archivo del Ministerio de Relaciones Exteriores, as well as those at the Biblioteca Nacional in Santiago. Archivists at the International Institute of Social History in Amsterdam also made my research visit pleasant and introduced me to Luis Thielemann, who happened to be there at the same time and looking at the same boxes.

I have also had the opportunity to present my research at a number of venues where I received feedback. Thank you to those who participated in and commented on panels at the following conferences: the American Historical Association (2021, 2020, 2018, 2017), the European Social Science History Conference (2018), Stony Brook University Latin American and Caribbean Studies Center Graduate Student Conference (2017), and the Columbia Graduate Student Conference (2014). I also received critiques and suggestions from talks at the Pontificia Universidad Católica del Peru and at the Pontificia Universidad Cátolica de Chile.

Throughout the process of turning the dissertation into a book and finding a publisher, Kate Marshall has been quite helpful. From an initial phone conversation to answer my numerous questions about process, she has worked to make this a reality. Kate also put in the time to find excellent reviewers for the manuscript and worked with me through multiple drafts. Heidi Tinsman and Chuck Walker provided both feedback and support that has helped me to sharpen the analysis. The third reviewer pointed out a few problems with the manuscript, and although this is not the volume they imagined, I hope it is better than what they initially read. The fourth reviewer pushed me to rework the arguments. I have not taken up all of the suggestions by Heidi, Chuck, and the third and fourth reviewers, but the finished product is much improved thanks to your reviews. In conjunction with Kate, Enrique Ochoa-Kaup at UC Press has helped with moving the process along. In addition, Carlos Dimas kindly read chapter 3. Ray Craib assigned the intro and chapter 1 to his History/Geography/Theory class, as well. Over the years a number of friends and colleagues have read and commented on earlier versions of portions of the book at conferences, workshops, and one-on-one meetings. Thank you to Kyle Harvey, Elena Guzman, Emily Hong, Youjin Chung, Denisa Jashari, Brandi Townsend, Joel Stillerman, Paul Gootenberg, Lex Heerma van Voss, Amie Campus, Fernando Galeana Rodriguez, Nick Myers, Kevan Antonio Aguilar, Miguel Costa, Claudia Rosas, Pablo Whipple, and Barbara Weinstein.

My family has been supportive of my academic ambitions for years, even if everything I explained to them about what I was doing when I returned home during breaks often did not make sense. Academia has taken me to places I would never have lived in nor visited, but that has also meant missing years with my family. Both of my grandfathers saw me begin this journey, and neither of them is here now to see the publication of the book. I am forever thankful for the love and encouragement of my family back in the IE.

Funding for the research came from a Walter and Sandra LaFeber grant through the Department of History at Cornell, a Dissertation Proposal Development Fellowship through the Social Science Research Council, a Graduate Research Fellowship through the Institute for the Social Sciences at Cornell, an International Research Travel Grant from the Mario Einaudi Center at Cornelll, a Research Travel Grant from the Graduate School at Cornell, an Ihlder Fellowship from the History Department at Cornell, and a Fulbright Institute of International Education fellowship. Writing was supported through a Provost Diversity Fellowship from Cornell University and a Dissertation Fellowship through the Ford Foundation.

I am sure mistakes remain, and some might question parts of the analysis. As the author, those are my responsibility, not that of the generous people who have accompanied me on this journey.

*Introduction*

IT WAS JANUARY 1881, and Manuel González Prada had locked himself in his home. González Prada had begun to visit Lima more often when the War of the Pacific erupted two years earlier in 1879. Soon thereafter he completely abandoned a life of reading and translating on a hacienda in the Mala valley, moved to Lima, and joined the effort to defend the country against the invading Chilean armed forces. During his youth González Prada spent time in the Chilean port city of Valparaíso in the mid-1850s, so this was by no means his first time engaging with Chileans. Still, the Chilean invasion brought out elements of González Prada's national pride. In 1881 he decided on a way of resisting the Chilean occupying forces: a self-imposed house exile. In the almost two years of his exile, González Prada left his home on only a few occasions. Once he ran into a former classmate from Valparaíso. He refused to acknowledge the classmate. For Luis Alberto Sánchez, the compiler and editor of González Prada's complete works, "from this incident arose González Prada's nationalist and patriotic vocation."[1]

In the years after the War of the Pacific came to a close, González Prada wrote and presented his work to the public in Lima, becoming one of the most influential writers on politics and literature of his generation. The War of the Pacific awoke something in him. He turned to Spain's invasion of the Peruvian coastline in the mid-1860s to help him think through what it meant to be Peruvian. Although the Spanish attack "gave us our own life, renown, and raised the national spirit," many in Peru remained "intellectually dependent" on the legacy of the Spanish literary tradition.[2] For González Prada, this created "the indefinite prolonging of childhood."[3] If the Spanish invasion produced a Peruvian "national spirit," it was one that confronted a different, and perhaps more unified, nation in the War of the

Pacific in the form of Chile. The war revealed both the limitations of the concept of the Peruvian nation and the deep internal hierarchies across the country. While the Chilean military brought with them their "araucanian ferocity" and "instinct of race" to fight against Peruvians, both suggestive of the internal coherence of the Chilean nation, Peruvians confronted the invaders as "a series of individuals attracted by their individual interests."[4] The Chileans arrived with the name of their country in their mouths, only to find Peruvians fighting in the name of a caudillo: local strongmen associated with personal, not national, power and politics.[5]

González Prada's interpretation of the War of the Pacific, and the place of nationalism more broadly, shifted dramatically in the following decades. In the direct aftermath of the war, he recognized the inequalities built into the economic system in Peru. There existed "two patrias" and two classes in Peru: the rich and the poor, owners and the dispossessed.[6] After traveling through Europe, González Prada moved toward an explicitly anarchist political orientation. And he now looked toward Chile with new eyes. Rather than a solidified national body full of "araucanian ferocity," the Mapocho River crossing Santiago, Chile split social classes similar to how the Rímac River did in Lima.[7] Rather than poor soldiers and marines of one country fighting poor soldiers and marines of another, they would do better to turn their guns around, for their "real *enemies* are not in front of them."[8] Instead of a war between states, the real conflict involved internal inequalities and hierarchies. By turning the popular conception of the war around, González Prada linked together nonelites in Peru and Chile, showing nonelites that their "real enemies" might share their national affiliation. This foray into González Prada's life and writings offers a way into thinking about the relationship between Peruvians and Chileans in the late nineteenth and early twentieth centuries. Indeed, it is suggestive of the two central arguments of this book.

From an emphasis on nationalist divisions to envisioning parallels that connected nonelite Peruvians and Chileans, González Prada's political trajectory reveals the possibility of cooperative relationships across the Peru-Chile border. Many people in both countries held onto a nationalist view built in part on antagonism toward the people of the neighboring country during and after the War of the Pacific. Within the scholarship on Peru-Chile relations, this perspective centering national conflict has been a structuring element, a presupposition upon which historical inquiry rests. Yet starting from the premise of conflict necessarily forecloses the idea that cooperative relationships could have existed in the past, or implies that they are not worthy of study. This book, though, begins from the idea that Peruvians and Chileans interacted and thought of each other in many other forms. From everyday interactions at work to transnationally organizing through labor unions, some Peruvians and Chileans created their own relationships that were not bound by the ideological prerogatives of the nation of their birth. That historians and other scholars have viewed Peru-Chile interactions through antagonism is partly a result of perspective and not necessarily how some Peruvians and Chileans lived before and after the War of the Pacific. By not assuming conflict, this book tells the story of people who were unconcerned with the national origins of their coworkers, who collaborated with professionals across the border, or who developed class solidarity regardless of location. The historiographical emphasis on the war and antagonism in the following decades overlooks their lives from the outset.

This reimagining of the Peruvian-Chilean relationship requires an additional, prior step. An underlying argument of this book is that Peruvians and Chileans created what I call a South American Pacific world that allowed for the production of relationships not bound by nationalist divisions. Maritime and port workers, medical professionals, and police in Peru and Chile all relied on the labor and methods of people from across the world. These relationships, moreover, developed in large part through the Pacific Ocean. In calling attention to the South American Pacific, this book uncovers quotidian forms of circulation between Peruvians and Chileans in the nineteenth and early twentieth centuries. By circulation I mean the movement of people, ideas, and diseases, among other things, primarily between Peru and Chile through port cities along the littoral, but also connected to other places across the Pacific. From the nineteenth century onward, these connections increased and created a more linked system than in previous centuries.[9] Even when not directly connected through, for instance, a job site, remarkably similar processes played out in both countries in similar situations. This geographical framework pushes a transnational and oceanic perspective as essential for understanding Peruvian-Chilean relations. While transnational history of Peru-Chile is nothing new, much of the time it has been used as a way of assigning blame in the War of the Pacific. The Peru-Chile relationship also tends to be studied from the contested land border, the Tacna-Arica region. But a transnational and oceanic perspective interested in the construction of the cosmopolitan world created through the Pacific brings into focus people and processes that otherwise would be overlooked. The South American Pacific, then, is the base through which the book builds historical circulation and the possibility of imagining non-conflictual relationships between Peruvians and Chileans in a history so heavily marked by conflict.

By centering circulation and not assuming antagonism, *Beyond Patriotic Phobias* opens new routes of scholarship, offering a more complete vision of the South American Pacific in the nineteenth and early twentieth centuries. Manuel González Prada's story is well known as a literary figure, involved in politics from numerous angles, with connections to the labor movement, and as a director of the National Library; it would be difficult to study Peru and not at least read about him at a minimum. Those involved with the War of the Pacific and its aftermath, too, have received plenty of attention from scholars. But so many more Peruvians and Chileans lived and labored across the decades of the mid-nineteenth and early twentieth centuries than those directly connected with the war. Some worked the ships connecting trade between the two countries, others read with interest the criminological strategies of the police in the neighboring country, and a few followed cholera's travels and the doctors researching how to impede its spread. Many of these stories have not been told; when they have, it has often been as a self-contained history focused on one particular topic, such as the history of cholera. But when brought together under the umbrella of the South American Pacific, their sum shows a new way of conceptualizing Peruvian-Chilean relations, one that emphasizes circulation as a foundation and cooperation as a possibility. And considering how much has been written and spoken about the relationship between Peru and Chile centered on division and conflict, this is a significant reevaluation.

## THE WAR OF THE PACIFIC

The War of the Pacific is indeed a central part of Peruvian-Chilean relations, and it is no coincidence that much of the field has studied it and its aftermath in such depth. Although this book charts a different path, a brief review of the history will help to put into relief the central arguments on circulation and cooperation. With independence from Spain, many former colonies accepted boundaries determined by Spain under the concept of *uti possidetis*, or "as you possess." In the 1820s the desert running from northern Chile through Bolivia's access to the Pacific was not of particular importance for either state, which meant that neither state was interested in defining the exact border. By the mid-nineteenth century, however, the importance of this region changed with the mining of guano and then nitrates. Despite successive negotiations in the midst of a large Chilean migration to southern Bolivia and Peru and one instance in 1861 of Chilean forces occupying the Bolivian port of Mejillones, the governments of Bolivia and Chile could not come to an agreement on the location of the border. Meanwhile, in 1873 the Bolivian government signed a secret military treaty with the Peruvian government. In August 1874 the Bolivian government set the border at the twenty-fourth parallel south, which the Chilean government agreed to as long as the Bolivian government did not raise taxes for twenty-five years. A new government in Bolivia, combined with complaints by Chileans of unfair treatment and a difficult economic scene, resulted in new taxes on Chilean mining; in turn the Chilean military occupied the Bolivian port of Antofagasta on February 14, 1879. Bolivian President Hilarión Daza declared war on Chile less than two weeks later. Although the Peruvian government tried to help mediate to avoid a war, by April the Chilean government had declared war on Bolivia and Peru, and the War of the Pacific had begun.[10]

The War of the Pacific proved to be especially violent, shocking, and important for all countries involved. The Chilean Navy and Army, which had gained experience in military combat during colonization efforts against indigenous people in the Araucanía region of southern Chile, quickly moved north, securing Bolivian and then Peruvian territory. As the Chilean military occupied cities, they pillaged, razed buildings, and raped women. In at least one case they followed advice from above to not take prisoners; in other words, to kill the wounded and those who had surrendered.[11] This style of warfare did not change much when the Chilean military took over Lima after the battles at Chorrillos and Miraflores, south of downtown Lima. The Peruvian military planted mines to help protect Lima, which according to historian William Sater angered the Chilean military and pushed them to continue with their take-no-prisoners approach.[12] Less than sixty years after expelling the Spanish from Lima, limeños found themselves occupied by a foreign power yet again. At the same time, political forces within Peru split along a few lines. In the north, Miguel Iglesias, a general with war experience at Chorrillos, warmed to the idea of signing a treaty with Chile, called the Treaty of Ancón (1883). Another political line followed the path of Andrés Cáceres, a general who fled into the Andes and helped lead a guerrilla insurgency against the Chilean forces. The Treaty of Ancón brought official peace between Peru and Chile, but the resistance led by Cáceres continued beyond the signing of the treaty. The campaign in the Andes was particularly brutal. Chilean soldiers were given the green light to "exterminate" Peruvians involved with the resistance: they inflicted collective punishment on towns, razed churches and towns, and took hostages. Peruvians in the resistance engaged in their share of violence, too, sometimes killing soldiers and then mutilating their bodies.[13]

The Treaty of Ancón and a peace settlement with Bolivia in April 1884 would forever change the South American Pacific. Bolivia lost its access to the sea, becoming one of two landlocked countries in South America. The Treaty of Ancón gave the department of Tarapacá to Chile and temporarily handed over the department of Tacna and the province of Arica as well. The Tacna-Arica portion of the treaty loomed large in the minds of those negotiating it, as well as among the populace of both countries, and would continue to be a bitterly contested issue in the postwar world. Although the treaty laid out a path that required a plebiscite to determine which state would permanently hold the territories, when that vote would take place—at the ten-year mark or at some point after ten years—was less clear. In addition, Chilean efforts to chileanize the region through changes to schooling, nationalist newspapers, and reducing the power of Peruvian priests—not to mention mass violence by patriotic Chileans against Peruvians—made the entire process much more akin to a second war than anything else.[14] Both states signed the Treaty of Lima in 1929, allowing Tacna to return to Peruvian hands and Arica to officially become Chilean. But the Chilean annexation of previously Peruvian territory and the war more broadly remained on the minds of many.

Beyond the physical territory that switched hands after 1884, the war also changed political, economic, and cultural elements within and across Peru and Chile. Many Peruvians began the search to reconstruct the idea of the nation through political writings, speeches, and cultural production in the aftermath of the war, as José Luis Rénique has shown. For Carmen McEvoy, the war changed the character of republicanism in Peru. While occupying Lima, the Chilean forces confiscated, stole, and sent back to Chile thousands of documents, books, statues, and artwork. Some of these pieces made their way to cities across the country to be displayed in plazas; Luis Montero's 4.2-by-6-meter oil painting *Los funerales de Atahualpa*, for instance, was taken all the way to the Chilean senate before being returned to Peru in 1885. Some books remained in Chile well into the twenty-first century; in 2007 the Chilean state returned close to four thousand books to Peru. The war also brought to the fore racist and masculinist ideas of the other: white Chileans had a duty to civilize the racially other Peru, a Peru filled with effeminate men involved in sexually deviant behavior. Some of these ideas already held sway in the minds of people prior to the war; the war simply helped solidify and enact them in a way unimagined before. Economically, the Peruvian state lost its access to valuable nitrates, from which Chile now profited on a global scale. The war also deeply damaged the Peruvian banking system, and "exports bottomed out at a quarter of prewar levels." To this day, "memory jolts of the war" continue to play out in Peru and Chile around issues of Chilean companies operating in Peru, the debates on the origins of the brandy pisco, and the YouTube comments on a Chilean-produced documentary miniseries on the War of the Pacific.[15]

Academics and popular writers have produced libraries' worth of material on the War of the Pacific and its aftermath. Contemporaries of the negotiations over Tacna-Arica complained of the inability to read the vast amount of literature produced on the topic. A writer for the Valparaíso-based *South Pacific Mail* wrote in 1925:

> In the course of forty years, Tacna-Arica literature has accumulated to an unmanageable extent. It is not the kind of question in which the average man takes interest and nobody would deliberately wade through the flood of books, pamphlets, political documents and newspaper articles dealing with it for pleasure. A really complete study of the history of the problem—it began long before the War of Independence and is still "going strong"—would require, in the first place, a competent knowledge of Spanish (including Peruvian, Bolivia and Chilean variants), very considerable geographical and historical information, and an acquaintance with Latin-American mankind that could only be attained by a life adventure spent in the Southern continent.[16]

Although the writer certainly wades into hyperbole, the overall sentiment rings true even for 1925. But perhaps one of the most classic examples of debate centers on the Chilean military's success in their campaign in the Andes when confronting the insurgency. Similar to González Prada's writings directly after the war, historian Heraclio Bonilla has argued that elite class fractures and vast inequalities in Peru meant that those oppressed by elite Peruvians felt no allegiance to Peru as a concept; while some peasants fought against the Chileans, they were just as likely to confront local elite landowners.[17] Responding to Bonilla, historians Florencia Mallon and Nelson Manrique agreed in large part about the inequalities within Andean society and peasant organizing against both Chileans and Peruvian elites.

But they pushed further, suggesting that these moments and actions were connected to a longer history of rural, peasant, and indigenous organizing that proposed its own form of nationalism, one produced locally and that included their hopes and desires.[18]

Despite these differences in opinion, the discussion points to a foundational problem in the literature on the subject: much of the time continual conflict between Peru and Chile is presupposed as the baseline from which to begin. The literature on the War of the Pacific—while adding much to our knowledge of the social history of the war; the political discussions before, during, and after it; and the ins and outs of how both states managed to engage in the war—has largely reproduced an image of Peru and Chile as two states inevitably on a path toward repeated conflict. This body of work also extends this state of conflict beyond the War of the Pacific, stretching from the early nineteenth century to the present. In many of these cases, the War of the Pacific functioned as the central node in making sense of binational relations, with far-reaching consequences for how scholars think of the pre- and postwar eras. Such scholarship, and the memory of the war, seeped deep into the lives of people across Peru, too; one need look no further than José María Arguedas's 1958 novel *Los ríos profundos*, in which schoolchildren in Abancay, a city in the Andes between Cusco and Ayacucho, played "Peruvians versus Chileans," a performance of nationalism in which "the Peruvians always had to win."[19] Recent Chilean fiction also returns to the War of the Pacific as a key marker in national history for both adults and schoolchildren. These accounts critically tell of the ways the War of the Pacific is used to continually teach young people about the "never ending battle with Peru and Bolivia."[20] In a sense, the war has largely determined the relations between the two countries, and in turn how each country is conceptualized before the study even begins.

But there are other ways of writing the connected histories of Peru and Chile. González Prada's critique of the internal hierarchies within Peru and his comparative approach to thinking through these inequalities, for instance, point to a different understanding of the historical relationships between Peruvians and Chileans. In this view differences *within* each country sowed the possibility for oppressed groups to rebel against the elite in their respective countries and, perhaps, forge bonds of solidarity across state lines.[21] Even within some of the literature emphasizing conflict, moments of international cooperation emerge.[22] Union organizing by Chilean, Peruvian, and Bolivian miners during a mining strike in the province of Tarapacá in

1907 is one episode many have pointed to as an example of internationalist solidarity.[23] Scholars today are pointing to the need to see both the differences *and* similarities between the two countries and to write histories with "wider perspectives and more positive directions that do not necessarily negate the past" of war and occupation.[24] This is a project that cannot simply wish away the War of the Pacific, yet it also cannot allow "this past [to] occupy the entire horizon of possibilities for future generations."[25]

Beginnings matter. How a historical project is conceived and where that history begins influence the types of histories produced. By centering the transnational and oceanic circulations between Peru and Chile and not positing conflict as foundational, *Beyond Patriotic Phobias* brings together many histories that help to overturn the traditional narrative on Peruvian-Chilean relations. One might, for instance, read an 1864 letter sent from Chile to Peru in a different light. Written in the midst of the Peruvian and allied South American governments' efforts to fend off the Spanish government's attempt to retake guano islands, the letter's Chilean author offered support in the form of a place to repair the Peruvian *Amazonas* frigate.[26] Given the "sympathies that the Republic of Chile has manifested to Peru," the author wrote, it should not prove difficult to speed up the repair process in Valparaíso. Although the Peruvian state did not take up the offer, the letter reveals an attempt to show the cooperative relationship between the two states. What makes this exchange even more significant is the author of the letter, one Patricio Lynch.[27] Lynch had just rejoined the Chilean Navy, having worked in the British Royal Navy during the Opium Wars and later with the Chilean Navy up to 1851. After composing the 1864 letter, he became the maritime governor of Valparaíso in 1867. And most important, Lynch would become the commander in chief of the occupation of Peru in the middle of the War of the Pacific.[28] Or we could call attention to a 1922 letter from the Santiago branch of the Industrial Workers of the World (IWW) directed to the workers of Peru. Armando Triviño, the author of the letter and an active member of the IWW, had recently met the young Víctor Raúl Haya de la Torre, a student organizer exiled from Peru and future founding member of the American Popular Revolutionary Alliance (APRA).[29] Triviño and the IWW recognized the crimes of the War of the Pacific. Instead of resorting to nationalist division, his analysis led him to write of the "affinity and sympathy with the workers of all regions and countries, including all of you, [rather] than with the capitalist governments of this world."[30]

*Beyond Patriotic Phobias* brings together stories like those of the younger Lynch and Triviño and Haya de la Torre to build the South American Pacific. Peruvians and Chileans did not always push for transnational collaboration against global capitalism; sometimes they simply labored alongside one another. The War of the Pacific certainly was important for many of them. But it also did not have the same meaning for all, and the necessity of working to live meant that sometimes they shared space on a ship or in the city. Even if the people populating this book represent somewhat atypical experiences, they are the ones who "cut across or swam against" the "fundamental currents" of what a historian might expect to find when studying Peru-Chile relations.[31] To help decenter the war as the central element in this relationship, the book begins in the 1850s and ends in the 1920s, a time frame that runs counter to much of the literature, which either leads up to the war or begins directly afterward. This periodization reveals a certain amount of continuity of circulation and collaboration that undercuts the war as the major historical event of the era.[32]

## OCEANS AND ANARCHISM AS METHOD

Influential in how I approach this book is the recent turn toward oceans as sites of historical study. By centering oceans, scholars are producing new work that crosses terrestrial borders, studies that take into account politically, culturally, socially, and economically intertwined stories. While oceans connect, they also do not necessarily form a united, total unit; as Braudel suggested in reference to the Mediterranean, the sea can simultaneously "share[] a common destiny" and be thought of as a space in which "there is hardly a bay . . . that is not a miniature community, a complex world in itself."[33] These miniature worlds of the bay that are part of the broader sea are connected, for Braudel, "not by the water, but by the peoples of the sea."[34] For this study, circulation between Peruvians and Chileans was facilitated, at least in part, by the Pacific Ocean. The transnational framework provided by a Pacific lens brings into the story the everyday people, ideas, and organisms of this world: maritime and port workers, doctors, cholera, and criminological theories, among others. It also reveals how these people, ideas, and organisms helped produce transnational relationships without losing the specificity of place. If they created a transnational scale, they did so in particular places. The approach, then, is one of multiple, simultaneous scales built by a variety of actors, who traversed both land and oceanic spaces.[35]

The South American Pacific offers a geographic opening up of the study of Peru and Chile as well. Much of the work on Peru and Chile treats both countries as states wherein history occurs on land, and much of the historical narrative in this study does indeed take place on land. But it is also a land that is deeply influenced by the ocean.[36] To take one example, the point in the War of the Pacific wherein the Chilean state turned the tide of the war is generally seen as the Battle of Angamos and the Chilean capturing of the Peruvian ironclad *Huáscar*.[37] The ocean, and in this case the military battles on it, is central to understanding the trajectory of the war. For both Peru and Chile, exporting goods overseas was a key aspect of their economic growth—however unequal across society—in the nineteenth and twentieth centuries.[38] Even more to the point, Peruvian guano, perhaps the key export in the nineteenth century, depended on birds that lived off the fish from the ocean. The ocean also extends the national borders outward into the Pacific, connecting Peruvian and Chilean history to slavers in Oceania, the colonization of Rapa Nui, later called Easter Island, and the many people and ideas that crossed the Pacific in any number of ways. In order to fully think through the oceanic connections and geography of cooperation, the narrative moves from littoral to island, from port to port, and from capital back to sea.

The oceanic perspective also questions some of the emphasis on nationalism so prevalent within Latin American historiography. For years scholars wrestled with the concept of nationalism, of why people in disparate parts of what would become the nation might join together in a common feeling of belonging.[39] Rightfully so, many critiqued earlier studies for an elitist approach to the topic, and some began to put forward nonelites as the producers of a particular kind of nationalism in their own right.[40] Although one might enter the archive and look for and find nonelite nationalism, this search inadvertently reproduces nationalism as a central category of analysis. One of the major challenges to this convention has been the study of anarchism, an ideology that by definition is antagonistic toward the nation-state. Even when anarchists have written or acted in favor of national liberation, they have done so out of an anti-colonial politics and with an eye toward the inherent contradictions within and across nation-states.[41] Oil workers in the Mexican Huasteca, for instance, developed a class consciousness based in part on their placement in a job site hierarchy built on national identity and in part on their differences with labor politics emanating from Mexico

City. As a marker of the end of their anarcho-syndicalist union organizing, they exchanged their red and black flag for the green, white, and red flag of Mexico. "One by one, hundreds of reds pricked their fingers with a pin and let their blood drip onto the white middle stripe of the flag around the eagle and the serpent." It was, as historian Myrna I. Santiago points out, the "death of anarcho-syndicalism in favor of nationalism."[42] Their collective identity formed around a common anarcho-syndicalist idea over and above a nationalist one—indeed, their protest showed that these were two incompatible allegiances.

Methodologically, the anarchist struggle helps with what we might term a suspicion of the nation (and state). Although anarchism is not the subject of every chapter, the entirety of the study takes this suspicion seriously. All of the people in the book labored and lived within national laws, had state police around the corner from them, and were affected by the economic situation in their country. They were not nation- or stateless. But some did find ways of relating to people from other parts of the world that were built on professional contacts, similar interests, or a politics based on destroying the state. In other words, instead of assuming nationalism and the nation—and thus reifying them—the ocean, transnationalism, and anarchism come together to methodologically find other ways of belonging.

## CHAPTER BREAKDOWN

The chapters do not represent a chronological movement: the first two cover the 1850s to 1920s, the third the 1880s, the fourth the 1910s and 1920s, and the fifth the 1870s to the 1920s, and the epilogue jumps to the 2000s. Rather, each chapter focuses on a particular analytical slice with built-in connections to other chapters. These bridges across chapters will hopefully draw the reader into the overlaps between the people, ideas, and ideologies that shaped this period. More broadly, the entirety of the book is connected through two central claims: first, that Peruvians and Chileans created a shared space through circulation; and second, that their co-created space produced the possibility of collaboration and parallel developments.

The first two chapters dive directly into the Pacific Ocean and Peru and Chile. Taking a somewhat synchronic form, I bring together a variety of archival materials, including ministry reports, working-class newspapers, ship rolls, judicial cases, and novels, to explore what it meant to live and labor in the Peruvian and Chilean Pacific from the 1850s to the 1920s. I begin by showing, through the example of the Peruvian *Amazonas*, how on some ships Peruvians and Chileans worked side by side. From there, the chapter pulls Peru and Chile well into the Pacific Ocean and circulation within it and by doing so emphasizes the need to center the Pacific when studying either country. Maritime life required the people to work the ships, and much of the first two chapters focuses on these people, answering the following questions: How did people sign up for ship work? What did laboring on a ship entail? How homosocial was the maritime world? What types of sexual relations helped sustain the people working ships and working ports? Chapter 2 delves into these last two questions, analyzing conceptions of masculinity and leftist militancy, and closes with Chilean state anxieties over supposed Chilean racial degradation as a result of Peruvian-Chilean male-male intercourse. Instances of cooperation or solidarity make occasional appearances in this portion of the book. More central to these two chapters is an analysis of how Peruvians and Chileans circulated and interacted within the Pacific. They were central to the creation of the Peruvian-Chilean Pacific through their life trajectories. They labored and lived in a hierarchical and cosmopolitan world, often in shared spaces. In some cases, strikingly similar projects and policies developed in parallel in Peru and Chile.

While searching in the Rare Manuscript room in the Biblioteca Nacional in Lima, Peru, I ran across a *memoria* written in the Peruvian port of Callao that mentioned the slowing of shipping from Chile due to a cholera outbreak in central Chile. While I was not interested in cholera at the time, the subprefect also wrote that this might have an effect on port and maritime workers because they would, in turn, have less work. As I continued to research in Peru and Chile, I kept this bit of information in mind. After seeing repeated references to the 1880s cholera outbreak in Chile, I decided to pursue the topic in more depth. Chapter 3 is a result of this decision. In this chapter I use the cholera outbreak to argue that the incomplete medical knowledge about this disease triggered a part of state formation in both Chile and Peru in the form of infrastructure and the central state spreading out geographically. Here we also see the states working together through the circulation of cleaning agents, international regulations on shipping, and doctors themselves. In the second half of the chapter I follow the path of David Matto, a doctor originally from Cuzco, who was sent to Chile by the Peruvian state to conduct research alongside Chilean doctors. I argue that through the sharing of equipment and laboratories, Matto and his Chilean counterparts created what I call a "science without a nation," or a transnational scientific community based on research above and beyond nationalist conflicts.

Split into three sections, the fourth chapter jumps from Mollendo, Peru, to Valparaíso, Chile, and back again to Mollendo, covering 1916 to 1928. By moving back and forth, the chapter argues for the need to historically analyze the specifics of each port *and* the transnational connections simultaneously. Although the port of Callao would be the Peruvian analog to Valparaíso in Chile during this time period, the archival trail of connections and solidarity brings the narrative to Mollendo. I begin with the buildup to and resolution of a 1918 strike by port workers in Mollendo, in the process of which workers realized their power as port workers instead of individual craft unions. Meanwhile, back in Valparaíso maritime and port workers had aligned themselves with the newly created branch of the IWW. They organized around local and national issues, while at the same time seeking to create links to maritime and port workers across the world, especially along the Peruvian littoral. The third section discusses these efforts. The chapter closes with a new organizing drive in Mollendo in the 1920s, the relationships built between Peruvians and Chileans, and the Peruvian state's response to these purportedly antipatriotic links.

Police tactics in the attempted suppression of the Mollendo labor movement lead directly into the subject of the fifth chapter: policing. If maritime workers circulated with ships, they also carried along with them, and disseminated to others, ideas that many within both states found to be dangerous. With the international movement of workers, ideas, and common criminals, police in Peru and Chile sought new ways to track these circulations, surveil radical workers, and develop methods of identification and archiving of this information. The chapter examines the discourse around this "población flotante," the specific needs—according to the police—required to control a cosmopolitan port city, and different identification systems—anthropometry and dactyloscopy—used to support their policing efforts. Instead of seeing these systems as competitive or as one replacing the other, I view them as two complementary systems that correspond to two different temporal moments in policing. These new policing techniques, too, meant financing, new material things, and infrastructure, and in turn, a reformulating of the state. And importantly, this reformulation was a direct response to both the Pacific world and increasingly militant maritime and port workers.

The epilogue jumps forward to the 2000s, specifically 2008. In January 2008 the Peruvian government initiated a case at The Hague against the

Chilean government regarding its maritime border. The legal case turned on the 1929 negotiated settlement of the Tacna-Arica dispute, a direct result of the War of the Pacific, and the prolonged plebiscite that was to take place after the war. Instead of recounting a legal history of the case, I use the arguments around the maritime border to show how each national government drew from particular historical discourses to produce a narrative beneficial to its contemporary legal case. To an extent, both state governments relied on nationalist divisions. I juxtapose these discourses with a newspaper article that appeared while the case was being litigated. The article discusses the transnational ties, cooperation, and mutual aid between fishers in the ports of Arica, Chile, and Ilo, Peru. In their ties to the sea across the border and their mutual support, these fishers recall bonds between Peruvians and Chileans that stretch back to the nineteenth century and that form the basis of this book.

ONE

# *A South American Pacific*

FROM THE COLONIAL PERIOD to the nineteenth century, Peru and Chile were part of a globalizing world. Indeed, recent genetic research shows that before the arrival of Europeans in South America, indigenous people in the Americas—probably from what is today northern Peru, Pacific Colombia, and southern Peru and Bolivia—built vessels that transported people and potatoes to the easternmost portion of Oceania.[1] Even for those who did not venture into Oceania, the Pacific played a key part in agricultural production through the use of guano, a fertilizer developed from bird excrement and the fish on which the birds preyed.[2] During the colonial period, cartographers for the early modern Spanish empire produced representations of the Pacific in an effort to prove that the western Pacific belonged to the Spanish realm.[3] With independence from Spain in the early nineteenth century and then the expansion of guano and later nitrate exports, and with the key place of Valparaíso in shipping (especially before the construction of the Suez Canal and the Panama Canal), Peru and Chile became even more connected to the Pacific than before. The Pacific Ocean was a central part of the long history of both Peru and Chile.[4]

This chapter takes as its starting point these connections to the Pacific world. Importantly, it emphasizes the internationalness of the maritime world, from merchant ships to warships. More specifically, it analyzes the Peruvian and Chilean maritime world in the Pacific from the mid-nineteenth to the early twentieth centuries. It shows the cosmopolitan nature of ships and port cities along the South American Pacific littoral. These locations bring out the broad connections built through the maritime world, from the Peruvian Andes to Tahiti, Rapa Nui/Easter Island to Manila, and importantly from the Chilean coast to the Peruvian coast. The cosmopolitan nature of the Pacific means that even when the nationality of all people involved in a scenario is not given, much of the shared experience discussed throughout happened in settings within which they probably interacted through living quarters, labor regimes, and port life. Living and working together need not necessarily result in cooperation all of the time, but it does mean that they had to get along well enough for the continued functioning of a ship or the life and commerce of an urban port like Callao. And even when seemingly separate, similar historical processes occurred in both countries' port cities in more or less the same time period.

The maritime world encompasses numerous aspects. This chapter deals with the quotidian aspects of this world for maritime workers, both at sea and in port. It analyzes the enrollment of workers on ships, reports from foreign diplomats, letters written on board ships, ministerial letters and reports, and the anarchist press to uncover what it meant to work on and around ships. This was a world constructed through contradictions. For some the ocean and work in the maritime industry meant freedom. For Manuel Rojas, a twentieth-century Chilean novelist and anarchist who spent a good portion of his life connected to the maritime world, the sea allowed people to "choose their own destiny" (elegir mi destino), whether that be Panama, Honolulu, or Guayaquil; as opposed to the defined pathways of land, the ocean was "a large path" with "amplitude, solitude, freedom, space, yes, space."[5] On the other hand, many found their way onto ships as unfree laborers alongside contracted workers, both living and breathing under strict hierarchical discipline. These contradictions or paradoxes open up space to examine the complex world within which thousands of people lived, worked, fought, organized, and died.[6]

## SHIP COMPOSITION: MULTINATIONAL CREWS AND THE CASE OF THE *AMAZONAS*

The ships that traversed the various ports of the Pacific flew the flag of only one nation, but their crews were anything but nationally homogenous. The crew of the Peruvian frigate *Amazonas* in the mid-nineteenth century reflects the multinational nature of crews in that era. Built in London from 1850 to 1852 in the Wigram shipyard, the *Amazonas* displaced 1,320 tons, measured 200 feet in length, and carried around 360 crew members.[7] Departing from the Peruvian port of Callao on October 25, 1856, the *Amazonas* began a journey to circumnavigate the world. The trip took the ship across the Pacific ocean to Hong Kong, Calcutta (where some thirty-nine crewmembers died from cholera), Saint Helena Island in the African Atlantic (where they visited the tomb of Bonaparte), London, Rio de Janeiro, Talcahuano (Chile), Arica (Peru), and finally back to Callao on May 28, 1858.[8] In 1863 the *Amazonas* made stops in Valparaíso, Iquique (at this point still a part of Peru), and Callao to recruit maritime workers. Although the records from these stops do not show the entire crew, they do cover a decent amount of the composition of the ship, as 123 new workers joined in Callao and 131 in Valparaíso and Iquique, or 34 and 36 percent, respectively, of the approximately 360 total crew members on the ship. As seen in tables 1 and 2, a plurality of the new crew members in Callao came from Peru: 40 of 123 identified as Peruvian, meaning that over two-thirds of those who boarded in Callao were not Peruvian. In Iquique, a Peruvian port city that would become Chilean after the War of the Pacific, all 11 of the new crew members were foreign born (8 from England, 3 from the United States). The new crew members who were picked up in Valparaíso leaned heavily Chilean (59), followed by British (30), after which the total numbers decline significantly, but the nationalities represented vary from the United States to the Philippines to Germany. The second largest group to board in Callao were Chileans, followed by Filipinos and British, and a mix of Mexicans, Portuguese, and South Asians. The multinational crew of the *Amazonas* of the 1860s meant that people worked across differences of language and national background. Maritime crews must have learned ways of working on a ship with people who may not have spoken their language. The crew most likely learned about other cultures on board, too. Even if some of these Chilean and Peruvian crew members never made a trip away from the South American Pacific littoral, they experienced a part of South and Southeast Asia and Europe through living and working with crew members from these locations. The national origins of those picked up in Callao, Iquique, and Valparaíso also reveals that the South American Pacific strongly leaned toward the Pacific Rim and Europe, without a single mention of a person from the Latin American Atlantic. This was a ship with a multinational crew, but one that pulled from specific places: the Pacific Rim and Europe. Significantly, Peruvians and Chileans worked together in tight quarters on board ships like the *Amazonas*. The cosmopolitan nature of crews remained consistent over time, as well. In a case from 1918, for instance, when the sailboat *San Joaquín* picked up crew members from the Peruvian sailboat *Helvecia* after

TABLE 1  Workers Picked up in Callao by the *Amazonas*, 1863

| Country | Total | Average Age | Marital Status | | |
|---|---|---|---|---|---|
| | | | Single | Married | Widowed |
| Peru | 40[a] | 24.4 | 32 | 8 | 0 |
| Pacific & others[b] | 20[c] | 30.9 | 20 | 0 | 0 |
| Chile | 12[d] | 24.3 | 12 | 0 | 0 |
| Philippines | 9 | 30.3 | 9 | 0 | 0 |
| England | 9[e] | 25.3 | 9 | 0 | 0 |
| Greece | 8 | 28.6 | 8 | 0 | 0 |
| Ecuador | 8 | 22.1 | 8 | 0 | 0 |
| Colombia | 5[f] | 24.0 | 5 | 0 | 0 |
| United States | 7[g] | 31.0 | 7 | 0 | 0 |
| Holland | 4 | 23.3 | 4 | 0 | 0 |
| Spain | 1 | 29.0 | 1 | 0 | 0 |
| | Total: 123 | Overall Average: 26.7 | 115 | 8 | 0 |

SOURCE: Table attached to letter to Sr. General Ministro de Estado en el despacho de Guerra i Marina, Callao, 30 Jan. 1863, AHM, Callao, Peru, Buques, Amazonas, Fragata, Perú, 1863, caja A17, sobre A134, fol. 5, 9–11.

[a] The document lists 39, but the count is 40.
[b] Labeled as "de las islas del Pacífico y otros paises," the category contained Panama (3), Mexico (5), Singapore (1), India (2), Portugal (5), Scotland (2), Ireland (1), and illegible (1).
[c] The document lists 23, but the count is 20, including 1 illegible.
[d] The document lists 11, but the count is 12.
[e] The document lists 8, but the count is 9.
[f] The document lists 6, but the count is 5.
[g] The document lists 6, but the count is 7.

it sank, the workers hailed from Peru, Chile, Russia, Mexico, Costa Rica, Colombia, and Spain.[9]

Differences existed within the same national group of workers, and it may have been the first time some had met a fellow countryman from a specific location. When the *Amazonas* picked up Peruvians in Callao in 1863, the keeper of the ship's manifest noted their origin from within Peru (see table 3). Of the forty Peruvians, ten came from the far northern city of Piura near the port of Paita, with others coming from places such as Islay in the south and Arica in the far south, as well as a few hailing from the Andes (Huancayo, Jauja, Huaráz, and Cusco). This multiregional Peruvian crew on the *Amazonas* was not unique. After a failed rebellion on the steamship *Lerzundi* in 1865, the Peruvian state took note of where the people sentenced to prison or forced work came from, as well as their physical

TABLE 2  Workers Picked up in Valparaíso and Iquique by the *Amazonas*, 1863

|  |  |  | Marital Status | | |
| --- | --- | --- | --- | --- | --- |
| Country | Total | Average Age | Single | Married | Widowed |
| Chile | 59 | 23.2 | 53 | 5 | 1 |
| England | 38 | 28.5 | 31 | 6 | 1 |
| United States | 8 | 27.9 | 7 | 1 | 0 |
| Peru | 7 | 26.1 | 5 | 2 | 0 |
| Germany | 7 | 24.5 | 6 | 1 | 0 |
| Portugal | 3 | 21.0 | 3 | 0 | 0 |
| Philippines | 2 | 23.5 | 2 | 0 | 0 |
| Italy | 2 | 41.0 | 1 | 1 | 0 |
| Austria | 2 | 25.5 | 1 | 1 | 0 |
| Colombia | 1 | 22.0 | 1 | 0 | 0 |
| Mexico | 1 | 21.0 | 1 | 0 | 0 |
| Ecuador | 1 | 25.0 | 1 | 0 | 0 |
|  | Total: 131 | Overall Average: 25.5 | 112 | 17 | 2 |

SOURCE: Table attached to letter to Sr. General Ministro de Estado en el despacho de Guerra i Marina, Callao, 30 Jan. 1863, AHM, Buques, Amazonas, Fragata, Perú, 1863, caja A17, sobre A134, fol. 5–8.

TABLE 3  Origins of Peruvians Picked up in Callao by the *Amazonas*, 1863

| Location in Peru | Total |
| --- | --- |
| Piura | 10 |
| Pasco | 4 |
| Paita | 4 |
| Callao | 4 |
| Lima | 3 |
| Huancayo | 2 |
| Islay | 2 |
| Casma | 2 |
| Tacna | 1 |
| Arica | 1 |
| Chincha | 1 |
| Lambeyeque | 1 |
| Chorrillos | 1 |
| Huaráz | 1 |
| Cusco | 1 |
| Jauja | 1 |
| Huarochiri | 1 |
|  | Total: 40 |

SOURCE: Table attached to letter to Sr. General Ministro de Estado en el despacho de Guerra i Marina, Callao, 30 Jan. 1863, AHM, Buques, Amazonas, Fragata, Perú, 1863, caja A17, sobre A134, fol. 5, 9–11.

appearance and scars. In some cases, the exact location is not clear, as they are listed as being from "Peru." Others, though, were identified as being from Ayacucho, Arequipa, Cuzco, Jauja, Ica, and Huaura. They were also from various racial backgrounds, if we can believe the classifications assigned to them: seven of them are listed as indigenous, two as mestizos, one pardo, one white, one mulato, and one zambo.[10] In other words, these were ships populated by people from around the world, and even when workers came from the same country, their origin within that country varied. In another case, when Peruvian workers, and many others, died or were saved after ships sank in a windstorm in Valparaíso in 1903, the list of birthplaces shows the continuance of the broad geographic range of maritime workers from Peru. Many came from Callao, but others were born in Quisque (in the Andes between the coast and Huancayo), Chiclayo, Piura, Arica, Paita, Andaray, and Chira.[11]

When maritime workers arrived at port, they also stepped into cosmopolitan cities. The port of Callao in the early twentieth century provides such an example. Despite inherent problems with census taking at the time—even the census administrators in 1920 proposed error coefficients ranging from 1 to 6 percent depending on location—censuses do offer some of the only quantitative data on population.[12] Between 1876 and 1920 the port added fewer than 20,000 inhabitants, rising from just under 35,000 to a little under 53,000, with a dip of around 5,500 at the end of the 1890s. According to the 1905 census, of the 33,879 residents of Callao, 3,449, or 10.18 percent, were foreigners. Of the Peruvian population in Callao, women were a slight majority (15,941 to 14,489), while the foreigner population was overwhelmingly male (2,503 to 946). Peruvian residents of white (13,122) and mestizo (13,338) background made up most of the city, with indigenous (5,276), Afro-Peruvian (1,317), Asians (719), and those without data (107) making up the rest.[13] The low percentage of Afro-Peruvians and Africans was a change from earlier periods, when Callao could easily be described as a port of the Black Pacific.[14] Non-Peruvians came from a number of places. Men and women from across the Americas had made their way to Callao, including 354 Chileans and 296 Ecuadorians, the two greatest numbers from the Americas (see table 4). Europeans also found a home in Callao, with the largest numbers made up by Italians (850) and the English (257). Of the 719 Asians counted by the census, 697 were Chinese and 22 Japanese.[15] By 1920 the percentage of foreigners in Callao had dropped slightly from its 1905 level, but there were still 4,032 foreigners in a population of 48,226 (8.36%).

TABLE 4  Foreigners in Callao, 1905 and 1920

| Country | 1905 | 1920 | % Change | Country | 1905 | 1920 | % Change |
|---|---|---|---|---|---|---|---|
| Argentina | 37 | 62 | 67.6 | England | 264 | 280 | 6.1 |
| Barbados | — | 2 | | France | 167 | 111 | −33.5 |
| Bolivia | 34 | 43 | 26.5 | Germany | 143 | 101 | −29.4 |
| Brazil | 4 | 7 | 75.0 | Greece | 22 | 22 | 0.0 |
| Canada | — | 2 | | Holland | 4 | 6 | 50.0 |
| Colombia | 59 | 81 | 37.3 | Hungary | — | 1 | |
| Chile | 354 | 288 | −18.6 | Italy | 850 | 662 | −22.1 |
| Costa Rica | 1 | 11 | 1,000.0 | Norway | — | 54 | |
| Cuba | 10 | 8 | −20.0 | Poland | — | 6 | |
| Ecuador | 296 | 247 | −16.6 | Portugal | 40 | 14 | −65.0 |
| El Salvador | 3 | 3 | 0.0 | Russia | 8 | 19 | 137.5 |
| Guatemala | 1 | 1 | 0.0 | Serbia & Montenegro | — | 8 | |
| Haiti | — | 1 | | | | | |
| Jamaica | 20 | 15 | −25.0 | Spain | 103 | 198 | 92.2 |
| Martinique | — | 2 | | Sweden | 20 | 20 | 0.0 |
| Mexico | 15 | 21 | 40.0 | Switzerland | 12 | 12 | 0.0 |
| Nicaragua | 1 | 4 | 300.0 | Turkey | 2 | 1 | −50.0 |
| Panama | 33 | 34 | 3.1 | Yugoslavia | — | 14 | |
| Paraguay | — | 2 | | | | | |
| Puerto Rico | — | 4 | | Armenia | — | 3 | |
| Uruguay | 3 | 9 | 300.0 | China | 697 | 613 | −12.1 |
| USA | 99 | 160 | 61.6 | India | — | 4 | |
| Venezuela | 4 | 5 | 25.0 | Japan | 22 | 804 | 3,554.5 |
| | | | | Philippines | — | 8 | |
| Austria | 77 | 27 | −64.9 | Syria | — | 5 | |
| Czechoslovakia | — | 6 | | Africa | 3 | — | |
| Denmark | 11 | 12 | 9.9 | Australia | 3 | 7 | 133.3 |

Total for 1905: 3,422

Total for 1920: 4,030

SOURCES: *Censo de la Provincia Constitucional del Callao, 20 de Junio de 1905* (Lima: Imprenta y Librería de San Pedro, 1906), 114–15; and *Resúmenes del Censo de las Provincias de Lima y Callao, levantado el 17 de Diciembre de 1920* (Lima: Imp. Torres Aguirre, 1921), 27–28.

Of those from the Americas, Chileans (288) and Ecuadorians (247) still outweighed their counterparts, as did the British (280) and Italians (662) when it came to Europeans. Between 1905 and 1920, the category of Asian expanded to include Armenia, the Philippines, India, and Syria, and the number of Japanese (804) exceeded the number of Chinese (613). Both the 1905 and 1920 censuses also detail the birthplace of Peruvians in Callao. In both 1905 and 1920 the vast majority of Peruvians were local, from either Callao (14,499 and 23,010) or Lima (7,106 and 9,155) (see table 5). The rest

TABLE 5  Origin of Peruvians in Callao, 1905 and 1920

| Departments | 1905 | 1920 | % Change |
|---|---|---|---|
| Amazonas | 25 | 49 | 96.0 |
| Ancash | 1,652 | 2,231 | 35.0 |
| Apurímac | 35 | 105 | 200.0 |
| Arequipa | 723 | 1,968 | 172.2 |
| Ayacucho | 236 | 426 | 80.5 |
| Cajamarca | 288 | 508 | 76.4 |
| Callao | 14,499 | 23,010 | 58.7 |
| Cuzco | 150 | 257 | 71.3 |
| Huancavelica | 83 | 155 | 86.7 |
| Huánuco | 93 | 206 | 121.5 |
| Ica | 1,135 | 1,675 | 47.6 |
| Junín | 776 | 1,065 | 37.2 |
| Lambayeque | 413 | 628 | 52.0 |
| Libertad | 768 | 1,304 | 69.8 |
| Lima | 7,106 | 9,155 | 28.8 |
| Loreto | 19 | — | — |
| Madre de Dios | — | 3 | — |
| Moquegua | 137 | 294 | 114.6 |
| Piura | 1,107 | 1,373 | 24.0 |
| Puno | 109 | 227 | 108.3 |
| San Martín | — | 26 | — |
| Tacna | 394 | 1,228 | 211.7 |
| Tarapacá | — | 1,371 | — |
| Tumbes | 62 | 175 | 182.3 |
| Born abroad and naturalized | — | 41 | — |
| Unknown* | 642 | 673 | 4.8 |
| Total | 30,452 | 48,153 | |

SOURCES: *Censo de la Provincia Constitucional del Callao, 20 de Junio de 1905* (Lima: Imprenta y Librería de San Pedro, 1906), 116; and *Resúmenes del Censo de las Provincias de Lima y Callao, leventado el 17 de Diciembre de 1920* (Lima: Imp. Torres Aguirre, 1921), 26.

*This category is called "without specification" in 1905 and "ignored" in 1920.

spanned nearly the entirety of Peru and areas in dispute with Chile. Several departments registered numbers exceeding 1,000, such as Ancash, Arequipa, Ica, Piura, Tarapacá, La Libertad, and Junín. Hundreds of residents had been born in Ayacucho, Cajamarca, and Lambayeque, as well. And some came from departments in the Amazon jungle region, such as Amazonas, San Martín, and Madre de Dios.[16] As a whole, more than 15,000 Peruvians in Callao were born outside of Callao and Lima. While these figures might not be completely accurate, they do show both the high number of foreigners living in Callao as well as the large numbers of Peruvians from other parts of the country living and working in the city. In other words, the crews working ships and the people living and laboring in port cities were both international and intranational.

In some cases, despite years of working in multinational crews, maritime workers found it difficult to find work due to their limited language skills. In 1913 the Chilean Ministry of Foreign Relations relayed to Santiago dismaying news on Chilean maritime workers in Europe. While the Chileans had worked alongside people speaking various languages and made it across the Atlantic with them, some ships would not hire them because many could not speak English, French, or German. Ship captains also had to contract for Chilean maritime workers through the Chilean consulate, an added burden many wanted to avoid entirely.[17] Even if they did not speak numerous languages fluently, many workers were able to transcend language limitations. Many on the *Amazonas* in 1863 did not speak Spanish, for instance, yet they did not have any trouble working together in a disciplined and orderly fashion.[18] Some also knew enough of another language to get by, to exchange the information necessary to continue living their daily lives. Ships and ports were, after all, cosmopolitan places. When a vagabond (vagabundo) in a Chilean port heard a marine ask him if he was hungry in English, he understood the question and knew how to respond in English. "A tramp [atorrante] from the port," Rojas wrote in 1929, "could not know English, but one could never be forgiven not knowing enough English to ask for food from one who speaks that language."[19]

## OCEANIA IN LATIN AMERICA

While the nationalities of the crew members who boarded the *Amazonas* along the South American littoral point toward a Pacific Rim world, Oceania (or what is sometimes called the Insular Pacific) played a part in the South American Pacific as well. One of the major ventures into the Pacific during this era was the forced movement of people from Pacific Islands to Peru and back between 1862 and 1864. In the aftermath of the abolition of slavery in Peru in 1854 and the 1856 suspension of the "coolie" trade, some in Peru began to look toward the Pacific Islands as a place to recruit laborers— through liquor, food, false promises, and violence. Sometimes men did volunteer, most likely due to a La Niña event running from 1860 to 1863, resulting in drought, which made the prospects of laboring elsewhere seem like a good option.[20] Some died en route to Peru, many ended up working on sugar estates, and others returned home after facing brutal work conditions. Slavers depopulated islands, like the Tokelaus, of perhaps close to 100 percent of their male inhabitants, who they thought could labor in Peru.[21] Although they arrived in Peru, some of the ships, captains, and crew members involved in this venture of "slaving in paradise" were Chileans or Europeans residing in Chile.[22] Indeed, some ships flying a Peruvian flag began their trip with a Chilean flag. With a Chilean state and media campaign against the slave trade and warnings that any enslaved person stepping foot in Chile or on Chilean ships would gain their freedom, many shipowners transferred their ships to Peruvian owners to continue their slaving missions.[23] Over two decades prior to the official annexation of Rapa Nui/Easter Island by the Chilean state in 1888, Chileans established a relationship of oppression and violence with the indigenous population of the island, a trend that continued for decades.[24]

Slaving in paradise and the annexation of Rapa Nui also created a basis on which people working the maritime circuit from Valparaíso to the island could meet and develop a sense of common interests. Despite an 1890 decree declaring Rapa Nui/Easter Island a legal part of the Gobernación Marítima and of the Intendancy of Valparaíso, in 1897 the authorities on the island still needed extra military force, including a war ship, to show "'National authority' to the people on the island."[25] As late as 1902 the legal jurisdiction over the island was still a topic of discussion for some within the Chilean state.[26] Five months later the Chilean state sent three guardianes to the island. One of them, Manuel Antonio Vega, returned to Valparaíso in 1904 and quickly built links with the local labor movement. Vega arrived with stories of abuses committed against both the indigenous people of the island and Chileans working there, which made clear to him the violence of Chilean control over the island. He even reported these abuses to the press, which in turn caught the attention of the French state since some of these figures came from French colonial possessions. Working-class organizations in the port of Valparaíso organized meetings on the situation in Rapa Nui and wrote a manifesto on the topic, and workers in a few other cities held rallies on the same day as one attended by four hundred people in Valparaíso. They proposed sending a commission made up of members of various working-class organizations and the press to Rapa Nui to investigate the situation, called for the return of land to the indigenous people of the island (though how much and to whom exactly is unclear), and sought to initiate monthly communications with people in Rapa Nui.[27] Although these calls to action did not change the relationship between the Chilean state in South America and Rapa Nui in Oceania, the protests and discourse show the construction of ties between the organized working class and people in Rapa Nui that explicitly recognized Chilean state imposition over Pacific Islanders.

Along with Chilean colonial rule of an island in Oceania came particular ideas of the problems of Rapa Nui and how to solve them. In a 1915 report, the commander and surgeon of the corvette *Jeneral Baquedano* described an indigenous population upset at foreigners taking over their ancestral lands, working for subsistence rather than trade, and women ready to engage in sex work. Including sex in the list of problems drew from a long history of non-Oceanians viewing Oceanian women as open for sexual trade.[28] This situation, in particular subsistence work, reminded the authorities of the indigenous population of southern Chile of decades past, and they hoped that with the Panama Canal, more ships would stop at the island and encourage the inhabitants to produce more than just what was necessary for subsistence.[29] They would, in turn, move from being subsistence laborers to commodity-producing people subject to the market. While the changes to indigenous agriculture in southern Chile might have been an exaggeration, the discursive connection shows one way in which in the decades after an extreme expansion of the Chilean state—the "Wars of Pacification" in the south, the War of the Pacific in the north, and the annexation of Rapa Nui in the west—some Chilean authorities had created a mental geography of Chile that directly linked Rapa Nui with lands south of the BioBío River, the historical marker of the beginning of indigenous territory in Chile.

The Pacific links expanded farther than Rapa Nui/Easter Island, too. In the early twentieth century some Tahitians had migrated to Rapa Nui/Easter Island. Verónica Mahute, Matias Otu, and Vicente Pont professed their desire to return to Tahiti, where they claimed to own property. They were receiving low wages for their labor harvesting sweet potatoes and bananas, raising cows for milk, and in carpentry; had either experienced abuse or seen others being abused by the Chilean authorities; and did not see a future for themselves on Rapa Nui. Mahute, half French and half Tahitian, landed in Rapa Nui in 1889 and lost much of what she had arrived with after her husband passed away. Afterward she and her children may have been forced to work under the threat of lashings. Though the Chilean government claimed Mahute's, Otu's, and Pont's petitions had no merit, they created a report on the connections between Rapa Nui, Tahiti, and other Pacific Islands.[30] Tahiti remained to an extent part of the Chilean vision and network; when novelist Manuel Rojas narrated a strike in his 1951 novel *Hijo de ladrón*, he described the meeting of two people as follows: "I do not know him, nor does he know me and does not know if I am a foreigner or countryman, a Turk or from Aragon [Spain], from Chiloe [in southern Chile] or a Tahitian."[31]

Even those who never left the continent experienced the Pacific character of the maritime world. As the "slaving in paradise" ships from Pacific Islands set sail for Peru, some of the indigenous laborers fell sick. Upon arrival in Peru, they were transferred to local hospitals, sometimes in Callao. In October 1863, for instance, the lazaretto in Callao received sixty-nine Pacific Islanders with smallpox, an infectious disease in part responsible for the large-scale demographic collapse during the early years of colonization in the Americas.[32] Peruvians and other people in hospitals or the lazaretto surely noticed groups of sick people arriving, people who did not speak Spanish, and probably talked among themselves about the newcomers. Prior to this wave of Oceanians passing through the port of Callao in the 1860s, some Pacific Islanders joined whaling ships in Hawaiian ports as early as the 1840s. Some boarded ships as workers in the thriving whaling industry, others as migrants. They helped create a Hawaiian diaspora across the Pacific. Some of them reached Valparaíso in the 1840s, and though it is unclear how long they stayed or what they did while in port, their movement shows Oceanic connections to Chile prior to the annexation of Rapa Nui.[33] In this way—as well as interacting with them on estates along the coast or through relayed messages by those who had traveled to Oceania, as mentioned earlier—many people who may never have set foot on a boat dealt and interacted with a broader Pacific world.

Beyond Oceanians, Chinese and later Japanese also formed part of the South American Pacific world. In the mid-nineteenth century increases in coastal agricultural production, demand for guano on the world market, railroad construction, a lack of domestic servants, and the abolition of African slavery and indigenous tribute after 1854 pushed Peruvians to search for a new source of cheap labor.[34] In 1849 the Peruvian government passed an immigration law that would help fund a grand immigration plan, and although some within Peru sought European laborers, most of the people who arrived at Peruvian ports were Chinese.[35] The trade ceased in 1856 after mistreatment of coolies became known across the world, only to pick up again from 1861 until 1874. Across this time frame, from 1849 to 1874, as many as 100,000 Chinese indentured laborers made the trip to Peru, a long and grueling journey with mortality rates ranging from 2 to 40 percent in any given year.³⁶ Some of these Chinese laborers found themselves working on the guano islands.

Living and laboring on coastal plantations and the guano islands meant long hours of tough work, sometimes with little food, and strict discipline imposed by the overseers. As Gregory Cushman has noted, "thousands ended up working as virtual slaves alongside convicts and debt peons on the guano islands."³⁷ Although some higher ups on the guano islands suggested that Chinese laborers were treated quite well since they had constructed places to pray in their downtime, visitors told of hearing the constant sound of workers being punished and listened to stories of abuse against workers, including the Chinese.³⁸ A few years after the end of large-scale Chinese immigration, many Chinese migrants in Peru both fought for their rights as laborers and were on the receiving end of mass violence by Peruvians during the War of the Pacific.³⁹ Even after the official coolie trade had ended and Chinese migrants were theoretically free laborers, abuses continued.⁴⁰ Considering that Chinese immigrants spread out across the country after completing their labor contracts or fled from such labor conditions, many Peruvians began to experience a part of the broader Pacific world as well.

The transpacific movement was not only from the Western Pacific to the Eastern Pacific, though. As Ana Maria Candela has so lucidly shown, coolies and free laboring Chinese immigrants crossed back and forth in person and via letter. In 1866 and 1871, Chinese laborers in Peru petitioned the Qing government to investigate their treatment in Peru. After their 1871 request, the Qing government set up a committee that included one person who had been drugged and robbed in Macao, placed on a ship to Peru, worked through the completion of his contract, and then returned across the Pacific to China.⁴¹ With the transition from coolie labor to free labor, a new Chinese elite class with agricultural interests and commercial connections across the Pacific emerged. These new elites took part in the exploitation of rural laborers, helped sow transpacific ties, and acted as community leaders.⁴² For Candela, these transpacific connections beginning in the mid-nineteenth century helped to create China as China, Peru as Peru, and the modern Pacific.⁴³

This was a process of deepening ties between both Peru and Chile to the Pacific, which required the labor of people from both countries. To be clear, Peruvian and Chilean workers, and people from a number of other places, labored together in the often violent removal and transportation of people from across the Pacific to the eastern Pacific. The idea is not to downplay this part of these multiple migrations. In addition to the hierarchical form of migration, this circulation helped to bring the Pacific to Peru and Chile while at the same time pushing Peruvians and Chileans into the Pacific. The aim of the collaborative labor by Peruvians and Chileans working ships carrying Pacific Islanders or Chinese back to South America was rather different than the goal of building a more equal world as envisioned by anarcho-syndicalists (discussed in chapter 4). Still, this points yet again to the cosmopolitan world of the Pacific and how some of it functioned only because Peruvians and Chileans were able to work with one another.

## DESERTIONS, DISCIPLINE, AND LABOR

Within the maritime Pacific, people from various national backgrounds shared living quarters, spent long hours working side by side, and saw and experienced new places together. They also fled from these same ships when necessary. Chileans regularly deserted their ships or stayed in port after a work trip, particularly in Peru. With the rise of guano exports from the Chincha Islands off the coast of Peru in the mid-nineteenth century, many Chileans sailed northward to work in the booming industry. They worked alongside Peruvians and later Chinese, and some also decided to set their own, less grueling schedules. The governor of the Chinchas claimed that groups of Chileans arrived without the desire to work the necessary hours, labeling them "vagrants" and alleging that they may have organized "disturbances." The governor asked that the central Peruvian government better screen the people going to the islands.[44] But even if improved screening had been implemented, smuggling people onto the islands would not have been much of a problem. In a similar situation in Tarapacá, Peru in 1874, officials in Iquique asked the Chilean government to offer free repatriation trips south for out-of-work Chilean nitrate miners. The request came, in part, from a fear that with too much time on their hands and facing a hard economic situation, miners might turn into bandits. The Chilean government declined the offer on this occasion.[45]

In the years after the War of the Pacific, Chileans on the Peruvian coast regularly made the trip back south to Chile. As nitrate mining become an important part of Chilean exports and as large-scale state projects expanded, the Chilean state sought to bring "back home" Chileans from Peru and the Pacific. In 1888, for instance, the Chilean government asked Chilean state offices in Peru to publicize free trips to Chile through the Compañía Sud Americana de Vapores (CSAV; South American Steamship Company). Many of the Chileans on the Peruvian coast, though, were maritime workers who had deserted their ships and were living a "transient" life, and the Chilean officials in Peru seemed unconvinced that they would want to return to Chile only to work at difficult job sites. They instead mentioned the numerous Chilean peons in the Pisco, Ica, and Cañeta valleys of Peru.[46] Sometimes these letters mentioned Chileans across the Pacific coast without any other geographic referent, perhaps extending the search for Chileans northward through Ecuador and Colombia.[47] The conversations regarding bringing Chileans back to Chile continued in the following decades, with the Chilean state telling Chilean workers that Peru and Panama offered no real work for them, and that it was best to stay in Chile.[48] The maritime industry and the circulation of crew members opened up new sites of work for many, and in a sense industries within Chile faced the competition and possibility of Chileans moving abroad for work. Although the Chilean state in 1912 knew that many of the Chileans in Peruvian ports had deserted their ships—some to recuperate their health, some due to problems with the law—the authorities also argued that because of the tense international political situation with Peru at that moment, it was the patriotic duty of the Chilean state to provide temporary housing for them until they could be brought back to Chile.[49] Occasionally Peruvians and others looking for work asked to join repatriating Chileans. In two cases from January 1907, the lists included more Peruvians (fifty) than Chileans (thirteen).[50]

Some of the maritime workers thought of as "deserters" were men fleeing unjust treatment on board ships. According to a navy report, 734 Chilean maritime workers deserted their ships in 1911, around 14 percent of the total "embarked men during the year." The Chilean Navy thought that a new increase in wages would counteract this high rate of desertion, and if it failed to do so, that officers should be strict in punishing deserters.[51] Though the report did not interrogate the treatment of workers on board—perhaps because many of the complaints involved private companies—it did recognize the significant numbers of maritime workers deserting ships. Aurelio Veas, a Chilean helmsperson, for instance, refused to return to the British Pacific Steam Navigation Company (PSNC) ship *Chile* in 1915. Veas claimed to "have been treated badly, both through words and actions, by the captain." Rather than reboarding the *Chile*, the Chilean consulate in Peru helped him embark on the Chilean steamship *Mapocho*, destined for

Valparaíso.[52] Slightly over a week after Veas had complained of bad treatment on the *Chile*, Jorge Ocarranza Heredia deserted the same ship in the port of Balboa, Panama.[53] Though the letter from the minister does not explain the reason for the desertion, considering the case of Veas, Ocarranza may have left the ship due to his experience onboard with the captain. Peruvian maritime workers faced similar difficulties with the PSNC. In 1904 the Peruvian consulate in Valparaíso wrote back home with stories of Peruvian maritime workers complaining of treatment aboard PSNC ships. According to them, PSNC ships used their own on-board rules, which allowed the heads of the ship to easily dock or withhold wages due to workers. Each worker had a labor contract, but the contract was written in English, a language many Peruvians did not read. In one incident, five Peruvians received permission to disembark in Panama, only later to discover that the ship had left port without them. The Peruvian consulate in Panama put them on another ship to Callao, where they rejoined the same PSNC ship. On arriving at Valparaíso, they asked for their pay, but the captain denied their request, claiming they had "deserted" in Panama. The consular authority suggested that Peruvian maritime regulations adopt Chilean rules, whereby the captain must go to the Enganche Office and sign the labor contract with the maritime worker, with clear stipulations about pay and duties on board, and whereby maritime workers could only leave the ship with written permission.[54] Considering the high rate of Chilean desertions, the change may not have resulted in much of a real difference in treatment on board, but it may have because the consular authority claimed that Chilean maritime workers labored in much better conditions than Peruvians. Helpful here is a comparison to the Brazilian Navy of the second half of the nineteenth century made by historian Zachary R. Morgan, who argues that the act of desertion meant a "temporary removal from a particular situation" on board, a situation often infused with grueling work and punishment.[55] Desertions in the cases of crewmembers of PSNC boats may relate directly to broader themes of abuse in the maritime world. These cases also show that Peruvian state bureaucrats observed and took inspiration from Chilean laws when proposing changes to Peruvian regulations.

Working on a ship meant discipline, a supply of food, and the clothing necessary for oceanic ventures. Sometimes these elements mixed, with good behavior resulting in more food. On the *Amazonas* the crew was rewarded with a larger ration of butter and sugar for "their good behavior" in October 1859. Though those in charge of the ship knew that the previous level of butter and sugar was not sufficient for the crew and saw a need to increase the ration, the good behavior of the crew offered them an additional reason to double it.⁵⁶ Food also brought ship crews together. In one case in 1911, thirty Chilean and seventeen Peruvian maritime workers refused to return to work on the British steamship *Guatemala*, run by the PSNC, after the captain of the ship repeatedly denied them their third meal of the day while at port in Ancón, Panama.⁵⁷ In this case, the lack of food inspired solidarity among, and a collaborative strike of sorts by, Peruvian and Chilean shipmates. Similar to food, clothing on the *Amazonas* was found lacking in the mid-nineteenth century. When Francisco Sanz, the commander of the *Amazonas*, wrote to the head of the Peruvian Navy in early 1861 on conditions of the crew, he explained that many did not have the basic clothing required for living and working on the frigate. Although they were sent some items, by May some of the crew wore deteriorating nine-month-old coats that would not protect them from the winter cold. Sanz requested 260 coats, pants, and hooded coats made of flannel, as well as 260 blankets and backpacks. Sanz also made it clear that crews on other ships in the Peruvian fleet faced a similar situation.⁵⁸ Indeed, in brief reports on seven Peruvian ships three years later in 1864, the crews of five ships—the *Amazonas, Lerzundi, Tumbes, Sachaca,* and *Chalaco*—reportedly needed new clothing.⁵⁹ The lack of clothing aboard ships remained almost a constant throughout the remaining decades of the nineteenth century and into the early twentieth century.⁶⁰ In an 1889 regulation for maritime workers in Chile, clothing was mentioned in multiple articles. In one article, crew members were not allowed to debark if they had become indebted to the ship, and one of the ways of accruing debt was through the acquisition of clothing while on board.⁶¹ This suggests that maritime workers laboring under the 1889 Chilean law did not always have sufficient clothing for the job and were forced into debt while acquiring it. Though the heads of ships expected the utmost discipline and strict work ethic from their crews, the crews themselves often lacked the bare essentials of clothing and food while on board.

Even when the crew had the materials necessary to perform their work, they labored within a world of heavy materials and dangerous situations. Throughout these years, ships took on water or sank, leaving the crew to save each other from drowning. In 1903 the winds in the port of Valparaíso caught maritime and port workers off guard. Multiple ships crashed against the malecon, and many sank. And many workers lost their lives.⁶² Beyond drowning, crew members dealt with other risks inherent to their labor.

Miguel D'Angello, for instance, was contracted to work on the *Magallanes*, a ship owned by the Braun and Blanchard Company and run by Duncan Fox and Cia, as a fourth-level engineer. This rank required him to work the boiler on the ship and perform a few related tasks. But during his contract he was forced to rebuild, install, and repair the steam engines, labor assigned only to first- and second-level engineers. As D'Angello worked on an engine, he hurt his hand dealing with a large bolt weighing around forty kilos, and as a result the doctors in Valparaíso amputated a portion of his thumb. The lack of a full thumb made his years of training and education irrelevant since his work required a certain amount of precision, which he could no longer guarantee.[63] In some cases accidents at work resulted in death: a Peruvian maritime worker named Mario Isaac died in a workplace accident while laboring on a Chilean steamship while in Valparaíso in 1918, for instance.[64]

In port, too, workers transported loads that could easily hurt those carrying them. Port workers in mid-nineteenth-century Valparaíso relied on their own muscles and skills to load and unload ships. Some port workers, called *aguateros*, labored with the bottom half of their bodies in the water while loading and unloading goods, work that probably "could not be done for many years as sickness and age would have impeded them from continuing to perform labor that required such great physical capacity in order to support such extreme labor conditions."[65] In 1918 Manuel Dávila, a jornalero in Valparaíso, was loading a cart with bales of sacks when a bale fell and landed on his right foot. A doctor who checked Dávila suggested that he stay out of work for twelve days to recover from the injury.[66] Rubén Darío, one of the great modernist literary figures of the late nineteenth and early twentieth centuries, who worked in the customs house of Valparaíso, picked up on the dangers of working in the port, as well. In a short story included in his 1888 book *Azul*, Darío tells the story of Tío Lucas, a boatman the narrator meets after a day of working on the dock, despite having sprained his ankle earlier in the day. After a harrowing experience working as a fisher with his son, they both decided to labor as stevedores. Darío's description of their work speaks to the dangers of port labor and foreshadows the possibilities of injury and death: "Yes, stevedores! On the big black, flat ships, they would hang from the shrieking chain that dangled like an iron serpent from the massive crane, which resembled nothing more than the hangman's gibbet."[67] When Tío Lucas woke one day with joint pain and sore bones, his son went to work on his own. Other stevedores loaded a large bail and pulled on the chain to raise it. "The bale, the enormous, heavy bale, slipped from its ropes, like a dog that slips its collar, and it fell on Tío Lucas's son, who lay now crushed between the bale and the guardrail of the boat, his kidneys ruined, his backbone fractured, black blood flowing from his mouth."[68] Forced out of school in order to help support the family, Tío Lucas's son met his end as a stevedore on the docks of Valparaíso.

Discipline on ship was often arbitrary and dictatorial. In 1863 Roberto Ureña, a cabin boy on the Peruvian *Amazonas*, attempted to take his own life. In the subsequent meeting on the *Amazonas* about his fate, José M. Marquina, a lieutenant on board, noted that the navy had no rule on hand to punish the act. Nonetheless, it warranted punishment, one that would show the rest of the crew the consequences of any other attempted suicides and one that could "moralize" Ureña. Marquina sentenced Ureña to two years in prison. A few weeks later the navy reviewed the case, reducing the sentence to six months in prison or another place that would also serve the purpose of "moralizing" Ureña. The rationale was that Ureña had received a flogging—apparently without cause—on board, and this surely had caused him to attempt to take his own life.[69] Even without a law on attempted suicide, the officers on board still had the right to punish Ureña. In another case of arbitrary discipline, the captain of the German steamship *Alexandria* docked in San Francisco, California, and brought two Chilean sailors to court for breaking rules while on board. The judge ruled in favor of the sailors. Unhappy with the outcome, the captain took them before the federal authorities, who sent the sailors to jail in Alameda, California. The Chilean consulate in San Francisco noted in its letter that this style of authority was common for the German company Kosmos. Another captain sent a Chilean worker to Angel Island in San Francisco Bay for twenty-three days as punishment for purported "disturbances" on board the Kosmos-run steamship *Salatis*.[70] These types of actions continued well into the 1920s, with complaints about flogging after taking part in a political rally and a captain asking for fines and prison for crew members requesting extra pay for extra work.[71] While work on an eighteenth-century ship in the north Atlantic has been described as "virtual incarceration" in which "the seaman was forcibly assimilated into a severe shipboard regimen of despotic authority, discipline, and control," it is clear that in some cases not much had changed by the early twentieth century.[72]

The maritime world relied, in part, on contracted labor. Before the cabin boys and sailors worked the ships, they had to sign up for the work. An essential element, or system, for recruiting workers was the enganche system, which was also used to attract peones and itinerant laborers to larger work sites, such as mines, railroads, or estates. On land, the enganche system—*enganche* meaning hook—provided cash up front in exchange for the promise of higher wages at the new work location. Yet they also became indebted for the cost of transportation to the new work site where, even if they received a higher wage compared to their previous work, they may have found themselves in a far worse economic situation because of a higher cost of living or were paid in tokens for the company story, a common practice in the nitrate mines. But the system also allowed rural people the choice to stay in their current location or work somewhere else, and sometimes to negotiate the price of their labor. Even so, as Edward Melillo emphasizes, this should not take away from or "obscure the fact that enganche was a form of unfree labor."[73] Further, in some cases these labor contracts were signed under less than ideal conditions for the laborers, such as after consuming large amounts of alcohol.[74]

Although the Chilean Ministry of the Navy set up extensive guidelines for how exactly the enganche should function, in practice the process sometimes looked quite distinct.[75] In one 1914 incident, an acquaintance of an *enganchador*—the person who hooks the worker—invited three people living in the northern Chilean port city of Antofagasta out for a drink. Completely drunk, they blacked out and fell asleep. They woke up on board the Finnish frigate *Samoena* and discovered that while drunk they had signed a labor contract with a cash advance of four pounds, ten shillings, though none of them had the money. After the almost four-month journey to Hamburg, Germany, their monthly salary was reduced to help pay for their work clothing and their cash advance. Four other sailors leaving from Tocopilla, a port north of Antofagasta, had a similar experience.[76] In some cases crew members who had signed on to a ship found their working conditions and pay unsustainable and made their position known. In late 1920, Peruvian crew members on the steamship *Iquitos* organized what authorities called a riot in response to treatment on board. The crew on a previous trip to Europe from Montevideo on the *Iquitos* had demanded a new work contract with increased wages and more food, which they received. Although the authorities in Montevideo thought that the next crew were well taken care of on their trip to Rosario, Argentina, they also noted that the ship did not have any medical staff and that some had become sick on the journey. Some of the crew had deserted during the trip, too, suggestive of some of the conflicts that may have transpired at sea.[77] Whatever may have been the case, the crew members found their labor situation unbearable and sought to renegotiate their contracts.

Beyond the enganche, many working on ships did not sign on to the workforce at all, whether willingly or in the middle of a night of drinking. The state often used prisoners as free laborers on ships. On the *Amazonas* the practice of using prisoner labor, including those who had deserted ships, became so generalized that by 1864 the commander of the ship worried that soon "the day will arrive when our war ships become converted into actual prisons."[78] The courts sentenced one person in December 1859, for instance, to "four years of service to the Nation, with rations and without a wage, in a warship."[79] In 1851 authorities in the navy proposed detaining people presumed to be vagrants or criminals in Chiclayo, sending them to Callao and forcing them to work on board ships. They reasoned that the local population of Chiclayo feared known criminals, allowing the suspects to find an easy way out of the judicial process since the court system had a difficult time finding witnesses willing to testify against them.[80] In some cases, too, people sentenced in Peruvian courts appealed to the authorities to serve their sentence on board a ship instead of in prison. In 1857 Eduardo Guzman, a prisoner at the Casasmatas in Callao, asked to serve as a mechanic in the Peruvian Navy to help serve the nation and keep his skills up to date after taking so much time to learn the trade.[81] Guzman may have also sought relief from the Casasmatas jail, which was made up of two rooms of 250 square meters and housed up to 200 male prisoners, and in which their forced work included the physically draining task of stone cutting.[82] The authorities rejected the appeal, claiming that it was against national law to send him to work on a ship. Nearly two decades later, a judge in 1876 explicitly rejected the idea of finishing a prison sentence working on a ship, writing that ships were neither "places of detention nor of punishment."[83] This may have signaled a shift within the judicial system away from prison labor on Peruvian ships, but it is not clear. Although the courts ruled against sending these prisoners to work on Peruvian ships, many prisoners served their sentences out as free labor for the Peruvian nation. If prisons in Lima-Callao were "bastions of authoritarianism and exclusion," prisoner labor on ships extended this carceral regime into the ocean, where a different type of authoritarianism could take place.[84]

Another group of people also worked on ships without volunteering: teenage males. Young people labored in various forms, from urban street vendors to rural agricultural work, throughout the nineteenth and twentieth centuries. For the historian Jorge Rojas Flores, the practice was so common that very few Chileans noted it in their writings, taking it as a normal part of life.[85] But for some, laboring as a teenager was the product of a system of punishment meant to reform young people. The first reformatory in Chile, founded in 1896 in the southern port of Talcahuano, for instance, sought not only to correct the moral behavior of the young but also to prepare them for work in the maritime world.[86] In Peru the courts sentenced young boys to labor on navy ships from the beginning of the republic.[87] In other cases the parents of young males seen as disobedient sometimes handed over their children to the navy to instill discipline. In 1875 Antonio Budinich's father sent him to work on the Peruvian corvette *Unión*, seeing the strict work regime on the ship as a place that might discipline his child. The practice of sending young males to work on ships as punishment was relatively common, the commander noted.[88] In another case, Adolfo Fellería's father sent his son Oscar Fellería to work on a ship sometime in the mid-1870s. Oscar either fell ill or injured himself on board, for he eventually landed in the hospital. He fled the hospital and returned to his family, where the navy later tracked him down.[89] Perhaps he returned to his family and changed his behavior so as to avoid being sent back to the ship by his father; whatever the case, it is clear that ship life and work was not where Oscar Fellería wanted to be in 1877. Comparatively, regarding the Brazilian Navy, Zachary R. Morgan combed through 344 court cases from 1860 to 1893 and found that the average age of the enlisted men was eighteen and that 158 had enlisted prior to turning eighteen.[90] With ships almost becoming mobile prisons, worked in part by men who signed up while drunk, as prisoners, and as young males sent there as punishment by their parents, circulation in the maritime world also meant confinement. As the historian Sunil Amrith recently noted, "In the age of sail, mobility embraced captivity."[91]

Nonetheless, for some the maritime world offered a type of relief and freedom. The tight spaces of the ship, the common features of work at sea, and a relatively homosocial world helped create bonds of cooperation and solidarity.[92] *La Voz del Mar*, the major newspaper of the maritime portion of the IWW on the Chilean coast, repeatedly printed articles on meetings between radical workers on board ships. Whenever the IWW needed help funding something—such as a new printer or help with an urgent situation—it ran the numbers of people donating from the sea. Ship crews often respected and supported the strike lines on arriving in port. The experience of the being on the ocean also produced a sense of vastness that easily lent itself to the idea of the openness of life and the future. For Manuel Rojas, the maritime world opened up opportunities not available on land.[93] "The ocean had all of the grandeur and beauty that one knows and supposes," he wrote.[94]

The paradox of the Pacific world—of strict discipline and the lack of food and clothing combined with the possibility of freedom—both forced and drew men in to participate as crew members. Workers on board labored alongside prisoners, woke up on the ship having signed away their labor after too much drinking, and transported unfree laborers from Oceania to work on a new continent. Yet the maritime world also allowed some to venture away from their place of birth for opportunities to work elsewhere or to understand the potential of radical organizing within the space of the ocean. Though at times the limitations of language inhibited connections, the multinational crews aboard ships allowed for mingling across national lines in the South American Pacific.

## CONCLUSION

In studying the Pacific, the interactions between the people on board ships or in port during the period of colonization tend toward radical difference. They spoke different languages, carried with them distinct cultural and spiritual assumptions and values, and engaged in labor practices often seen as being from two different worlds.[95] This was certainly sometimes the case in the nineteenth and early twentieth centuries. But it does not appear to have been the rule. If Chilean deserters lived and worked along the Peruvian coast, they did so not as the beachcombers of Greg Dening fame—as stepping out of one culture and into another, of figuring out the translation of culture—but rather as people who spoke the same language, perhaps shared the same religious ideas, and came from a similar political system.[96] Throughout these decades the interactions and circulation of ships created a South American Pacific where many Peruvians and Chileans worked alongside one another, faced similar disciplinary regimes on board ships, and passed through the same neighborhoods in port. Even though both the Peruvian and Chilean national states may have thought of themselves as taking part in a conflict over national land and pride, the circulation of goods and laborers required multinational crews on board ships. Stepping on board a ship or walking through the streets of Callao or Valparaíso would have entailed not only Chileans and Peruvians working and living side by side, but also a cosmopolitan world filled with seafarers, migrants, and commercial agents from any number of places across the world.

Writing on Māori and Oceania, the literary critic Alice Te Punga Somerville called attention to the ways in which Māori living in what is today the nation-state of New Zealand have often been thought of as tied to land and not a part of Oceania or the Pacific, despite long historical connections. For some Māori, the realization of being part of the Pacific occurs when they leave New Zealand and are recognized as belonging to the Pacific. In turn, they forge new (and historic) connections to the Pacific and develop a new sense of region.[97] Historian Ernesto Bassi has taken up the arduous work of tracing the trajectories of ships, captains, and sailors in the Caribbean during the late eighteenth and early nineteenth centuries. By following their routes, Bassi shows that these maritime people regularly crossed imperial borders and, in the process of doing so, created a maritime-centered region. This Greater Caribbean emerged out of the experience of people on ships and at ports.[98] For the South American Pacific littoral examined in this chapter, the feelings and thoughts of many of the people working the ships and docks were not recorded; indeed, that was never the mission of state record keeping. It is, then, unclear if Peruvians and Chileans experienced the transformation described by Te Punga Somerville. But we may imagine what it meant for a young man from rural Chile to travel to a regional port and work on ships traveling across the Pacific, conversing with new people in a Peruvian port and seeing commonalities and differences. This laboring journey may have helped them form a sense of a larger world, one connected through ships and the Pacific. In this case, their experiences on board and in port formed a part of the South American Pacific of the nineteenth and early twentieth centuries.

TWO

*Gender and Sexuality in the Pacific*

AS MARITIME WORKERS on board ships circulated in the South American Pacific, they did so in a rather homosocial space. By and large these were men making the rounds from port to port. Where full crew lists are extant, state bureaucrats wrote about events on board, and the working-class press published about the boat or dock as worksite, the vast majority of the characters in these discussions were men. Had one walked from downtown Callao or from one of the various cerros in Valparaíso to the port, one certainly would have recognized the lack of women working on the ships. To paraphrase the geographer Doreen Massey in a different context, these were spaces "entirely given over" to men.[1] This was, indeed, a man's world. And this must be taken into account when writing about the Peruvian-Chilean Pacific.

Yet it was also a man's world built in relation to women.[2] All of these men spent time in port among both men and women. Some were married and had families; some were single with long-term girlfriends; and some traveled from port to port and visited brothels to sing, drink, and pay for sex with sex workers. These women are important because they formed part of this oceanic world; they both interacted with men and helped men form ideas around gender, sexuality, and self. The relational, co-constitutive process of creating gender ideologies is central to the experience of the Peruvian-Chilean Pacific. Scholarship examining class formation has shown how workplaces are thoroughly gendered spaces where perspectives on how men and woman should or should not live are formed. As Thomas Miller Klubock has demonstrated for the case of copper miners in twentieth-century Chile, male class formation occurred in part through masculine ideas of hard work and in relation to women as wives or as providers of goods or sex. While at work the "miners expressed their overcoming of alienation and danger ... in the language of masculine pride and sexualized conquest."³ Although they labored in a rather homosocial environment, these male miners developed a sense of themselves and a vision of overcoming their own oppression through a gendered lens that included both men and women. Women may not have been laboring in the mines, but they certainly were around the mines.⁴ As Matthew C. Gutman has noted, male "[h]omosociality exists in relation to women."⁵

Homosocial spaces on board ship and at the dock also helped maritime and port workers create their own norms when it came to gender relations and sexuality between men. In areas where the ratio of men to women skewed heavily male, social activities that tended to include both men and women had to conform to new circumstances. When a journalist visited the nitrate mines of northern Chile in 1904, he witnessed a dance organized by a mutual aid society at which many of the people present were men who drank and danced with one another. "My partner was extremely polite," the journalist wrote, "and possessed of such strong muscles, that instead of my leading 'her,' 'she' led me as if I were a feather."⁶ In the maritime world, this meant constructing specific ideas about what it meant to be a man—such as working hard, developing muscles, speaking with a loud voice, and, as Pablo Ben has remarked, "one's capacity to submit other men and women to one's own sexual desire"—and what it meant to be other.⁷ The category of other in the Peruvian-Chilean Pacific is both specific and capacious, targeted and shifting over time. From the perspective of self-presenting masculine workers or the state, the other might include an effeminate port worker, someone racialized as of African or indigenous descent, a woman, or someone engaging in male-male sexual relations in the supposed "passive" position. These positions within the category of other often intersected, as well. And just as important, these were also relationships built within a hierarchy of power.

This chapter discusses some of the ways in which men in Peru and Chile constructed ideas of themselves through gendered, class, and national lenses. Working within a relatively homosocial environment, male workers produced ideas of what it meant to be a working-class man, such as strength and, sometimes, allegiance to the labor union. These conceptions of masculinity were also founded upon the idea of males carrying more value than women. Whether they saw women as wives or as sex workers, many working-class men and men in positions of political power clearly envisioned their role as controlling women, either through placing themselves as the main source of income for the family or by restricting the affairs of female sex workers.

While a comprehensive history of gender ideologies along the South American Pacific littoral is beyond the scope of this chapter, it should be noted that these gender ideologies are constructed and reproduced in conjunction with the spatial arrangements—the material architecture, that architecture's history, and how people interact with it—of the ship and port.[8] Given the cosmopolitan nature of the maritime world and the extensive interaction between Chileans and Peruvians, discussed in the previous chapter, they surely mixed and learned from one another on board and in port. Many of the sources, however, only tell one side of the story, providing a somewhat comparative perspective. At other points the stories intersect, and we see moments of appreciative influence and possibly affect, in addition to conflict.

## GENDER AND SEXUALITY IN THE PACIFIC

Multinational and working under different sets of labor rules, the crews did exhibit one element of homogeneity: they were overwhelmingly male and single. As seen in the case of the *Amazonas* (see tables 1 and 2 in chapter 1), not a single worker picked up at Valparaíso, Iquique, and Callao can be identified as female. Perhaps some women performed a male role and made it onto a ship's crew, as Elizabeth Hutchison shows in other types of work on early twentieth-century Santiago.[9] But the work of a woman performing male industrial work in urban Santiago—where one could go to work and then return home, away from the work site—was much different than ship life: where work and home were spatially condensed into the same location.[10] The vast majority of the men working on these ships were not married. Only 17 of the 131 men picked up in Valparaíso and Iquique were married (13%), and only 8 of the 123 picked up in Callao had wives (6.5%). The crews on these ships were, then, entirely male and overwhelming unmarried men at that. To enter into this world one had to either know the rules of male work or be open to learning them and, in the process, to reproduce the gender ideology of the ship.

Nonetheless, women did occasionally make their way on board ships. In a letter asking for the appropriate rations of food for the crew of the Peruvian *Amazonas* in 1863, for instance, the commander named the battalion on board as well as the "one hundred twenty-eight women who belong to the mentioned unit" who sailed on the *Antonio Elias*.[11] Months later, 173 women traveled on the *Amazonas*, "belonging" to two military groupings.

One of the women gave birth while on the ship.[12] When the Peruvian steamship *Perú* arrived at the port of Pisco in 1886, 23 women, possibly passengers, disembarked, and 67 "rabonas" did as well.[13] The word *rabona*—from the word *rabo*, meaning tail—and a few others (such as *cantinera*) were used to describe women who ventured along with soldiers, often to cook, clean, and perform other gendered work. This was a common practice within the Bolivian and Peruvian armed forces at the time, and during the War of the Pacific many Chilean women traveled north with the military. Some rabonas also took part in the male world of military fighting.[14] In a photograph of Irene Morales, a Chilean rabona in 1881 during the Chilean occupation of Lima, she carries a rifle in her right arm and firmly holds a dagger in her left hand. While these might have been props used for the photograph, she also appears to feel comfortable with the weapons, suggesting a familiarity with their presence and probably their use.[15] Even if the maritime world involved mostly men working on ships, some women also labored on these ships.

Men and women in port cities engaged in sexual relationships that sometimes conformed to the rules of marriage and at other times fell outside of those bounds. In a study on "children of war" in Lima during the War of the Pacific, historian María Lucía Valle Vera discusses baptismal records that reveal quite a number of children born from Chilean fathers and Peruvian mothers from 1882 to 1883, during the Chilean military occupation of Lima. Since the occupation of some of the fathers is left blank, and since hundreds of Chilean men lived in Lima prior to the war (720 according to the census of 1876), it is unclear how many children may actually be classified as children of war. Some of the fathers may have been military men, and some may have been civilian Chileans. But what these records do show is that across the two years of the study, 150 children were born of Chilean-Peruvian relationships, and the majority of the relationships were between people of lower social status. According to Valle Vera, these children were "products of consensual relationships, which suggests a form of 'horizontal collaborationism,' 'sentimental' or 'intimate' of some Peruvian women towards some Chilean men."[16]

For some maritime workers, their sexual lives in the nineteenth and early twentieth centuries involved many partners in numerous places. One of the ways of tracking sexuality, or at least of providing a sense of it, is through reports on venereal infections. In 1884 the Junta de Higiene del Puerto in Valparaíso formed a commission to study venereal infections. They asked for reports from the heads of both Chilean and foreign ships on their crews, as well as collecting information from local medical institutions. The resulting numbers show that of the eight ships consulted, on average just under 55 percent of the crew carried a venereal infection.[17] The same report consulted the records of the local Hospital San Juan de Dios and found that of the 853 maritime workers who passed through the hospital from 1882 to 1883, 397 of them—or just under half (46.5%)—had a venereal infection.[18] The sample of eight ships and 853 maritime workers in the hospital might be limited in size and skewed toward those already in need of medical attention. Still, it does point to high rates of venereal infection among maritime workers in Valparaíso in the 1880s. And this seems to have remained an issue for decades. In a 1908 report in Chile, for instance, the director of the navy estimated that up to 60 percent of the crews on various boats had contracted a venereal infection. He even claimed that the British Navy instituted new rules for Valparaíso, which the navy considered the most dangerous of ports in terms of venereal infections.[19] The situation was similar in Peru, where it appears that in the first decade of the twentieth century, some ships' captains did not allow their crews to disembark in Callao due to the danger of their acquiring venereal infections.[20]

Concerns over venereal diseases in ports and the broader maritime world continued well into the twentieth century. In 1933, for instance, Benigno A. Callirgos completed a thesis at the medical school of the National University of San Marcos in Lima analyzing venereal infections in Callao. Over a three-year period, Callirgos consulted on 1,220 cases, a significant number considering an estimated population of 75,000 in Callao.[21] In analyzing the data, Callirgos shows that people in the seventeen to twenty-six age range were the most likely to have an infection. Just over half of the people treated were mestizos (50.49%), followed by white (25%), indigenous (19.10%), Black (5.25%), and Asian (0.16%). The number of Asian subjects is most likely much lower than it should be because, as Callirgos noted at the time, many avoided the state-run health-care system and visited other types of medical healers, such as herbalists or Chinese healers.[22] Some of the poor also did not make it to the state-run hospital and turned to other types of medical help since the Sociedad de Beneficencia del Callao had begun to charge for health visits.[23] Still, Callirgos's data provides an in-depth examination of venereal infections in Callao. The vast majority of cases involved people from Callao (900 cases, or 75%). In addition to these, 87 cases (7.25%) were people from other coastal areas of Peru, 79 (6.58% percent) were from the Andes, 59 (4.9%) were from Lima, and 51 (4.25%) were foreigners.[24] Even though foreigners represented the smallest grouping in the study, Callirgos still emphasized the international and cosmopolitan nature of the port of Callao as a reason for the high rates of venereal infection: "In a place like Callao, where the density of the population is much higher than in other regions of Peru, with its importance as the first port of the republic and for this reason naturally containing a cosmopolitan population, there is an importing and exporting of sick people with all types of conditions."[25] Callao was a port where "individuals from across the world embark and disembark, from all social conditions," carrying with them "the most varied of venereal diseases."[26] Although Callirgos did not include the profession of each patient, considering the importance of the port to the incoming and outgoing of people in Callao, many of the patients probably worked in the maritime industry. While most of the patients seen by Callirgos were Peruvian, the list also included people from Chile, Italy, Russia, England, Yugoslavia, France, India, Poland, Turkey, Germany, the United States, Spain, Austria, Bolivia, Romania, and Haiti.[27] In major ports, maritime workers from around the world engaged in sex with people while docked at the port, spreading venereal infections at high rates, while also connecting those who lived and worked in the city with the maritime world.

The realm of sex work lay at the center of both the 1908 Chilean report and the 1933 Callirgos thesis on Callao. For the Chilean commander, the lack of a specific space in hospitals for women sex workers meant that they could not have their health checked regularly. And since many maritime workers visited brothels as clients and sometimes formed relationships with sex workers, the lack of a space to treat sex workers created a maritime world rampant with venereal infection.[28] Indeed, one of Chilean Manuel Rojas's first novels, published in 1932, centers in part on the relationship between the port worker narrator, Eugenio, and Yolando, a sex worker in Valparaíso.[29] Callirgos called sex work "the primary and almost singular cause of the diffusion of venereal diseases" and categorized three different types of female sex worker: (1) those who did it through legal means, which entailed a medical checkup once a week; (2) those who did it clandestinely; and (3) those who did it to make extra money on the side or to have another lover, which might include married women, who could then spread the infection to their husbands.[30] Although Callirgos recommended better sexual education across the board, by seeing female sex work as the central node in the circulation of venereal infections, he reproduced a patriarchal view of the problem: it is not the men who frequented official and clandestine brothels, but rather the women who worked in them, who were to blame.

In a sense, Callirgos's take reaffirmed more generalized ideas on patriarchy. From discussions on sex work in the 1850s to its initial regulation in 1910, much of the discourse in Lima-Callao centered on how to control the location and practices of sex work so as to secure the health of men. Women would in turn also benefit, health wise, but it was their bodies—and not those of men—facing regulation.³¹ In 1888, the subprefect of Callao wrote about the need to create a special neighborhood for "women of the happy life [mugeres [sic] de la vida alegre]," which would facilitate police access to surveil and police the area and the women.³² In the Callao-Lima area, the subprefect's point about carving out a geographic area within which the sex trade would function and which the state could regulate fit into a broader discussion in Peru (and other parts of the world) about regulating sex work.³³ As Paulo Drinot has shown, intellectuals, politicians, members of the medical community, and others took part in decades of discussion in the second half of the nineteenth century around whether or not to legalize and regulate sex work, and if so, what exactly this might look like.³⁴ For elites, Drinot points out, regulating sex work functioned both as a "modern approach to *governing*" and as a way of "*polic[ing]* prostitution in order to improve it."³⁵ Callirgos's understanding of women sex workers as the main vector of venereal disease, the subprefect's suggestion of geographically cordoning off sex workers, and the 1905 decree officially regulating sex work all reinforced the social, medical, and geographic understanding of female sex workers as both a medical and a "moral contagion" for others.³⁶

In Chile, too, blaming women seems to have been relatively common. The second paragraph of the 1868 Reglamento del Ramo de Policia relativa a la prostitución (Police Regulation Relative to Prostitution) states in no uncertain terms: "Before everything, it is convenient to have in mind that there are recognized universal truths, across all time and people of the world: 1. that public women [sex workers] constantly produce moral and physical corruption, propagating contagious diseases and scandalizing with their bad customs."³⁷ The first article in the Reglamento created a council composed of a city council person, the head of the police, the director of the Office of Sanitation, and a medical inspector, who would together oversee sex work and workers in Valparaíso.³⁸ Regulations on these women workers included their only being able to work in places where they had registered, not "hid[ing] from the doctor a sickness they may have," forgoing public intoxication, and not changing residence without notifying the authorities.³⁹ In the forty articles of the Reglamento, only one mentions the males paying for the sex:

brothels were banned from allowing males under the age of eighteen on their premises.[40] The patriarchal view on sex work intersected with class as well. In one 1912 report to the intendant of Valparaíso, the police relayed dismay that due to the reconstruction of the Almendral area of the city—probably due to the 1906 earthquake—many brothels had popped up in the neighborhoods of "honorable families." The police offered a solution: ban all "brothels, houses of entertainment [casas de diversion], and hotels or boarding houses of a similar type" from the areas where these "honorable families" resided.[41] Perhaps this was forgotten by 1912, but in the direct aftermath of the 1906 earthquake, some women sex workers quickly set up new places of work in their temporary tents along major streets in Valparaíso.[42] Women sex workers in the port faced the realities of patriarchy through a policing of their lives and work and feared their removal from a well-to-do part of the city due to elite concerns over their private work and public presence, while also acting as a central piece of economic exchange in the port.[43]

The social atmosphere in the neighborhoods where sex work took place in Lima-Callao and Valparaíso seems to have been rather similar. Behind lights shining through red glass, in well-off establishments one might find a piano being played inside a house while patrons and workers danced between ordering booze. In these high-end houses, the furniture revealed the cost and profitability of the sex trade. In less high-end places one probably found a less festive common space and more individual rooms. Some women also worked local dance halls or even ice-cream parlors. The women and men in the establishment reflected the international connections of the city. Some women were local to the city or from the country more broadly, some had been trafficked from other parts of the world, and others may have been involved in sex work prior to migrating and sought to continue in the trade. Similarly, many of the men were surely local. In a port city like Valparaíso, though, many of them had only recently arrived aboard a ship. Rojas provides a panorama of one such group of men in 1930 Valparaíso, including local bakers and port and maritime workers, and seamen from Japan, England, the United States (yanquis), Germans, and Spaniards.[44]

Throughout these decades sex workers had their own ideas on how their worksite should function. As the Peruvian state created the new category of regulated sex worker, others fell outside of regulation and were considered to be clandestine sex workers. As Drinot discusses through an analysis of letters written by sex workers, sometimes registered sex workers wrote to the local government upset that they had paid their monthly fee to work while others flouted the fee. When the authorities in Lima decided to move sex workers to a new red light district in La Victoria, sex workers wrote letters protesting the relocation, while others were willing to abide by the move but wanted to make sure that it affected everyone equally.[45] I have not yet found letters of a similar quality in Chile. But there are hints at resistance to state regulation. Margarita Valdés, owner of a brothel in Valparaíso, was charged with selling liquor past the regulated hour on two occasions in 1913. When Valdés was called to appear for her hearing, she seems to have skipped out on the court appearance and did not sign any legal papers relating to the case. From the documents available, it appears that the local authorities did not arrest her or seek the fines for the violations.[46] The documents relating to repercussions could be lost, or I simply may not have found them while researching. But the lack of arrest or fines could also reflect a tacit understanding that Valdés's establishment was important enough to overlook legal infractions.

Beyond similarities between Lima-Callao and Valparaíso, visions of sex work and regulation directly connected Peru and Chile. Oddly enough, the War of the Pacific, and more specifically the Chilean occupation of Callao and Lima, created a cross-pollination of ideas on sex work. When the Chilean military arrived in Callao, leaders put into place some basic regulations on sex work even though sex work was still not regulated back home in Chile. In 1883 a local medical official in Callao built on the Chilean regulatory system in constructing his own proposal for regulation, which included spatially limiting brothels, registering sex workers, medical inspections, and hospitalization for those found to have a venereal disease.[47] The subprefect may have drawn from elements of this proposal in the 1888 letter discussed earlier. Just a few years later, in 1892, a subprefect in Lima proposed a new plan to regulate sex work. As Drinot shows in his reading of the proposal, it drew on not only regulations from Europe and across the Americas, but also previously produced proposals in Lima and Callao, including the 1883 proposal which, in turn, was based on the regulations put into place by Chileans during the occupation.[48] By 1899 one physician in Lima "lamented the failure of any of the proposals to have led to effective regulation" in Peru. "In spite of our resentments as eternal rivals," the physician had to praise the regulations on sex work put into place by the Chileans.[49]

If the men on board ships described in chapter 1 helped to create a sense of a region called the South American Pacific through their circulation in the ocean, then the women discussed here were also part of that creation.

Whether moving around the port from their homes to a brothel or traveling with the military, their labor was foundational for the functioning of a geographically broader circulation in the Pacific. In her study of Liverpool, anthropologist Jacqueline Nassy Brown questions why men crossing national boundaries seem to dominate port histories. Women, Brown points out, moved as well, "but apparently they were not moving *far enough* out of place to have their travels ... recognized as momentous and transformative."[50] Considering the numerous conversations on regulation versus abolition of sex work, of what exactly regulation should entail, of the place of the brothel in literature and social life, of women as central to the functioning of the military, and of the place of the family in labor negotiations (discussed in chapter 4), women also made up an essential part of the South American Pacific.

### MASCULINITY AND SEXUALITY

A constitutive part of maritime patriarchy was the concept and material life of masculinity. Maritime and port workers produced a view of masculinity that one can read in both culturalist *and* materialist ways.[51] The case of Gregorio Buendía, a sailor on the Peruvian steamship *Mairo*, offers an insight into both cultural and materialist readings of masculinity. In 1874 the commander of the *Mairo* sent Buendía to the "Insane Hospital" after he cut his own right leg with a broken glass bottle, "the first object he had by his hand." While at the hospital the medical team discovered scars on his body, for which they blamed excessive drinking. According to the witnesses, he cut himself with the bottle to prove his valor, and in the process yelled out "I am brave!" Clearly Buendía found it necessary to prove his valor by cutting his own leg with the broken bottle, however misguided the effort may have been. But behind this performance lay a history of work and labor. Buendía had previously been sent from the Chincha Islands for being a "vagrant," something many on the islands could be classified as if perceived as not working hard enough by the authorities.[52] While on board the *Mairo*, some of the crew or the commander may have chided Buendía for the "vagrancy" charge, a direct challenge to his ability and desire to work on the ship. In that situation, men worked hard while on board, while less manly men sat back and worked less than necessary. To show his manliness, Buendía cut himself, an action created out of the culture of masculinity—to show valor to other men—and the material realities of class—as a counter to being labeled a "vagrant" sent from one place to the next.

By the 1910s and 1920s radical Chilean maritime and port workers had developed a clear idea of what it meant to be a man and a leftist worker. Much of this entailed being a worker, active in and faithful to the union, and who completes his work with vigor, force, and expertise. For many radical writers in Valparaíso, these were foundational elements of masculinity. They also consistently spoke of holding the correct political line, which meant, in part, respecting the militancy of their class. If workers of a certain industry or work site in the port city struck, a working-class man could not cross the picket line, otherwise he would transform into a strike breaker and a "beast," a "rabid dog," who should receive punishment for his abandonment of working-class masculinity.[53] Calling someone a rabid dog in 1920s Valparaíso brought along with it very specific connotations, since bites from rabid dogs had long been a problem in the port. The typical method of dealing with a rabid dog entailed the police finding the dog and sometimes cutting off the head, which would then be sent to Santiago for study.[54] To be called a rabid dog was a serious label. At the end of a strike by workers employed by the CSAV in 1925, the editors of a newspaper for metalworkers wrote of the "men" who had shown their "discipline" in the struggle, "men" ready for the next fight.[55] For maritime Wobblies, those who ran away from the task of organizing were characterized as lacking manliness (falta de hombría); when approached by organizers, they pretended to be busy with something else, always postponing until tomorrow the necessity of organizing today.[56] In the midst of worker mobilization, one writer directed a few key words to the authorities: "Mister Governors, you protect the interest of capitalism, and we protect our muscular power and happiness in our homes."[57] They were muscular men who took care of their families while combating capitalism and standing up to the boss. Even if involved in a union, one could not call oneself a man if he fought against other radical unions.[58] Indeed, the detractors of the IWW in Valparaíso were called "ex-men that vegetate under the sun," for real men organized with the IWW and worked for a living.[59] Comparatively, turn-of-the-century port workers in Buenos Aires in the Federation of Maritime Workers (FOM) dismissed strike breakers from their union-family.[60] Chilean copper miners conducted their own trial of a strikebreaker in 1942, meting out the punishment that he had to dress like a woman to perform his unmanliness.[61] And in the Pacific Northwest of the

United States, union militancy in the IWW was intimately connected to white and Asian masculinity in the early twentieth century.[62]

Rather than being a purely pessimistic view of their lack of masculinity, though, some thought that through education—both in terms of ideology and in organizing with unions—their manliness could be reborn, and a new age of collective action might take hold. In one June 1925 article in the IWW maritime worker newspaper *La Voz del Mar*, the author makes precisely this point: "Convinced that the world evolves, and convinced of our class's lack of ideology, it is necessary to dedicate ourselves to purifying our spirit, and once our minds are overflowing with truth, courage and manliness [hombría] will come to only us, and we will lose the egoism that makes us feel like a privileged class, and that induces us to forget and look with disdain at the worker who is and will always be the principle factor of all collectivity."[63] With education and organizing, then, the innate relationship between man and worker—"it is necessary that the workers do not forget that beyond being workers, they are men"—would allow for a broader view and concern for the world, and the organizing necessary to change it.[64] Hutchison might be correct that some anarchists in the 1920s took a more conservative turn in their politics toward women, seeing them less as a revolutionary category and more as a hindrance to revolution.[65] Anarchists connected to the maritime industry, though, put forth a critique of *men* as another reason the movement was not as strong and unified as it could have been. Nonmilitant men—whether or not they took care of their families—lacked the proper masculinity of their sex, weakening the labor movement as a whole. Though their concept of masculinity left little room for negotiation, anarchist port and maritime workers' analysis of masculinity reveals an interrogation of men that linked masculinity directly with leftist, working-class militancy.[66]

Connected to these conceptions of masculinity and patriarchy is that of male-male sex. Since much of the evidence on male-male sex does not come directly from the people engaged in the sex—and even when it does, it is often filtered through the purview of the judicial process—it is rather unclear whether specific people did it out of sexual desire or out of a desire for power; in other words, questions of intent, sexual identity, and other aspects of sexual relations are difficult to ascertain with the archival documents left to historians.[67] Rather, the evidence brings together the ways in which patriarchy and homophobia may have played out within the Peruvian-Chilean maritime world. It also allows for some slippages within this landscape, moments when ambiguity about male-male sex reigned and possibilities abound.

While maritime workers along the South American Pacific littoral took part in heterosexual relations with girlfriends, wives, or women sex workers, they also engaged in male-male sexual relations. In October 1883 a court in the port of Iquique, Chile, tried the case of Tomas Jhones—probably Thomas Jones—for the crime of sodomy with a boy of ten or eleven years old. Although Jones had most recently worked as a peon, in previous years he had worked on ships, as an "hombre de mar" or a man of the sea. Jones claimed that he had drunk too much that day and that when he drank, he became mad and sometimes did weird things. But he also testified that even if he had engaged in male-male sex, it was nothing outside of the ordinary. For a former maritime worker, male-male sex was the norm: "I should also add that I have been a man of the sea for a long time and that on board ships the vice of sodomy is frequent." Though described as a vice, the act was a completely normal and routine one for Jones. These words came back against Jones two months later in his conviction, with the judge citing them in conjunction with other testimony.[68] On the one hand, Jones's description of male-male sex as a vice suggests a broader, societal condemnation of the act. On the other hand, referencing his previous life as a maritime worker and the frequent occurrence of male-male sex on board reveals a nonchalant casualness about male-male sex within the maritime world; though viewed as a vice, it was also normal according to his experience. As Zachary R. Morgan has suggested in the case of the Brazilian Navy, male-male sex was probably so commonplace that it was "generally acknowledged and overlooked."[69] By the early twentieth century, police in Santiago reported (and police in the port of Valparaíso reprinted) that criminals sometimes used the slang "cabro" as "the nickname they use to call someone a sodomite," a linguistic creation that would only make sense if the practice were somewhat common.[70] Though Jones's testimony unveiled male-male sex as an integral part of the maritime world, this should not distract from the age difference and power differential in this case; perhaps this is what David M. Halperin has called "sex as hierarchy, not mutuality," a relation built out of a "systemic division of labor."[71] Although many times the men in court cases on sodomy and pederasty may have formulated testimony to "exculpate themselves," Jones saw no need to do so.[72] The law, though, was less interested in the quotidian forms of maritime life and much more concerned with the law of the land.

The politics of male-male sex within radical working-class circles comes out most clearly in Rojas's semiautobiographical (or autobiographical fiction) tetralogy following the life of Aniceto Hevia.[73] Although published decades after the main period of study here, considering the relationship between autobiography and fiction in Rojas's work, it is likely that the tetralogy reflects elements of the first two decades of the twentieth century.[74] In the tetralogy—made up of the novels *Hijo del ladrón* (1951), *Mejor que el vino* (1958), *Sombras contra el muro* (1964), and *La oscura vida radiante* (1971), and republished as two volumes in 2015 under the title *Tiempo irremediable*—gay men are present throughout, not as a piece of the setting or as spectacle, but rather as part and parcel of the everyday life of a working-class port. While describing sleeping in a *conventillo* (a tenement), for instance, Rojas writes of the many different people who fill up the conventillo, including "*maricones*."[75] Whenever Rojas writes about conventillos, he discusses them as distinctly working-class housing, with people from various backgrounds: workers trying to sleep after a long day of laboring, people returning from police custody, the sick, murderers, and thieves. The characters often sleep among unknown others: "Nobody knew how many people lived in that room, nor how many slept there that night or tomorrow night; one could know who had slept there, but since there was no interest in knowing it, the mystery remained, without it being important to anyone."[76] Gay men were merely one of many different working-class people staying in the conventillos due to economic circumstances. Although this suggests a familiarity and openness to male-male sex, Rojas also portrayed them as different. In one case, calling someone a homosexual, and in a sense questioning their masculinity, could have resulted in a fight.[77] At one point one of the characters worried that others would question his heterosexuality after he did not make it to a date with a woman he had been courting who had agreed to have sex with him.[78] Familiarity, then, meant an accepting of gay men's presence as long as one's own sexuality and masculinity remained thoroughly heterosexual and manly.

The idea of anarchists possibly being gay—or even of heterosexual men engaging in male-male sex—is almost out of the question for Rojas.[79] El Chambeco, one of the characters in *La oscura vida radiante*, for instance, "was not a bad person, he didn't have any tendencies towards crime nor towards homosexuality."[80] Though homosexuality is not a crime in the description, it remained within the same discursive realm as a crime. Later, when the character Gutiérrez offered to look for a place to stay with Aniceto,

Gutiérrez asked several questions regarding how Aniceto slept. Since they would have to share one mattress, the sleep questions were fundamental for Gutiérrez. After asking about dreams, whether he screamed or laughed in his sleep, or even sleepwalked, the conversation turned much more serious in preparation for the last question: "Do you have homosexual tendencies? Don't answer: I don't think so, I think that I don't, I'm not sure, nor maybe, because if that is the case, there is no room and no bed. Yell NO! with all of your mouth." Aniceto yelled "¡NO!" and Gutiérrez agreed to look for a room with Aniceto.[81] Perhaps in the latter part of his life Rojas turned toward a more critical view of homosexuality, for *La oscura vida radiante* is the last book in the tetralogy, and none of the earlier works contain such clear pronouncements against it. This turn in Rojas in a book published in 1971 maps onto some of the homophobia within the left in Chile and elsewhere in Latin America at the time. At a meeting of the Chilean Revolutionary Left Movement (MIR) in San Francisco in 1975, for instance, the official position of the group was that "in the MIR, there are no gays."[82] As Gastón Carrasco has suggested, the world Rojas constructs is indeed "heterogeneous and complex," but it is also a "homo-affective and heteronormative heterogeneity."[83] Still, in these pieces from the tetralogy, homosexuality as a sexual orientation is both consistently present and characterized as something alien to the radical left.

Yet Rojas left some ambiguity in regard to male-male sex in his work. While anarchists were neither "drunks nor homosexuals," and though it may have been "inconceivable that an anarchist be a homosexual," Rojas opened up the possibility of a hidden homosexuality within anarchism as long as it was not "declared and active."[84] Perhaps the largest ambiguity and openness about male-male sex in Rojas comes in his first novel, *Lanchas en la bahía* (1932), a story of port workers, unions, and sexual attraction in Valparaíso. In the novel, a character named Eugenio asked a man near him the name of the ship entering port, and from there they began a friendship. Alejandro, a capataz de cuadrilla (gang foreman), offered Eugenio a job as a lanchero if he joined the IWW. Although Eugenio feared he lacked the necessary strength and manliness required of the lanchero position, Alejandro convinced him that he was more than capable of the work. Alejandro introduced Eugenio to his fellow lancheros, who quickly brought Eugenio into the masculine world of port work: "This is the voice of a man, comrade," the lanchero Rucio del Norte told Eugenio while "forcefully hitting his chest," "and not the voice of a boy, like yours." With Eugenio visibly tired after his first day of work as a lanchero, Alejandro mentioned to him that if he did not have a place to sleep for the night, he was welcome to stay with him. "I have a wide bed, queen sized, almost bigger than the room. I bought it when I had the idea of having a woman, and the bed lasted longer than the woman.... Useless costs that one does." After taking in the panorama of the city from Alejandro's apartment window, they laid down together in silence, "with soft movements, as though we feared the shooing away of our tiredness." They turned off the lights and said "until tomorrow, compañerito" to one another, and before the sunrise the next morning they had already eaten breakfast and were on the dock ready to work.[85]

This brief portion (and other parts) of *Lanchas en la bahía* touches on many of the issues of gender and sexuality discussed earlier. Rucio del Norte quickly heard the childlike voice of Eugenio and offered to teach him a manly voice, in part through a show of physical strength and durability in the striking of his chest. Men's bodies were made up of muscles, too: Rojas describes Rucio del Norte as "completely filled with muscles, spreading through his body like roots of a tree."[86] Their working-class status meant the men lacked the money to rent a place to live, pushing Eugenio to dorm with Alejandro after work, a practice that appeared earlier in the novel as well.[87] And in terms of male-male sex, Alejandro opened the conversation with a mention of his sexual past involving a woman, but the bed had lasted longer than his previous relationship. As they laid down to fall asleep, they gently moved together, and the next day they headed directly back to work on the docks. Though no mention is made of male-male sex, the language of lying together in a shared bed and moving gently with one another would have been recognizable by many men of the era, for in court cases on sodomy, men often explained the appearance of sodomy from afar as nothing more than two men moving with one another.[88] In this brief moment in *Lanchas en la bahía*, Rojas invoked the common phrasing of the encounter as a gesture to the possibilities of male-male sex without explicitly stating it.[89]

The Chilean state also paid close attention to male-male sex on board ships in the Pacific. In particular, authorities looked toward what this sex might do to their international reputation and the future of the Chilean race. In 1910 Antonio Agacio of the Chilean consulate in Panama wrote back to Santiago with concern about the "terrible development of the vice of sodomy that one observes in our merchant marine." In three years of serving the Chilean consulate in Panama, Agacio was aware of numerous cases of male-male sex between crew members from various countries on board

Chilean merchant ships. Sometimes the actions involved males of fourteen to eighteen years of age who labored on board without a wage as general help. Working almost as a servant to groups of maritime workers, they were exposed to abuses, including sexual ones. Beyond this abuse, the use of these young males occasionally caused maritime workers to fight with one another due to jealousy over access to the young helpers. In Panama, too, people involved with the trafficking of women had begun to entice these young males with "flattering wages and good treatment on land," and many of them left the ship life for one on the land, "beginning a depraved existence" in Agacio's eyes. As a partial solution, Agacio suggested that Chilean merchant ships no longer allow the enganche of males less than eighteen years of age.[90]

But for Agacio the banning of employing underage males on Chilean merchant ships was only one element in solving the problem of sodomy on board. Just as important, if not more so, were Peruvians. According to Agacio, the problem of male-male sex on Chilean ships began with the Chilean occupation of Peru during the War of the Pacific. During the Chilean occupation, Agacio claimed, Peruvian men introduced the concept of male-male sex to the Chilean Army and Navy. The problem was particularly acute in Lima. Agacio quoted the definition of the word *maricón* from a Spanish dictionary published in Paris in 1894:

> "Maricón".—An effeminate and cowardly man. One who spends their time on women's work.—They use this word in LIMA to describe certain men that imitate womanly manners, inclinations, and, sometimes even dressing as women, becoming them in their most shameful or lewd acts [actos más impúdicos].[91]

Though "actos más impúdicos" could mean a variety of things in other contexts, within the definition, coming as it did after describing effeminate actions and dress, Agacio linked it directly to sodomy. In reproducing the idea of limeños as effeminate and possibly engaging in male-male sex, Agacio tapped into a much longer history of a similar discourse. In the late colonial and early republican period in Peru, foreigners and locals alike depicted the abundance of men in women's clothing in public places, often racializing them as African or of African descent. These discourses brought together a critique of masculinity (or lack thereof) in Peru (and Lima in particular) and brought attention to the African aspect of it, creating an image of effeminate and unmanly Afro-Peruvians.[92] During the War of the Pacific, too, some Chilean soldiers and others within Chile continued this characterization of Peru—and again, particularly of Lima—as full of effeminate and possibly gay men, in part as a rhetorical move to justify Chilean aggression. Rather than focusing on the Afro-Peruvian, they set their sights on the indigenous population as the problem.[93] And in the 1920s, before the issue of Tacna-Arica had been settled, the local press in Tacna and Arica published articles that characterized Peruvians as of African descent and, sometimes, as a way of reinforcing the Peruvian as other and less than.[94] Agacio did not mention Afro-Peruvians or indigenous Peruvians; instead he homogenized Peru into one national unit, undivided: *all* Peruvians should be feared. According to Agacio's reading of ship documents, with at least five to ten Peruvians working on each crew, and given the 1894 dictionary definition of maricon and the "public fame" of Peruvians, male-male sex on board Chilean ships was an inevitability; these conditions "naturally produce" the problem. Agacio could hardly have made the case for the seriousness of male-male sex—between men and underage males, and between Chileans and Peruvians—on ships clearer than when he posited that the continuation of such acts "could affect the virility of the Chilean race." In a sense, Agacio saw male-male sex purportedly propagated by Peruvians as a means through which to contaminate the Chilean race.[95] Agacio suggested the banning of all Peruvians on Chilean ships, similar to the restrictions on underage male helpers. It is unclear, though, how the authorities in Chile responded to these suggestions.[96]

## CONCLUSION

Agacio's letter on male-male sex on board Chilean ships offers insight into one way Chileans and Peruvians interacted at sea and in port. While some of these acts undoubtedly involved coercion or a performance of bringing newcomers into the family fold of the ship, some also surely took place between consenting adults. For the British sailor Jones, male-male sex on board was a common occurrence, and as Rojas shows in his works, gay men hung out and slept in the same places as many maritime and port workers. As Agacio's report relates, these relationships occurred across the Pacific littoral. If the post–War of the Pacific Chilean state worried about an internal coherence, about the possibility of losing the annexed territories of the north due to Peruvian sentiments, then the male-male sex on board ships between Peruvians and Chileans meant the possibility of the "peruvianization" of

Chileans, a fear that persisted from the years of the War of the Pacific through the early twentieth century.[97] If elites in Chile sought to forge a nation built first on the prowess of the mixed-race "roto" in the aftermath of the War of the Pacific and then on the prospect of a white nation connected to European immigration, then the idea of Chilean men engaging in sexual relations with Peruvian men, thought of as indigenous and of African descent, was the exact opposite of their envisioned country.[98] It is unclear whether or not these men formed the same type of community that historian George Chauncey wrote regarding the navy in Newport, Rhode Island, or if these forms of sexual relations created a maritime family structure like that off the south China coast, as historian Dian Murray discusses.[99] But given the numbers of Chilean and Peruvian men working on the same ships, interacting at ports, or crossing paths in brothels, they clearly built ideas of class, gender, and sexuality with one another. Agacio's letter was certainly produced with plenty of exaggeration and xenophobia. Yet it also points to the possibility of some Chilean and Peruvian maritime workers forming some type of bond through their mutual desire and pleasure in male-male sex within their rather homosocial world aboard ships.

THREE

*Transnational Cholera*

IN NOVEMBER 1886 residents of the Chilean port city of Valparaíso began to read stories about cholera on the Atlantic coast of South America. Published in the main daily of the country, *El Mercurio*, short articles related the number of dead in certain areas, the precautions prescribed for the population, and measures different Atlantic states took to fend off cholera. In one case, a British doctor suggested that maritime quarantines were entirely unnecessary since England had largely escaped the wrath of cholera without their use, while some places in Europe with a quarantine in place knew all too well the effects of the disease.[1] The public read that the Brazilian state had instituted a maritime quarantine, and they followed the debates within Argentina concerning the right of movement within the country versus the need to protect against the spread of cholera.[2] *El Mercurio* even reported on a plan to raze the entire Buenos Aires neighborhood of La Boca in order to "save the rest of the municipality from the lash of such a terrible whip."[3] Those not reading the newspaper must have known something was afoot because local authorities in Valparaíso began to call for sanitary changes throughout the city.[4] Despite the advance notice, it would be only days before the first cases of cholera were reported in Chile.

Recent studies on cholera analyze it within larger frameworks based for the most part on social and political differences. For individual countries scholars have used cholera to bring into relief, for instance, class and/or racial differences and the political responses to these inequalities or state responses.[5] In colonial contexts the spreading of cholera and perceptions of its movement pushed a wedge between colonizer and colonized, as well as between elite and nonelite, both within and across borders, sometimes resulting in sanitation conferences.[6] These works, especially those of historians

Eric Tagliacozzo and Valeska Huber, are foundational for how this chapter thinks about and uses cholera. As Huber remarks, cholera marked both the "unification of the globe by disease" and the "unification of the globe *against* disease."[7] In particular, I lean on scholarship that emphasizes political discussions across borders. Rather than using cholera as a wedge in already existing conflictual relationships—in other words, as a vehicle to explore conflict—here it acts as a binder, bringing together doctors and medical professionals from two countries into one community.[8] The fear of cholera spreading brought people together across political boundaries.

Linked to cholera's spread throughout Chile and the fear of its reaching Peru are material elements of state formation. Ever since Philip Abrams argued that the state is not a material object but rather a "third-order object, an ideological project," wherein the study of the material is in reality the study of a reified form rather than the ideological process that created it, historians of Latin America have tended to emphasize the cultural and ideological portion of state formation rather than material aspects. For Abrams, to study the material—that is to say, a physical object, such as a "human ear"—is to miss the ideological and cultural processes that produced it.[9] While many within this turn engage with the material, the dialectic tends to initiate with the cultural and ideological and can at times drift into the realm of idealism. But the material is central to any process of state formation. The cholera bacteria, a material thing, and interpretations of it, triggered specific responses by Chileans and Peruvians; the items and people crossing borders in a time of quarantine mattered for state authorities and port populations; and the material tools required to conduct research on cholera allowed specific people to work together. While the argument here does not go as far as calling the state "in the last analysis, fiscal mechanisms of one kind or another," it does emphasize the material in processes of state formation.[10]

## CHOLERA'S TRAVELS

Chilean authorities in Santiago sought to protect the country from cholera. After receiving news that cholera had begun to spread westward across the Argentine pampas toward Mendoza, the Chilean Ministry of the Interior ordered the closing of all communication through the Andes between Argentina and Chile, on December 4, 1886.[11] Although by no means easy, the trip from Mendoza to Santiago was one that many people, animals, and ideas had traversed for centuries.[12] Indeed, both states were in the process of planning the transandean railroad from Mendoza to Santiago.[13] The closing of the border was not taken lightly, but authorities in Chile must have had in mind a recent smallpox epidemic, which had left tens of thousands dead across Chile just a few years earlier.[14] Within the press, some criticized the move by the state, calling it an authoritarian power grab by the recently elected president of Chile, José Manuel Balmaceda. Others, particularly the Valparaíso editions of *El Mercurio* and *La Union*, supported the move as a necessary measure to save the population from cholera's ravages.[15] Ships leaving from Argentina also faced closed ports in Chile. On December 4, 1886, the Ministerio de Marina declared that all ports in Argentina and Rio de la Plata would be considered "infested ports," "with the exception of Montevideo."[16] Despite these public debates over the power of the central state, the fear of even more death in all likelihood pushed the Ministry of the Interior to call for the blocking of all communication with Argentina through the Andes.

Canceling all communication, though, is much easier declared than completed. On December 6, just two days after the decree, Eulojio Allende composed a letter from his home in Talca, a city about 250 kilometers south of Santiago, concerning the closing of the border with Argentina. Allende requested the Ministry of the Interior send twenty men to Talca to help stop traffic across the Andes.[17] Any reply to this request no longer exists in the archive, but it suggests the substantial efforts—of workers, of money, of transportation, and of room and board—required to attempt to block movement between Argentina and Chile. (Indeed, in January 1887 the local government of Valparaíso quickly realized that the troops they sent to maintain the sanitary cordon required a change of shirts and hats to protect them from the summer sun.)[18] Despite these efforts, cholera began its destructive course in San Felipe, a town just under 90 kilometers north of Santiago, by the end of December 1886. The Chilean state again attempted to stop cholera's spread by instituting a sanitary cordon in San Felipe.[19] These efforts would be in vain.

Meanwhile the Peruvian state began to receive cables from Chile on the spread of cholera. How it would respond depended on previous decades of discussions within the Peruvian medical community. The outbreak of cholera in 1880s Chile was not the first time the Peruvian state had confronted the possibility of the disease reaching its shores. In 1833, for example, after hearing of cholera in Mexico and Central America, the young Peruvian republic instituted a maritime quarantine on all ships coming from infected areas.[20]

In 1857 a student at the San Fernando Medical School of the National University of San Marcos defended a thesis in which he argued that cholera was endemic to certain places in the world. Moreover, cholera was infectious but *not* contagious, a distinction that in turn meant any use of sanitary cordons, lazaretos, or quarantines did not help fend it off and could actually cause more harm, considering the economic consequences of such barriers.[21] More importantly and to the point of cholera in Chile in late 1886, Lizando Maurtua defended a thesis on medical-social issues in Callao in 1885. Maurtua had worked in hospitals in Callao while researching, and much of his thesis relied on an understanding of the port and port life more broadly. For Maurtua, Callao was "one of the unhealthiest places man could live." Much of this categorization as unhealthy emanated not directly from the soil, though it was certainly part of the equation, but rather from how people had changed the environment in ways that did not account for the health of the population. Industrial waste mixed with water from nearby farms and excrement in the insufficient canals, and the jetty, constructed with granite rocks, though useful for ships, made it difficult for water to circulate, resulting in the fermentation of organic substances from the ships' crews (excrement, food, and other materials), creating "a permanent center of putrid emissions" and sickness.[22] Although in 1885 cholera had not yet reached Callao, the city had experience with yellow fever, and its arrival tended to coincide with maritime traffic. As such, Maurtua argued for the need to impose quarantines on ships, in addition to disinfecting water and planting eucalyptus and other plants to freshen the air.[23] The people of Callao had also lived through a recent hit from smallpox, which claimed more victims than yellow fever. Though smallpox remained a constant threat in Callao, it had not reached the level of an epidemic through the 1870s. This changed, though, with the beginning of the War of the Pacific; during the Chilean invasion one of the troops "imported the smallpox venom," and from there it ravaged the port.[24] If the structure of Callao—both on land and in the port—created an atmosphere apt to spread diseases, the main route of arrival for nonendemic diseases was the ocean.[25]

Initially all ships leaving Chile, regardless of point of origin, were barred from all Peruvian ports. Throughout January and February 1887, however, the Junta Suprema de Sanidad (Supreme Council on Sanitation) in Lima proposed various revisions to the total closure of Peruvian ports. The Junta Suprema de Sanidad "irregularly functioned from the middle of the nineteenth century" and was involved with checking the health conditions of ships, passengers, and crews.[26] Its proposals ranged from a quarantine of twenty days before docking in port to allowing ships from the far southern port of Punta Arenas to proceed to Peruvian ports as normal, as long as they had not docked at any other Chilean port.[27] These efforts of port closure and quarantine were part of a global conversation around the spread of diseases in the nineteenth century, particularly with the new speed of steamships.[28] Indeed, in the South American context, throughout these years Ecuador, Colombia, and Brazil would all institute varying forms of regulations on ships leaving from Chilean ports.[29] Within weeks of the first cables to Peru with the news of cholera in Chile, authorities in Lima learned what many dreaded: cholera had reached not only Santiago, but also Valparaíso. The news worried Peruvian authorities. At the time, the ocean acted as the main surface on which the two countries communicated and exchanged goods. Officials knew that once ships began leaving Valparaíso northward for other Chilean ports, cholera's geographic spread would continue north and possibly reach the Peruvian coast.

Similar to the Chilean effort to close the Andean border with Argentina, the banning of ships proceeding from Chile by the Peruvian state proved difficult to enact. In December 1886 the Italian steamship *Washington* arrived, and the local authorities in Callao ordered that it not be allowed to dock. In the press rumors circulated that small, privately owned ships had made contact with the *Washington*, creating fear within parts of the population that the people leading the charge of maintaining the quarantine—in this case the head of the Peruvian steamship *Peru*—had failed in their mission. It appears the crew members of the *Peru* had indeed succeeded in keeping up the quarantine, but the doubt expressed by the local press is easy to understand given the difficulty of the operation. They first had to restock their coal supplies in the amount of forty-eight tons; they then escorted the *Washington* five miles away from the port, situating it downwind from the *Peru*, per the regulations of the Junta de Sanidad. The crew of the *Peru* had to stand watch over the *Washington* day and night, and when a ship or boat needed to communicate with the *Washington*, they had to make sure contact took place at a reasonable distance and always upwind from the ship. Since several small ships approached the *Washington* with provisions for the crew, some in Callao may have interpreted these interactions as a breaking of the quarantine, even if the ships passed through fumigation at the port.[30]

In some cases the new regulations contained loopholes allowing for a partial breach of the ban. The steamship *Coquimbo*, for instance, left the

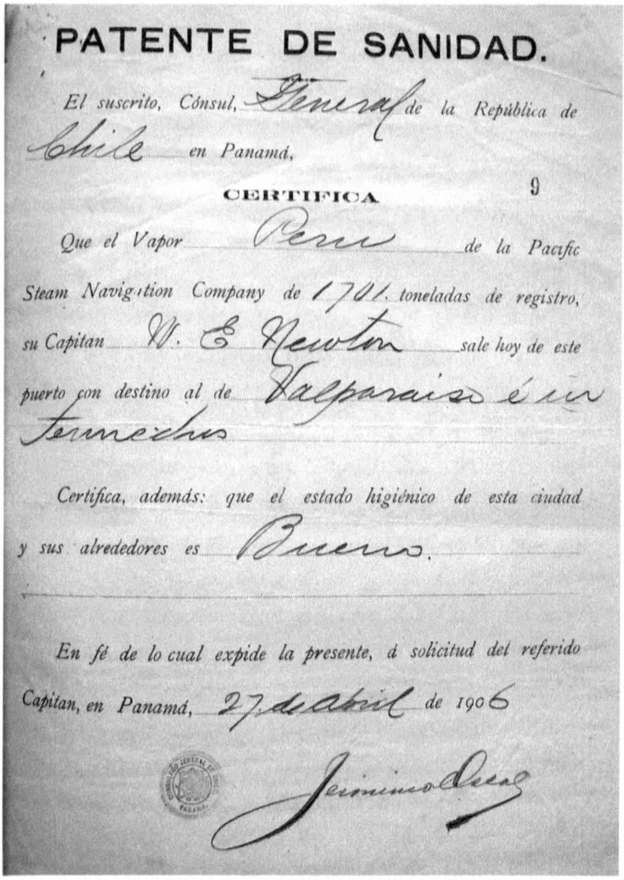

**PATENTE DE SANIDAD.**

El suscrito, Cónsul, *General* de la República de *Chile* en Panamá,

**CERTIFICA**                                                    9

Que el Vapor *Peru* de la Pacific Steam Navigation Company de *1701* toneladas de registro, su Capitán *W. E. Newton* sale hoy de este puerto con destino al de *Valparaíso é in termedios*

Certifica, además: que el estado higiénico de esta ciudad y sus alrededores es *Bueno*.

En fé de lo cual expide la presente, á solicitud del referido Capitán, en Panamá, *27 de Abril* de 190*6*

FIGURE 1. Patente de sanidad for the British steamship *Peru*, dated 27 April 1906, two decades after the cholera outbreak. *Source:* Archivo Nacional de la Administración, Santiago, Chile, Ministerio de Relaciones Exteriores, vol. 1327.

port of Valparaíso just as the population of the port city began to experience cholera for the first time. The Peruvian consulate in Valparaíso quickly sent a cable to Lima notifying authorities of the ship's departure. The authorities in Lima performed a study on the *Coquimbo* and determined that, even though it carried a *patente sucia* (unclean bill of health), it fell within a provision that allowed ships with European goods destined for Peru to continue on, and the *Coquimbo* proceeded on with its business.[31] (For examples of patentes from 1906, see figures 1 and 2.) On the other hand, ships arriving with a *patente limpia* (clean bill of health) sometimes faced a

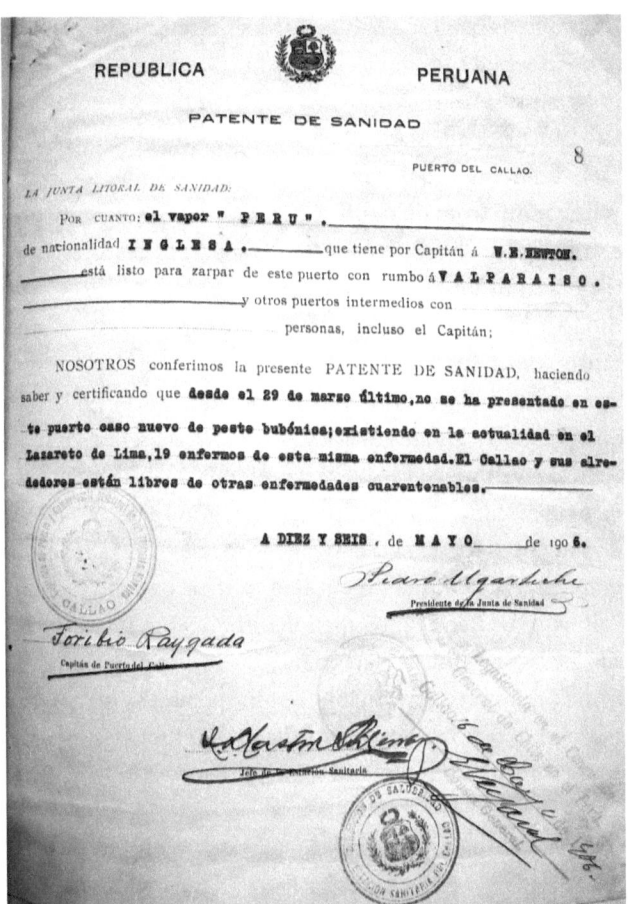

FIGURE 2. Patente de sanidad for the British steamship *Peru*, dated May 16, 1906, two decades after the cholera outbreak. *Source:* Archivo Nacional de la Administración, Santiago, Chile, Ministerio de Relaciones Exteriores, vol. 1327.

tough process at port. When the French ship *Vauban*, which had been taking on water at between thirty-five and forty centimeters per hour, arrived in Callao in March 1887, the authorities quarantined the boat downwind near San Lorenzo Island, just off the coast of Callao. Although the ship carried with it a patente limpia, it had begun its journey from a Chilean port, and authorities in Peru decided to exercise caution. Considering the danger of taking on water, the Junta Suprema de Sanidad and the Junta Litoral (Littoral Council), in conjunction with the French consulate and the shipping company, agreed to allow the ship to unload the nitrate cargo onto small boats while the crew made the necessary repairs. The Junta Litoral put in place measures to "completely impede the communication of the ship with the mentioned island [San Lorenzo] and the port." By April 4, after the lack of any signs of cholera on board, the Junta Suprema de Sanidad released the ship from quarantine.[32] Peruvian authorities worried about incoming ships from Chile as late as June 1888, months after cases of cholera in Chile began to drop drastically.[33]

According to historian Lauren Benton, ships acted as "vectors of law thrusting into ocean space," simultaneously as "islands of law with their own regulations" and as part of the sphere of "municipal legal authorities."[34] Similarly, historical sociologist Renisa Mawani has argued that ship manifests operated as "technolog[ies] of jurisdiction," which attempted to "render oceans to be intelligible and thus potentially governable."[35] In these cases, the legal documents produced and signed in Chile held value on board, but authorities in Peru determined, according to their own prerogative, how to enforce their own medicolegal regulations. The vector of law of the patentes left Chilean shores and functioned on board as a way of making the sanitary conditions intelligible and governable, but the patentes also had to be recognized and respected by those on land. Whatever authorities at port may have decided, these ships forced the legal and regulatory hands of authorities in both Peru and Chile.

The ocean played a significant role in the cholera outbreak, paradoxically functioning as both threat and savior. The oceanic connections sowed fear in Peruvian authorities. Not only did they begin to pay closer attention to the patentes of ships arriving in Peruvian ports; they also sought to create a new international system of agreements in regard to how states treated shipping in a time of epidemic diseases. When representatives from Peru, Chile, Bolivia, and Ecuador met in Lima for a Sanitation Conference early in 1888, they agreed upon 136 articles dealing with cholera, of which 9 spoke to general issues, 12 dealt with land crossings, 3 discussed rivers, and 115 detailed the sanitary policing of the maritime world.[36] International trade relied heavily on shipping in the 1880s, and with 115 of the 136 articles dealing with the maritime world, fear of cholera traversing oceanic space revealed both the need to regulate the maritime world and the fundamentally oceanic nature of these Pacific states. Indeed, in the months leading up to the planning of the Sanitation Conference, Cesáreo Chacaltana Reyes, the minister of foreign affairs of Peru, mentioned the desire to not hurt international commerce through maritime quarantines.[37] Thus, in this scenario, the ocean acted as the transporter of a deadly disease, as a threat to people and business.

The ocean, however, could also be a savior from the disease. Even though the municipal government of Valparaíso thought quite highly of the sanitation of the port, it developed a plan to clean the *cerros*, the hills that surround the small flat portion of the city leading into the bay.[38] At its December 20, 1886, meeting, the intendant proposed the idea of pumping ocean water with gas engines valued at 10,000 pesos from the bay into the cerros. Though the specifics of the plan are less than clear and it never came to fruition, the premise was to let water out at specified locations in the cerros and then have it course down through the problem areas (particularly the ravines), taking with it the hygienic threats to the city.[39] Perhaps the government was aware of a plan devised in 1832 in New York City in which fire hydrants would be opened multiple times a week as a means of cleaning the streets.[40] Though it does not seem that the idea ever materialized, the plan itself shows the central place of the ocean for Chileans in Valparaíso. In this case, the ocean became, quite literally, a cleansing force.[41]

As soon as cholera crossed the Andes from Argentina, the Chilean state began to import medicine and disinfectants from Peru. Just as the fear of cholera spreading to Peru dealt mostly with the oceanic connections, the flow of anti-cholera materials from Peru arrived via the ocean. The Chilean state began to import disinfectants—phenol, calcium chloride, and corrosive sublimate (mercuric chloride)—from Peru as early as December 18, 1886.[42] Not counting the aforementioned shipment on December 18, the Chilean diplomat in Peru sent 206 packages with disinfectants to Valparaíso in December 1886, shipped through the CSAV.[43] In the coming months, the Chilean delegation in Peru sent numerous packages and barrels of materials to Valparaíso, much of it aboard the steamship *Ayacucho*.[44]

Cholera was a business. Coordinating all of these shipments, as well as communicating the status of cholera, also meant paying for telegrams, for example close to 500 pesos to cover the telegrams for the first half of January 1887.[45] In March 1887 the Chilean delegation in Peru sent 14,780.40 pesos' worth of disinfectants to Valparaíso, perhaps the largest shipment of materials.[46] Within Chile the state also had to pay for the loading, unloading, and shipping of materials to various parts of the country. In May 1888, when new cholera cases dropped significantly compared to late 1887, the state paid 477.42 pesos for the distribution of materials within Chile, paid out in fifty-six transactions, mostly to the CSAV (twelve), Compañía Inglesa de Vapores (seven), and H. Gomez (twenty-two).[47]

Cholera, and the fear of its spreading northward via ships, invigorated state formation in Chile and Peru. In Chile, fending off cholera meant the sending of men to various parts of the country to enforce quarantines, the construction of new lazarettos in numerous locations, and funding people to work in the lazarettos. By December 1887, the Ministry of the Interior contracted with the West Coast Telephone company to install telephone lines with the intention of increasing communication concerning cholera. These lines connected various sanitation places, a hospital, and the personal homes of Dr. Patiño Luna and Dr. David Mesa, whom the state contracted with in February 1887 to conduct research on cholera, including detailing the geographic distribution and spread of cholera and the relationship between cholera, climate, and hygiene.[48] In Peru, the arrival of the *Vauban* made clear that a quarantine without a lazaretto made little sense. Cholera set in motion the construction of a lazaretto in Callao and one on the island of San Lorenzo by November 1887, with the latter being completed by the end of December. The idea of creating a lazaretto on San Lorenzo stretched back to at least 1833, when the Peruvian government had noticed the southward movement of cholera from Mexico and Central America.[49] The lazaretto in Callao, though, seems to have taken much longer to construct, since eleven months later the Dirección de Obras Públicas (Public Works) was still allocating funds to two state engineers to work on the lazaretto.[50] Additionally, on the heels of the cholera epidemic, Chilean president Balmaceda created the Consejo Superior de Higiene (High Council on Hygiene) as an institution to protect against future epidemics.[51] Although cholera seems to have never spread in Peru as it did in Chile, the mere idea of a possible cholera epidemic, the speculation about it, created the need for changes in policy and the creation of new material things—telephone lines, lazarettos, sanitation rules, and hygiene on board, among others—that situated the state as the agent to protect society from the ravages of cholera.[52]

All of this is part of what I am referring to as the materiality of the state: the way in which cholera spread, the lazarettos built, and the people enacting social health programs all fit within this broad category of "material." Of course people carry with them not only their bodies but also their minds and years of education and cultural experiences, and this informs how material things are interpreted. But that interpretation is intimately linked to the material itself. The materiality of the lazaretto, the bodies of the people conducting the work of the state, the architecture of housing, and the urban geography of sickness all interact with the cultural/ideological to help in the formation of the state and social movements created out of the cholera outbreak.[53] In this case, the nonhuman in the form of cholera is essential to understanding the historical moment. Regardless of whether cholera had historical "agency," as the bacteria moved from city to city it pushed the state to respond to its advances.[54] There was no intent to change the course of human history immanent to cholera, but in order to continue as bacteria, cholera needed to spread. And contemporaries' ideas on cholera, sanitation, shipping, and international relations intertwined to create the transnational processes of state formation. The historian E. P. Thompson summed up this interaction of material and cultural ideas quite well: "The wood imposes its properties and its 'logic' upon the joiner as the joiner imposes his tools, skills and his ideal conception of tables upon the wood."[55] Similarly, cholera allowed for specific types of actions by state authorities, doctors, and maritime workers.

Neither state authorities nor doctors in Chile and Peru in the 1880s knew the totality of the material life of cholera. According to Federico Puga Borne—a doctor and member of congress named by the minister of justice and public instruction in 1887 to help fend off cholera and who acted as the Chilean state's representative at the Sanitation Conference in Lima in 1888— "the essential cause of cholera ... is still not determined."[56] In an 1886 coauthored pamphlet, Dr. Cárlos Killing, a member of the Junta de Salubridad de Valparaíso, wrote that even though Dr. Robert Koch had discovered the basis of cholera, the work of Rudolf Virchow, which emphasized certain "atmospheric and ground conditions" in the spread of cholera, still held sway over much of the medical community in Chile.[57] In Peru and in Chile (as well as in many other countries), medical thought on cholera (and yellow fever) was divided, for the most part, on whether it spread via person to person contact or through environmental factors, such as urban sanitation.[58] In the case of disinfecting items possibly contaminated with cholera, doctors and scientists offered a number of solutions, from the use of chloride of lime or sulfuric acid to fumigate items or spaces to lengthy exposure to the circulation of air.[59] Even Puga Borne contradicted his own arguments on the effectiveness of fumigation, calling it a false hope in need of condemnation just before going on to describe processes of sanitation that read as fumigation.[60]

The result of this uncertainty about the life of cholera pushed the state in an expansionist direction. If the specific ways cholera spread were unknown, the state interpreted this gap in scientific knowledge as a need to expand and intensify its multiple forms of materially controlling the situation. Expansion came in the form of sending people across the country to help create and maintain sanitary cordons. Similar to the case of Talca mentioned previously, the authorities in the southern city of Moquegua, Peru, asked the School of Medicine of the National University of San Marcos in Lima for more men to enforce new sanitation rules.[61] In January 1887 Manuel Barros Borgoño, the president of the Sociedad Médica (Medical Society) in Santiago, produced six lists with the names of doctors and medical students willing to help the government in its fight against cholera across Chile. These lists ranged from full doctors to "students whose course work has not been possible to verify." Although the listed doctors all desired to remain in Santiago, for licenciados, sixth-year students, and those with "lower level courses" named more varied locations, though still leaning toward Santiago.[62] In order for the state to expand in response to cholera, it tapped into a vast store of laboring bodies, even those who might not have been suited to help, bringing people and territory into the state fold.

Intensification meant digging in where the state already had a strong camp, as in Santiago, Valparaíso, and Callao. In Santiago, the Ministry of the Interior paid for new telephone lines, and Puga Borne argued for the need to check on water drainage and food, sending suspected sick people to lazarettos, the creation of "monitoring committees," and the naming of medical inspectors "to make daily visits to the houses of the city."[63] The intendant of Valparaíso, with eyes on the idle hands of workers as the result of a downturn in the shipping industry due to shipping restrictions meant to impede cholera's international travels, asked the Ministry of the Interior for 40,000 pesos to pay the jobless to repair public roads in the province.[64] Facing a similar problem in Callao, the subprefect worried that the lack of work "could be the cause of frequent and numerous criminal acts," even if they had not yet occurred. The subprefect reasoned that this lack of crime was due to the "well known morality of the people from Callao [chalacos]" as well as the work of the local police. Despite this confidence, he asked the prefect to increase the number of men policing both the urban port and the rural portions outside of the city. (The subprefect also helped the Concejo Provincial in implementing new hygiene regulations, including the visiting of homes and, seeing the number of Asian, probably Chinese, immigrants living in tight quarters, personally destroying the "scaffolds" where they slept.)[65] Connecting the expansion and intensification of the state, one new rule in Peru called for any person who "circumvented" sanitation procedures to be sent back to the border with Chile, and the person's "luggage, goods, or packages" were to be incinerated in the "public plaza wherever they were apprehended."[66] This functioned both as a public lesson to the people of the city and to show the importance of material items in the spread of cholera and the state's control of them.

With the arrival of cholera in Chile and the fear of its traveling to Peru in ships, both states initiated new material forms of state formation. This is not to suggest that either state possessed the material, ideological, or cultural means to produce a state capable of attaining total hegemony or the wholesale stopping of the spread of cholera. Taking a cue from international debates on the spread of cholera through the consumption of fruit, and perhaps with knowledge of authorities in neighboring Argentina burning orchards in the western province of Tucumán during the cholera outbreak there, authorities in Valparaíso set their sights on fruit sales.[67] After the government officially banned the sale of fruit in the port, close to ninety local fruit and legume vendors wrote a letter of protest against the measure, calling it an overreach of the state.[68] Shortly thereafter the vendors' petition succeeded, and the ban was lifted by the Intendancy.[69] In a way this was a debate about the reach of the state versus the rights of individuals, a discussion in full force during the epidemic.[70] But in some cases cholera created enough fear that people across class lines agreed on the need to enforce the sanitary cordon or even asked the state to enact one where it had not yet done so. In the port of Arica, annexed by Chile in the wake of the War of the Pacific, members of diplomatic missions, merchants, members of unions representing port workers, individuals, "and all of the inhabitants of this miserable port"—ninety-six signatories in total—lodged a petition asking for the central government to institute a ban on the docking of all ships from south of Arica.[71] This was a case in which the state "was invited in."[72] Thus while the centralizing political force of the Balmaceda presidency may have lent itself to the structure of public health in Chile, many on the ground welcomed and asked for the state to increase its presence.[73]

## MICROSCOPES AND MICROHISTORY: DAVID MATTO AND TRANSNATIONAL MEDICINE

Peruvian doctors in Lima could hardly not know of the devastation of the War of the Pacific. Indeed, it hit close to home for them: the Chilean army used their medical school as a station during the occupation of Lima. Three years after signing the Treaty of Ancón (1883), which formally ended the War of the Pacific, doctors at the medical school were still trying to catalog exactly what the Chilean Army took back to Chile during its takeover of the school.[74] And since doctors helped during the war, in 1886 the Concejo Provincial de Lima (Provincial Council of Lima) attempted to compile a list to reward all those who had provided "humanitarian services" in their "patriotic" duty.[75] Given the Chilean military's occupation of their school, and the language of patriotism in the last letter, doctors at the School of Medicine very easily could have allowed these experiences to lead them down a path of medical hermeticism in relation to Chile. But with the threat of cholera reaching Peru, they saw a very real need to engage with Chilean diplomats and doctors in their efforts to better understand cholera and stop, or at least impede, its spread.

Outside of the recent events of the War of the Pacific, Chilean doctors associated with the *Boletín de Medicina* displayed some elements of a nationalist sentiment. When the German-born Eduardo Wagner received the post of cirujano mayor of the Navy, the *Boletín* quickly published an editorial against the move. It reminded the public of the sacrifices Chilean doctors had made, from their studies in Chile and Europe, only to see the high medical post go to a foreigner. Although Wagner had supported Chile during the War of the Pacific, his actions did not change the fact that he was German and that equally qualified Chileans—indeed, *more* qualified since part of the qualifications, in their eyes, was being Chilean—deserved the position. The *Boletín* blamed this appointment on a "strange love for the foreign" in Chile and hoped the Chilean state would take a cue from the Catholic Church's rules requiring that bishops be born in the country in which they practiced.[76] The irony of critiquing the "foreign" Wagner while many in the medical community had either studied in Europe or looked to Europe (and particularly France) as the center of the medical world did not faze the authors.[77] Although not directed toward Peruvians, the article shows a definite Chilean nationalism within the medical community. Despite these nationalistic tendencies, when confronted with an epidemic disease like cholera, many Chilean doctors displayed a willingness to work across borders.

Throughout the cholera years, Chilean and Peruvian doctors and diplomats consistently communicated with one another, sharing medical information on cholera. Besides the numerous cables between consulates along the Pacific coast delivering information on which city or town had recently

FIGURE 3. Portrait of David Matto. Source: *El Perú Ilustrado* (Lima, Perú), 11 Feb. 1888.

shown the first signs of cholera, pamphlets and publications were also popular items sent across the maritime border. In October 1887 the decano of the School of Medicine in Lima received "some recently completed publications in Chile on cholera" sent by a Chilean diplomatic agent. Members of the School of Medicine then agreed upon sending two copies of these publications to the collections of the Academia Libre de Medicina in Lima.[78] Two months later the Chilean plenipotentiary sent three copies of the memoria of the Junta Central de Vacuna de Chile, which were to be distributed to anyone who might be interested in them, and stated that if similar publications were produced in Peru, he would appreciate copies being sent to Chile.[79]

Particularly telling is the Peruvian government's commissioning the young doctor David Matto (see figure 3) to visit Chile and "study the advances of the cholera epidemic." Born in Cuzco, Matto eventually moved to Lima when his sister, the writer Clorinda Matto de Turner, brought him with her to take advantage of opportunities available in the capital. During the War of the Pacific Matto used his medical knowledge to support the Peruvian military at the battles of San Juan and Miraflores. Matto also helped found the Sociedad Médica "Unión Fernandina" in 1883, a group that published *La Crónica Médica*, the most important medical journal in Peru at the time and for which Matto served as an editor until his trip to

Chile. Having worked as a "médico de polícia," reporting on the sanitation and health aboard ships to the Ministro de Beneficencia, Matto's medical trajectory blended quite well the experience of seeing a nationalist war firsthand with the life and circulation of the maritime world.[80]

The government assigned Matto the job of going to Chile to study cholera, to "impede the importation of the terrible guest."[81] It is unclear exactly what Matto thought about taking on an assignment that required him to conduct research in the midst of a cholera outbreak. He may have had in mind the life of Daniel A. Carrión, a sixth-year medical student from Cerro de Pasco who had injected himself at the age of twenty-six with what at that point was called the verruga peruana. With a Chilean doctor studying the verruga peruana, Carrión, according to his medical student friends, thought that the Peruvian disease should be studied and a cure found by Peruvians, not anyone else. (Some of this nationalist ideology may have come from Carrión's having served in the Battle of Miraflores during the War of the Pacific.) Carrión extracted the disease from a female patient and injected himself twice in each arm. After thirty-eight days, he died. The verruga peruana then became known as Carrión disease, and Carrión the medical student transformed into a national symbol for Peruvian medicine.[82] Some at the time did indeed place Matto's research alongside that of Carrión.[83] Some doctors also viewed their job as healing the nation in the aftermath of the War of the Pacific.[84] There is, too, a glimpse of how other doctors perceived the task given to Matto. Doctor Francisco Almenara Butler, for instance, wrote of Matto's new duty as "fulfilling the glory of our national medicine." Paradoxically, Butler's emphasis on Matto's research "illustrating to us" the specifics of cholera as part of Peruvian national medicine entailed research *abroad*.[85] In a sense, in the case of cholera research, national medicine required transnational medicine.

Matto stayed in Chile from December 1887 to July 1888. Over the course of those months he traveled to numerous cities, sent information on cholera and the Chilean state's response to it back to Lima, and conducted research with Chilean doctors. Matto's first reports from Chile—which were initially not published in the press so as to not cause the Peruvian public to panic—show a Chilean state allowing almost free movement across the country, with little to suggest that cities or provinces were securely cordoned off.[86] In an "imperfect" map attached to a letter, Matto used red to color in swaths of land between Santiago and Valparaíso and Angol (a city in the southern province of Malleco) to show the route cholera had taken. Traveling in perpendicular directions from Santiago, cholera most likely had hopped on the train with passengers, since the red areas of the map hugged the railroad, Matto noted. Whether coincidence or not, the movement of people, items, and cholera across this area revealed a situation in which cholera surely would continue to spread. In Valparaíso, a port with documented cases of cholera, Matto wrote that ships still left the port for other parts of the country that cholera had not yet reached: "The referenced port has not taken any precaution to impede the transmission of cholera to the ports of the North and South." Steam ships in Valparaíso "freely sail for Iquique and Arica where they are immediately put into free communication" and "nobody stops" a passenger who might be carrying and spreading cholera.[87] Considering Peru's closing of its ports to ships incoming from Chile, as well as Matto's previous work overseeing ship sanitation, it is clear that many in Peru arrived at the conclusion that securing the oceanic spread of cholera was essential to stopping cholera's advance to Peru.

Part of Matto's work in Chile seems to have been to relate to people in Peru not only the course of cholera, but also how the Chilean state responded to it. In a certain sense, Matto interpreted the Chilean state as doing relatively little, as seen in the previous paragraph. But Matto did go into great detail on the specifics of the Chilean state's procedures, as well as the state structure to deal with cholera. A "Comisión Directiva," headed by Dr. Wenceslao Díaz, led the "sanitation services" of the country, and the commission fit under the umbrella of the Ministry of the Interior. It created thirteen sanitary stations throughout Santiago, each with "one or two doctors, a pharmacist, and a first aid kit," and each station produced a daily report on "the infected, the dead, the cured, etc.," which it sent to the commission. Matto went on to describe disinfection methods, conducting house visits, and the functioning and material composition of lazarettos.[88] Although the Chilean state employed house visits, Matto thought the method "impossible" to implement, and suggested that the Junta de Sanidad in Peru focus on the "multiplication of houses of assistance and lazarettos."[89] In a way, Matto's suggestion of forming casas de asistencia and lazarettos stayed the course of the treatment of epidemics in Lima: during the 1868 yellow fever epidemic, the government moved away from treating the sick in their homes in the midst of the outbreak.[90] This type of transnational reporting by Matto reads as a "how to" (or "how not to") guide for state officials in Peru. If cholera acted as a catalyst for parts of Chilean state formation, these actions, as reported by Matto, also put into motion similar processes in Peru.

Matto's research in Chile and his reports back to Lima also function as a working-through of transnational medicine. In his first report, Matto told the story of two women with cholera. One woman from Valparaíso allowed a friend fleeing cholera in Quillota to stay at her house, and they shared the same bed for the night. "The next day both friends had cholera and were sent to the lazaretto of Valparaíso, where after twelve hours, the sick woman from Quillota died."[91] Although he had just arrived, Matto already had access to patients at the "Baron" lazaretto of Valparaíso, suggesting that he must have formed some connections to the local medical community. These connections, in turn, meant access to subjects to study. It also meant being a part of a social community around and within which medical professionals congregated. On January 3, 1888, for instance, the Santiago medical community held a banquet in honor of Matto that fifteen doctors and eleven others attended, with some doctors sending cards or messages saying that, due to various reasons, they could not attend. "The banquet went on, in the midst of the most frank and cordial cheerfulness, until eleven at night."[92]

This transnational medical world was in large part a man's world. Although an article in *La Crónica Médica* does not delve into the details of the discussions at the banquet, it is significant that entrance into the event was gendered: every person who attended as a guest on January 3, 1888, was male. If you were a doctor in 1880s Chile, it was almost a certainty you would have been male. As historian María Soledad Zárate points out, in the 1885 census, of 625 doctors across Chile, only 12 women could count themselves as part of the community. The medical community of doctors formed a homosocial world in which the foundations of the profession involved "masculine virtues," wherein the "man of science" of academic texts meant just that: man as exclusive owner of medical science and practice.[93] In Peru, too, the medical community was largely populated by men, a gendered atmosphere that would not change in any major way until the second decade of the twentieth century. And even when gender dynamics shifted, they tended to route women to medical subfields (such as odontology, pharmacy, and nursing), and men most likely viewed their female colleagues as less-skilled practitioners.[94] Matto's entry into the medical community in Chile, while partially formed around a mutual idea of medical research, also relied on masculine assumptions about who could practice medicine.

In mid-December 1887 Matto began working with Dr. Cárlos Killing in Viña del Mar. Killing, as mentioned previously, had cowritten a pamphlet on cholera in 1886 and was a member of the Junta de Salubridad de Valparaíso.

According to Matto, Killing was a chemist "very knowledgeable in micrography," the ability to photograph through a microscope.[95] In Killing and Augusto Villanueva G.'s 1886 report on cholera and hygiene, after detailing the relation between cholera and the environment, including topography, hygiene, and water, they offered a final comment on the future of studying public hygiene and epidemics, arguing for the creation of a "Municipal Laboratory, similar to those that, with great success, [function in] the principal cities of Europe."[96] Moreover, original research on cholera in Chile was minimal, according to Killing and Villanueva, resulting in their need to rely on studies produced in Europe; this new laboratory, though, would help fix this lack of in-depth study in Chile.[97] Despite the absence of a municipal laboratory, Killing did have access to scientific equipment, and with this equipment he and Matto conducted research on cholera. Together, Killing and Matto collected a small sample of diarrhea of a patient with cholera, and they used Killing's microscope to view the sample. In describing cholera organisms under the microscope, Matto wrote that "in the proper environment . . . , they live perfectly, they move rapidly, and they are presented in all of their forms and states." Matto continued: "It is quite an enchanting spectacle, the world of the infinitely small, whose law is 'destroy to live,' that pass through the area of the microscope by the hundreds and thousands, quickly moving in all senses, in incessant activity. The observation of these tiny beings, in their full vitality, is so appealing, without a doubt similar to what it must be for astronomers to contemplate the sky through the telescope." Under the microscope, these "tiny beings" possessed their own life and logic to Matto, an observable process that Killing and Matto probably discussed at length. After these initial days of working together Matto and Killing prepared two samples to send to Lima, though they were never sent because Matto feared that the fumigation process in Arica would damage them.[98] Matto brought some of these initial samples to Viña del Mar, resulting in a sixteen-hour delay between the collection of the samples and the viewing of them through Killing's Zeiss lens–equipped microscope.[99] A week later Matto and Killing produced photos of cholera in Killing's laboratory. Although the resulting photographs were not of the highest quality, Matto relayed a high regard for Killing's ability to prepare the sample and gelatin tubes.[100]

Part of this transnational medical cooperation found its basis in the material instruments of the profession. Matto traveled to Chile without any scientific instruments: "I did not have even a watch glass, much less a microscope."[101] In a different context, historian of science Kapil Raj shows how British scientific interventions in South Asia entailed much less a science *over* South Asian science and society and required the interaction, though in an extremely hierarchical form, of British scientists and local science and bodies.[102] While it is unclear whether or not the research by Matto and Killing produced a new type of knowledge, as Raj proposes for South Asia, it is clear that despite the scientific premise of Matto's trip to Chile, he brought none of the material instruments required for his research. Thus the connections between Matto and Killing, as well as others, and Matto's ability to produce scientific knowledge on cholera to inform the Peruvian state of both its spread in Chile and ways to stop or impede its arrival in Peru, necessitated close working relationships between Peruvians and Chileans, which revolved around access to scientific instruments.

After a month of working together, Matto and Killing finally performed an autopsy on the body of someone lost to cholera. On January 13, 1888, only ten minutes after the person passed away, Matto began to collect intestinal contents, and Killing worked on the culture. They prepared three separate samples: one placed in a humidity chamber, another in gelatin on a plate, and one in gelatin tubes. The humidity chamber produced cholera "in all of its life, surprising to the observer with its rapid movements and incessant activity" in only one day; the samples in gelatin on a plate were visible within two days; and cholera cultivation in the gelatin tubes succeeded after three days. Their results paralleled the recent work undertaken by Salazar at the Naval School in the port so much that Matto attached a photo of cholera captured by Salazar back to Lima in his correspondence (see figure 4). At one point in describing some of the processes used in the lab, Matto resorted to the use of analogy: "The microbes seen in the prepared plates, with the water having been taken out, are dry, like the *raisin* with respect to the *grape*, if the comparison is permitted."[103] Perhaps a small flourish of the pen. But it is also part and parcel of a lengthy description of how to conduct similar research in Lima, of resorting to a familiar scenario to relate an unfamiliar scientific procedure; it is a use of analogy in order to help foment new medical research techniques in Peru, techniques that were learned in Chile. It was a moment in the transnational history of medicine.

In February Matto left central Chile and headed south, mostly in the company of Dr. Patiño Luna. Cases of cholera in central Chile steadily declined in January, while in southern Chile the number of cases continued to increase. Around the same time, the Comisión Directiva del Servicio Sanitario

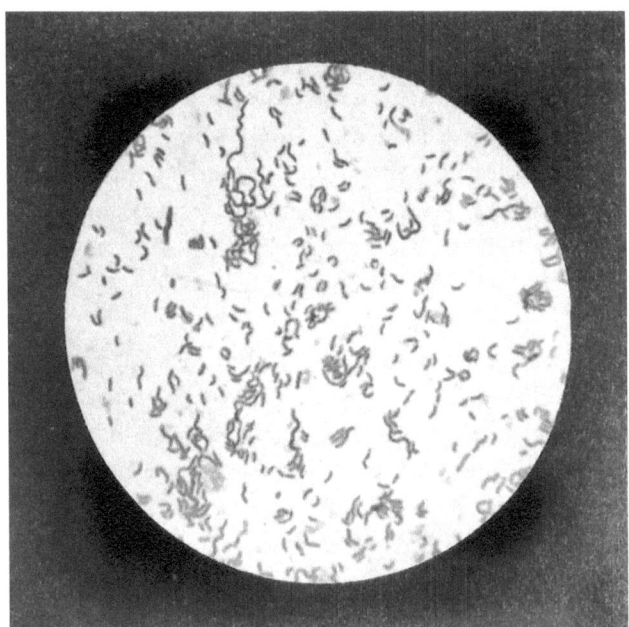

FIGURE 4. Spirillum *Cholerae Asiáticae* in hard gelatin, at a magnification of 500, after forty-eight hours at an average room temperature of 26°C. *Source:* A. E. Salazar and C. Newman, *Notas sobre el espirilo del cólera asiático (Bacillus Coma de Koch)* (Valparaíso: Imprenta del Universo de G. Helgmann, 1888). Biblioteca Nacional de Chile.

(Commission of Sanitation Services) in Santiago called upon Patiño Luna to travel in order to "inspect the medical services in the South."[104] Patiño Luna, as mentioned earlier, had received a new telephone line directly to his home in December 1887. While in southern Chile, Matto visited Talca, Chillán, Concepción, Talcahuano, Penco, Los Angeles, Angol, Los Sauces, Traiguen, Collipulli, Coronel, Lota, Laraquete, and Arauco, while also receiving messages on other areas, such as Mulchén, Nacimiento, and Santa Bárbara. Matto's reporting from his visit through the south reads as a description of cities and towns, mentioning climate, humidity, number of sites to receive patients, numbers of sick, mortality rates, and sanitation. As discussed previously, Matto found the Chilean state's efforts at making house visits ill-thought-out. Nonetheless, in Collipulli Matto went along with Patiño Luna on a number of house visits, including one he described as follows: "Visiting the sick in various houses, with doctor Patiño, we saw in one of them someone with cholera in a very bad state, laying on the ground, in a badly taken care of room, who had two children of a tender age on each side, in the same bed, and who vomited on top of them, wetting the floor of the room with their vomit. This scene proved to me yet again the difficulty and danger that is home assistance with this sickness, as in all sickness which are infectious by their nature."[105] In this case, working with a state-employed Chilean doctor following the state's guidelines of conducting house visits met with Matto's skeptical eye toward the procedure, and Matto made it clear to the doctors reading his letters in Lima that he would not advise such a system in Peru.

The spread of cholera soon began to slow in Chile. The structure of Matto's reports shifted from discussing a traveling bacteria to showing the geographical and numerical contraction of patients. In one letter Matto reproduced a table showing an overall drop in people entering and dying in the San Borja lazaretto. After a steep rise from 41 entering in October to 211 in November 1887, 154 entered in December, followed by 106 in January and 68 in February. Deaths in the lazaretto dropped from 123 in November 1887 to 19 in February 1888.[106] Matto reported similar trends in other places, as well. With the diminishing of cholera, and having completed the task given to him, it was time for Matto to return to Lima.[107]

Matto arrived in Lima on July 11, 1888, after almost seven months of research in Chile. Before his return, the editorial board of *La Crónica Médica* in Lima asked the public to donate to a fund in order to bestow upon Matto a gold award for his service.[108] Announcing his return on the cover of the journal, the editorial board wrote of Matto's ability to "conquer the appreciation and sympathies of the most select society of Chile," many of whom helped facilitate his research, and they thanked their Chilean counterparts with "deep appreciation." They even reproduced, word for word, the "farewell" printed in the Santiago-based *Boletín de Medicina*, in which the authors used the same language as the board of *La Crónica Médica*: Matto "has managed to conquer the appreciation and esteem of his Santiago colleagues." The Sociedad Médica of Santiago also named Matto a "corresponding member" in Lima and hoped that "this proof of respect and sympathy will contribute to the strengthening of ties between those in Peru and Chile, of those who dedicate themselves to medical studies."[109] Despite the clear transnational medical and scientific ties that allowed Matto to conduct research in Chile, the Concejo Provincial de Lima decided to honor Matto by delivering a gold medal to him on "the 28th of July, 67th anniversary of National Independence," tilting his work in the direction of a nationalist service.[110] Nonetheless, in the same issue of *La Crónica Médica*, Matto expressed, in his last published letter of correspondence on cholera, his thanks to the medical community of Chile: "Within the medical community in Chile I found all types of facilities to complete my commission, and to the people a special distinction to those whose help went beyond the simple duty of professional fraternity."[111]

In *Affective Communities*, Leela Gandhi suggests that a Manichean view of colonialism does not allow for the space to incorporate and think through anti-colonial persons from the colonial center. Gandhi, drawing on vegetarian groups in turn-of-the-century London, argues that some people built bonds across the colonial divide through an emphasis on a non-speciesist perspective on the world. As such, they created an anti-imperial subculture within empire.[112] To be clear, the Chile-Peru relation was not the same as that of England and South Asia. But Gandhi's argument resonates with the transnational medical community analyzed here. While their attitudes may not have reached into the realm of a critique of the War of the Pacific, to the taking of land, or to the racialized and gendered rhetoric of the war, their active partnership in researching cholera, of borrowing material instruments, seeing the same bacteria through the same microscope, and working toward a common goal that functioned less as a tool of nationalism and much more as a push for a science without a nation (to rework the anarquismo sin adjetivo of the late nineteenth century) approaches the outlook of some of the vegetarian groups discussed by Gandhi.[113] Similar to Paul S. Sutter's argument on entomological workers in the Panama Canal, the veracity of their scientific research is less important than the ideologies these doctors brought to their work.[114] At a time in which nationalist ideologies emanated powerfully from many on both sides of the border, these doctors enacted a "science without a nation" that countered such nationalist dogmas.

Gandhi places her historical subjects in the category of "affective cosmopolitanism," and although her definition of the term is more suited for the colonial relationship of England and South Asia, the idea of one putting "friend over country" is particularly apt here.[115] In his last correspondence on his research in Chile, Matto made it clear that while the medical community in Chile helped facilitate his work, they also formed part of his personal, affective community. Matto concluded his letter by mentioning Chilean doctors "and to the people a special distinction to those whose help went beyond the simple duty of professional fraternity." Matto continued: "For that, now outside of that republic, from the distance, I make present and public my thankfulness."¹¹⁶ Though similar in form to many late nineteenth-century letters that ended with appreciation for the receiver of the letter, Matto's language of gratitude for the relationships he built outside of the laboratory, and displaying this to the public at large in Peru, suggest that at least one Peruvian and more than a few Chileans created a medical and affective community in the midst of the 1880s cholera outbreak. It was a community less interested in the marker of nation and much more interested in research and friendship.

In such a close look at Matto, the question of historical importance arises. Was his experience a singular, atypical, fascinating yet exceptional history, considering the purportedly larger trend of nationalism in the aftermath of the War of the Pacific? The question, though, is a false beginning, leading directly back into the teleological logic this book seeks to disrupt. Matto, Killing, and the other Chilean doctors with whom he worked "swam against" the "fundamental currents" of the time and, as such, make up what Lara Putnam has called a "telling example." For Putnam, when there is "a strong presumption of *absence*" within the literature, and we find a few examples that contradict this presumption, "one or more instances of *presence* [are] something to write home about."¹¹⁷ And write home about it Matto certainly did.

## CONCLUSION

In December 1888 the intendant of Valparaíso met with a group of twenty-six doctors to discuss the recent cholera outbreak and the sanitary conditions of the port city. The doctors reported that although recently some had fallen ill to smallpox or fevers, there had not been one case of cholera. They assured the intendant that "the state of sanitation in Valparaíso was highly satisfactory," a phrasing suggestive of a low possibility of cholera's return. Nonetheless, the intendant called for the formation of a medical commission that would coordinate any type of response to a new medical emergency. The doctors present agreed, and they voted on a commission made up of Francisco Javier Villanueva, Georg Thiele, and Juan Edwin Espic.¹¹⁸ Villanueva was a well-known doctor in Valparaíso since the 1840s, when he had worked at the San Juan de Dios Hospital, later working for the Servicio de Sanidad Naval and the expanded San Juan de Dios in 1879, and a member of the Junta de Salubridad during the cholera outbreak; Thiele trained as a doctor in Berlin and had arrived in Valparaíso in 1873; and Edwin Espic would work as a doctor in the maternity ward of San Agustín Hospital in 1894.[119] The intendant and doctors clearly saw the need to prepare for the possibility of another cholera outbreak, bringing together the power of the local government and some of the most well-established members of the medical community.

But securing Chile—or at least doing everything possible to secure Chile—from future cholera epidemics also required the funds to finance these efforts, and the spaces in which to do it. In 1890, two years after the Sanitation Conference in Lima, the Chilean Ministry of Foreign Relations in Peru wrote an urgent letter to the Ministry of the Marina. Although the vast monetary cost of upgrading and maintaining Chilean sanitation facilities might seem exorbitant, the Chilean state needed to keep in mind the economic effects of ports being closed to ships departing from Chile, as had just occurred a few years before. Even if other Pacific coast countries failed to put in their fair share of money and resources to help impede the spread of diseases, the Chilean state possessed enough old ships to create a maritime sanitation fleet that could potentially satisfy authorities in other ports.[120] The suggestion, however, does not seem to have moved beyond this discussion. In July 1903 representatives from seven shipping companies servicing the coasts of Chile and Peru met in Valparaíso to discuss the closing of ports to ships leaving from Chilean ports. Yet again, the closing of ports directly affected their ability to ship goods and people, and in turn their economic bottom line. In conjunction with the intendant of Valparaíso, they argued against long periods of quarantine and in favor of full disinfection at the port of all people and things on ships, which the companies would pay for, and even offered to oversee the procedure or propose other methods of control.[121]

A year later, in 1904, the Cámara de Comercio in Guayaquil, Ecuador, sent a letter to its equivalent in Valparaíso concerning the circulation of bubonic plague in the Pacific. The Cámara had recently bought a new machine to disinfect ships, their contents, and the people working on them in port. If each port in the Pacific bought one, the letter stated, "we would all be totally free from the risk" of the plague and thus allow for the continual flow of goods from port to port.[122] A few years later, at the 1908–9 Pan-American Scientific Congress in Santiago, Chile, delegates returned to the emphasis on the need to establish "quarantine stations for all incoming vessels" in port cities.[123] And at the Pan-American Scientific Congress held in Washington, D.C., in 1915–16, a Uruguayan delegate pointed out new regulations regarding the reporting of disease on board ships. Second on the list of diseases was cholera, which should be reported immediately instead of within a twenty-four-hour window like many of the others.[124] These efforts show a clear understanding of the importance of public health and sanitation in port cities. They also reveal a vision of state-scientific power to dominate processes out of their control. Underlying all of these concerns, yet somehow absent from the conversation, was the fact that maritime circulation, the basis of the power and importance of port cities, necessarily meant exposure to infectious diseases. Commerce lay at the heart of port cities; as Karl Marx wrote in the mid-nineteenth century, "The circulation of capital is at the same time its becoming, its growth, its vital process." For Marx, "if anything needed to be compared with the circulation of the blood," it was the circulation of capital.[125] Even if these measures held up the dream of a sanitized or at least controlled Pacific in order to both save lives and maintain trade, the efforts went against the very logic and purpose of port cities.

The months of research in Chile seem to have affected how Dr. Matto conceptualized medicine, as well. If during his time working with Dr. Killing in a laboratory in Viña del Mar he observed cholera as "tiny beings," this vision of the microbe world remained with Matto in the following years. In 1891 Matto finished his doctoral thesis on tetanus. Much of the thesis is a state of the field report, without much laboratory research of his own. In his introductory remarks on the work, though, Matto resorted to a language of describing medical researchers examining bacteria that was remarkably similar to his phrasing when discussing cholera. These new researchers, Matto wrote, "have risen in all parts, to explore through diverse means and in all senses, this kingdom of the infinitely small." Medical researchers' work involved studying the bacteriological world, a process that Matto compared to "interviewing" these tiny beings.[126]

In later years Matto remained committed to some type of cooperative relationship with Chile. From December 1908 to January 1909, scientists from across the Americas met in Santiago for the Fourth Latin American Scientific Congress. In preparation for the conference, Matto wrote a brief book detailing the history of medical teaching in Peru. A broad work of synthesis stretching from precolonial times to the present, much of the work dealt with the types of classes required of medical students and some of the important names in the field. Matto mentioned the havoc the War of the Pacific had caused for the Medical School and the efforts to rebuild thereafter.[127] But with the continent-wide congress ahead of him, Matto also referenced the treaties Peru had with various countries that allowed for medical training to transfer from one place to the other. In particular he singled out Chile, with whom Peru had signed an agreement in December 1907, and he included the entirety of the agreement as one of his appendixes. In his closing paragraphs Matto "applauded" the congress's push to "unify" the teaching of medicine across the Americas. Finding "equivalences" and pushing past "obstacles" "is the ideal to which we, all of the North and South *Americanos* should aspire."[128]

The cholera years of 1886 to 1888 created panic across the South American Pacific, as well as throughout the Atlantic world. Sanitation and health commissions created new quarantines, called for the construction of new medical facilities, and oversaw the public health response. Cholera's movement, from Argentina to across the Andes, and its rapid travel within Chile, combined with the scientific debates around the specific life of cholera, fomented these material forms of state formation. Cholera also brought together the medical communities of Peru and Chile just a few years after the end of a bitter war between the two countries. Many of these medical professionals, such as David Matto, had themselves taken part in the war. But the necessity of researching cholera, how it traveled, and how to prevent it from continuing to spread allowed them to put aside antagonistic nationalisms and work together. Even if some of the state recommendations from the era failed to survive past the end of the outbreak, this collaborative scientific work magnifies the efforts of looking past borders and toward a science without a nation.

FOUR

## *Comparisons and Connections in Pacific Anarchism*

IN LATE 1924 Chilean anarchist Luis Toro and a fellow shipmate named Rodriguez disembarked in the port of Callao, Peru. Before arriving, crew members warned Toro of the violence and repression that awaited Chileans in the Peruvian port. They told "stories of prisons, beatings, and abuses that others have had to experience in Callao, all only for being Chileans." Despite these stories, Toro and Rodriguez walked to the local office of the Union Marítima y Terrestre de la Compañía Peruana de Vapores y Dique del Callao (UMT). After listening to Toro explain the reasons for his visit, UMT members told him his timing was perfect—"la hora no podía ser mas oportuna"—since a meeting of the *Mantaro*'s crew was scheduled to take place shortly thereafter. They discussed a worker's proposal of supporting the political candidacy of a worker from Callao with a solid reputation of backing working-class aims. The crew and UMT members "coldly listened" to the idea before shooting it down as a waste of time. The anti-electoral political position of the workers revealed an ideological link between workers in Callao and Wobblies in Chile. Toward the end of the meeting Toro spoke with the Peruvians about the history of their union and their labor struggles, and they found much common ground on political positions.[1]

Afterward R. Orellana, the president of the Callao union, sent a letter back home with Toro. He emphasized the desire of the UMT to strengthen connections with the Chilean IWW in order to better organize "against the abuses that constantly surround us." Orellana thanked Toro and Rodriguez for visiting the union office, expressed his hopes that they would return and discuss the relationship between the two unions, and urged them to actualize their ideological internationalism by creating relationships with unions in "both regions." It was, after all, in each government's "interest to maintain a latent division between the two peoples." Should Chilean readers of *La Voz del Mar* find themselves in Callao, Orellana urged them to leave their ships and visit the union office, to help create "the road towards our ideal of universal fraternity."[2]

This chapter delves into the ways in which maritime and port workers in Chile and Peru organized, circulated radical politics, and built solidarity across the border. Much of the literature on labor movements in Peru and Chile is limited by national boundaries.[3] In some cases a text may follow one or two organizers into other countries, but the story is tangential to the main argument.[4] Rather than being a critique of such scholarship, this chapter shows what types of historical narratives a transnational history of labor might open up.[5] By homing in on Mollendo, Peru, and Valparaíso, Chile, this chapter shows both the specifics of each port and the workers there as well as the ways Peruvian and Chilean workers and their struggles mixed at various points. Workers had complaints that dealt with their situation in their ports or on their ships, yet these problems were similar to those of workers across the South American Pacific, and when workers—in this case specifically anarchist workers—interacted, their workplace issues and politics of industrial unionism created the conditions through which to produce a transnational, maritime labor movement. The transnational perspective allows for these stories to come into focus, but it can also run the risk of ignoring the nation or state, as though movement or connections cast the national to the side. But workers, even those who moved around the Pacific or worked with people from around the world, lived and labored under the laws of a specific state. And in some cases, transnational circulation reinforced national states.

Local and national issues, then, mixed with the transnational maritime world of the early twentieth century. The overarching narrative must follow both the transnational and the local simultaneously. As some working on maritime connections have argued, while the space of the ocean offers a certain amount of unity, there is a difference within unity. Each bay in the Mediterranean, Fernand Braudel argued, was its own "miniature community, a complex world in itself"; the Pacific, Matt Matsuda showed, might best be thought of as "multiple seas, cultures, and peoples" that are part of a "historical assemblage of smaller elements."[6] Transnational history should also "sink back deeply into place," as David Sartorious and Micol Seigel have suggested, cognizant of the various scales at play and the co-constitutive nature of the local and transnational.[7] With this in mind, the chapter looks closely at the local and national issues affecting workers, how they interpreted these concerns, and why they organized in particular ways.

Struggles over wages and hours in Mollendo are discussed in the first and third sections of this chapter, and maritime Wobblies in Chile organizing around labor recruitment and social laws are covered in the second section. Their concerns were first and foremost the elements of the local and national. In a sense, these are parallel moments of organizing along the South American Pacific littoral. But due to workers' mobility on ships and their interaction with people from abroad at ports, many developed a politics of internationalism. Similar labor issues and a politics of anticapitalism that viewed state conflict as mere distraction for working-class organizing helped create transnational maritime and port worker solidarity. And significantly, this transnational organizing occurred while the Peruvian and Chilean states were still engaged in negotiations over the future of the disputed land of Tacna and Arica.

## MOLLENDO, 1916–1918

The crew of the Chilean steamship *Cachapoal* may have been taken by surprise when they approached the port of Mollendo on March 17, 1918. Normally, the *Cachapoal* would have been met by stevedores, who unloaded materials from the ship onto *lanchas*, small boats. On these lanchas, lancheros received the materials and steered the lanchas to the dock, where they would work with jornaleros to unload the cargo and passengers onto the dock. If crew members had been working a smaller tonnage ship, izaderos (called playeros in other ports) would have been responsible for much of the unloading of the cargo, as well as any passengers.[8] All of this work required, to an extent, some type of collective process, of knowing that each job depended on the one before and after it. Despite differences in pay, the process of loading and unloading cargo and passengers meant that workers most likely knew that their job was but one link within the chain of shipping.

But this was no normal day. Instead of being greeted by stevedores, marineros were sent to the ship by the capitán del puerto, Victor V. Valdivieso. This probably signaled to the crew that the port of Mollendo was not functioning as it typically did. The crew may have had similar experiences in the past or at least heard of them from other crews. When jornaleros in Callao went on strike in 1917, demanding an increase in pay after some of them were injured while loading cement, the shipping company W. R. Grace & Co. requested marineros to replace the jornaleros.[9] Whatever the case may

FIGURE 5. Mollendo, Peru, date unknown. *Source:* Unknown photographer, n.d., glass plate negative, 1996.00009.X93485, Keystone-Mast Collection, UCR/California Museum of Photography, University of California, Riverside.

have been, marineros unloaded the cargo of the *Cachapoal* without any difficulties. In the following days, marineros performed the same labor on the Chilean steamship *Mapocho*, as well as on the CSAV steamship *Palena*.[10]

Mollendo was a relatively new port in 1918 (see figure 5). One visitor in the early 1870s described it as a city with a "sufficiently numerous population" that, only a "few years ago... was a barren, and uninhabited rock."[11] The neighboring port of Islay was the second most important port in Peru after Callao until 1874, when a new railroad connected the provincial capital of Arequipa to the coast and, in effect, established Mollendo.[12] Shortly thereafter, in 1880, Chilean soldiers "pillage[d] the city" after finding a store of liquor, destroying the dock, railroad station, and other buildings during the War of the Pacific.[13] After the war Mollendo was the main port for southern Peru, as well as for Bolivia, particularly for wool, mostly from alpaca and sheep; from 1916 to 1930, wool represented 73 percent of all exports through Mollendo, even with a sharp fall in the 1920s.[14] Beginning in 1914 with the completion of a railroad connecting La Paz to Arica, Chile, exports from Bolivia had a new route to the global market, and Mollendo had a new (Chilean) competitor for Bolivian exports.[15] Still, in 1918 the quantity of goods exported through Mollendo continued to increase.

The March 1918 Mollendo strike built on over two years of organizing by port workers. On January 26, 1916, members of various shipping companies, the capitán of the navy and port, and two foremen of the laborers' union (*gremio de jornaleros*) met to sign an agreement on port work in Mollendo, Peru. They set the workday at 6:00 a.m. to 6:00 p.m., with one hour of the day for rest and to eat and daily wages at 3 soles for normal days and 4 soles for holidays, with an extra 0.60 sole and some type of food distributed to jornaleros for work done after 6:00 p.m. In addition, for hourly workers, who probably had a much less consistent work schedule, their wage was placed at 0.50 sole per hour on normal days and at 0.60 sole on holidays. Jornaleros would also receive 0.30 sole per ton of coal or coke in bags moved, with bulk coke paying 0.40 sole per ton due to the increased labor required to move it.[16] In this agreement, a typical day of labor for a jornalero meant eleven hours of work with only one hour of rest.

By the end of the next year, port workers in Mollendo petitioned for a new agreement. In a letter with forty-eight signatories, they claimed the right to an eight-hour workday paid at 4 soles; an extra 0.80 sole for working between 6:00 and 7:00 a.m., 11:00 a.m. and 1:00 p.m., and 5:00 and 6:00 p.m.; double pay for work on holidays; and no work at night.[17] Discussion ensued between local authorities of the state in Mollendo and in Callao. Officials in Mollendo thought the demand for an eight-hour workday, "as established in Callao," just and achievable considering that it worked in Callao, a much larger and busier port. Authorities in Callao disagreed: "There is no reason to alter the established."[18]

Some petitions also drew upon notions of gender and the family to persuade the recipients in their favor. In November 1917 the lancheros union of The Mollendo Agencies Company (also called Casa Grace) petitioned for an eight-hour workday, a ban on working on holidays unless paid double, and increases to their pay for working on lanchas. All of this was just from their perspective because as "fathers of families" the continuing low pay for their labor directly affected families in the port, making it "impossible to attend to the necessities of our homes." They even asked that the state contact a doctor and senator from their department who would vouch for their claims.[19] Valdivieso refuted most of their arguments, but he never mentioned the discourse on the family.[20] Nonetheless, their use of a gendered discourse—of lancheros as male heads of households and of the family as an important social unit in the port—shows that they perceived this type of argument as powerful enough to sway the state. These very claims drew from a much longer history of honor, class, and the concept of a male head of house in the department of Arequipa (and Chile).[21] Their petition linked, in a direct way, pay and work in the port with the material well-being of women and children in their homes. They connected and intertwined their class concern with their conceptions of gender and family. As heads of households, they had the responsibility—and duty—to provide the necessary finances for the support of their families.[22]

In between these two petitions—the first in January 1916 and the second in November 1917—other unions in Mollendo wrote, signed, and delivered their own sets of demands. In April the Gremio de Izaje requested higher pay per ton of material they moved, and in May stevedores asked for double pay on holidays and to be given the sole right to load and unload any material sent on the state-owned railroad or on cabotage boats.[23] On August 15, 1917, both unions agreed to different increases in pay: the stevedores, led by Juan Vargas and Fermin Carpio, won a 75 percent increase in their pay rate, as well as an increase of 75 percent on holidays, and the izadores, led by Manuel Torres and Emilio Chirinos, signed a deal for a 75 percent increase in holiday pay.[24] Izadores did not win their demand for a higher pay rate per tonnage, perhaps because Valdivieso had little esteem for the izadores' work, characterizing it as the "lightest with relation to the other maritime services" just before their negotiations.[25]

The central state in Callao weighed in against these local agreements. The response by authorities in Callao reveals a legal rationale, a logic of labor-private company exchange, and national economic interests. Izadores and stevedores, they argued, were not legal maritime unions, their work being subject to free negotiation between individual workers and the people employing them.[26] Stevedores were classified in a similar manner.[27] With negotiations directly between workers and companies, the state had no place within these private affairs, and therefore they did not see a reason for the state to intervene.[28] Some even responded that since they had begun to examine the situation of the izadores, they now realized that there were far too many izadores for the workload, and they suggested a slashing of their numbers.[29] Moreover, raising the cost of labor in any way would result in less commercial traffic through Mollendo. Companies and state authorities argued that any increase to the cost of shipping through Mollendo would push commercial traffic south to Arica, providing an economic boost to Chile. Maintaining shipping costs, in this case the price of labor, was a "patriotic obligation."[30]

Combined, these sets of negotiations reveal several different types of relationships in the port of Mollendo. For port workers, it is clear that while they respected the local representative of the state, Valdivieso, they also did not see him as either the final decision maker or the person who would weigh in on their side of the negotiations. Behind the scenes, authorities in Callao held a much stiffer line in the negotiations, but it is doubtful that the unions knew this, and from the beginning of the strike they continued to look to the central state as an arbiter on their behalf. After unsuccessful individual petitions, different classifications of port workers began to organize together. Some signatures on petitions by one union, Valdivieso noted, were from workers not associated with the specific union submitting the petition, suggesting that communications across job classification were taking place.[31] Considering the cooperation across different job classifications necessary to load and unload and move goods and people at the port, the cross-job communication makes sense. By March, after individual rejections, the petitioners turned toward their power as *port* workers, rather than as stevedores or izadores.

On March 16, 1918, after several labor unions had petitioned for various sets of increases in wages and changes in work scheduling, the unions sent in a notice of their intention to strike.[32] But before declaring the port-wide strike, they attempted one last petition. Signed by the Gremio de Jornaleros, Gremio de Izaje, Gremio de Lancheros, and Gremio de Chaluperos, the petition framed their local protest within the global situation: the war in Europe had created a increases in the prices of goods, yet their wages had not risen to compensate for these changes.[33] Although wool exports in 1918 were still high and had not yet fallen off, as they would in the 1920s, and while many elites lived quite well in the aftermath of World War I due to these exports, these were also years in which the cost of living across Latin America (and the world) had increased.[34] Workers in Mollendo knew this economic reality firsthand. The Mollendo Agencies Company and Pacific Steam Navigation rejected their petition in three days.[35] Valdivieso relayed the news of the impending strike to authorities in Callao, telling them that he was ready for anything that might come.[36]

Valdivieso did not overestimate his preparedness for the strike. Although several unions struck together, he called upon marineros to help load and unload materials in the port.[37] Valdivieso consistently wrote to Callao to convey the tranquility of the strike, even remarking that some workers "very respectfully" declined his suggestion to return to work. Nonetheless, local authorities called in military help for the strike.[38] By March 23 *hombres de infantería* (infantry) and the guardia civil were on their way to Mollendo, along with gente de mar strike breakers.[39] Unfortunately for the shipping companies and Valdivieso, port workers spoke with the potential strike breakers and convinced many of them to honor their strike. Some of the new workers who crossed the strike line were unfamiliar with the work routine of the port and injured themselves at the worksite.[40]

By the end of March, shipping companies, unions, and the state finalized an agreement to end the strike. Lancheros employed by The Mollendo Agencies Company received an increase from 19 soles for lanchas to 28 soles (a 47% increase), from 0.40 centavo per ton of coal to 0.50 centavo, and an increase from 0.50 centavo per ton of ballast to 0.60 centavo. Lancheros of the Compañía Inglesa received increases for each lancha size, ranging from increases of 3 soles for the largest (25 to 28 soles) to 2.5 soles (7.50 to 10 soles). Similarly, stevedores of both companies won increases according to the size of the lanchas; izadores got a flat rate for all things they unloaded instead of different rates for cargo and ballast; donkeros moved from a daily rate of 2 soles to a monthly pay of 75 soles plus 25 centavos for overtime; cuadrilla de tonelaje pay was set at 40 centavos for all goods; the conductores' monthly wage went from 75 to 90 soles (a 20% raise); and jornaleros fixed their pay rates across the different hourly work schedules.[41] These were large gains across the board for port workers. Their struggle—in individual petitions, striking together, and arriving at a contract in which some workers almost doubled their pay and others saw increases of 20 percent—must have shown them their power when organizing across job classifications. It unveiled and proved to them their strategic power as port workers.

In settling the strike, a long list of names of those representing different interests appears at the beginning and end of the agreement. The names in the first large set all come from shipping companies, followed by a set of names of workers negotiating the terms of the agreement for various unions. Having been involved from the beginning, Juan Vargas and Fermin Carpio were present as two of the three representatives for the stevedores' union. Directly after their names, one Don Benigno Quintana appears for the cuadrilla de Tonelaje. Up to this point, Quintana had not appeared in any other document, and his role in any of the organizing over the 1916 to 1918 period is unclear. As a signatory of the final agreement, Quintana must have taken part in organizing in some capacity during the lead-up to the strike, since it is unlikely that he sat at the negotiating table if port workers more broadly did not view him as a trustworthy worker, as someone who would look after their interests while signing the document ending the strike. Nonetheless, Quintana's organizing, and his political beliefs in general, can only be inferred from his difficult-to-read signature on this 1918 document. With no police reports on his activities in the year prior to and through the signing of the deal, it is safe to assume that Quintana's politics fell squarely within the range of acceptable, working-class politics. Seven years later, during another round of organizing in the port of Mollendo, however, Quintana's anarchist politics would be much clearer to other workers in Peru, the police in Mollendo, the authorities in Callao, and perhaps Chilean maritime workers as well.

### THE CHILEAN MARITIME WORLD, 1917–1927

While Quintana and other port workers were organizing for raises and improved work hours in Mollendo, port and maritime workers in Valparaíso were in the midst of their own battles. In 1913 they went on strike alongside railroad workers and numerous others to fight against a new law requiring portraits of all state-employed railroad workers. The law did not directly affect them as port and maritime workers (though behind closed doors state authorities did think about including them in a portrait law); they joined out of a sense of solidarity.[42] In 1917 they organized another strike, in part against a similar portrait law, as well as around work hours, load weight, and working conditions.[43] Throughout these years, Juan Onofre Chamorro was one of the key local labor union organizers. Before 1911 Chamorro was a member of the Democratic Party, a somewhat social democratic party, before moving toward anarchism. Around this time Chamorro began to serve as the president of the Sociedad de Estibadores y Gente de Mar and worked part time both in the port and in a butcher shop. From around 1912 onward Chamorro was at the center of labor organizing in Valparaíso, from speaking at rallies to helping to organize both the 1913 and 1917 strikes. He seems to have been a key node in the circulation of radical politics.[44] It is no wonder that the intendant ordered special police surveillance on Chamorro in December 1913.[45] Although Chamorro and port and maritime workers lost their effort to combat the portrait law after their six-day strike in April 1913 and then another in July–August 1917, they turned the momentum of the moment into the founding of a new organization. They sought a new method of organizing, and in late 1919 they formed a branch of the IWW.[46] From its founding through 1927, the IWW acted as a central force of labor organizing in Valparaíso, as well as some other ports in Chile, and was one of the targets of the Sanfuentes regime's repression of 1920.[47] Although membership waxed and waned with state repression, successful and unsuccessful strikes, and political disputes, maritime workers in Valparaíso consistently leaned heavily toward the IWW as their union. In June 1925 William Vergara, an inspector with the Oficina del Trabajo (Labor Office), estimated that at least 70 percent of maritime workers in Valparaíso were members of the IWW.[48]

Influenced by local organizing and developments in Chile and connections to the IWW in the United States, the Chilean IWW might best be characterized as anarcho-syndicalist. Anarchists in Chile and elsewhere tended to define their ideology as being critical of hierarchy, focusing in particular on capitalism, the state, and religion. In late nineteenth-century Buenos Aires, anarcho-feminists added in the category of gender as central to the construction of hierarchies. The syndicalist portion of the identifier meant that labor unions were both a key in organizing against the current system and possibly a place from which to build a new world. In these early decades of the early twentieth century, and especially after the Russian Revolution, many in Peru and Chile turned to communism. Although some of the militants of these different political orientations and practices may have had ideological differences with the others, many also found much overlap in their everyday organizing. Divisions existed between these leftist positions, but at points they also collaborated in what Raymond Craib has called a capacious left.[49]

From the late 1910s through 1927, much of IWW organizing centered around both local and national issues. Many of the strikes that historian Peter

DeShazo outlines deal with demands for increased wages and better working conditions in the port. Nationally, they also confronted new laws, many of which the state instituted in direct response to working-class mobilization and organizing. The "redondilla" system—wherein a union had control over who worked which shifts and what type of work was to be done, and designed to evenly distribute work across the labor force—came under attack by the Arturo Alessandri Palma government in October 1921 after employers began a lockout of maritime workers.[50] Employers argued that the system did not align with the interests of the industry, forced "unknown" workers onto their worksites, made fulfilling the duties of unloading and loading ships difficult and unreliable, and harmed the work process, as the redondilla did not take into account the physical abilities of workers, distributing work evenly across all those within the labor pool. Some workers, on the other hand, complained about the wages earned under the system. Others complained of ideological and financial issues with the system, telling the Oficina del Trabajo that preference was given to those affiliated with the IWW and that Luis Toro, the secretary of the Federación de Jente de Mar, required small bribes of between 5 and 20 pesos in order to assign a shift of work.[51] Whatever the problems of the redondilla system, maritime workers—those affiliated with the IWW and those with other organizations—consistently organized to reimplement the system, claiming it helped in times of high unemployment, gave them more control of the work site in general, and allowed them to receive their full wages instead of giving a portion of it to pay a middleman charged with overseeing the contracting of workers.[52] The abolition of the redondilla system in Iquique caused such large problems that Moises Poblete Troncoso, the head of the Oficina del Trabajo in Santiago, and Alfredo Weber, the head of the regional office in Valparaíso, were sent north to talk with workers and companies to study different systems of work and develop a plan for labor relations in the port.[53] If a part of the essence of the state is the ability to produce rules and regulations of some sort to govern society, then elements of this state formed not out of preconceived, already formed ideological motivations, but rather from the material organizing and force of working-class groups, and in this case, the IWW.[54]

One law in particular drew ire from the IWW and many other organized workers. Law 4054, the Law of Obligatory Social Security, passed as one part of seven labor laws brought forth during a military junta on September 8, 1924.[55] The law required workers to pay 2 percent of their wages into a social security fund, which was widely seen as an overreach by the state and, in essence, a pay cut for workers.⁵⁶ In some cases, workers refused to allow their employers to deduct the 2 percent from their pay, and in one case the CSAV agreed to pay the 2 percent instead of collecting it from the crew members of the *Palena*.⁵⁷ In early 1926 workers in Valparaíso even formed a committee specifically against Law 4054.⁵⁸ The IWW, Federación Obrera de Chile (FOCH), and others met on several occasions to discuss the possibility of a general strike against the law, with "independent" (or nonaffiliated) workers upset over the law as well.⁵⁹ Although the IWW protested against the new social legislation in general, it targeted Law 4054 over and above the other laws and maintained an active presence in anti–Law 4054 organizing.⁶⁰ In conjunction with protests, some Wobblies in Valparaíso attended meetings at which state representatives from the Oficina del Trabajo explained the new laws to workers, and instead of silently listening, they slowed down the presentations (perhaps through asking tough questions), making the state representatives' job much more difficult. And when the official meeting ended, Wobblies stayed afterward to disparage the new laws to anyone who remained.⁶¹ All of this fit into a larger analysis by the IWW, which proclaimed itself antilegalist (*antilegalistas*), calling the social laws different ways of fooling, robbing, and oppressing workers, and arguing that the broader umbrella of these laws was a legal form of "social repression."⁶² The IWW in Valparaíso was intensely concerned with national laws and organizing locally to confront them.

Maritime Wobblies looked into the Pacific, as well. A view of the Pacific came in part through those deported from other countries. It appears that Australia regularly deported radicals across the Pacific to Chile. When Tom Barker, an IWW member in Australia, and seven others were deported to Chile in 1918, they initially planned on not leaving the ship in the hopes of eventually arriving in Great Britain. But to their surprise, they saw Julius Muhlberg, an Estonian carpenter in the maritime industry who had worked in Sydney and whom the Australian state had also deported. Muhlberg assured them that they were "amongst friends" in Valparaíso, and they went to the local union hall, where they were set up with a place to stay, food, and some cash. Juan Chamorro lunched with them on their first day, and thereafter they held collective dinners and parties for them.⁶³ With common ideas of industrial unionism and having either experienced or seen deportation due to organizing, their immediate friendship and political discussions fit into a broader conception of the geography of Pacific organizing.⁶⁴ Even prior to this exchange in 1918, anarchists in Valparaíso paid close attention to anarchist organizing in other parts of the Pacific. When the Japanese state arrested and then executed twelve activists after the police claimed to have discovered a plot to assassinate the emperor in 1910 and 1911, Valparaíso anarchists used a portion of their two-page paper to express their solidarity with two Japanese anarchists, Kotoku Shushui and Kanno Sugako. Kotoku had written a book on imperialism and translated the Russian anarchist Peter Kropotkin, Kanno helped to bring in a feminist perspective on hierarchy, and both were active in broader networks of radical Asian politics.[65] For the editors of the paper in Valparaíso, Kotoku and Kanno were killed because of their "sublime ideas of the emancipation of unredeemed humanity." Their Japanese comrades were part of a global struggle, linking them to anarchists in Chicago and to the notorious Montjuich prison in Spain. Anarchists across the world would keep their struggle alive and continue to move forward.[66]

Anarchist workers in Valparaíso also sought to make connections northward to Peru. During the 1913 strike discussed earlier, Chamorro and many others in Valparaíso organized heavily around the Peruvian anarchist Eulogio Otazú, who had been detained and then deported by the Chilean state.[67] By the mid-1920s they had begun to actively reach out to maritime and port workers in Peru. Letters referencing political discussions with Peruvians in November 1924 in the port of Supe (north of Callao), for instance, mention meeting workers "close to our ideas on proletarian emancipation." A small group of workers, they represented the remnants of the Federación Obrera Marítima de Supe (Maritime Workers Federation of Supe), previously affiliated with the Federación Obrera Regional Peruana (FORP; Peruvian Regional Workers Federation), an anarchist organization formed in 1913 and dissolved in 1921 due in part to government repression. They nostalgically conversed in an article published in *La Voz del Mar* about the days of the FORP and of organizing, while also "lamenting the indifference of their brothers of misery." Since the dissolving of the Federación Obrera Marítima de Supe, they had "lived with their face to the sea" in hopes of hearing that they were not alone in their political desires. Despite—or perhaps because of—this, the author of the article implored other members of the IWW to continue the work of organizing across the maritime border with Peru:

> Here, camaradas, the moment has arrived to demonstrate to our brothers of Supe that we are united with them in a tie of international solidarity. We must demonstrate to them that patriotic phobias have not contaminated us, and that across prejudices and borders, we fraternally hold their hand so that, united, we can struggle in common against our common enemy: capitalism.

That each steam ship crew that touches this port, have voices of encouragement for this group, that although reduced in size today, could be strong and potent with the international cooperation of the Industrial Workers of the World (I.W.W.).[68]

Although the author affirmed the idea that they had not been "contaminated" by a patriotism of one nation against another, the relationship between the Chilean IWW and the workers of Supe seems quite superficial. It is clear that this was the first time these particular Chileans had met up with those particular Peruvians, though all may have had some type of knowledge of the other organization's history.

The Chilean-Peruvian anarchist connections continued in the coming weeks. Take for instance the experience of Luis Toro in Callao. Toro previously had served as the secretary of the Federación de Jente de Mar, helped publish the anarchist newspaper *Campaña Nueva*, may have been the author of the above mentioned letter concerning Supe, and had long-running connections with maritime and port workers, though some of them not agreeable to all.[69] Toro is also the anarchist with whom the chapter began, dismissing rumors of repression for being Chilean in Callao, meeting workers at the offices of the UMT, and returning with a letter from the president of the Peruvian port union urging the creation of closer ties between port and maritime workers in Peru and Chile.[70]

From Toro's lengthy report and letter from Callao, we can arrive at a few conclusions. First, the power of rumor probably dissuaded many Chileans from venturing too far away from their ships in the port of Callao. In one case from 1912, Chilean maritime workers did experience violence in Callao, but instead of its being state led, the fighting resulted from a dispute between crew members and recently repatriated Peruvians from Tarapacá.[71] Without evidence from many other cases, it appears that rumors of violence and persecution on the part of Peruvians against Chileans held sway for many on the ship, and many may have never passed a vague spatial line into the city of Callao. Whether or not the rumors were true, they certainly restricted the movement of Chileans in port.[72] Second, these two movements in Peru and Chile met along similar ideological grounds. Both articles emphasized as much ideological equivalency as possible, an important point since writers for *La Voz del Mar*, the newspaper of maritime Wobblies, were rarely afraid of critiquing other organizations, particularly other anarchist groups and the Partido Comunista (PC; Communist Party), and there is no reason to believe they would shy away from doing so here as well. Though the particular people meeting and talking had not previously met, they were familiar with the history of the larger labor federations. To mention the FORP with little historical background meant that the readers of *La Voz del Mar* surely had some familiarity with the organization.

Third, and perhaps most importantly, they both clearly saw the need to work across national borders, with other maritime workers, against nation-state based patriotism, and as working-class people without national affiliation. And this connection across national lines became more solidified discursively in January when *La Voz del Mar* published an article on Peruvian government repression against Peruvians. Toro accused the Augusto Leguía regime in Peru of persecuting students and looked to Víctor Raúl Haya de la Torre, who had spent a year in exile from Peru, as a key case.[73] Haya de la Torre had participated as a university student leader in the massive general strike in Lima-Callao in late 1918 and early 1919, a strike with anarchists at the forefront and which ended with a new law on the eight-hour workday.[74] Toro pointed out that many other Peruvian students had also left Peru, and that their exile helped to clearly show "the limits of the two patrías [fatherlands]: bourgeoisie and proletarian." Further, "they [the Peruvian students] and us belong to the latter and we fight to defend it." For Toro, the bourgeoisie used "the story of Tacna and Arica and 'the indistinguishable hate of the Peruvian people'" as a means of dividing the working class. But, as Toro pointed out, "we maritime workers that in our mass movements across the sea in search of bread have been cordially welcomed in working class and student organizations in Peru, we that due to our work are in continual contact with the people of the north, we who go with the pulse of the heartbeat of these people, we have known how to find groups of men who think like us on this coast, and that cordially shake our hand, camaradas and brothers of capitalist exploitation." Maritime work forced interactions between working-class Chileans and Peruvians, and through these interactions they had seen in action the importance of organizing across national borders as a class: camaradas in their state of exploitation and camaradas in their fight against capitalism, a system that did not distinguish between Peruvians and Chileans. Moreover, Chilean workers and students had recently experienced repression with "the assault and sacking of the Federación de Estudiantes in Santiago, and the assailants, after their work of vandalism, drunk of enthusiasm, went to [the offices of] the magazine 'Zig-Zag' where they took a picture with their trophies of conquest 'in such a glorious action.'" Toro even drew a direct parallel between the Peruvian students' Universidad Popular González Prada and the Chilean Universidad Popular Lastarria, two student initiatives in which students and workers could continue to build an alliance through students (and professors) offering classes on a broad range of topics to workers.[75]

These conversations and exchanges in late 1924 and into 1925 between Chilean Wobblies and Peruvian port and maritime workers are also significant because of Peruvian-Chilean relations at the state level. After decades of failed negotiations and a series of diplomatic breaks, the Peruvian and Chilean states had agreed on allowing the US government to arbitrate the Tacna and Arica dispute. The Peruvian and Chilean governments submitted their cases in April 1924, just a few months prior to the conversations discussed earlier, and the ruling would not come until March 1925.[76] All of this was happening, too, just a year after the Chilean state had expelled numerous Peruvians from Tacna and Arica in preparation for a plebiscite to decide on the territories.[77] In other words, Chilean and Peruvian port and maritime workers were creating new political conversations and friendships and supporting labor actions (discussed later) at the exact same time that political leaders in both countries eagerly waited for the United States to rule on a forty-year-old, bitter border dispute.

Although Wobblies involved with *La Voz del Mar* published only a few articles related to Peru, the Chilean branch of the IWW continued to interact with Peruvian maritime and port workers. When Chilean Wobblies arrived at Peruvian ports, they brought with them copies of *La Voz del Mar* and occasionally sold copies to those in port. During these years the Chilean IWW also sought donations to help their movement and purchase a new printer. Nearly half of all financial reports (sixteen of thirty-four) in *La Voz del Mar* show sources of money from the Peruvian coast, sometimes with multiple sources in the same ledger. The precise percentage of money incoming from Peruvian sources varies widely, from 1.17 percent (issue 23) to 10.16 percent (issue 34). Significantly, Chilean Wobblies spread their campaign across the Peruvian coast, selling issues or receiving donations from the ports of Supe, Huacho, Pacasmayo, Salaverry, and Mollendo.[78]

The ledger of *La Voz del Mar* only tells part of the story, though. When workers purchased a copy of the newspaper, they sometimes passed it along to another person either at the same port or at another port. In 1925 the police in Mollendo confiscated a March 24, 1925, copy of *La Voz del Mar* and transcribed an article on Peru into their notes.[79] The ledgers for *La Voz del Mar*, though, do not show any incoming money from Mollendo until

March 1926. The discrepancy between the ledger of *La Voz del Mar* and the date of appearance in Mollendo shows that the newspaper did in fact circulate across the Pacific in ways that cannot be read solely from the ledger of the newspaper. Thus, even if the idea of stretching the Chilean movement northward dropped off the radar in *La Voz del Mar*, perhaps to focus on the movement within Chile, the newspaper and its ideas continued to reach Peruvian shores, and Peruvians bought the paper or donated to the movement through the mid-1920s.

## MOLLENDO, PORT OF PACIFIC ORGANIZING

After the strike of 1918, unions and different radical groups in Mollendo continued to organize. Although the local authorities thought of the port as rather tranquil in the years between the strike and the mid-1920s, not all organizing occurs in the streets. Organizing can be a slow process, requiring many conversations in union halls, houses, or during lunch breaks; it can require patient coalition building across political lines; and it may involve productive and generative failures.[80] The bursts of energy in a march or strike might suddenly catch the eye of the authorities, but this should not mask the quotidian reality of organizing. Mobilization is not the same as organizing.

Quintana serves as an example of the effects of organizing over years. The documentary trail is thin in terms of his life, but we can make some inferences through state records and petitions. Born in 1888 in the northern Peruvian city of Piura, Quintana made his way to Mollendo sometime in 1905.[81] As mentioned previously, the first instance of Quintana participating in any type of organizing is the signing of the agreement concluding the 1918 port worker strike. As someone signing—and perhaps negotiating—the agreement, Quintana probably was held in some esteem by the ranks of port workers. Along with the other signatories of the agreement across different maritime and port unions, Quintana most likely had already participated in some type of organizing in the port of Mollendo, though the length of his previous experience in politics at this point in 1918 is unclear. The content of Quintana's politics, and of many others in the port, is also less than explicit in this time period. In none of the state documents are there references to anarchism, socialism, or any other type of radical ideology, suggesting that the politics of the strike may have been more syndicalist broadly construed, as a round of organizing for the material improvement of the working-class people of the port without pretensions to an overturning of society. Even though troops were sent to Mollendo during the protests and stayed on after the strike ended, the urban violence seen in other strikes in previous years in Pacific ports seems not to have taken place in Mollendo.[82] While violence may not necessarily reveal a revolutionary character underneath a movement, the generally amicable situation between workers and authorities, and the total lack of any mention of radical political ideas in state documents, suggests that the political intentions of many of those organizing in Mollendo probably fell well within the bounds of acceptable politics in the eyes of the state.

Between 1918 and 1925 this acceptability drastically changed. Some of this happened as port and maritime workers organized and won gains throughout these years. The strike of 1918 concluded with significant gains for all job classifications in the port, a result that surely created new ideas of collective power for port workers. In 1923, after some jornaleros lodged a complaint against the urban comisario of Mollendo, the state replaced the comisario for someone else they likely thought more acceptable to jornaleros.[83] Organizing tends to escalate over time; a group might initially ask for something—increased wages, a different supervisor, etc.—and if rejected move on to a different action, such as a rally, and perhaps eventually a strike. In this case it appears that a complaint was sufficient to replace a state functionary. In late 1924 jornaleros again petitioned the subprefect of Mollendo, asking him to speak with the capitán del puerto concerning their right to work on the Peruvian steamship *Tres Hermanos*. The capitan del puerto had refused the jornaleros previously, but the subprefect conversed with him and received assurances that he would in turn talk to those above him to allow the jornaleros to work the ship.[84] In both of these cases, jornaleros employed a rather low-risk form of changing their work environment and received exactly what they asked for in the end. If the 1918 strike had taught port workers about their power, they mobilized their strength in 1923 and 1924 for improved working conditions and for the right to work. Through their own organizing, they learned and relearned their own power.

Looking south, workers in Mollendo found common political practice with Chilean Wobblies.[85] The idea of organizing across job classifications, of "one big union" that united all workers in an industry (an industrial union), fit within their experience over the previous decade. If the lead-up to the 1918 strike proved anything, it was that a port-wide strike could force the hand of the state and shipping companies. It is no wonder, then, that sometime in 1925, workers in Mollendo formed a local of the IWW. Without any local working-class newspapers and only vague references to radical ideologies by the police, it is difficult to ascertain exactly how workers in Mollendo conceptualized anarchism. But their actions—moving from individual union action to a port-wide strike, steadily becoming more radicalized in their analysis of social problems according to police reports, and questioning the nationalistic politics of both states—pulled them closer and closer to identifying with anarchism and the form of anarcho-syndicalism practiced by the IWW. Wobbly politics mirrored their organizational experience and connected them to fellow maritime and port workers who had organized along the South American littoral as well.[86] The methods of organizing and direct action were indeed easy to understand, but they also required workers to recognize the power in industrial unionism.[87]

*La Voz del Mar*'s politics of anarchism on the waterfront, too, probably appealed to them not only through the articles, but also through its use of imagery. Over the course of the three-year run of *La Voz del Mar*, the masthead changed only once, and both versions centered port and maritime workers. The first masthead (see figure 6) shows a person pushing a cart of sorts with the phrase "Join the IWW," flanked on the left by a ship docked at port, and on the right by a lighthouse. The lighthouse, as the tallest figure in the image, dominates the scene, and from up top, the lens beams out the words *La Voz del Mar* on one side and I.W.W. on the other side. In the second masthead (see figure 7), a hooded worker on the far left looks out toward the dock, where another worker helps with a bale on land and two others load a bale on board a ship suggestively named *Emancipación*. The hooded worker's gaze also looks directly at the lettering for the name of the newspaper and the initials for the IWW. In the background, ships circulate in the bay. In both mastheads, port and maritime labor feature prominently, and in the second the worker's upward look provides a sense of pride in his labor. And in both images, the paper's affiliation with the IWW is clear.[88]

Connections between Peruvian and Chilean maritime and port workers in previous years seem to have been limited to discussions of politics, forming new bonds across the Pacific, and the possibilities of a broader littoral movement. In 1925 these discussions turned into material action. The exact date of the founding of the IWW in Mollendo is unclear. But it probably is not a coincidence that after a manager with the Peruvian Corporation

FIGURE 6. First *La Voz del Mar* (Valparaíso, Chile) masthead, 1st half of Nov. 1924. *Credit:* International Institute of Social History (Amsterdam).

FIGURE 7. Second *La Voz del Mar* (Valparaíso, Chile) masthead, 1 May 1926. *Credit:* International Institute of Social History (Amsterdam).

unjustly suspended three railroad workers in February 1925, the railroad union called for a strike, which port and maritime workers quickly joined. With port workers on strike, the authorities in Mollendo called on the crew of the steamship *Rapot* to unload the cargo.[89] Again invoking their gendered roles, they called attention to the "three homes" that would be affected by the suspension of these workers, that they were three "fathers of families" who had lost their "right to live and be able to bring a pieces of bread home for their tender children."[90] As the Chilean steamships *Mapocho* and the *Cachapoal* and the Peruvian *Mantaro* approached the port of Mollendo, the crew must have immediately noticed the change in work regime in the port, similar to during the 1918 strike. (It just so happens that the *Mapocho* was the exact same ship that had arrived during the early days of the 1918 Mollendo strike.) Strikers in the port must have communicated with the crews of both ships, perhaps through the use of lanchas, for the crews of both ships refused to cross the strike line, an action one called a *gesto viril* (manly/virile expression).⁹¹ Either shipping companies or the state brought in strikebreakers to try to keep the commercial activities of the port going. Within a week of the first day of the strike, though, the strikers had won their demand for the return to work of the suspended railroad workers.⁹²

In the aftermath of the strike, local authorities hit the IWW and others hard. If working-class organizing mixed with anarcho-syndicalist politics frightened the state and companies, this was their attempt at dissolving class consciousness and solidarity.⁹³ The police attempted to capture two members of the IWW but were unsuccessful, as they had purportedly fled to the border with Chile. One of the men, Nacriso Cuadros, "lives with a woman of Chilean nationality," the police wrote, gesturing toward Chile as a refuge (away from the police of Mollendo) and as a love interest of radical Peruvians. Indeed, within the "working class home," according to their description of an anarchist recently deported from Mollendo, "Patria [fatherland] does not exist, nor a rivalry of any sort."⁹⁴ The subprefect complained to the prefect of a lack of resources to combat the rise of radical organizations and the less than stellar work of police before the strike, but nonetheless noted the use of a now-demolished house where Peruvian and Chilean workers met, "in a stealthy manner deep into the night and early morning."

Deporting leaders of the movement seemed to have worked in the past, the subprefect suggested, hinting at a possible option for the state in future actions.⁹⁵ Over the course of his eleven-year rule (1919–30)—commonly referred to as the *oncenio*—President Augusto Leguía had deported many political and labor organizers.⁹⁶ In other words, deportation was a common state technique to deal with political dissidents. And in the case of Mollendo, local government officials took up this option: in May the state deported Mariano de Olazabal, one of the founders of the Mollendo IWW local.⁹⁷ Olazabal, Andrés Cuba (discussed later), and a few others may have been sent to Chile, but authorities there did not allow them to disembark, sending the deported along to somewhere else.⁹⁸ In other cases, local authorities sent labor organizers into internal exile, often to "la montaña," a geographic referent often referring to the eastern slopes of the Andes, but which was not specified in the remaining archival documents.⁹⁹

The state's plan, however, was sometimes much more complicated than capturing and deporting labor organizers. There were people the state knew had actively engaged in organizing actions and were members of anarchist groups, but they did not pass the imaginary line to the land of those to be deported. Here we return to Benigno Quintana: a signatory at the end of the 1918 strike, a negotiator for a labor contract for lancheros in June 1922, an organizer, and possibly a member of the IWW in 1925. State agents wrote several letters concerning his ideas and actions. All of these letters on Quintana describe his ideas as dangerous and against the general will of the nation.[100] Yet when asked to include Quintana in the list of workers to be captured and sent to Lima in early 1926, the local authority replied that it was not an opportune time to do so. Even though "I do not like him one bit, I do not think it is the time to remove him from here," he wrote. Despite Quintana's activities in 1925, at the moment his political convictions and organizing did not threaten the city or the state, and he was a hard worker at the customs house. When the situation changed, and port workers might not have the same political zeal, however, they could deal with Quintana, or, as they phrased it, "clear him" out of the port. But instead of detaining and sending him to Lima, the author referenced an "old saying": "For the enemy, you must build a bridge of silver in front of them across which to march." Taken from Cervantes's *Don Quixote*, the phrase calls for offering enemies a route of escape, pushing direct confrontation off the table.[101] In this case, rather than arresting and sending Quintana to the northern coast of Peru (direct confrontation), the writer proposed concocting a budgetary issue, essentially making up a reason for the state to move Quintana's job to another location, and by doing so, remove him from Mollendo and neutralize the threat without exposed conflict.[102]

This argument was ignored. In early March the subprefect of Islay received a letter with the names of thirteen men and their professions on it. All were to be detained and sent to Lima, by order of the minister of the state. Recognizing that this move could cause some urban unrest, the central state offered to send troops.[103] Along with Quintana, the list included Eugenio Neira, a jornalero who appeared next to Quintana in a list from June 1925 naming three people with "subversive ideas" and "anti-social anarchist ideas," and characterized as "insolent Bolsheviks."[104] Manuel Escalona also made an appearance on the list. Authorities had accused Escalona, an employee with the Subprefecture of Islay, of passing confidential documents from state officials to workers in Mollendo and Chilean radicals. Authorities called this an act of "espionage."[105]

These are the last letters on Quintana. His fate is unknown. But it is likely that the authorities in Mollendo bent to the will of the central state in Callao. In similar cases, officials in Mollendo facilitated the capture and internal deportation of labor organizers. Take Andrés Cuba, a jornalero, for instance. In February 1923 Cuba signed a letter of protest supporting jornaleros in their petition requesting more workers and the return to work of seven of his coworkers. One of the other signatories to the petition was Neira.[106] Two years later Cuba signed the agreement ending the port strike of 1925.[107] It appears that Cuba was already well known in the local labor scene, for within a day of the 1925 strike his name appeared in a list of the "Bolshevik" organizers, along with Quintana and Neira.[108] By March 1926 Cuba found himself on yet another list of agitators the central government wanted captured and was sent to Lima.[109] In November 1926 the local authorities in Mollendo were again angry over Cuba's organizing. They had deported him from Mollendo three times already, but every time he was sent somewhere else, he returned home to Mollendo and continued agitating among port workers. Even though deportation had not worked in the past as they desired, they issued the call to deport him a fourth time.[110] This last effort may have served its purpose, for one month later the authorities suspected Cuba's involvement in a disturbance, but after investigating, discovered that he was then in Lima.[111]

Nonetheless, repression could not entirely stamp out the spirit of organizing. The experience of organizing side by side with coworkers, demonstrating together, and seeing Chilean workers decide to not cross the strike line inspired continued agitation. Although the authorities captured and deported Quintana in June 1925, Cuba's organizing is a testament to the continuation of the struggle in Mollendo. In Arequipa, the capital of the department that included Mollendo, workers set up a regional federation to support their aim of "Liberty and Justice," and port workers in Mollendo almost struck to defend a suspended coworker.[112] Students at San Agustín University in Arequipa also pushed for secularization of their education while employing the radical organizational form of naming a facilitator of each meeting rather than electing a long-term president or leader. In one case, students invited the important indigenista scholar Luis Valcárcel to speak on their campus. In their introduction to the event, a student connected the politics of Vladimir Lenin, the Mexican educator José Vasconcelos, the Cuban revolutionary José Martí, and the writings of Peruvian anarchist Manuel González Prada.[113] And in January 1928, jornaleros in Mollendo petitioned for an increase in pay.[114]

## CONCLUSION

One could say that the Valparaíso Pacific "lived and breathed with the same rhythm" as the Mollendo Pacific.[115] The labor struggles of people in Mollendo and Valparaíso, and how they came together in the 1920s, demonstrate the framework of oceanic connections, which included both comparison and unity. In the episodes analyzed here—from the labor organizing in Mollendo in the 1910s to the Wobblies in Valparaíso and the move toward adopting the IWW platform in Mollendo in the mid-1920s—port and maritime workers patiently built organizations based on local needs. Their political orientation and interactions with those from across the border brought them to the idea of connecting their struggles. They learned and built from one another. A decade of organizing in Mollendo had shown them that when they acted industrially instead of within craft lines, they had more power. When Chilean Wobblies arrived and spoke of industrial organizing, they took on the model not necessarily due to the persuasiveness of the Chileans, but rather because their program fit within their local experience in Mollendo. The local built the transnational, just as the transnational built on the local.

The historical anthropologist Greg Dening wrote that "from a beach, it is possible to see beyond one's horizons. Beaches breed expansiveness."[116] For Chilean novelist Manuel Rojas, the ocean offered the entirety of human thought to people: "You can think or imagine what you would like, that which is and which will be, that which can be and cannot be." The ocean helped him imagine the possibilities of anarchism, even if it was "nothing more than a desire" and might not come to fruition.[117] "Look," Rojas wrote in *Sombras contra el muro*, "I never belive more in anarchism than when I sit here, looking at the ocean."[118] These maritime and port workers lived and put into practice the expansiveness of Dening in the anarchist ocean of Rojas. The ocean does not necessarily mean expansiveness or freedom. As Leon Fink has noted in the context of the North Atlantic during the first decades of the twentieth century, "The translation of solidarity from rhetorical commitment to international union practice had ... proved an uneven process."[119] Even for the subjects of his book, their organizing centered on grievances concerning pay, work hours, and national labor laws, a testament to the power differentials in place. But for many along the South American littoral at the time, the ocean offered a certain expansiveness and opportunities for enacting their ideology of global proletarian organizing. Across a still unsettled post–War of the Pacific border, they looked beyond the horizon of chauvinistic nationalism, toward a working-class transnational solidarity.

FIVE

*Pacific Policing*

IN THE FIRST ISSUE of the newly founded *Revista de la Policía de Valparaíso*, the editors published a short article on the rationale of the journal and on the police in Chile more broadly. The police in Valparaíso, the most important port of Chile, had a double mission: they must "watch over lives and property in Valparaíso" and must act as a dignified institution within society.[1] Each individual within a state had duties and obligations, many of which required knowing the limits of their freedom and happiness in relation to that of others. The police, as an institution of the state, helped citizens find this balance between individual and collective, providing a space within which people could live in peace. Modern Chile, however, need not imitate Europe or the United States—which "provide light to the world and lessons to humanity"—but rather could "mold the form of being to the real necessities of Valparaíso."[2]

This chapter details the ways in which police in Chile (particularly Valparaíso) and Peru (particularly Callao) incorporated new elements into their labor of surveillance and repression. It is a story of local ideas and practices, in conjunction with international conferences and transnational activities and concerns. The police and the people above them in local government, first and foremost, had to deal with their own cities, in this case port cities. They wrote of concerns about certain parts of the city, worried about protests, and regarded working-class foreigners in their city with suspicious eyes. Of course many of these concerns were not new. But in the late nineteenth and early decades of the twentieth centuries, with the increase in the circulation of goods and people in port cities, a more solidified labor movement, and rising discussions on the "social question," the police turned toward new methods of control.[3]

The labor of policing in the early twentieth century involved mixing tried-and-true techniques, looking abroad for methods from other locations, as well as a reliance on locally tested methods. For many, new techniques such as the Bertillon system of identification or photographing criminals meant a more precise way of policing. Putting these systems into practice at the local level meant training and resources. And to do so across state lines, from Valparaíso to Buenos Aires, from Montevideo to Callao, required reproducibility. If policing were to be modern, it needed to be measurable and reproducible. But in cities with limited budgets, martial arts, spying, and planting evidence could just as readily play a part in police work and help detain and arrest individuals. These approaches, the modern-scientific and the physical training-footwork, were not mutually exclusive and functioned in tandem. Differences of method existed even within each approach. Still, these differences amounted to complementary means to the same end: struggling to (re)take control of the city.

Perhaps city as a descriptor is not accurate. The chapter is mostly concerned with *port* cities. Valparaíso and Callao were at once both cities with local populations, industries, and political structures, and ports bringing in people, ideas, and goods from around the world. The cosmopolitan nature of ports was central to the police's discourse as well as how they practiced policing. In these ports, too, working-class people organized labor unions and resistance societies to fight for gains in wages and improved working conditions and to battle specific state laws. They also reached across state lines to forge bonds of solidarity with their class comrades from afar. While the police consistently sought to apprehend criminals of various sorts, they also focused on the labor movement. Labor organizing, in other words, pushed the police to reform their ways and introduce new methods of policing into practice. If the radical wing of the labor movement, most visible and concentrated in the politics of anarchism, posed a threat to port cities and society as a whole, according to the police, they had a mission to "organize the common defense" against it. And "the State, as is its duty," must cooperate with the police to defend society.[4] The mythical duty of the state created a goal, yet an unreachable one that moved ever further along a rhetorical temporal line. This unreachability allowed for the reproduction of the police force as a larger and broader arm of the state in its fight against a common enemy. Police actions removed organizers from the political scene, their reports trickled from local to national authorities, their discourse helped shape cultural ideas of crime, and they pushed for new equipment to keep pace with their criminological techniques.

Police discourse in both Valparaíso and Callao emphasized the recording of physical features, but with their gaze toward the Pacific, they tended to emphasize nation over race. This is not to suggest that race was not a central element of criminology. In the case of Peru, race was written into the 1924 penal code, and many people from radically different political perspectives relied on specific ideas on race when thinking about criminology.[5] But it appears that, similar to what Nathan Perl-Rosenthal found for the late eighteenth-century northern Atlantic, many in Callao and Valparaíso centered nationality and the cosmopolitan nature of their port cities in their policing.[6]

## POLICING TECHNIQUES

As the police expanded numerically, they also sought to improve their ability to police. More feet on the ground meant they could cover more square kilometers of the city, which may have resulted in increased arrests and perhaps even less crime in general due to the frequency of police passing through the city. But the police also knew that modern policing required modern techniques. While sheer quantity might make the streets safer for a while, labor organizers, criminals, and potential criminals changed their methods to circumvent the typical police officer. What was needed were new methods in policing, a qualitative change in their form.

Part of these new techniques came in the form of police training. While in the port of Yokohama, Japan, in late 1909 or early 1910, the crew of the Chilean corvette *Jeneral Baquedano* sought out instructors of jiu-jitsu. The police in Yokohama were required to learn jiu-jitsu—a martial art based on chokes and putting pressure on limbs and joints in such a way as to diminish the challenge of different sizes of people in combat—to help them apprehend suspects. In one case, a police officer quickly brought a man suspected of robbing one of the commercial houses in the port to the ground through a wrist and elbow hold. The use of jiu-jitsu in a port city and around the commercial houses must have made an impact on the Chileans, since they were dealing with similar issues back at home. The commander of the ship contracted with Kunio Kawada and Kinkichi Okura in Yokohama to teach the Chilean Navy jiu-jitsu. One of the Chileans who learned some of the martial art had the opportunity to test it out when the ship arrived in Sydney and an Australian athlete challenged the Chilean official. Though the Chilean warned his opponent against making any sudden moves during their bout, the Australian yanked his arm from a hold, dislocating it in the process.[7] Similarly, in March 1911 the government of Peru signed an agreement with a jiu-jitsu instructor named I. Matzuura, who would lead classes, along with two other instructors, for police officers in Lima over the next year. Up to twenty-five police officers would learn jiu-jitsu over a series of two-hour-long classes, training in the "Japanese sport" that police officers in Europe had already begun to learn, a skill that allowed "one to dominate with relative ease, an individual without causing them any harm."[8] The police in Valparaíso also looked to boxing as a possible new weapon in their arsenal. In 1908 new physical education classes for police were instituted in Santiago, which included boxing classes every day of the week (except holidays) for one hour. These new classes in boxing and jiu-jitsu, the Valparaíso police noted, should be a part of the port city's offerings as well, since it was "absolutely indispensable that the police be sure of their physical strengths" and their ability to "calmly" fend off "an attack or accurately hit someone with vigor."[9] Though learning to box required repeated movements, which some found monotonous, after learning the straight punch and bobbing and weaving, the rest of the sport came easily. In helping police officers defend themselves, boxing and jiu-jitsu also had the advantage of being cheap to learn and could be performed as long as the officer was physically capable of continuing, since it only required using one's hands—though the injuries that might result from hitting another person were not taken into account.[10] By 1913 the police in Valparaíso could enroll in workshops on boxing, jiu-jitsu, Greco-Roman wrestling, fencing, and saber handling.[11] Jiu-jitsu, boxing, and wrestling required only training, no new weapons or costly bullets, and though swords and sabers were needed for fencing and saber handling, these were items that could be reused repeatedly. These were cost-effective measures and training that could potentially alleviate some of the difficulties of policing port cities with limited budgets.[12]

Police also sought to better demarcate the use of the city by protesters. Controlling the paths protests might take and how they would use the different spaces mattered. In flat plazas, use of raised platforms allowed the voice of the speaker to reach a larger number of people; relegating orators to even terrain with the crowd meant fewer people would hear their words. In an era when police regularly described speeches as subversive or against the order of society, cutting off the aural reach of orators might help lessen the impact of their ideas. After a protest in Valparaíso in 1913 during which the crowd damaged trees along the street, the group arrived at the Plaza de la Victoria. According to the police report, the protesters broke ten podiums and ruined the grass.[13] In response, the intendant of Valparaíso decreed that only the military and police choir would be allowed to use the small stage or platform in the Plaza de la Victoria. Anyone not belonging to these groups was banned from using the stage, and the police were instructed to ensure the decree was followed by those in the plaza.[14] The decree quickly expanded to the use of pavilions, as well as prohibiting people from stepping onto benches or climbing monuments, which were both common ways of extending the range of a speech by gaining even a small amount of height.[15] All of this transpired *prior* to the large anti-portrait strike of October 1913.[16] After the strike, the police sought to require any group of protesters to notify the police with the name of one person or a committee of people who would be responsible for the gathering. They also pointed to the need to protect gardens, monuments, and public decorations. The right to protest remained, but the local government and police put into place new rules and regulations to ensure public space would be used as they thought it should be used; it was a state and police perspective on respecting public space while abiding by the constitution and local ordinances.[17]

If railroad workers in Valparaíso feared the use of obligatory photography in 1913, the police saw much potential in the new technology. According to historian Vania Cárdenas Muñoz, Chilean police began to take photos of suspected petty thieves in 1899, and in 1903 the police in Valparaíso started to photograph a broader array of individuals, expanding beyond petty thieves and including anyone who was found guilty in court. In later years the photographing of individuals spread to not only criminals, but also people in specific jobs, such as street vendors and drivers.[18] In Valparaíso the police ran through all of their photographic materials in 1907 and 1908 and requested increased funding from the state for photography.[19] By 1910, 8 percent of the monthly budget of the Investigative Section of the police in Callao went to office supplies, photographic materials, or incidentals, and by 1912 they had amassed close to a thousand photographs.[20] A modern and professional police force required not only reproducible methods but also the material things necessary to perform those functions, such as photographic paper and office supplies.[21]

But portraits of those arrested or detained were not created through a simple process of point and shoot. The police had to set up the scene, and do so in a similar way to those in other locations. Born from concern regarding transnational criminals and anarchists and the need to find common ground from which to surveil them among the police of South America, representatives from Santiago, La Plata, Buenos Aires, Rio de Janeiro, and Montevideo met in Buenos Aires in October 1905.[22] They agreed on the need to share information across borders, and one of the types of information shared would be portraits of individuals. Police officers would take two pictures, one from the front and another of the individual's profile. Their face, measured from the middle of the hair line to the bottom of the chin, needed to take up no more than 32 mm of the 9 x 13 cm photographic plate—the standard size plate used in Rio de Janeiro and La Plata. The camera would be set at a decent distance from the subject so as to not distort their features. The photo should also capture the suspect in their normal, everyday appearance, with the police ensuring that their clothes and facial hair looked as they would when encountered on the street. Somewhat more difficult to achieve, they also had to capture the suspect's everyday "attitude" on the plate.[23] When police delegates met in 1920 to revise and geographically extend their agreement (this time including Peru, Paraguay, and Bolivia), the size of the photographic plate remained the same, but they allowed for the size of the subject's portrait to vary when a person had a large head, since it would distort the rest of the image.[24] While building an archive of portraits of suspects may have helped in policing transnational subjects, who could give a different name in each location, the practice of producing such a database required a transnational technical reproducibility.[25]

Reproducibility in photographing suspects tied into a longer trend in attempts to produce a more scientific and, for the police, precise functioning of criminology. In the case of Chile, the president of the Sociedad Médica, Augusto Orrego Luco, commissioned Pedro N. Barros Ovalle "to study the Bertillon system of physical attributes [filiación] and contribute to the dissemination and learning of this new system of identifying criminals."[26] In 1900 Barros Ovalle published his *Manual de antropometría criminal i jeneral* (Manual of criminal and general anthropometry), a textbook designed to explain criminological theories and practices, as well as to outline the how-to of these theories. For Barros Ovalle, photographs were to be taken from the front and the profile, with the light source coming from the left of the subject for front pictures and the light filling the face for the profile shot.[27] Even with these photographs, though, Barros Ovalle warned of their inability to account for how people's appearance changes over time or is manipulated, such as through the shaving of a beard or the changing of one's hair color.[28] Photographs, even if taken in exactly the same way by different officers, could not tell the full picture of a person as they aged or as they changed their appearance to evade the police.

In order for a more precise identification of a person across the years, Barros Ovalle supplied two additional measurements based on the Bertillon system: filiación antropométrica and filiación descriptiva. The anthropometry system entailed measuring body parts, with particular interest focused on the size of the head since "it cannot be altered by the individual."[29] The filiación antropométrica also meant measuring other parts of the body, such as the ears, height, and arms, according to the instructions in the manual, and people new to the task of measurements would practice on the same individual three to four times to hone their skills.[30] The filiación descriptiva dealt with describing particular characteristics of the subject's body. In this set of descriptions, eye color was central since, similar to the size of one's head, "it is impossible... to alter or hide this element." This exercise in description also required a certain reproducibility; eye color, for instance, should be taken with the person 30 cm directly in front of the subject.[31] But sometimes description required more than simply seeing the color of the eye or type of nose: in the case of tattoos, the practitioner might benefit from talking with the subject on the meaning behind a date, name, or image, and this conversation would help in describing the physical characteristic.[32] And to help standardize descriptions, as well as to allow the practitioner to write quickly, Barros Ovalle supplied a list of terms and their abbreviations, most translated from French for the first time.[33] In subsequent years, Barros Ovalle continued his criminological work, contributing articles to the *Revista de la Policía de Valparaíso*; his manual, far from being a theoretical treatise read and discussed by those interested in the theories of criminology, was a book meant to be used by police officers, and some of it was published in an outlet that police officers read.[34] Barros Ovalle's manual, then, brought together photography, body measurements, and physical description of suspects in order to triangulate the identity of the subject.

The issue of reproducibility and consistency hung over the field of criminology. Barros Ovalle argued that practitioners should work through the entirety of a procedure on the same person three to four times to learn the proper way to take the measurements and describe the subject. In order to teach these techniques, he included drawings of the various procedures (see figures 8 and 9). Even if the person conducting the procedure was not familiar with how to measure certain body parts or the different types of noses, the drawings attempted to create clear categories. The system also allowed for the broad splitting of categories, typically into large, medium, and small, which made it possible for a grouping of twenty-four thousand people to be put through successive splits of threes until the grouping was small enough to identify a person.[35] Even trained practitioners, however, made mistakes, and this required an additional chart of tolerances with respect to measurements and observations.[36] Nonetheless, all of this only worked if the categories made sense to those using them. While the police in Valparaíso do not seem to have questioned the Bertillon taxonomy, some did push back against other forms of categorization. In Lima, for instance, the police wondered why people charged with vagrancy and gambling were bunched with those charged with sedition within the broader category of "crimes against the public order."[37] Crime statistics and criminological techniques in turn-of-the-century Latin America were intimately connected; Juan Vucetich, the famed Croatian immigrant to Argentina who developed a new form of taking and classifying fingerprints (dactyloscopy), began his work in Buenos Aires as the director of statistics on crime, for instance.[38] At play in these years of experimenting with the Bertillon system was precisely the reproducibility of the techniques the system required, as well as the specific taxonomy the system presupposed.

At the time, another form of criminological method took root alongside the Bertillon system. The dactyloscopy system as developed by Vucetich in Argentina, based on a new method to "subclassify loops, for example, identifying an 'internal' inclination, or tracks leaning to the left with the outer ridge, to the right of the observer, as well as the reverse, 'external' inclining loops," which allowed for a simplified form of classification, spread across various Latin American countries in the late nineteenth and early twentieth centuries.[39] But rather than the Vucetich system overtaking the Bertillon system as a whole, the police in Valparaíso thought of them as complementary methods, as systems applicable to different types—or moments—in policing. Since the Bertillon system relied on physical features, the police could pick a suspect out of a crowd, "from the distance and within the multitude of large populations," and once they were apprehended, the Vucetich system would help the police "with amazing quickness and a mathematical assuredness" determine the identification of the suspect. Even if some physical attributes

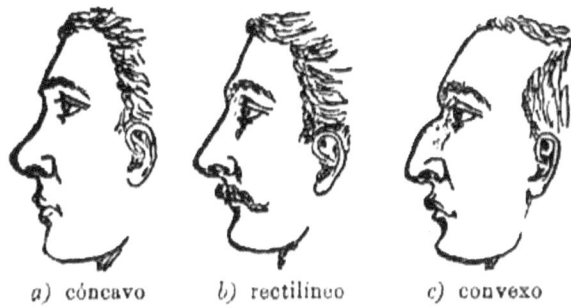

FIGURE 8. Profiles of the nose. *Source:* Pedro N. Barros Ovalle, *Manual de antropometría criminal i jeneral escrito segun el sistema de A. Bertillon para la identificación personal i destinado al uso de los establecimientos penitenciarios, autoridades judiciales, compañías de seguros, cuerpos, armados, etc., etc.* (Santiago de Chile: Imprenta de Enrique Blanchard-Chessi, 1900). Memoriachilena.gob.cl.

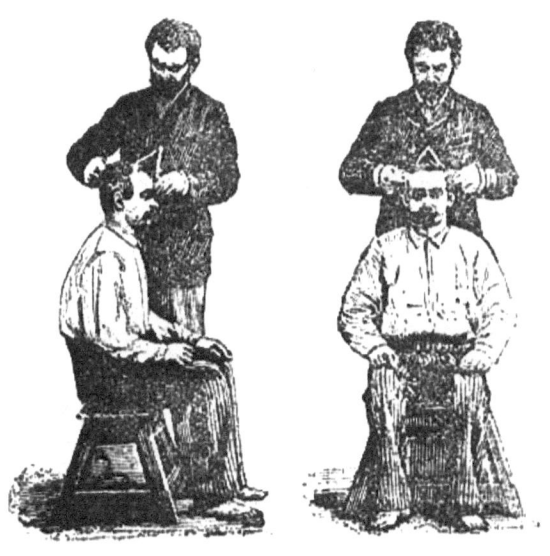

FIGURE 9. Measurements of the head. *Source:* Pedro N. Barros Ovalle, *Manual de antropometría criminal i jeneral escrito segun el sistema de A. Bertillon para la identificación personal i destinado al uso de los establecimientos penitenciarios, autoridades judiciales, compañías de seguros, cuerpos, armados, etc., etc.* (Santiago de Chile: Imprenta de Enrique Blanchard-Chessi, 1900). Memoriachilena.gob.cl.

might change over time, the Bertillon system allowed for the capture of an individual if the police had already conducted the bodily examination of the person; the dactyloscopy method was of no help in the investigation process, but rather only secured the identification of the individual *after* they were already in custody.[40] Together, both systems of identification, in theory, enabled the police to identify a person on the street (Bertillon) and confirm the assessment once back at the police station (Vucetich).[41]

These were decades of vast changes in the criminological world. Police and scholars—and police scholars—took up new methods, adapted them, and mixed them with other techniques in an effort to construct a more reproducible and translatable system of national and transnational policing. They were doing what Kirsten Weld has called the "most basic sense" of policing: building "an archive of society."[42] But these developments were no mere intellectual pursuits, simple theoretical discussions within small circles of police officers. Efforts at taking measurements of criminal bodies, of recording fingerprints, and tracking people made their way well into the popular world in Chile. By the early decades of the twentieth century, taking fingerprints of apprehended individuals had become so common that within the working-class population of urban Chile, many began to give it their own name: *tocando el piano*, or playing the piano.[43] They transformed the word *escrachar* from a verb meaning to destroy or break to one that referred to having their photograph taken: "in the Police Department lo escracharon."[44] Some even developed ways of distorting the appearance of their faces in photographs, subverting the consistency of identification.[45] And when Julio Vicuña Cifuentes collected and printed a book on slang used by Chilean criminals in 1910, he included the words typically used to refer to being imprisoned and the prison as *archivado* and *archivo*, respectively, both referring to the practice of archiving and the location of the archived material.[46] The bodies of imprisoned people had become the source of archival material for the police, and labor organizers, criminals, and suspects were quite aware of it.

## TRANSNATIONAL POLICING, 1905 AND 1920

The 1905 police conference in La Plata took place after years of transnational police cooperation between Buenos Aires and Rio de Janeiro. Local police forces witnessed the movement of suspected criminals from Buenos Aires to Rio de Janeiro and recognized the need for better cooperation between the police of both cities. For the 1905 conference, they invited the police of Montevideo and Santiago, forming a broad Southern Cone network of information exchange stretching from the Atlantic to the Pacific. When they reconvened in 1920, the political geography of the participants extended northward, bringing Peru, Bolivia, and Paraguay into the fold. At the 1920 conference, the Chilean delegation sent Luis Manuel Rodríguez, the same delegate who had participated in the 1905 conference, producing a continuity across the fifteen-year gap. Though they disagreed on some proposals, the overall atmosphere of the meetings was one of cooperation and solidarity. The Argentine Elpidio González, for instance, appealed to a "spirit of solidarity" between the police of South America in their "social function."[47] Francisco Eulalio do Nascimento e Silva Filho, the Brazilian delegate, called their work a "functional solidarity, creating a homogenous system of prevention and repression, founded in conscious and faithful collaboration between all police organizations."[48] And Victor Abento Haedo, the Paraguayan delegate, after hearing some of the speeches from the other participants, spoke of their work across borders as "healthy and useful work for humanity, and for this reason the actions of the police, in their preventative and repressive functions, should not recognize borders."[49] These police officers and representatives of different states knew quite well that "in the war for survival, cooperation, not competition, was key."[50]

Still, how exactly transnational police solidarity would actually function presented difficulties. As the previous discussion on photography shows, a certain amount of reproducibility and uniformity of method across borders was required so that the object being exchanged could be read, interpreted, and used as a police tool in another location. Transnational policing also meant the transfer of material things: pictures, paper documents, fingerprints, reports, and the like. The delegate from Uruguay at the 1920 meeting suggested the creation of a central office for much of this information. The other delegates objected to the idea, however, arguing that such an office might be prohibitively expensive to sustain, and that the transferring of police archival documents from various locations, "some of them contain[ing] hundreds of thousands of criminal records," to one central office might take years to complete.[51] And despite the emphasis on transnational solidarity and cooperation between police forces, some of their provisions made these efforts difficult, if not impossible, to achieve. If the police decided to deport someone, for instance, they needed to notify the country to which that person was heading, sending along information on the individual, the date of their expulsion, the ship or train on which they would arrive, and their destination. But the proposal also included language that would deny some of those expelled a passport, making entering a new country quite difficult.[52]

Nonetheless, in the case of Peru and Chile, police in both countries initiated and took part in the sharing of information. In late January 1903 the Peruvian consulate in Valparaíso sent back to Peru two pamphlets on policing in Chile and ten numbers of the *Boletín de la Policía de Santiago*.[53] Just over a month later, the consulate in Valparaíso sent another text on policing in Chile. Importantly, the mailing of police pamphlets by the Peruvian consulate was not an action taken without the knowledge of the Chilean authorities. The Intendancy of Valparaíso asked the consulate if it would mind asking the authorities in Peru to send a copy of their Reglamentos y Manuales de la Policía de Lima, something from which they hoped to learn.[54] In one case, a police officer from Santiago approached the Peruvian consulate in Valparaíso and asked if he could go to Lima and "lend his services" to the capital.[55] It is unclear if the Peruvian government took him up on the offer.

Despite increased tension between Peru and Chile in the 1910s and 1920s, police and state figures in both countries exchanged information on suspects and, in some cases, put through extradition orders. In 1915 the authorities in Peru, for instance, asked the Chilean police in the port of Iquique to arrest and detain suspects in a bank robbery that took place in Arequipa until they could complete the extradition paperwork, a request the Chilean police agreed to.[56] A few years later, in 1918, Chilean authorities asked the Peruvian police to extradite a prisoner held preventively in the port of Callao, and authorities in Callao put the prisoner on a ship run by the CSAV to return him to Chile.[57] These were cases in which the identity of the suspect was clear. But what happened when the suspect did not have identification papers? When a man named Vergara appeared on a ship in late 1926 without any documentation to confirm his identity, the authorities were left to "presume" his nationality and a possible repatriation.[58] In another extradition discussion, the police in Valparaíso detained a Uruguayan suspect whom the government of Uruguay requested for extradition. But when the police in Valparaíso spoke with him, he declared that he was not the person wanted by Uruguayan authorities. On learning of these new developments, authorities in Uruguay sent seven pages of background information on the suspect and a letter from the Investigative Police in Montevideo to prove the man's identity. A month later, the suspect still awaited his fate.[59]

## "I ASÍ, LA MAR"

The emphasis on policing transnationally developed out of the circulation of people, goods, and ideas in the late nineteenth and early twentieth centuries, and much of this took place within the maritime world. The shipment of goods required the safe and secure transfer from customs house to dock and then ship, and vice versa, from ship to dock and then the customs house. If a ship docked and had to hold goods on board for a later unloading, the materials could fall prey to thieves. In Valparaíso, thefts on ships, which were sometimes referred to as piracy, were so prevalent that in 1907 the police created a new unit designed specifically to watch over the bay. The Special Guards of the Bay helped lower the incidence of theft on board Grace Company ships in its few months of existence, and to demonstrate its gratitude, the Grace Company donated $200 to the police, which it hoped would be distributed to the officers of the unit.[60] Although the new unit stemmed theft for a time, "pirates" soon found holes to exploit, as the small police unit could only cover "one hundredth" of the total area of the bay, according to the police.[61] The opening pages of Chilean novelist Manuel Rojas's first novel, *Lanchas en la bahía* (1932), centers on the narrator Eugenio protecting ships on the dock of Valparaíso as the night watchman, or, as the term became in Spanish, the *guachimán*.[62] Similarly, British shipping companies complained to the Peruvian government about stolen goods along the Peruvian coast in 1919, and just as in Chile, the response was the creation of a new policing unit specializing in overseeing merchant ships, especially in Callao.[63]

If goods being stolen worried authorities, the people working on the ships and those living in port cities caused just as much consternation. Maritime workers consistently disembarked and stayed past their time in port. In 1874 the Peruvian Ministry of Foreign Relations complained of sailors from the United States ignoring the time limits of their off-ship permission. The police in Callao, in turn, had to spend time looking for, detaining, and sending them back to their ships. They had to do the same for sailors from other countries, too. But sailors were getting help in violating their permission to be on land, for they needed to find temporary housing in Callao. The Ministry of Foreign Relations, in turn, blamed owners of inns who did not check the sailors' written permission slips.[64] Overstaying their time in port could turn into desertion, which also required the local police to take action.[65]

Even if maritime workers abided by all applicable laws, state officials still sometimes viewed them with suspicion. Police in Callao, for instance, perceived the *población flotante* (floating population) in the port as one reason to continue funding the Sección de Investigaciones, identificación i estadística in 1913.[66] This población flotante was a group of people who had not committed any crime, but their lack of attachment to any fixed location placed them in a broad category of possible criminals. In another case in 1918, the police in Callao detained the second mate working on the Chilean steamship *Huasco*. After interrogating him at the local police station, it became clear to the second mate that part of the real reason the officer had detained him could be found on his left hand: a tattoo.[67] Again, the maritime worker had not done anything wrong, legally speaking. But the police interpreted the vocation of maritime worker and the presence of a visible tattoo as signs of a possible criminal in their port. Even before these cases, within the criminological world tattoos were often characterized as a symbol of a return to the savage past, an idea reproduced by the Italian criminologist Cesare Lombroso and circulated in Latin America by people like Barros Ovalle.[68] The police probably knew that within Peru, tattoos were much more common along the coast, perhaps due to the relationship with maritime workers from other parts of the world. They may have also been aware of the frequency of tattoos among incarcerated people in early twentieth-century Peru. Just a year prior, in 1917, Marino C. Alegre y Pacheco had published a book based on his bachelor's thesis, a study of tattoos in Peruvian prisons. Of the many people Alegre interviewed, an unnamed maritime worker with tattoos related to his work—a 5 × 4 cm anchor with a heart and an arrow, another heart and arrow of similar size, and two clasped hands with a rising sun behind them (see figure 10)—was one of the only men who, when offered the possibility of removing the tattoos, rejected the suggestion (*negó rotundamente*), being completely "content with his tattoos."[69] For the anonymous prisoner, his tattoos may have brought him memories of life at sea, of places visited, or of friendships formed. Whatever his reason, and despite the attention they surely brought, he knew he wanted to keep them.

The maritime world presented particular problems for policing along the South American Pacific littoral. The crews of ships docking at port hailed from around the world, and the police and local authorities viewed this población flotante as a difficult sector of port society to keep under control. The police in Valparaíso called attention to the "cosmopolitan" nature of their port city, "where, day in and day out, flow a considerable number of foreigners," as a prime reason for the necessity of having a fully funded and functioning police department.[70] In Callao, the category of población

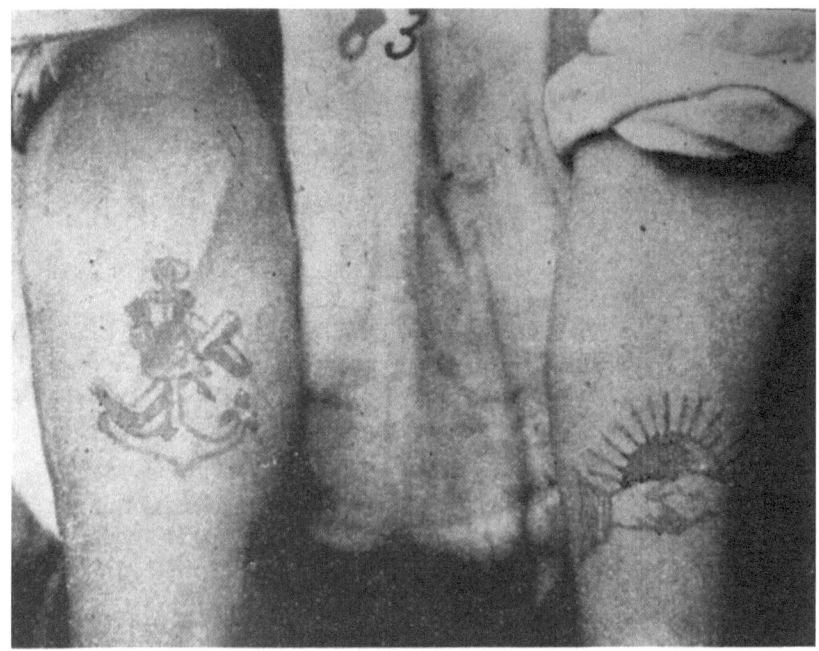

FIGURE 10. Tattoos on a prisoner. *Source:* Marino C. Alegre y Pacheco, *Los delincuentes tatuados de la penitenciaria nacional* (Lima: Tip. Y Encuadernación de la Penitenciaria, 1917), 43.

flotante spread across decades, from at least the 1870s and into the 1910s, at once both homogenizing a rather heterogeneous population and discursively producing a population to be surveilled. In 1891 local authorities in Callao referenced this población flotante in calling for more and better trained police for the port; in 1903 the prefect of Callao characterized this población flotante as made up mostly of maritime workers who, "due to necessity or bad instincts, frequently commit robberies or attempted robberies that sometimes contain the characteristics of true assaults," and who occasionally committed crimes in neighboring Lima and fled to Callao in search of refuge in a ship leaving port; and in 1913, as mentioned previously, the población flotante lay at the center of the argument around the continued funding of the Sección de Investigaciones, identificación i estadística.[71] In many ways, the maritime población flotante mirrored a similar population moving around within each country.[72] The port of Valparaíso, by the sheer fact of being Chile's main port, was seen as harboring a nefarious population. According to the police, "there is a group, quite numerous, in Valparaíso, of well-known thieves, pickpockets, vagrants..., swindlers, accessories to theft, buyers of things of suspicious providence, and, in other words, the sea [i así, la mar]."⁷³ Though they recognized different types of crimes, the ocean lay at the center, as the nexus, of crime, linking them all together. The brevity of the end of the sentence—"i así, la mar"—acted as an almost ominous closing to the list, and the abruptness of the period lends itself to being read as an ellipsis, indicating the extensiveness and elusiveness of the ocean.

Part of the problem of policing was the geographical space of the port, particularly in Valparaíso. The police repeatedly referenced the difficult terrain of the port, characterized by flat land near the downtown and port, surrounded by hills with steep and winding streets and staircases (see figure 11). These streets "appeared to have lost themselves in the hills, and that turned around and around, rose and came down, as though looking for themselves."[74] The topography and the way people built their lives into the hills resulted in a port with "thousands and thousands of hiding places" for criminals, with streets and passageways "full of crossroads and intricate pathways," making it easy to commit a crime and escape, a city "twice as difficult" to police.[75] Even if a police officer had a decent knowledge of the streets, there were places that people had carved out for themselves. In 1903 the police in Valparaíso reported on "subterranean cavities" from which "pickpockets and people of bad lineage" or "vagrants" gathered and assaulted pedestrians.[76]

In order to police this población flotante across the social and physical geography of the port, the police in Callao and Valparaíso had to develop policing methods appropriate for their ports. Police in Callao sought to create a special police unit in the 1870s, primarily to prevent crime and pursue criminals in a port city with a cosmopolitan población flotante. The local press learned of the formation of what they called a "secret police," and the authorities demanded apprehension of the journalist who broke the story because the order to create the unit was confidential.[77] This type of policing appears to have made its first appearance in Callao decades before a similar policing unit in Lima. In Valparaíso, the police suggested incorporating dogs and horses into the policing of the city to help them cover the difficult terrain. Part of this move developed out of the police paying attention to police in other locations using dogs to aid in their work.[78] These police officers were probably not aware of it at the time, but police and security agents of various types had used dogs for centuries, especially with regard to slavery.[79] Dogs would allow for police officers to not have to patrol with another human officer; when two officers patrolled together they often talked, and

FIGURE 11. General view of Valparaíso, Chile, date unknown. *Credit:* Unknown photographer, n.d., glass plate negative, 1996.00009.X128744. Keystone-Mast Collection, UCR/California Museum of Photography, University of California, Riverside.

the conversation distracted them from their duties. Patrolling with a dog would remove this distraction. And importantly, horses could be used "during large parties or popular revolts."[80]

This turn to thinking more concentratedly about popular movements in the first decades of the twentieth century reshaped police forces in Callao and Valparaíso.[81] In both cases the police had dealt with labor unrest for decades, but it was not until the early twentieth century that the militancy of labor, and the frequency of its public protests, forced authorities to carefully consider how to police the city in an era of increasingly organized workers. During the 1905 police conference in Argentina, the list of people they sought to track included numerous types of criminals, but it also mentioned labor organizers. As protesting, marching through the streets, and using the space of public plazas increased in Valparaíso, police looked to the local government to create new regulations on the use of plazas as a way of legally bounding public spaces.

Within each port city, the police also reworked their specific policing techniques. Part of this was in the form of new police units and a restructuring of the internal dynamics of the police hierarchy. In Callao, authorities pushed an early version of this in the 1870s, as mentioned previously, though it is unclear if this new unit actually formed and functioned. With the población flotante category of people circulating in Callao, police also saw the need to track people within the group, and in particular those who had participated in labor protests, especially after the successful port strike of January 1913.[82] In response to the strike (and the numerous other workers who went on strike after port workers won their demands), and building from years of discussions within elite circles on how to conceptualize and deal with labor in modern Peru, President Guillermo Billinghurst established the short-lived Secciones Obreras (Labor Sections).[83] These Labor Sections would be run out of police stations, which had been tasked since at least the late nineteenth century with similar document processing and registering, such as in the case of domestic workers.[84] As Paulo Drinot notes, they were tasked with a wide variety of data collection, including statistics on industrial establishments, workers, wages, working-class housing, population density, cost of living, workplace accidents, and labor actions, as well as with registering and officially recognizing worker societies.[85] Significantly, the Chilean state was well aware of the establishment of the Labor Sections. Frias Collao, the head of the Chilean Labor Office (Oficina del Trabajo), wrote to the director of the Labor Section in Lima about the new grouping and sent along some publications written in the name of the Labor Office. Collao hoped they could "establish cordial relations and frequent communication with the new administrative organism." The Labor Section in Lima was so new, though, that it did not have any equivalent publications to send in return.[86] In previous years, the Peruvian consulate in Valparaíso sent back home reports on labor actions in the port, which may have been instructive to authorities in Peru on how to relate to labor and the social question.[87]

Of particular interest is the directionality of the Labor Sections. They were, first of all, created in response to a strike wave set off by port workers in Callao. Second, the very form in which the Lima branch of the Labor Sections recorded information on workers—including where they worked and physical features such as age, height, race, eye color, facial hair, hair color, and the shape of the person's nose, lips, mouth, face, and forehead—developed

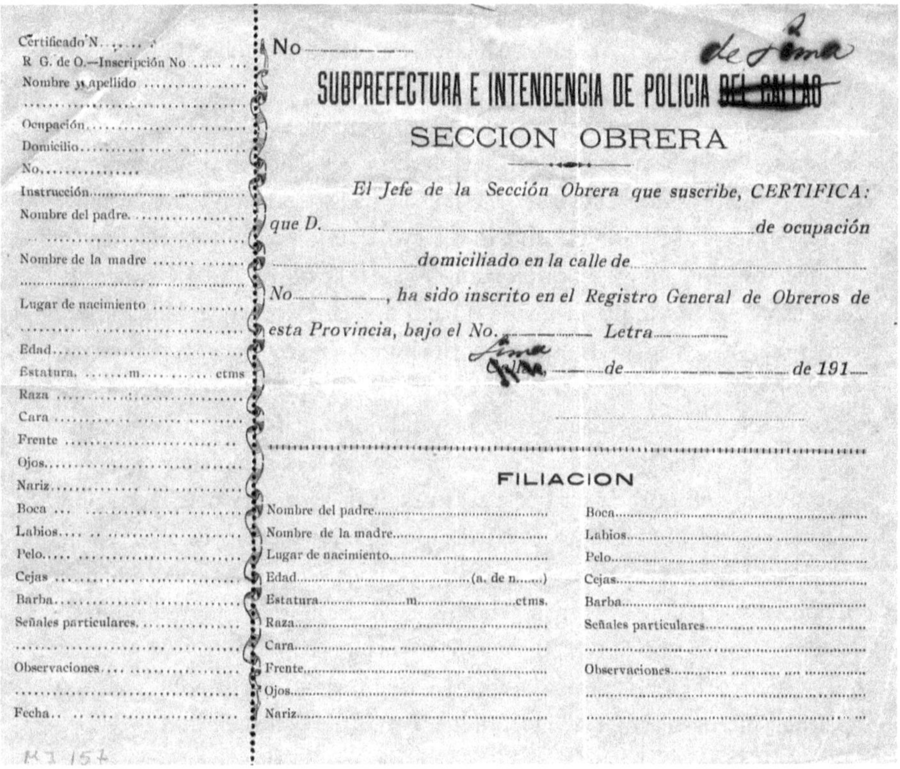

Certificado N.
R. G. de O.—Inscripción No
Nombre y apellido
Ocupación
Domicilio
No
Instrucción
Nombre del padre
Nombre de la madre
Lugar de nacimiento
Edad
Estatura ... m ... ctms
Raza
Cara
Frente
Ojos
Nariz
Boca
Labios
Pelo
Cejas
Barba
Señales particulares
Observaciones
Fecha

No ... de Lima

SUBPREFECTURA E INTENDENCIA DE POLICIA ~~DEL CALLAO~~

SECCION OBRERA

*El Jefe de la Sección Obrera que suscribe, CERTIFICA: que D. ... de ocupación ... domiciliado en la calle de ... No ..., ha sido inscrito en el Registro General de Obreros de esta Provincia, bajo el No. ... Letra ...*

*Lima ~~Callao~~, ... de ... de 191...*

FILIACION

Nombre del padre
Nombre de la madre
Lugar de nacimiento
Edad ... (a. de n. ...)
Estatura ... m ... ctms.
Raza
Cara
Frente
Ojos
Nariz

Boca
Labios
Pelo
Cejas
Barba
Señales particulares
Observaciones

FIGURE 12. Lima Police filiación form, based on the form created in Callao. *Source:* Pedro Saenz to sub-prefecto é Intendente de Policía, 18 Jul. 1913, AGN, Prefecturas, Lima, 1913. Courtesy of the Archivo General de la Nación de Perú.

first in Callao and was then transported to Lima. As seen in figure 12, the Lima branch of the Labor Sections took the Callao form, scratched out "Callao," and wrote in "Lima."[88] Port worker strikes and this specific form of collecting statistics and data on individual workers, then, had their birth in Callao and spread to nearby Lima.

The police also used more qualitative policing methods. In Valparaíso, police used multiple connected actions to disrupt labor organizing. A foundational aspect of this was the use of police spies. A police spy could be counted as a participant in just about any major demonstration or public union meeting in Valparaíso. The spies reported on who said what in meetings, took notes on the speeches of organizers during a protest, and alerted the authorities—typically in a letter to the prefect, who then paraphrased or quoted the most important parts of the report and sent it to the intendant—about what the local movement might do in the coming days and weeks.[89] Similarly, much of what was discussed on Mollendo in the previous chapter came directly from police spies.

Even with reports from the inside of meetings, the police still needed other, sometimes extralegal, methods to throw a wrench into labor organizing. In 1920 Enrique Caballero, the police chief in Valparaíso, for instance, ordered the planting of dynamite in the IWW union office so that when the police raided it, they would have ample evidence of the IWW's subversive ambitions.[90] During a strike by Las Habas shipyard workers in Valparaíso in late 1924, metalworkers claimed that the police secretly placed a syringe into a labor leader's pocket, which experts claimed showed his criminal intentions. This was, the workers wrote, "a well-known maneuver" on the part of the police.[91] (The police were, of course, not always completely organized and disciplined in their efforts. Residents in the port city of San Antonio, Chile, complained in 1917 that the local police were constantly drunk while on the job and abused their powers. Four of them had recently been demoted for raping a woman. The inspector filing the report suggested a total reorganization of the police in San Antonio.)[92]

Whether the police called upon detailed forms, sent in police spies, or planted incriminating evidence, policing maritime workers and their protests cost money. Throughout these early decades of the twentieth century the police in Callao and Valparaíso referenced the need to either maintain or increase their funding. They also took great care to document exactly how much policing protests cost. After the May 1903 strike by maritime workers in Valparaíso, in which workers, police, and armed residents fought in the streets, the police budget had largely been exhausted. During the strike the police had to place more officers on the streets throughout the city, feed the extra officers and the horses, and repair their weapons. The police asked the state for more funds to help replenish their budget, as well as new guns, a switch from Winchesters to Mausers.[93] After a city-wide strike in 1907, the police in Valparaíso argued that the increase in crime across the city was a direct result of reassigning police to watch over a local strike. A raise in police wages might, they suggested, bring in more officers.[94] The idea of potential labor strife also encouraged police expansion. In February and March 1913, just months before the strike against portraits, police in Valparaíso wrote to the intendant about the poor state of affairs within police supplies. Although they counted 1,176 police officers, they only had 322 rifles. To partially cover this gap between the total number of rifles and officers, they requested an additional 250 Mauser rifles. The motivation behind the letters of request was working-class actions: a "violent strike," "subversive movements," a normal "strike," and to help catch "bandits."[95]

Increased resources also meant the installation of new technological devices to control labor organizing. In Callao in 1913 the local authorities sought to improve their ability to police strikes through the installation of new telephone lines. They argued for the need to install direct lines between the prefect in Callao and various offices within the state government, including the Guardia Civil, police intendant, and Dirección de Gobierno, and between the intendant and the barracks. They were even worried that telephone company employees might be organizing and, in turn, not relay information during a strike. Again, working-class organizing allowed the local authorities to push for new, private lines between government offices.[96] In 1912 the police in Valparaíso noted the benefits of having their telephone lines running out of the central office of the prefect since 1906. But they also saw the need to replace the older phones because they required the use of two hands, which meant that apprehended people could attempt an escape while the officer made a phone call.[97] Though this particular instance is not specific to labor organizing, the police in Chile clearly made a connection between communication technologies and labor strife. In 1920 authorities in Chile conducted a study on installing radiotelegraphy—a method of wirelessly sending telegrams—that would connect the Moneda (the house of the executive branch of the government) with various parts of the country, in large part due to "current moments of internal agitation and external threats." The August 1920 study and plan came seven months after a port worker strike in Magallanes, only one month after another strike in Taltal and the campaign against "subversives" in Santiago and Valparaiso, and during continued worker mobilization in Punta Arenas. By October 1920 the authorities were still figuring out how to proceed, but radiotelegraphy remained an "urgent necessity."[98]

The state also had recourse to a militarized form of policing. Beginning in the colonial period in Latin America, people attached to the military often—particularly after the Bourbon Reforms—fell within the jurisdiction of the military rather than civil authorities. During the late colonial period, this fuero militar allowed some people to escape prosecution from civil authorities and created a juridical "class apart" from others in society.[99] After independence in the early nineteenth century, the fuero militar remained but became less an avenue of protection and much more a tool of control.[100] Maritime workers in Peru, in order to officially be a member of a state-sanctioned union, technically fell within a branch of the military. This legal position meant that authorities higher up the chain of command could remove maritime workers from their matriculado status, which gave them a right to work as part of the union. A brief struggle between local port workers (*fleteros*) in the Peruvian port of Paita in 1917 offers an illustration of how this relationship may have played out on other occasions, and how the fuero militar was used as a method of control by the state over port workers. When the steamship *Chile* docked at port on June 17, 1917, fleteros approached the ship to help unload passengers, as they normally would do. From there the story changes depending on the narrator. According to the workers, the Sr. Ayudante de la Capitanía, one César Valdivieso, became enraged at their boarding the ship, ordered them back to land, imprisoned a few of them for twenty-four hours, tortured them with a method dating back to the Inquisition, and removed them from their jobs.[101] According to Valdivieso, the fleteros were told not to board the ship since there were few passengers and during the trip valuables had been stolen, and local port officials wanted to investigate before adding any new people to the ship. In the process of disobeying Valdivieso, the workers hurt a passenger, argued with Valdivieso, and raised some "rebellious voices." Due to these actions, Valdivieso removed them from the list of matriculados and sent them to military court.[102] Whatever happened on the dock, port workers went on strike in order to bring their coworkers back onto the matriculado list and allow them access to port work again. Even though local authorities argued that the workers had broken the rules of port work and wrote to the military judge that many of the workers expelled from the matriculado list were known for being thieves, "bad elements," or even leaders of the movement, the judge reenlisted the men.[103] In the end, the fuero militar helped these workers return to work. But significantly, of the eight workers sent to the fuero militar, four of them fled the court.[104] Even though the court ruled in their favor, the idea of going to the military court may have scared them enough to want to flee, suggesting their weariness with the system. If Valdivieso could unilaterally remove them from the gremio, the military court could just as easily uphold the decision, leaving them out of a job.

Throughout the early decades of the twentieth century, police and state authorities concerned with control over their populations used two broad categories of people as a rationale for learning, adapting, and improving upon criminological techniques. One group the police and reformers focused on was urban criminals, who had purportedly perfected their craft and whose population increased by the year.[105] The second group, who had formed connections with organized labor, fomented protests and street violence, and created and maintained connections to people with similar beliefs and political mobilization, were the anarchists. At the 1905 police meeting in Argentina anarchists figured prominently as a threat. And at the 1920 meeting, the actions of anarchists, as well as Bolsheviks, weighed heavily on many of the attendees. Luis Manuel Rodríguez, the Chilean delegate at both the 1905 and 1920 meetings, for instance, drew a line between acceptable organizing—what he called "gremios del pueblo" that were part of the "evolutionary force of social life and within the law"—and that which "pretend[s] to impose solutions contrary to order and the normal regime of the life of the State."[106] The Chilean delegation sought to differentiate what they called "political crimes and acts connected to them" from "acts of anarchism and maximalism directed against the bases of social organization." They understood the former as *electoral* politics, and by doing so cut off the possibility of politicians from being extradited for their crimes. Anarchism and maximalism, on the other hand, were "not be understood as political crimes," and therefore those suspected of such acts would face extradition.[107] And delegates more generally worried about anarchists; the very first article of the convention on sharing information across state lines emphasized "anarchist acts" and "the alteration of the social order."[108]

The police in Chile and Peru dealt with the perceived threat of anarchism in similar ways. In both countries the state deported people, internally and externally. In the case of Mollendo, Peru, labor organizers were routinely detained and sent into the Andes. Internal deportation, officials thought, would not only remove the individual from the scene but also reduce class conflict in the port.[109] On other occasions, local authorities in Peruvian ports were less careful with their internal deportation, allowing for suspects to leave the city without their knowledge. In one case, a governor ordered the removal of the Spanish citizen Luis Cebrian from the port of Ilo. Cebrian, a "pernicious foreigner," decided to clandestinely board the steamship *Maipo*, which was heading north. On the way, a ship official noticed him on board without the proper paperwork and kicked him off the boat while docked in Mollendo.[110] Although the local authorities in Ilo sought to deport Cebrian, their surveillance team could not keep track of him, and even though he left of his own accord, the ship officials simply deposited him in another port city. In Chile the government passed the Ley de Residencia in 1918, giving the state the ability to both limit the entrance of and expel foreigners thought of as subversives, a term that included anarchists, socialists, communists, and others.[111] The idea for the Chilean Ley de Residencia developed, at least in part, from a similar 1902 law in Argentina, which ironically had had the adverse effect of pushing "subversive" immigrants to Chile. When Simon Radowitzky killed the chief of police and his secretary in Buenos Aires with a bomb in November 1909, police in Valparaíso called for a Ley de Residencia to be enacted "immediately" in Chile, noting that the Argentine version of the law had produced an "anarchist horde, naturally pushed to our country by the whip of Argentine laws."[112] The people of Valparaíso, wrote one police officer, feared the "anarchist invasion."[113] And just a year later, in 1910, Peruvian President Augusto Leguía, with an eye toward Buenos Aires, "proposed a law that would allow the authorities to expel 'pernicious foreigners'" from the country. The law did not pass, though, due to lack of support from the legislature, according to Peter Blanchard.[114] Nonetheless, in 1913 authorities in Peru worried about "rufianos" from Argentina looking to Peru as a possible destination after the Argentine Ley de Residencia and the crackdown on anarchists in Chile and Bolivia.[115]

Anarchism brought together some of the most important and pressing issues of the social question within one category of people and thought. It allowed the police to attack resistance societies as the locus of radical thought, scrutinize immigration of nondesirables, push for more police officers and especially for preventative policing, drive a discursive wedge between acceptable and unacceptable protests, and launch rhetorical attacks on neighboring Peru.[116] To fend off anarchism, the strong arm of the police was not enough, however. Police needed to learn about the origins of anarchism, its ideology, and only then would their chances of defeating the "anarchist invasion" increase. For Hugo de la Fuente Silva, the events of the present required a historical understanding of anarchism. Thus he linked the 1909 events in Argentina to the founding of the International Workingmen's Association (IWA) in 1862, the IWA meeting in Geneva in 1866, Mikhail Bakunin and his revolutionary catechism, various anarchist figures in France and Germany, and their violence against leaders of states across Europe.[117] In this trajectory, from Europe in the 1860s to South America in the 1900s, anarchism was clearly the foreign ideology many within the state had claimed. A cursory understanding of the historical trajectory of anarchism, combined with the tried and true techniques of police spies and the new criminological methods of anthropometry and dactyloscopy, were the necessary ingredients to quash anarchism as an ideology and movement.

But perhaps a more appropriate phrasing is that of medicine. Barros Ovalle, the author of the anthropometry manual, described the situation thus in 1906: "As in the case of diseases, the best procedure to cure them is to prevent their appearance, the most efficient form of impeding crime is to prevent the causes that create it."[118] These were preventative (inoculation) measures, using and improving on scientific knowledge and its application (criminology) and putting into play the medicine required (police spies) to cut off the "social gangrene that is called anarchism."[119]

### CONCLUSION: POLICE AND THE STATE

Even though the police and authorities in Peru and Chile worried about the transnational movement of criminals, anarchists, and undesirables, some still constructed stiff barriers to working together across national lines. The police in Valparaíso, for instance, consistently referenced the War of the Pacific, placing it as an important moment in Chilean history and as interlocked with policing Valparaíso because many police officers had been military men either before or after their work in the police department.[120] State authorities in Chile also had a tendency to believe wild and elaborate stories about international connections between radicals and the Peruvian state.[121] In one case, when people with "anarchist characteristics" gathered in 1920 in Montevideo to protest the Chilean state, authorities immediately blamed the protest on Peruvian propaganda, instead of on people upset with the Chilean state's arrest of anarchist Julio Rebosio.[122] The nationalism of the police, and of some state authorities, continued in the midst of transnational cooperation.

Still, and more important for the argument here, authorities in Peru and Chile developed, almost simultaneously, similar methods and techniques of policing. Police in both countries recognized the cosmopolitan nature of their port cities and the rise of more militant labor organizing, and they pushed for increased funding, better tools, and more and different training for their officers. They also made connections to police officers from across South America through international conferences, which entailed attempts at creating identification procedures that were easily reproducible across borders. Beyond this, some officials and local officers sought to create more direct connections from city to city. These were decades of parallel developments and police-led transnational cooperation. Moreover, these connections mirrored, and were in part inspired by, similar local and transnational relations developed by working-class people in the early twentieth century.

If the cholera epidemic of the 1880s pushed both the Peruvian and Chilean states to rely on and create new material objects, the police of this chapter were also part of this material world of the state. Their work certainly entailed particular understandings of culture—the study of tattoos, of slang, or of the social geographies of the port—in order to surveil, patrol, and secure city space and to arrest suspects. But none of this would have been possible without the police officer, the photographic plates, the policing manuals, and the instructors of boxing, jiu-jitsu, anthropometry, and dactyloscopy. In her book on transnational policing in the twentieth century, Micol Seigel argues that the "police realize—they *make real*—the core of the power of the state."[123] Police and state authorities in the nineteenth and early twentieth centuries in Peru and Chile, with an eye toward an increasingly cosmopolitan world and the rise of militant labor organizing, knew that they needed to create new criminological methods and improve old ones. By enforcing state laws, creating new laws to deport or extradite suspects, and creating an archive out of the bodies of suspects and imprisoned people, the police made the state real. And they did so in parallel ways in Peru and Chile.

# Epilogue

OF PARALLELS

WHEN ALLAN WAGNER, the former minister of defense and minister of foreign relations, presented the Peruvian state's case at the International Court of Justice (ICJ) in The Hague in January 2008, Peruvians were already well aware of the international lawsuit.[1] For weeks on end *El Comercio*, the most important newspaper in Peru, had published article after article on the lead-up to the presentation of the formal complaint against Chile. Wagner, according to *El Comercio*, called the appointment to lead the Peruvian delegation "the biggest challenge in his career."[2] Readers were told that the process could take between five and six years to resolve, that the main issue up for debate was a still unsettled maritime border between the two countries, and that international law clearly backed up Peruvian claims.[3]

Still, despite the confrontation with Chile in the courtroom, many of the articles and quotes from key political figures emphasized the need to see Chile as more similar than different. Chile was no enemy, and there would be no war between the two countries. Alan García, the leading politician of Alianza Popular Revolucionaria Americana (APRA; American Popular Revolutionary Alliance) and president of Peru, told the Congress that to take a country to the ICJ was "not an unfriendly act, but to the contrary, shows the search for a peaceful solution to a juridical controversy." The relationship between the two countries, García said, should continue to be amicable, for Chile "is, in the end, a brother country from the beginning."[4] Another APRA member mentioned the importance of good commercial relationships between Peru and Chile, and a Chilean senator remarked that even though Chile would put forward its best case, he hoped that the legal conversations would take place "within the framework of good bilateral relations."[5]

Even though the border had been agreed upon by the 1929 Treaty for the Settlement of the Dispute regarding Tacna and Arica (the 1929 Treaty of Lima), the borderlands had remained a topic of discussion and possible war for decades afterward. On September 11, 1973, a military junta led in part by Augusto Pinochet overthrew the democratically elected Socialist Party President of Chile, Salvador Allende. With this radical reversal in national politics, what many would call a counterrevolution, relations with Peru also quickly turned bad. With heavy backing from the United States, the Chilean state had realigned its international political position; in Peru, the leftist dictator Juan Velasco Alvarado then looked to bolster that country's relationship with the USSR. Tensions between Peru and Chile rose, as did the possibility of a new war. Although some residents of the northern Chilean border city of Arica do not recall any worry about going to war with Peru, some remember hearing Peruvian military training in the distance and a shift in school uniforms to resemble War of the Pacific–era uniforms.[6] Pinochet was, after all, quite interested in the War of the Pacific, having previously been stationed in Concepción, a city next to the port of Talcahuano, which was the home of the Peruvian warship *Huáscar*, captured during the war.[7] Pinochet had also published his own study of the War of the Pacific just a year prior to the coup.[8]

The 2008 case at The Hague revolved around the question of delimiting the maritime border between Peru and Chile. For the Peruvian state, the 1929 Treaty of Lima only referred to the land border. Further, all agreements reached with Chile thereafter only recognized two hundred nautical miles of sovereign rights, shared by both Peru and Chile, and did not set forth a line separating Peruvian and Chilean sea rights.[9] The geographical layout of the coast leading to the land boundary, in which the Peruvian coast approached Chile via a southeastern diagonal and the Chilean coast more or less running north-south, meant that the two hundred nautical miles of sovereign rights in both countries, if drawn directly west for Chile and southwest for Peru, would overlap. As it stood, the Chilean state had claimed its right to the two hundred nautical miles of sovereign rights by drawing a "parallel of latitude extending from the terminal point on the land boundary" into the sea, resulting in what the Peruvian state called a "dramatic cut-off effect, or encroachment, on Peru's maritime entitlements."[10] The answer to these issues, they claimed, was to draw a general line along both coasts from the point at which the land border met the ocean, then create an equidistant line between the coastal lines, which they termed the equidistant methodology.

By doing this, the overall area of the sea would be split more or less evenly between Peru and Chile, at 84,782 square kilometers for Peru and 80,143 square kilometers for Chile.[11]

In their response to these arguments, the Chilean group claimed that the maritime border between the two countries had been settled for decades. First, they pointed to the mutual declaration of Peru and Chile to rights to two hundred nautical miles adjacent to their coasts in 1947 to fend off foreign fishing and whaling. Although not meant to draw a maritime border, the proclamation did delineate Chilean territory as a "mathematical parallel projected into the sea," which the Chilean state understood as a parallel of latitude.[12] This parallel of latitude into the sea as the maritime border, Chile argued, was reinforced in the Santiago Declaration of 1952, an agreement again reached in part due to fishing and whaling concerns.[13] Moreover, the Peruvian state's claim to an "outer triangle" made up of sea past Chile's two hundred nautical miles of sea but within Peru's same two hundred nautical mile line was an attempt to claim ocean with a "high-seas status" for one country.[14]

But perhaps more revealing of the relationship between Peru and Chile in these debates over maritime territory is how each state represented the historical justifications for its claims. For the Peruvian legal team, the history of Peru-Chile relations was one of conflict. During the colonial era, Lima had acted as the central node of politics and economics, connecting Peru with Chile, northern Argentina, and Bolivia. After independence, Chilean political leaders looked north with fear of a strong Peru, and thus statesmen like Diego Portales in the 1830s pushed for war and the eventual breakup of the Peru-Bolivia Confederation. In the Peruvian interpretation, Chile was the aggressor nation during the War of the Pacific. Peru simply acted as a loyal partner to Bolivia, whose military succumbed to Chilean aggression early in the conflict, leaving Peru to bear the brunt of the war. Although the negotiations and signing of the Treaty of Lima in 1929, which solidified the territorial border, were agreed to by all parties, the splitting of Tacna away from Arica involved a "disrupting [of] the natural economic unit formed by the two provinces," since Arica is "Tacna's natural harbor."[15] From independence through the signing of the Treaty of Lima, the Chilean state was built primarily through war, with a fundamental aim at cutting down the importance of Peru. To prove this, the Peruvian claim not only looked toward historical events, but also to Chilean historians. That the Chilean state was bent on destroying Peru through war was proven by none other than Chilean

National History Prize winner Mario Góngora and his *Ensayo histórico sobre la noción de Estado en Chile en los siglos XIX y XX* (Historical essay on the notion of the state in nineteenth and twentieth century Chile).[16] Still, in the decades after the Treaty of Lima, Peru and Chile worked together (sometimes with the help of Ecuador) to fend off foreign fishers and whalers and built strong economic ties, Chile joined the Andean Community, and both were members of the Asia-Pacific Economic Cooperation Forum.[17] Despite a nineteenth-century history of conflict, more recent history led toward cooperation for the benefit of both countries.

The Chilean version of this history is quite different. Indeed, Chile's countermemorial calls Peru's interpretation of nineteenth- and early twentieth-century history an "incomplete account of complex events."[18] The Chilean state, in this view, acted as a friend to Peru since independence. Chile, in the person of Bernardo O'Higgins, alongside Argentina in the form of José de San Martín, helped Peru in its independence struggle. Rather than the war against the Peru-Bolivia Confederation being one of aggression against an increasingly formidable Peru, it was the result of a binational alliance between Chile and a portion of the Peruvian army to defeat the power-hungry Andrés de Santa Cruz. Chile's cooperative nature appeared again during the defense of the Pacific coast from Spanish aggression from 1865 to 1866, for which Chile was punished by Spain attacking the port of Valparaíso.[19] The War of the Pacific is almost entirely absent from this history. The Chilean case also relied in part on the work of historians, though less heavily than the Peruvian case. In what can be read as a veiled reference to the War of the Pacific, the Chilean countermemorial argued that the nineteenth and early twentieth centuries involved a "protracted and often conflictual process through which nation-states came into being in Latin America." If the Chilean state had engaged in an unnamed "conflictual process," it was only part of a natural process of becoming a nation-state, just as it happened throughout Latin America. The footnote to the quote referenced an essay cowritten by Peruvian historian Cristóbal Aljovín de Losada and Chilean historian Eduardo Cavieres Figueroa, which made a broader claim about a history of cooperation and solidarity between Peru and Chile; for Aljovín and Cavieres, it was a history that cannot be boiled down to a replaying of the singular event of the War of the Pacific.[20]

These two presentations of the historical relationship between Peru and Chile portray both different and overlapping historical trajectories. For Peru, the relationship was one of conflict from independence through

1929, before taking on a much more cooperative turn from then onward. For Chile, cooperation and solidarity actually began in the years prior to independence and extended to the present, though with a lack of discussion of the events of the War of the Pacific or the Chileanization campaigns of the early twentieth century. These differences in opinion over the relationship show both the importance of cooperation and the idea that the best type of cooperation occurs under a banner of justice. For Peru, this meant a new maritime border; for Chile, a ruling in favor of the border in the form of a parallel of latitude. A concept of cooperative justice structured both arguments but could not work in tandem. The historical representations, despite their claims of cooperation, were seeped in nationalist divisions, of claims of acting first as the country of solidarity despite their best interests. More than anything, the gesture toward binational cooperation is one of appearances, for the countries are, in the end, arguing over the rights to exploit fisheries and have direct access to shipping lanes. The appearance of solidarity is underwritten with nationalist and exclusionary goals.

In December 2012, just under three years after Peru's initial formal memorial, a very different story made the press in Lima. William Afaraya, a fisher from the southern Peruvian port of Ilo, found himself in the northern Chilean port of Arica. Afaraya worked as the pilot of a small fishing boat named *Mariano*. In the search for fish, the boat crossed south into Chilean waters, passing the ports of Antofagasta and Caldera, before being detained near the port of Coquimbo. From there, the Chilean patrol took the boat back north to Arica. Hit with a massive fine (the equivalent of US$30,000), stuck in a port away from home, and with the food supplies of the ship destroyed according to international laws on food crossing borders, Afaraya needed help to sustain himself in Arica. This is where Sergio Guerrero, the president of the Sindicato de Pescadores Artesanales de Arica, stepped in. While at sea in 2005, Guerrero's ship wandered north into Peruvian waters, before winding up in Ilo. "I was treated like a king" by the Gremio de Pescadores in Ilo, Guerrero recalled. Now Guerrero and his union regularly come to the aid of Peruvian fishers detained in Arica. While in Arica, Guerrero offers Peruvians food and a place to stay, and the Chileans even work their networks to help reduce fines—in the case of Afaraya, they spoke with the Servicio Nacional de Pesca de Chile and lowered the fine from $30,000 to $6,000. The Chilean fishers also helped Peruvian fishers who ended up in jail. When Emilio Risalazo, the owner of the *Danibel*, crossed the maritime border and the Chilean patrol detained the ship and crew, the patrol sent Risalazo to jail in Arica, where he stayed for one month. During his time in prison, the Chilean fishers union sold all of the ship's cargo and gave the money to Risalazo. The inflow of cash allowed him to survive in Chile until he returned to Peru. "For all of this, Risalazo, in his humble cove, remembers with gratitude his southern colleagues." While specialized teams debated the historical, legal, and geographical rationales for determining where the Peruvian sea and the Chilean sea begin and end, fishers living on both sides of the border envisioned a very different sea. They knew that fish move from one place to another, and that to live and labor as fishers, one might have to cross the border from time to time. The article reporting Risalazo's story closed by referring to José Peñaloza, the secretary of the fishers union in Arica, and the help the union offers to Peruvians, writing that it "is the attitude of an experienced fisher, who knows that in the ocean, all men are equal."[21] They envisioned, navigated, and lived in a shared South American Pacific world.

Parallels, paradoxically and counterintuitively, are both divisive and connecting. In the debate between the Peruvian and Chilean states at The Hague, a parallel line into the sea marked both the supposed border *and* the very line and concept, in terms of historical-juridical interpretations, on which their competing claims to maritime sovereign rights centered. This was a parallel line of division, one that marked difference. Even though the geometric use of the term *parallel* refers to two lines that never meet, for the fishers in Arica and Ilo, the term might be used in a different sense. Laboring as fishers in ports near the border, they had experienced similar wanderings in their daily work. They knew the struggles of fishers, of the difficulties of state-defined borders at sea, of supporting one another when the security apparatus of the state caught, detained, and brought them up on charges. Their parallel situations allowed them to create a collective world of fishers. Parallels, in other words, connected.

And this is the main historical argument and narrative of this book. Despite over a century of writing—in the form of newspaper articles and editorials, partisan attacks, historical analysis that presupposes antagonism, and cultural battles, among others—some Peruvians and some Chileans, though cognizant of nationalist divisions, decided to take another path. They recognized similarity, saw analogous situations, and worked and organized side by side with those with whom they were supposed to be in conflict. Struggles over nation certainly were present, but to only see nationalist conflict is to reproduce a history that has been determined before research has begun. When Manuel González Prada, or David Matto, or anarchists in

Mollendo analyzed their position vis-à-vis the other, they reached a point at which other became similar due to parallel trajectories or structural positions, within capitalism or a fear of cholera, for instance. These stories of parallels creating connections offer precisely what Cristóbal Aljovín, Eduardo Cavieres, Daniel Parodi Revoredo, and Sergio González Miranda, as mentioned in the introduction to this book, call for when they argue that the War of the Pacific cannot be the event that undergirds the possibilities of relationships between the two countries.[22] The War of the Pacific need not act as the starting point of diverging histories that run parallel to one another. Rather, by recovering the actions and voices of those who created relationships of solidarity, we can write a history of parallels that connect and a history against patriotic phobias.

# NOTES

## INTRODUCTION

1. Luis Alberto Sánchez, "Prólogo sobre don Manuel González Prada," in Manuel González Prada, *Obras*, tomo 1, vol. 1 (Lima: Ediciones COPÉ, 1985), 11 ("from this incident"); and David Sobrevilla, Introduction to *Free Pages and Other Essays: Anarchist Musings*, ed. David Sobrevilla (New York: Oxford University Press, 2003), xxv–xxvii. For an in-depth take on González Prada in the aftermath of the war, see José Luis Rénique, *Imaginar la nación: Viajes en busca del "verdadero Perú" (1881–1932)*, 2nd ed. (Lima: Instituto de Estudios Peruanos, 2016), 29–76. All translations, unless otherwise noted, are my own.

2. Manuel González Prada, "Perú i Chile," in *Obras*, tomo 1, vol. 1, 93 ("gave us"); and González Prada, "Conferencia en el Ateneo de Lima," in *Obras*, tomo 1, vol. 1, 53 ("intellectually dependent").

3. González Prada, "Conferencia en el Ateneo de Lima," in *Obras*, tomo 1, vol. 1, 53.

4. González Prada, "Perú i Chile," in *Obras*, tomo 1, vol. 1, 94 ("ferocidad araucana"), 105 ("instinto de raza"); and González Prada, "Discurso en el Politeama," in *Obras*, tomo 1, vol. 1, 88. Araucanian refers to the indigenous in southern Chile.

5. Manuel González Prada, "Discurso en el Politeama," in *Obras*, tomo 1, vol. 1, 88–89. This is a rather abbreviated form of thinking about caudillos. Their power and strength required some type of popular support as well. On this, see, for instance, Hilda Sabato, *Republics of the New World: The Revolutionary Political Experiment in 19th-Century Latin America* (Princeton, NJ: Princeton University Press, 2018).

6. Manuel González Prada, "Las dos patrias," in *Obras*, tomo 2, vol. 3, 337. The exact year of this text is unknown. But it must have been written after December 1907, since González Prada references the recent massacre of miners in Iquique, Chile.

7. González Prada, "Las dos patrias," in *Obras*, tomo 2, vol. 3, 338.

8. González Prada, "Las dos patrias," in *Obras*, tomo 2, vol. 3, 339. Emphasis in original.

9. Jürgen Osterhammel makes the point that the "nineteenth century reflects is own emergent globality." See Osterhammel, *The Transformation of the World: A Global History of the Nineteenth Century*, trans. Patrick Camiller (Princeton, NJ: Princeton University Press, 2017), xvi.

10. This summary is based on William E. Skuban, *Lines in the Sand: Nationalism and Identity on the Peruvian-Chilean Frontier* (Albuquerque: University of New Mexico Press, 2007), 3–12; and William F. Sater, *Andean Tragedy: Fighting the War of the Pacific, 1879–1884* (Lincoln: University of Nebraska Press, 2007), 16–33.

11. Sater, *Andean Tragedy*, 91–92, 218–19, 244–45, 254–55.

12. Sater, *Andean Tragedy*, 288.

13. Sater, *Andean Tragedy*, 310–11, 317, 321–22, 327–28.

14. Skuban, *Lines in the Sand*; Sergio González Miranda, *Chilenizando a Tunupa: La escuela pública en el Tarapacá andino, 1880–1990* (Santiago: Dirección de Bibliotecas, Archivos y Museos, 2002); González Miranda, *El dios cautivo: Las ligas patrióticas en la chileanización compulsiva de Tarapacá (1910–1922)* (Santiago: LOM, 2004); and González Miranda, *La llave y el candado: El conflicto entre Perú y Chile por Tacna y Arica (1883–1929)* (Santiago: LOM, 2008). See also the forthcoming article by Evan Fernández on this process and its relationship to Pan-Americanism: "Pan-Americanism and the Definition of the Peruvian-Chilean Border, 1883–1929," *Diplomatic History*, forthcoming.

15. Rénique, *Imaginar la nación*; Carmen McEvoy, *Armas de persuasión masiva: Retórica y ritual en la Guerra del Pacífico* (Santiago: Ediciones Centro de Estudios Bicentenario, 2010); McEvoy, *Guerreros civilizadores: Política, sociedad y cultura en Chile durante la Guerra del Pacífico* (Santiago: Ediciones Universidad Diego Portales, 2011); McEvoy, "Civilización, masculindad y superioridad racial: Una aproximación al discurso republicano chileno durante la Guerra del Pacífico (1879–1884)," *Revista de Sociologia e Política* 20, no. 42 (June 2012): 73–92; McEvoy, *Chile en el Perú: La ocupación a través de sus documentos, 1881–1884* (Lima: Fondo Editorial del Congreso del Perú, 2016); Paul Gootenberg, *Imagining Development: Economic Ideas in Peru's "Fictitious Prosperity" of Guano, 1840–1880* (Berkeley: University of California Press, 1993), 182–83 (183 for "exports bottomed out"); Paulo Drinot, "Website of Memory: The War of the Pacific (1879–1884) in the Global Age of YouTube," *Memory Studies* 4, no. 4 (Oct. 2011): 370–85 (374 for "memory jolts"); Skuban, *Lines in the Sand*; Sater, *Andean Tragedy*; Daniel Parodi Revoredo, *Lo que dicen de nosotros: La Guerra del Pacífico en la historiografía y textos escolares chilenos* (Lima: Universidad Peruana de Ciencias Aplicadas, 2010); Glauco Seoane Byrne, *Revisando una historiografía hostil: Sobre el origen de la Guerra del Pacífico, la industria del salitre y el papel de la casa Gibbs de Londres* (Lima: Pontificia Universidad Católica del Perú/Instituto Riva-Agüero, 2013); Sergio Villalobos, *Chile y Perú: La historia que nos une y nos separa, 1535–1883* (Santiago: Editorial Universitaria, 2002); Mark Thurner, *From Two Republics to One Divided: Contradictions of Postcolonial Nationmaking in Andean Peru* (Durham, NC: Duke University Press, 1997), ch. 3; Ericka Beckman, "The Creolization of Imperial Reason: Chilean State Racism in the War of the Pacific," *Journal of Latin American Cultural Studies* 18, no. 1 (Mar. 2009): 73–90; Jeffrey L.

Klaiber, "Los 'cholos' y los 'rotos': Actitudes raciales durante la Guerra del Pacífico," *Histórica* 2, no. 1 (July 1978): 27–37; Julio Pinto Vallejos, Verónica Valdivia Ortiz de Zárate, and Pablo Artaza Barrios, "Patria y clase en los albores de la identidad pampina (1860–1890)," *Historia* 36 (2003): 275–332; Gabriel Cid, "De la Araucanía a Lima: Los usos del concepto 'civilización' en la expansión territorial del Estado Chileno, 1855–1883," *Estudios Ibero-Americanos* 38, no. 2 (July/Dec. 2012): 265–83; Milton Godoy Orellana, "'Ha traído hasta nosotros desde territorio enemigo, el alud de la guerra': Confiscación de maquinarias y apropiación de bienes culturales durante la ocupación de Lima, 1881–1883," *Historia* 44, no. 2 (July–Dec. 2011): 287–327; and Emilio José Ugarte Díaz, "La Guerra del Pacífico como referente nacional y punto condicionante de las relaciones chileno-peruanas," *Si Somos Americanos: Revista de Estudios Transfronterizos* 14, no. 2 (July–Dec. 2014): 159–85.

16. "Purposeful Provocation," *South Pacific Mail* (Valparaíso), 27 Aug. 1925, 1, 3 (quote on 1).

17. Heraclio Bonilla, "The War of the Pacific and the National and Colonial Problem in Peru," *Past & Present* 81 (Nov. 1978): 92–118.

18. Florencia E. Mallon, *The Defense of Community in Peru's Central Highlands: Peasant Struggle and Capitalist Transition, 1860–1940* (Princeton, NJ: Princeton University Press, 1983), esp. chs. 2–3; Mallon, *Peasant and Nation: The Making of Postcolonial Mexico and Peru* (Berkeley: University of California Press, 1995); Nelson Manrique, *Campesinado y Nación: Las guerrillas indigenas en la guerra con Chile* (Lima: Centro de Investigaciones y Capacitación, 1981), esp. ch. 11. See also the exchange between Bonilla ("The Indian Peasantry and 'Peru' during the War with Chile") and Mallon ("Nationalist and Antistate Coalitions in the War of the Pacific: Junín and Cajamarca, 1879–1902") in *Resistance, Rebellion, and Consciousness in the Andean Peasant World, 18th to 20th Centuries*, ed. Steve J. Stern (Madison: University of Wisconsin Press, 1987), and Bonilla's reflections on the debate in *La metamorfosis de los Andes: Guerra, economía y sociedad* (La Paz: Centro de Estudios para la América Andina y Amazónica Grupo and Editorial Kipus, 2014), 479–95.

19. José María Arguedas, *Deep Rivers*, trans. Frances Horning Barraclough (Austin: University of Texas Press, 1978), 47.

20. Nona Fernández, *Space Invaders*, trans. Natasha Wimmer (Minneapolis: Graywolf Press, 2019), 16. The War of the Pacific is also referenced on 21–22, 51, 56. Elements from this are also found in Fernández, *The Twilight Zone*, trans. Natasha Wimmer (Minneapolis: Graywolf Press, 2021), 169–70, 176. See also the discussion of the War of the Pacific in Robero Bolaño, *Distant Star*, trans Chris Andrews (New York: New Directions Book, 2004), 99–101.

21. It is no coincidence that Bonilla closed his article with a reference to González Prada's analysis of "'the suppurating wounds' of Peruvian society" and radical movements built, in part, out of this recognition. See Bonilla, "War of the Pacific," 118.

22. See, for instance, Seoane Byrne, *Revisando una historiografía hostil*, 61; and McEvoy, *Guerreros civilizadores*, 22. See also the summary of the turn toward new perspectives in Drinot, "Website of Memory," 374.

23. See Eduardo Devés, *Los que van a morir te saludan: Historia de una masacre; Escuela Santa María, Iquique, 1907* (Santiago: Ediciones Documentas / America Latina Libros / Nuestra America, 1989); Pablo Artaza Barrios et al., *A 90 años de los sucesos de la Escuela Santa María de Iquique* (Santiago: DIBAM / LOM ediciones, 1998); and Lessie Jo Frazier, *Salt in the Sand: Memory, Violence, and the Nation-State in Chile, 1890 to the Present* (Durham, NC: Duke University Press, 2007).

24. Cristóbal Aljovín de Losada and Eduardo Cavieres F., "Reflexiones para un análisis histórico de Chile-Perú en el siglo XIX y la Guerra del Pacífico," in *Chile-Perú, Perú-Chile en el siglo XIX: La formación del Estado, la economía y la sociedad*, comp. Eduardo Cavieres Figueroa and Cristóbal Aljovín de Losada (Valparaíso: Ediciones Universitarias de Valparaíso / Pontificia Universidad Católica de Valparaíso, 2005), 13. See also Eduardo Cavieres Figueroa, "Ni vencedores ni vencidos: La Guerra del Pacífico como análisis de conflicto y no del conflicto en sí mismo," in *Ni vencedores ni vencidos: La Guerra del Pacífico en perspectiva histórica*, ed. José Chaupis Torres, Juan Ortiz Benites, and Eduardo Cavieres Figueroa (Lima: La Casa del Libro Viejo, 2016), esp. 12, 16, 21.

25. Daniel Parodi Revoredo and Serio González Miranda, "Introducción," in *Las historias que nos unen. 21 relatos para la integración entre Perú y Chile*, comp. Daniel Parodi Revoredo and Sergio González Miranda (Lima: Fondo Editorial de la Pontificia Universidad Católica del Perú, 2014), 12. For other works that look at cooperative relationships, see María Lucía Valle Vera, "Los 'hijos de la guerra': Niños peruano-chilenos durante la ocupación de Lima (1881–1883), *Histórica* 41, núm. 1 (2017): 125–57; and Joanna Crow, "Photographic Encounters: Martín Chambi, Indigeneity and Chile-Peru Relations in the Early Twentieth Century," *Journal of Latin American Studies* 51, no. 1 (Feb. 2019): 31–58. For an example of cooperation before the war and conflict afterward, see Stefanie Gänger, *Relics of the Past: The Collecting and Study of Pre-Columbian Antiquities in Peru and Chile, 1837–1911* (New York: Oxford University Press, 2014), 203–50. For a work that brings together Bolivia and Chile, see Ivanna Margarucci and Eduardo Godoy Sepúlveda, *Anarquismos en confluencia: Chile y Bolivia durante la primera mitad del siglo XX* (Santiago: Editorial Eleuterio, 2018). Heidi Tinsman has also plotted a new path in the study of the War of the Pacific that emphasizes labor and race, bringing out the important role of Chinese immigrants and stories about them played in the war. See Heidi Tinsman, "Rebel Coolies, Citizen Warriors, and Sworn Brothers: The Chinese Loyalty Oath and Alliance with Chile in the War of the Pacific," *Hispanic American Historical Review* 98, no. 3 (Aug. 2018): 436–68; Tinsman, "Narrating Chinese Massacre in the South American War of the Pacific," *Journal of Asian American Studies* 22, no. 3 (Oct. 2019): 277–313.

26. On guano, see Gregory Cushman, *Guano and the Opening of the Pacific World: A Global Ecological History* (New York: Cambridge University Press, 2013); and Gootenberg, *Imagining Development*.

27. Letter from Patricio Lynch, in packet beginning with Ignacio Mariategui to Ministro de Estado del despacho de Guerra y Marina, Callao, 26 Aug. 1864, no. 907, Archivo Histórico de Marina, Callao, Peru (hereafter cited as AHM),

Buques, Amazonas, Fragata, Perú, 1864, caja A18, sobre A137, fol. 64–75 (67 for Lynch letter).

28. On Lynch, see William F. Sater, *Chile and the War of the Pacific* (Lincoln: University of Nebraska Press, 1986), 70; and Tinsman, "Rebel Coolies," 444.

29. See Peter Blanchard, *The Origins of the Peruvian Labor Movement, 1883–1919* (Pittsburgh: University of Pittsburgh Press, 1982), 153; Jeffrey L. Klaiber, "The Popular Universities and the Origins of Aprismo, 1921–1924," *Hispanic American Historical Review* 55, no. 4 (Nov. 1975): 693–715; and Iñigo García-Bryce, *Haya de la Torre and the Pursuit of Power in Twentieth Century Peru and Latin America* (Chapel Hill: University of North Carolina Press, 2018).

30. "Mensaje a los trabajadores del Perú," in Armando Triviño, *La I.W.W. en la teoria y en la práctica* (Santiago: Editorial Lux, 1925), 29–30.

31. Lara Putnam, "To Study the Fragments/Whole: Microhistory and the Atlantic World," *Journal of Social History* 39, no. 3 (Spring 2006): 618 (emphasis in original). See also Stuart B. Schwartz, *All Can Be Saved: Tolerance and Salvation in the Iberian Atlantic World* (New Haven, CT: Yale University, 2008).

32. One could, for instance, look no further than the long history of trade between the two countries from the colonial period through the twentieth century. See, in this case, L. A. Clayton, "Trade and Navigation in the Seventeenth-Century Viceroyalty of Peru," *Journal of Latin American Studies* 7, no. 1 (May 1975): 1–21; Gabriel Salazar, *Mercaderes, empresarios y capitalistas (Chile, siglo XIX)* (Santiago: Editorial Sudamericana, 2011), 490–98; Eduardo Cavieres Figueroa, *El comercio chileno en la economia mundo colonial* (Valparaíso: Ediciones Universitarias de Valparaíso de la Universidad Católica de Valparaíso, 1996), 77–100; and Villalobos R., *Chile y Perú*, 14.

33. Fernand Braudel, *The Mediterranean and the Mediterranean World in the Age of Philip II*, trans. Siân Reynolds (New York: Harper & Row, 1972–73) 1:14 ("shared") and 1:110 ("there is"). See also David Igler, *The Great Ocean: Pacific Worlds from Captain Cook to the Gold Rush* (New York: Oxford University Press, 2013), 4. Some have, rightly, questioned the foundational place of Braudel (and Bernard Bailyn) in oceanic studies. See, for instance, Suvit Sivasundaram, Alison Bashford, and David Armitage, "Introduction: Writing World Oceanic Histories," in *Oceanic Histories*, ed. David Armitage, Alison Bashford, and Sujit Sivasundaram (New York: Cambridge University Press, 2018), 2–3. For work on oceans influenced by Braudel, see K. N. Chaudhuri, *Trade and Civilization in the Indian Ocean: An Economic History from the Rise of Islam to 1750* (Cambridge: Cambridge University Press, 1985); Anthony Reid, *Southeast Asia in the Age of Commerce, 1450–1860*, 2 vols. (New Haven, CT: Yale University Press, 1988); Janet L. Abu-Lughod, *Before European Hegemony: The World System, A.D. 1250–1350* (New York: Oxford University Press, 1989); Eric Tagliacozzo, *Secret Trades, Porous Borders: Smuggling and States Along a Southeast Asian Frontier, 1865–1915* (New Haven, CT: Yale University Press, 2005); Alejandro de la Fuente, *Havana and the Atlantic in the Sixteenth Century* (Chapel Hill: University of North Carolina Press, 2008); James Warren, *Pirates, Prostitutes and Pullers: Explorations in the Ethno- and Social History of Southeast Asia* (Crawley: University of Western Australia Press, 2008); Matt K. Matsuda,

*Pacific Worlds: A History of Seas, Peoples, and Cultures* (New York: Cambridge University Press, 2012); Stuart B. Schwartz, *Sea of Storms: A History of Hurricanes in the Greater Caribbean from Columbus to Katrina* (Princeton, NJ: Princeton University Press, 2015); and Edward Dallam Melillo, *Strangers on Familiar Soil: Rediscovering the Chile-California Connection* (New Haven, CT: Yale University Press, 2015).

34. Braudel, *Mediterranean*, 1:276.

35. Helpful in this has been Epeli Hauʻofa, "Our Sea of Islands," *Contemporary Pacific* 6, no. 1 (Spring, 1994): 148–61; Andrew Herod, "From a Geography of Labor to a Labor Geography: Labor's Spatial Fix and the Geography of Capitalism," *Antipode* 29, no. 1 (Jan. 1997): 1–31; Micol Seigel, "Beyond Compare: Comparative Method after the Transnational Turn," *Radical History Review* 91 (Winter 2005): 62–90; David Sartorious and Micol Seigel, "Introduction: Dislocations across the Americas," *Social Text* 28, no. 3 (Fall 2010): 1–10; Ernesto Bassi, *Aqueous Territory: Sailor Geographies and New Granada's Transimperial Greater Caribbean World* (Durham, NC: Duke University Press, 2016); Gregory Rosenthal, *Beyond Hawaiʻi: Native Labor in the Pacific World* (Oakland: University of California Press, 2018); Tore C. Olsson, *Agrarian Crossings: Reformers and the Remaking of the US and Mexican Countryside* (Princeton, NJ: Princeton University Press, 2017); Melillo, *Strangers on Familiar Soil*; Sanjay Subrahmanyam, "Connected Histories: Notes towards a Reconfiguration of Early Modern Eurasia," *Modern Asian Studies* 31, no. 3 (July 1997): 735–62; John D. French, "Another *World* History Is Possible: Reflections on the Translocal, Transnational, and Global," in *Workers across the Americas: The Transnational in Labor History*, ed. Leon Fink (New York: Oxford University Press, 2011); and Constance Bantman and Bert Altena, "Introduction: Problematizing Scales of Analysis in Network-Based Social Movements," in *Reassessing the Transnational Turn: Scales of Analysis in Anarchist and Syndicalist Studies*, ed. Constance and Bantman and Bert Altena (Oakland: AK Press, 2017).

36. Joshua L. Reid, *The Sea Is My Country: The Maritime World of the Makahs, An Indigenous Borderlands People* (New Haven, CT: Yale University Press, 2015); Andrew Lipman, *The Saltwater Frontier: Indians and the Contest for the American Coast* (New Haven, CT: Yale University Press, 2015); Hauʻofa, "Our Sea of Islands"; Renisa Mawani, *Across Oceans of Law: The Komagata Maru and Jurisdiction in the Time of Empire* (Durham, NC: Duke University Press, 2018); Tagliacozzo, *Secret Trades*; Philip Steinberg, *The Social Construction of the Ocean* (New York: Cambridge University Press, 2001); Steinberg, "Of Other Seas: Metaphors and Materialities in Maritime Regions," *Atlantic Studies* 10, no. 2 (2013): 156–69.

37. Sater, *Andean Tragedy*, 150–60.

38. Cushman, *Guano*; Paul Gootenberg, *Between Silver and Guano: Commercial Policy and the State in Postindependence Peru* (Princeton, NJ: Princeton University Press, 1989); Gootenberg, *Imagining Development*; Melillo, *Strangers on Familiar Soil*; Manuel Llorca-Jaña and Juan Navarrete-Montalvo, "The Chilean Economy during the 1810–1830s and Its Entry into the World Economy," *Bulletin of Latin American Research* 36, no. 3 (July 2017): 345–69; and Salazar, *Mercaderes, empresarios y capitalistas*.

39. The classic text is, of course, Benedict Anderson, *Imagined Communities: Reflections on the Origin and Spread of Nationalism*, rev. ed. (1983; New York: Verso, 2006). But see also Ernest Gellner, *Nations and Nationalism* (Ithaca, NY: Cornell University Press, 1983).

40. Partha Chatterjee, *The Nation and Its Fragments: Colonial and Postcolonial Histories* (Princeton: Princeton University Press, 1993). See also Mallon, *Peasant and Nation*; Charles F. Walker, *Smoldering Ashes: Cuzco and the Creation of Republican Peru, 1780–1840* (Durham, NC: Duke University Press, 1999); and Thurner, *From Two Republics to One Divided*.

41. See, for instance, Mikhail Bakunin's comments on Poland in the nineteenth century or the experience of Cuban anarchists in the late nineteenth century. Michael Bakunin, *Statism and Anarchy*, trans. and ed. Marshall S. Shatz (New York: Cambridge University Press, 2002); Evan Matthew Daniel, "Rolling for the Revolution: A Transnational History of Cuban Cigar Makers in Havana, Florida, and New York City, 1853–1895" (PhD diss., The New School for Social Research, 2010).

42. Myrna I. Santiago, *The Ecology of Oil: Environment, Labor, and the Mexican Revolution, 1900–1938* (New York: Cambridge University Press, 2006), 310. Although Benedict Anderson was at the center of studying nationalism, he also made the move to thinking about anarchism and the fight against the nation. See Benedict Anderson, *Under Three Flags: Anarchism and the Anti-Colonial Imagination* (New York: Verso, 2005).

## CHAPTER 1. A SOUTH AMERICAN PACIFIC

1. Alexander G. Ioannidis, Javier Blanco-Portillo, Karla Sandoval, et al., "Native American Gene Flow into Polynesia Predating Easter Island Settlement," *Nature* 583 (2020): 572–77.

2. Cushman, *Guano*, 1–8. For an excellent analysis of the production of guano, see Gregory Rosenthal, "Life and Labor in a Seabird Colony: Hawaiian Guano Workers, 1857–70," *Environmental History* 17, no. 4 (Oct. 2012): 744–82.

3. Ricardo Padrón, *The Indies of the Setting Sun: How Early Modern Spain Mapped the Far East as the Transpacific West* (Chicago: University of Chicago Press, 2020).

4. See Kristin A. Wintersteen, *The Fishmeal Revolution: The Industrialization of the Humboldt Current Ecosystem* (Oakland: University of California Press, 2021), ch. 1.

5. Manuel Rojas, *Hijo del ladrón*, in *Tiempo irremediable* (1951; repr., Santiago: Zig-Zag, 2015), 1:117.

6. For broader interrogations of this paradox of freedom and imprisonment at sea, see, among many works, James Frances Warren, *The Sulu Zone, 1768–1898: The Dynamics of External Trade, Slavery, and Ethnicity in the Transformation of a Southeast Asian Maritime State* (Kent Ridge, Singapore: Singapore University Press,

1981); Julius S. Scott, *The Common Wind: Afro-American Currents in the Age of the Haitian Revolution* (New York: Verso, 2018); Marcus Rediker, *Between the Devil and the Deep Blue Sea: Merchant Seaman, Pirates, and the Anglo-American Maritime World, 1700–1750* (New York: Cambridge University Press, 1987); David A. Chappell, *Double Ghosts: Oceanian Voyagers on Euroamerican Ships* (Armonk, NY: M. E. Sharpe, 1997); Peter Linebaugh and Marcus Rediker, *The Many-Headed Hydra: Sailors, Slaves, Commoners, and the Hidden History of the Revolutionary Atlantic* (Boston: Beacon Press, 2000); Leon Fink, *Sweatshops at Sea: Merchant Seamen in the World's First Globalized Industry, from 1812 to the Present* (Chapel Hill: University of North Carolina Press, 2011); Sunil S. Amrith, *Crossing the Bay of Bengal: The Furies of Nature and the Fortunes of Migrants* (Cambridge, MA: Harvard University Press, 2013); Alex Borucki, "Shipmate Networks and Black Identities in the Marriage Files of Montevideo, 1768–1803," *Hispanic American Historical Review* 93, no. 2 (May 2013): 205–38; and Greg Grandin, *The Empire of Necessity: Slavery, Freedom, and Deception in the New World* (New York: Metropolitan Books, 2014).

7. Rosendo Melo, *Historia de la marina del Perú*, tomo primero (Lima: Imprenta de Carlos F. Southwell, 1907), 208; and Estado General, al ancla, Callao, 26 Oct. 1863 (373 crew members); Estado General, al ancla, Callao, 4 Nov. 1869 (348 crew members); Estado General, al ancla, Callao, 21 Jul. 1863 (359 crew members), all in AHM, Buques, Amazonas, Fragata, Perú, 1863, caja A17, sobre A134, fol. 92–94.

8. Melo, *Historia de la marina del Perú*, 211–14.

9. Ministerio de Marina to Ministro del Interior, Santiago, 6 Nov. 1918, Archivo Nacional de la Administración (hereafter cited as ARNAD). Ministerio de Marina (hereafter cited as MM), vol. 2225, no. 549.

10. See letters and documents attached to Ministerio de Guerra y Marina to Ministro de Estado en el Despacho de Justicia, 11 Oct. 1865, Archivo General de la Nación, Lima, Peru (hereafter cited as AGN), Republicano, Ministerio de Justicia, Beneficencia e Instrucción (hereafter cited as MJBI), Poderes del Estado, Ministerios, Guerra y Marina 1827–1879, legajo 186. A few of the people also had scars from the plague. Though problematic and more complex, these racial categories would be defined as mestizo (half indigenous, half European or Creole white); pardo (part European or Creole white, indigenous, and African descendant); mulato (European or Creole white and African descendant), and zambo (indigenous and African descent).

11. E. Oyanguren to Ministro de Relaciones Exteriores, Valparaíso, 9 Jun. 1903, Archivo del Ministerio de Relaciones Exteriores, Lima, Peru (hereafter cited as AMRREE-P), correspondencia, caja 523, carpeta 3, código 8-10-G, 1903, fol. 110–15, 112–13 for the specific people and locations.

12. *Resúmenes del Censo de las Provincias de Lima y Callao, leventado el 17 de Diciembre de 1920* (Lima: Imprenta Torres Aguirre, 1921), 6.

13. *Censo de la Provincia Constitucional del Callao, 20 de Junio de 1905* (Lima: Imprenta y Librería de San Pedro, 1906), 96–97, 108–9.

14. Frederick P. Bowser, *The African Slave in Colonial Peru, 1524–1650* (Stanford, CA: Stanford University Press, 1974), 96–100, 126–29; Grandin, *Empire of*

*Necessity*, 239–40; Jay Monaghan, *Chile, Peru, and the California Gold Rush of 1849* (Berkeley: University of California Press, 1973), 79–80, 90; and Tamara J. Walker, "'That is How Whores Get Punished': Gender, Race, and the Culture of Honor-Based Violence in Colonial Latin America," *Journal of Women's History* 31, no. 2 (Summer 2019): 11–32.

15. *Censo de la Provincia Constitucional del Callao*, 110–11, 114–15.

16. *Resúmenes del Censo de las Provincias de Lima y Callao*, 26.

17. Ministerio de Relaciones Esteriores to Ministro de Marina, Santiago, 9 Oct. 1913, ARNAD, MM, vol. 1905, no. 2912.

18. Informe sobre la Inspección pasada á los buques de la Armada por el órden que se indica, Callao, 5 Sep. 1864, attached to Ignacio Mariategui to General Ministro de Estado del despacho de Guerra y Marina, Callao, 6 Sep. 1864, AHM, Buques, Amazonas, Fragata, Peru, 1864, caja A18, sobre A137, fol. 93.

19. Manuel Rojas, "El vaso de leche," in *Cuentos* (Santiago: Ediciones Universidad Alberto Hurado, 2016), 146.

20. Cushman, *Guano*, 86.

21. H. E. Maude, *Slavers in Paradise: The Peruvian slave trade in Polynesia, 1862–1864* (Stanford, CA: Stanford University Press, 1981), 73.

22. Milton Godoy Orellana, "Los 'colonos polinesios' en Sudamérica: La variante chilena en el tráfico de rapanui a Perú, 1861–1864," in *América en Diásporas: Esclavitudes y migraciones forzadas en Chile y otras regiones americanas (siglos XVI–XIX)*, ed. Jaime Valenzuela Márquez (Santiago: RIL Editores / Instituto de Historia, Pontificia Universidad Católica de Chile, 2017).

23. Godoy Orellana, "Los 'colonos polinesios' en Sudamérica," 495; and Maude, *Slavers in Paradise*, 147. For a discussion of the Chilean-owned ship *Ellen Elizabeth*, which went to the Gilbert Islands and returned to Lambayeque, Peru, see Maude, *Slavers in Paradise*, ch. 20.

24. On the role of southerners from the United States in blackbirding, see Gerald Horne, *The White Pacific: U.S. Imperialism and Black Slavery in the South Seas after the Civil War* (Honolulu: University of Hawaii Press, 2007).

25. Gobernación Marítima to Intendente de la Provincia, Valparaíso, 14 May 1897, Archivo Nacional Histórico (hereafter cited as ANH), Intendencia de Valparaíso (hereafter cited as IV), vol. 832, no. 58.

26. Washington Lastarria (Dirección Jeneral de Obras Públicas) to Ministro del Interior, Santiago, 26 Oct. 1902, no. 78; Gobernación Marítima de Valparaíso to Intendente, Valparaíso, 11 Nov. 1902, both in ANH, IV, vol. 1016.

27. Prefectura de Policía de Valparaíso to Intendente de la Provincia, Valparaíso, 22 Jul. 1904, ANH, IV, vol. 1106, no. 854; Prefectura de Policía de Valparaíso to Intendente de la Provincia, Valparaíso, 27 Jun. 1904, ANH, IV, vol. 1106, no. 880; and Prefectura de Policia de Valparaíso to Intendente de la Provincia, Valparaíso, 28 Nov. 1904, ANH, IV, vol. 1109, no. 1374. (Note: one of the dates in volume 1106 is incorrect, as the numbering on the letters does not match the dates.) On the French state and Vega going to the press, see Ministerio de Relaciones Esteriores to Ministro de Marina, Santiago, 3 May 1905, Archivo del Ministerio de Relaciones Exteriores,

Santiago, Chile (hereafter cited as AMRREE-C), Fondo Histórico (hereafter cited as FH), vol. 306 B, no. 398. The instances of violence on the island are the same as those discussed below.

28. Igler, *Great Ocean*; David A. Chappell, "Shipboard Relations between Pacific Island Women and Euroamerican Men, 1767–1887," *Journal of Pacific History* 27, no. 2 (Dec. 1992): 131–49; and Chappell, *Double Ghosts*.

29. Dirección Jeneral de la Armada to Ministro de Marina, Valparaíso, 5 Jul. 1915, ARNAD, MM, vol. 2033, no. 1767.

30. For the state report, see Armada Nacional to Director Jeneral de la Armada, Valparaíso, 12 Jan. 1905, AMRREE-C, FH, vol. 306 B, no. 76. Similar to the previous paragraph, the state agent claimed that Pacific Islanders (canacas) "have become accustomed to the idleness in which they have always lived, [and] look with disgust at all work even if it is paid work" (3). See also Sub-Marítima de la Isla de Pascua to Comandante Luis Gomez, Isla de Pascua, 16 Dec. 1904; Ministerio de Realciones Esteriores to Ministro de Marina, Santiago, 3 May 1904, no. 398, both in AMRREE-C, FH, vol. 306 B.

31. Manuel Rojas, *Hijo del ladrón*, in *Tiempo irremediable* (Santiago: Zig-Zag, 2015), 1:119.

32. Dirección de Beneficencia to Prefecto, Callao, 2 Oct. 1863, AHM, Prefecturas, Beneficencia Pública del Callao, 1863, caja 1, sobre 6, fol. 11. See also Cushman, *Guano*, 90; and Maude, *Slavers in Paradise*, 158-62.

33. Rosenthal, *Beyond Hawai'i*, 77, 232n49.

34. Humberto Rodríguez Pastor, *Herederos del dragón: Historia de la comunidad China en el Perú* (Lima: Fondo Editorial del Congreso del Perú, 2000), 35–36; and Cushman, *Guano*, 55.

35. Peter Blanchard, *Slavery and Abolition in Early Republican Peru* (Wilmington, DE: Scholarly Resources, 1992), 139–40.

36. Cushman, *Guano*, 55; Michael J. Gonzales, "Chinese Plantation Workers and Social Conflict in Peru in the Late Nineteenth century," *Journal of Latin American Studies* 21, no. 3 (Oct. 1989): 391, table 1; and Elliott Young, *Alien Nation: Chinese Migration in the Americas from the coolie era through World War II* (Chapel Hill: University of North Carolina Press, 2014), 30–31.

37. Cushman, *Guano*, 55. See also Vincent C. Peloso, *Peasants on Plantations: Sublatern Strategies of Labor and Resistance in the Pisco Valley, Peru* (Durham, NC: Duke University Press, 1999); Ana Maria Candela, "Nation, Migration and Governance: Cantonese Migrants to Peru and the Making of Overseas Chinese Nationalism, 1849-2013" (PhD diss., University of California, Santa Cruz, 2013), 60–67, 96; and Blanchard, *Slavery and Abolition*, 141.

38. Expediente sobre una publicación Aparecida en un diario de Estados Unidos de Norteamérica al mal tratamiento a los trabajadores que presten servicios en las islas guaneras del Perú, 1858, Biblioteca Nacional, Lima, Peru (hereafter cited as BN-P).

39. Tinsman, "Rebel Coolies"; and Tinsman, "Narrating Chinese Massacre."

40. Candela, "Nation, Migration and Governance," 105–14; Peloso, *Peasants on Plantations*; and Gonzales, "Chinese Plantation Workers."

41. Candela, "Nation, Migration and Governance," 63–66.
42. Candela, "Nation, Migration and Governance," 141–53.
43. Candela, "Nation, Migration and Governance," 2–3.
44. Juan M. del Mar (Ministerio de Gobierno, Culto y Obras Públicas) to Prefecto de la Provincia Constitucional del Callao, Lima, 28 Feb. 1858, AHM, Prefecturas, Ministerio de Gobierno, Culto y Obras Públicas, 1858, caja 18, sobre 151, fol. 32.
45. Amaro G. Tizón to Ministro de Estado en el Despacho de Relaciones Exteriores, Iquique, 21 May 1874, fol. 78; David Mac-Iver to Amaro G. Tizón, Iquique, 21 May 1874, fol. 80, both in AMRREE-P, correspondencia, caja 222, carpeta 17, código 2-0-E, 1874.
46. Consulado General de Chile en Callao to Augusto Matte (Ministro de Relaciones Exteriores), Callao, 7 Apr. 1888, ANH, Ministerio de Relaciones Exteriores (hereafter cited as MRREE), vol. 410, reproduced in [illegible] to Ministro de Marina, Santiago, 3 May 1888, ANH, MM, vol. 502. See also various letters on repatriating Chileans from Peru in ANH, MRREE, vol. 353.
47. Circular a los Cónsules de Chile en las costas del Pacífico, 23 Feb. 1888, ANH, MRREE, vol. 407, fol. 74–75.
48. J. Muñoz Hurtado (Director del Territorio Marítimo), Valparaíso, 16 Aug. 1904, AMRREE-C, FH, vol. 306 B, circular no. 121.
49. Consulado General de Chile to Ministro de Relaciones Exteriores, 8 Feb. 1912, Confidencial, AMRREE-C, Fondo Perú (hereafter cited as FP), vol. 347 C, no. 11-Sección C.
50. Consulado General de Chile to Intendente de Valparaíso, Callao, 12 Jan. 1907, no. 12; Consulado General de Chile to Intendente de Valparaíso, Callao, 22 Jan. 1907, no. 24, both in ANH, IV, vol. 1201.
51. Armada Nacional, Memoria de la Dirección del Personal, Valparaíso, 14 May 1912, ARNAD, MM, vol. 1812, secc. 1a, no. 666, p. 11/3.
52. Ministerio de Relaciones Esteriores to Ministro de Marina, Santiago, 15 Jul. 1915, ARNAD, MM, vol. 2032. The letter was forwarded in Ministerio de Marina to Director de la Armada, Santiago, 21 July 1915, ARNAD, MM, vol. 2044, no. 408.
53. Ministerio de Relaciones Esteriores to Ministro de Marina, Santiago, 23 July 1915, ARNAD, MM, vol. 2032.
54. E. Oyanguren (Consulado General del Perú en Valparaíso) to Ministro de Relaciones Exteriores, Valparaíso, 8 Feb. 1904, AMRREE-P, correspondencia, caja 538, carpeta 6, código 6-4, 1904, fol. 32–36.
55. Zachary R. Morgan, *The Legacy of the Lash: Race and Corporal Punishment in the Brazilian Navy and Atlantic World* (Bloomington: Indiana University Press, 2014), 99–102 (quote on 99).
56. Mayoria de Ordenes de la Escuadra to Jeneral Ministro de Estado en el Despacho de Guerra y Marina, a bordo de la fragata "Amazonas," Paita, 21 Oct. 1859, AHM, Buques, Amazonas, Fragata, Perú, 1859, caja A17, sobre A130, fol. 13–15.
57. Enrique A. Rodriguez (Ministerio de Relaciones Esteriores) to Ministro de Marina, Santiago, 27 June 1911, ARNAD, MM, vol. 1805, no. 2198. The complaint is reproduced in Ministerio de Marina to Director Jeneral de la Armada, Santiago,

30 June 1911, ARNAD, MM, vol. 1815, no. 313. The captain of the ship claimed that the upset crew members had debarked, gotten drunk at port, and returned to the ship at 9 p.m., much too late to wake the chef and prepare food for them. Even if this were the case, the collective action of a short-term strike across national lines reveals the power of food, access to it, and of its bringing people together collectively. For the captain's take, see Armada Nacional to Director Jeneral de la Armada, Valparaíso, 16 Nov. 1911, ARNAD, MM, vol. 1805, no. 2249.

58. See Nicolas Freire to General Ministro de Estado del despacho de Guerra y Marina, Callao, 25 Feb. 1861, fol. 21; Francisco Sanz to Capitan de Navio, al ancla, Arica, 18 Feb. 1861, fol. 22; Constantino Alvarez, Relación de las prendas de vestuario y equipo que necesita la espresada, al ancla, Arica, 18 Feb. 1861, fol. 23; Juan Antonio to General Ministro de Estado del despacho de Guerra y Marina, Callao, 24 May 1861, fol. 33; Francisco Sanz to Capitan de Navio, Arica, 3 May 1861, fol. 34; Mariano [illegible] Galdoz to Capitan de Navio Mayor Ordenes del Departamento, Callao, 10 May 1861, fol. 34r (on the deteriorating clothing); Mariano [illegible] Galdoz, Relación de vestuario que le falta al espresado, Callao, 11 May 1861, fol. 35, all in AHM, Buques, Amazonas, Fragata, Peru, 1861, caja A17, sobre A132.

59. Report following Ignacio Mariategui to General Ministro de Estado del despacho de Guerra y Marina, Callao, 6 Sep. 1864, AHM, Buques, Amazonas, Fragata, Peru, 1864, caja A18, sobre A137, fol. 91–99.

60. Percy Cayo Córdova, *Historia marítima del Perú. La República, 1906 a 1919*, tomo 13 (Lima: Instituto de Estudios Histórico-Marítimos del Perú, 2009), 758–66; and Jefe de la Sección de Capitanías to Director de Marina, 9 February 1891, AHM, Capitanías, Capitanía de Puerto del Callao, 1891, C18, exp. C147, fol. 18–19.

61. Reglamento jeneral de enganche de jente de mar, Santiago, 10 Jan. 1889, ANH, Fondo Emilio Bello Codesido, vol. 1, p. 25.

62. E. Oyanguren to Ministro de Relaciones Exteriores, Valparaíso, 9 June 1903, AMRREE-P, correspondencia, caja 523, carpeta 3, código 8-10-G, 1903, fol. 110–15.

63. ANH, Juzgado Civil de Valparaíso, caja 71779, exp. 44, 1919.

64. Consulado General del Perú en Chile to Oficial Mayor del Ministerio de Relaciones Exteriores, Valparaíso, 13 May 1918, AMRREE-P, correspondencia, caja 710, carpeta 7, código 8-10-G, 1918, fol. 75.

65. Aldo Yávar Meza, "El gremio de jornaleros y lancheros de Valparaíso, 1837–1859: Etapa de formación," *Historia* 24 (1989): 351–53 (quote on 352).

66. ANH, Juzgado Civil de Valparaíso, 9 Mar. 1918, caja 71779, exp. 24.

67. Rubén Darío, "The Bale," in *Selected Writings*, ed. Ilan Stavans, trans. Andrew Hurley, Greg Simon, and Steven F. White (New York: Penguin Books, 2005), 243–48 (quote on 245). Thanks to Daniela Samur for calling this short story to my attention.

68. Darío, "The Bale," 247.

69. Packet beginning with Comandancia General de Marina to Ministro de Estado del despacho de Justicia, Culto i Beneficencia, 21 Jan. 1864, AGN, Republicano, MJBI, Poderes del Estado, Ministerios, Guerra y Marina, 1827–1879, legajo 186.

70. Ministerio de Relaciones Exteriores to Ministro de Marina, Santiago, 31 May 1913, ARNAD, MM, vol. 1905, no. 1549.

71. "Secuestro," *La Voz del Mar* (Valparaíso), 28 Jun. 1925, 6; and "A bordo del vapor 'Fresia' de R. W. James y Co," *La Voz del Mar,* 8 Apr. 1925, 3.

72. Rediker, *Between the Devil and the Deep Blue Sea,* 159.

73. Melillo, *Strangers on Familiar Soil,* 126–29 (quote on 127).

74. On the enganche, also see Edward D. Melillo, "The First Green Revolution: Debt Peonage and the Making of the Nitrogen Fertilizer Trade, 1840–1930," *American Historical Review* 117, no. 4 (Oct. 2012): 1028–60, esp. 1048; Michael Monteón, "The *Enganche* in the Chilean Nitrate Sector, 1880–1930," *Latin American Perspectives* 6, no. 3 (Summer 1979): 66–79, esp. 67; Peter Blanchard, "The Recruitment of Workers in the Peruvian Sierra at the Turn of the Century: The Enganche System," *Inter-American Economic Affairs* 33, no. 3 (Winter 1979): 63–83; Michael J. Gonzales, "Capitalist Agriculture and Labour Contracting in Northern Peru, 1880–1905," *Journal of Latin American Studies* 12, no. 2 (Nov. 1980): 291–315; and Peloso, *Peasants on Plantations,* 44–46. For the nineteenth-century enganche in the maritime industry, see Gilberto Harris Bucher and Eugenia Garrido Alvarez de la Rivera, *La gente de mar en Chile y el exterior: Aspectos históricos, jurídicos y diplomáticos, 1818–1915* (Valparaíso: Puntángeles Universidad de Playa Ancha Editorial, 2004), 12–18.

75. See, for instance, "En la corte reunida en Osborne House, isla de Wight, el 28 de julio de 1856, presente S. M. la reina en consejo" and "Mensaje i proyecto de lei para el establecimiento, en los puertos de la República, de ajencias oficiales i responsables para el enganche de marineros," both in *Documentos parlamentarios: Discursos de apertura en las sesiones del congreso, i memorias ministeriales en los dos primeros años del segundo quinquenio de la administración Montt (1857–1858),* tomo 6 (Santiago: Imprenta del Ferrocarril, 1859), 214–18.

76. Legación de Chile en Londres to Ministro de Relaciones Exteriores, Londres, 24 Apr. 1914, ARNAD, MM, vol. 1978, no. 86.

77. Ministerio de Marina to Ministro de Estado en el Despacho de Relaciones Exteriores, Lima, 5 Nov. 1920, AMRREE-P, correspondencia, caja 741, carpeta 8, código 2-2, 1920, fol. 44; and letter to Director de Marina, Lima, 9 Nov. 1920, AMRREE-P, correspondencia, caja 754, carpeta 10, código 2-2, 1920, fol. 82–83.

78. Comandancia de la Fragata de Guerra Amazonas to Contra Almirante Comandante General de Marina, Callao, 21 June 1864, AHM, Buques, Amazonas, Fragata, Perú, 1864, caja A18, sobre A137, fol. 32.

79. José G. Zaramona (Prefectura de la Provinicia Constitucional) to Ministro de Justicia, Instrucción y Beneficencia, Callao, 22 Dec. 1859, AGN, Republicano, MJBI, Poderes del Estado, Prefecturas, Callao, legajo 203 (1856–1879).

80. Juan M. del Mar [?] to Gobernador de la Provincia litoral del Callao, Lima, 29 Mar. 1851, AHM, Ministerio de Gobierno, 1851, caja 16, sobre 142, fol. 35.

81. Eduardo Guzman to Coronel y Prefecto, Casas Matas, 22 Dec. 1857; Eduardo Guzman to Don José Pañino[?], Casas Matas, 30 Dec. 1857; Villraul[?] to Exmo. Sor., Lima, 15 Jan. 1858, all three in AGN, MJBI, Poderes del Estado, Prefecturas, Callao, legajo 203 (1856–1879).

82. On the Casasmatas, see Carlos Aguirre, *The Criminals of Lima and Their Worlds: The Prison Experience, 1850–1935* (Durham, NC: Duke University Press, 2005), 87–88.

83. Ministerio de Guerra y Marina to Ministro de Estado en el Despacho de Justicia, July 1876, AGN, Republicano, MJBI, Poderes del Estado, Ministerios, Guerra y Marina, 1827–1879, legajo 186.

84. Aguirre, *Criminals of Lima and Their Worlds*, 1.

85. For the case of Chile, see Jorge Rojas Flores, *Historia de la infancia en el Chile republicano, 1810–2010* (Santiago: Ocho Libros Editores, 2010), 75–78 (75 for Chileans not writing on it).

86. Rojas Flores, *Historia de la infancia*, 216.

87. Sarah C. Chambers, *From Subjects to Citizens: Honor, Gender, and Politics in Arequipa, Peru, 1780–1854* (University Park: Pennsylvania State University Press, 1999), 195.

88. Comandancia de la Corbeta "Unión" to Capitan de Navio, Grado Mayor de Ordenes del Departamento, Al ancla, Callao, 29 Mar. 1875, AGN, MJBI, Comandancia General de Marina, legajo 253. See also Morgan, *Legacy of the Lash*, 111.

89. Comandancia General de Marina to Cor. Sub. Prefecto de la Capital, Callao, 2 Jan. de 1877; Comandancia General de Marina to Subprefecto de esta provincia, Callao, 3 Mar. 1877, both in AGN, MJBI, Comandancia General de Marina, legajo 253.

90. Morgan, *Legacy of the Lash*, 110.

91. Amrith, *Crossing the Bay of Bengal*, 77.

92. For various takes on the closeness of organizing and tight spaces, see June Nash, *We Eat the Mines and the Mines Eat Us: Dependency and Exploitation in Bolivian Tin Mines* (New York: Columbia University Press, 1979); John Bergquist, *Labor in Latin America: Comparative Essays on Chile, Argentina, Venezuela, and Colombia* (Stanford, CA: Stanford University Press, 1986); Thomas Miller Klubock, *Contested Communities: Class, Gender, and Politics in Chile's El Teniente Copper Mines, 1904–1951* (Durham, NC: Duke University Press, 1998); and Julio Pinto Vallejos, *Trabajos y rebeldias y la pampa salitrera: El ciclo del salitre y la reconfiguración de las identidades populares (1850–1900)* (Santiago: Editorial de la Universidad de Santiago de Chile, 1998).

93. Rojas, *Hijo del ladrón*, 1:117.

94. Manuel Rojas, *Sombras contra el muro*, in *Tiempo irremediable* (1964; repr., Santiago: Zig-Zag, 2015), 1:353.

95. Various shades of this come through in Greg Dening, *Islands and Beaches: Discourses on a Silent Land. Marquesas, 1774–1880* (Melbourne: Melbourne University Press, 1980); Marshal Sahlins, *Islands of History* (Chicago: University of Chicago Press, 1987), ch. 4; Sahlins, *How "Natives" Think: About Captain Cook, for Example* (Chicago: University of Chicago Press, 1995); and Vincent O'Malley, *The Meeting Place: Māori and Pākehā Encounters, 1642–1840* (Auckland: Auckland University Press, 2012).

96. Dening, *Islands and Beaches*. Later, reflecting on *Islands and Beaches*, Dening wrote: "I had long wanted to write the history of Oceania in a double-visioned way. I wanted to write the history of Pacific islands from both sides of the beach." See Dening, *Beach Crossings: Voyaging across Times, Cultures, and Self* (Philadelphia: University of Pennsylvania Press, 2004), 17.

97. See Alice Te Punga Somerville, *Once Were Pacific: Māori Connections to Oceania* (Minneapolis: University of Minnesota Press, 2012).

98. Bassi, *Aqueous Territory*, esp. part 1.

CHAPTER 2. GENDER AND SEXUALITY IN THE PACIFIC

1. Doreen Massey, "Space, Place and Gender," in *Space, Place, and Gender* (Minneapolis: University of Minnesota Press, 1994), 185.

2. A classic text is Joan W. Scott, "Gender: A Useful Category of Historical Analysis," *American Historical Review* 91, no. 5 (Dec. 1986): 1053–75. See also Massey, "Space, Place and Gender."

3. Klubock, *Contested Communities*, 140.

4. For an important corrective to gender and mining, see Rossana Barragán Romano and Leda Papastefanaki, "Women and Gender in the Mines: Challenging Masculinity Through History: An Introduction," *International Review of Social History* 65, no. 2 (Aug. 2020): 191–230. See also Jane E. Mangan, *Trading Roles: Gender, Ethnicity, and the Urban Economy in Colonial Potosí* (Durham, NC: Duke University Press, 2005).

5. Matthew C. Gutman, "Introduction: Discarding Manly Dichotomies in Latin America," in *Changing Men and Masculinities in Latin America*, ed. Matthew C. Gutman (Durham, NC: Duke University Press, 2003), 5.

6. Quoted in Bergquist, *Labor in Latin America*, 46.

7. Pablo Ben, "Plebian Masculinity and Sexual Comedy in Buenos Aires, 1880–1930," *Journal of the History of Sexuality* 16, no. 3 (Sept. 2007): 445.

8. Doreen Massey, *For Space* (Los Angeles: Sage, 2012), esp. 10, 12.

9. Elizabeth Quay Hutchison, *Labors Appropriate to Their Sex: Gender, Labor, and Politics in Urban Chile, 1900–1930* (Durham, NC: Duke University Press, 2001), 1–2.

10. Women did occasionally do this, though. See Daniel A. Cohen, ed., *The Female Marine and Related Works: Narratives of Cross-Dressing and Urban Vice in America's Early Republic* (Amherst: University of Massachusetts Press, 1997).

11. Comandancia General de Marina to General Ministro de Estado del Despacho de Guerra y Marina, Callao, 1 July 1863, AHM, Buques, Amazonas, Fragata, Perú, 1863, caja A17, sobre A134, fol. 54.

12. Comandancia de la Fragata de Guerra Amazonas to Capitan de Navio Comte. Grāl de Marina, Callao, 4 Nov. 1863, AHM, Buques, Amazonas, Fragata, Perú, 1863, caja A17, sobre A134, fol. 86.

13. Juan Salaverry to Coronel Director del Ministerio de Guerra y Marina, al ancla, Callao, 3 Jan. 1886, AHM, Buques, Perú, Vapor, 1886, caja P4, sobre P60, fol. 1.

14. Sater, *Andean Tragedy*, 75–78, 81–84.

15. Portrait, Irene Morales, Chilena, 1881, Ocupación de Lima, AHM.

16. Valle Vera, "Los 'hijos de la guerra,'" 133.

17. Data from Antecedentes relativos a la presentación hecha por la Junta de Higiene al Excmo. Consejo de Estado, cited in Álvaro Góngora Escobedo, *La prostitución en Santiago, 1813–1931: Visión de las elites* (Santiago: Dirección de Bibliotecas, Archivos y Museos / Centro de Investigaciones Diego Barros Arana, 1994), 58.

18. Góngora Escobedo, *La prostitución en Santiago*, 59.

19. Ministerio de Marina to Ministro del Interior, Santiago, 30 June 1908, ANH, IV, vol. 1214, no. 561.

20. Paulo Drinot, *The Sexual Question: A History of Prostitution in Peru, 1850s–1950s* (New York: Cambridge University Press, 2020), 160, 172n68.

21. Benigno A. Callirgos M., "Algunas consideraciones sobre una estadistica venérea del Callao" (thesis, Universidad Nacional Mayor de San Marcos, 1933), 33 for Callao population. The thesis is housed in the Archivo de la Facultad de Medicina de San Marcos in Lima, Peru.

22. Callirgos M., "Algunas consideraciones," 79. See also Patricia Palma, "Sanadores inesperados: Medicina china en la era de migración global (Lima y California, 1850–1930)," *História, Ciências, Saúde-Manguinhos* 25, no. 1 (Jan.—Mar. 2018): 13–31; and Patricia Palma and José Ragas, "Enclaves sanitarios: Higiene, epidemias y salud en el Barrio chino de Lima, 1880–1910," *Anuario Colombiano de Historia Social y de la Cultura* 45, no. 1 (2018): 159–90.

23. Callirgos M., "Algunas consideraciones," 82.

24. Callirgos M., "Algunas consideraciones," 65 (age range), 69 (race), 70 (location).

25. Callirgos M., "Algunas consideraciones," 6.

26. Callirgos M., "Algunas consideraciones," 33.

27. Callirgos M., "Algunas consideraciones," 34–57. Worker societies in Callao seemed to recognize the large number of their own with sexually transmitted infections and the added cost of taking care of them. In one case, the Unión Industriales del Mercado del Callao explicitly stated in its statutes that the society would not help with "enfermedades venéreas." See Reglamento de la Socieadad, "Unión Industriales del Mercado del Callao" fundado el 31 de marzo de 1921 (Lima: Imprenta "El Progreso," 1921), 15, in AGN, Ministerio de Fomento, Expedientes Laborales, Gremios, exp. 30, 1924, art. 32.

28. Ministerio de Marina to Ministro del Interior, Santiago, 30 June 1908, ANH, IV, vol. 1214, no. 561.

29. Manuel Rojas, *Lanchas en la bahía* (1932; Santiago: Tajamar Editores, 2014).

30. Callirgos M., "Algunas consideraciones," 14 ("the primary" and categories), 16 (on weekly medical exams).

31. Drinot, *Sexual Question*, 187–89; and Lorraine Nencel, *Ethnography and Prostitution in Peru* (London: Pluto Press, 2001), 14–23.

32. "Memoria elevada por el Subprefecto de la provincia de Callao al prefecto," 1887–1888, BN-P.

33. See, for instance, Stephen Legg, "Stimulation, Segregation and Scandal: Geographies of Prostitution Regulation in British India, between Registration (1888) and Suppression (1923), *Modern Asian Studies* 46, no. 2 (2012): 1459–1505.

34. Drinot, *Sexual Question*, ch. 1.

35. Drinot, *Sexual Question*, 61. Emphasis in original.

36. Drinot, *Sexual Question*, 88–92, 123 ("moral contagion").

37. *Reglamento del Ramo de Policia relativa a la prostitución* (Valparaíso: Imprenta del Mercurio, 1868), 3.

38. *Reglamento del Ramo de Policia relativa a la prostitución*, 4.

39. *Reglamento del Ramo de Policia relativa a la prostitución*, 8–9.

40. *Reglamento del Ramo de Policia relativa a la prostitución*, art. 31, 3, p. 12.

41. Prefecto de Policía de Valparaíso to Intendente, Valparaíso, 2 Feb. 1912, ANH, IV, vol. 1305, no. 146.

42. Alcaldia Municipal de Valparaíso to Intendente de la Provincia, 26 Sep. 1906, ANH, IV, vol. 1172. On the 1906 earthquake, see Joshua Savala, "'Let Us Bring It with Love': Violence, Solidarity, and the Making of a Social Disaster in the Wake of the 1906 Earthquake in Valparaíso, Chile," *Journal of Social History* 51, no. 4 (Summer 2018): 928–52.

43. Comparatively, see Lara Putnam, *The Company They Kept: Migrants and the Politics of Gender in Caribbean Costa Rica, 1870–1960* (Chapel Hill: University of North Carolina Press, 2002), ch. 3; and Joanne M. Ferraro, "Making a Living: The Sex Trade in Early Modern Venice," *American Historical Review* 123, no. 1 (Feb. 2018): 30–59.

44. Drinot, *Sexual Question*, esp. 91, 98–104, 111–12, 126–32, 236–38; and Rojas, *Lanchas*, 65–80 (65 for the groups of men).

45. Drinot, *Sexual Question*, 115–16, 148–49.

46. Tercer Juzgado del Crimen de Valparaíso, contra Margarita Valdés por Infracción al Reglamento de Casas de Tolerancia, 30 Abr. 1913 ANH, Juzgado del Crimen de Valparaíso, caja 50015, exp. 18; Tercer Juzgado del Crimen de Valparaíso, contra Margarita Valdés por Infracción al Reglamento da Casas de Tolerancia, 24 Mayo 1913, ANH, Juzgado del Crimen de Valparaíso, caja 500115, exp. 19. These are both reproduced in ANH, Juzgago del Crimen de Valparaíso, caja 50014, exp. 44 and 45.

47. Drinot, *Sexual Question*, 43–44.

48. Drinot, *Sexual Question*, 50.

49. Drinot, *Sexual Question*, 57–58.

50. Jacqueline Nassy Brown, *Dropping Anchor, Setting Sail: Geographies of Race in Black Liverpool* (Princeton, NJ: Princeton University Press, 2005), 237. Emphasis in original.

51. Ulrike Strasser and Heidi Tinsman, "It's a Man's World? World History Meets the History of Masculinity, in Latin American Studies, for Instance," *Journal of World History* 21, no. 1 (Mar. 2010): 75–96.

52. [Diego?] de la Haya to Ministro de Estado en el Despacho de Guerra y Marina, Callao, 22 Dec. 1874, fol. 136; Federico Alramora[?] to Capitan de Navio Comandante General de Marina, Callao, 16 Dec. 1871, fol. 137; Manuel A. Villarifencio[?] to Capitan de Navio, al ancla, Callao, 15 Dec. 1874, fol. 138, all in AHM, Buques, Mairo, Vapor, Perú, 1872, caja M2, sobre M17.

53. Metalúrgico, "Metalúrgicos de Valparaíso ¡Alerta!," *El Obrero Metalúrgico* (Valparaíso), no. 7, 28 Dec. 1924, 3; "Box. Nicanor Rojas," *El Obrero Metalúrgico*, no. 10, 30 Mar. 1925, 2; and "El Boycott a la Casa González Soffia," *El Obrero Metalúrgico*, no. 12, 1 Oct. 1925, 4.

54. On rabid dogs and the process, see Prefectura de Policía de Valparaíso to Intendente de la Provincia, Valparaíso, 18 June 1905, ANH, IV, vol. 1148, no. 848; Prefectura de Policía de Valparaíso to Intendente de la Provincia, Valparaíso, 14 Mar. 1908, ANH, IV, vol. 1225, no. 217; Prefectura de Policia de Valparaíso to Intendente, Valparaíso, 2 Apr. 1912, ANH, IV, vol. 1306, no. 384 (this volume contains at least three more); Prefecto de Policía de Valparaíso to Intendente, Valparaíso, 13 June 1913, ANH, IV, vol. 1332, no. 424; Dr. Damian Miquel, "Auxilio que deben prestar los guardianes a las personas victimas de accidentes," *Revista de la Policía de Valparaíso* (Valparaíso) (hereafter cited as *RPV*) 1, no. 2, 30 Nov. 1906, 44; Aquiles Dell Aquila, "Tratamientos veterinarios de las enfermedades infecciosas," *RPV* 2, no. 23, 31 Aug. 1908, 13; and "Instrucciones para los casos de mordeduras por animales hidrófobos," *RPV* 7, no. 99, 1 Apr. 1914, 57–59.

55. "La huelga del personal de Maestranza de la C.S.A. de V.," *El Obrero Metalúrgico*, no. 10, 30 Mar. 1925, 2–3.

56. "Los que pasarán mañana: Un palo para los rehacios," *La Voz del Mar*, 2a Quincena de Julio de 1924, 2. According to the historian Laura Caruso, the Federación Obrero Marítimo (Federation of Maritime Workers; FOM) in Argentina dismissed the strike-breaking male from its "family." See Laura Caruso, *Embarcados: Los trabajadores marítimos y la vide a bordo: sindicato, empresas y Estado en el puerto de Buenos Aires, 1889–1921* (Buenos Aires: Imago Mundi, 2016), 44.

57. Armodio, "De potencia a potencia," *Mar y Tierra* (Valparaíso) 1, no. 11, 1a Quincena de Julio de 1917, 2.

58. "Como se nos combate," *La Voz del Mar*, 1a. Quincena de Noviembre de 1924, 5.

59. "Un año de vida," *La Voz del Mar*, 1 May 1925, 3.

60. Caruso, *Embarcados*, 44.

61. Klubock, *Contested Communities*, 150–51, but also see 140–50.

62. Kornel Chang, *Pacific Connections: The Making of the U.S.-Canadian Borderlands* (Berkeley: University of California Press, 2012), 135–46.

63. R. P. M., "Hombría," *La Voz del Mar*, 6 June 1925, 5.

64. Ejemplo, "Obreros, pero también hombres," *La Voz del Mar*, 6 June 1925, 3.

65. Elizabeth Quay Hutchison, "From 'La Mujer Esclava' to 'La Mujer Limón': Anarchism and the Politics of Sexuality in Early-Twentieth-Century Chile," *Hispanic American Historical Review* 81, nos. 3–4 (Aug.–Nov. 2001): 519–53.

66. Compare to Jeffrey D. Glasco, "'The Seaman Feels Him-self a Man,'" *International Labor and Working-Class History* 66 (Fall 2004): 40–56, esp. 45–46. See also Valerie Burton, "A Seafaring Historian's Commentary on 'The Body' as a Useful Category for Working-Class History," *Labor: Studies in Working-Class History of the Americas* 4, no. 2 (2007): 55-59.

67. For a discussion of this, see Pete Sigal, "(Homo)Sexual Desire and Masculine Power in Colonial Latin America: Notes toward an Integrated Analysis," in *The Infamous Desire: Male Homosexuality in Colonial Latin America*, ed. Pete Sigal (Chicago: University of Chicago Press, 2003), 9.

68. Juzgado del Crimen de Iquique, contra Tomas Jhones, causa Sodomia, 27 Oct. 1883, ANH, Juzgado del Crimen de Iquique, caja 596, exp. 14, 1883, fol. 3–4 for Jones's testimony, fol. 10 for the use of his testimony against him. Carolina González U. also briefly discusses this case in "Entre 'sodomitas' y 'hombres dignos, trabajadores y honrados': Masculinidades y sexualidades en causas criminales por sodomía (Chile a fines del siglo XIX)" (Tesis para optar al grado de Magíster, Universidad de Chile, 2004), 81. Early in the Mexican Inquisition, sailors were prosecuted for sodomy. See Martin Nesvig, "The Complicated Terrain of Latin American Homosexuality," *Hispanic American Historical Review* 81, nos. 3–4 (Nov. 2001): 696.

69. Morgan, *Legacy of the Lash*, 119.

70. Guillermo Avila Money, "Clave de los criminales," *RPV* 1, no. 8, 31 May 1907, 248.

71. David M. Halperin, "How to Do the History of Male Homosexuality," *GLQ: A Journal of Lesbian and Gay Studies* 6, no. 1 (2000): 97.

72. Martin Nesvig, "The Lure of the Perverse: Moral Negotiation of Pederasty in Porfirian Mexico," *Mexican Studies/Estudios Mexicanos* 16, no. 1 (Winter 2000), 13 ("exculpate themselves"), 23; and González U., "Entre 'sodomitas,'" 61–62. On pederasty, see Nesvig, "Lure of the Perverse"; González U., "Entre 'sodomitas,'" 77–82; and Peter Beattie, "Conflicting Penile Codes: Modern Masculinity and Sodomy in the Brazilian Military, 1860–1916," in *Sex and Sexuality in Latin America: An Interdisciplinary Reader*, ed. Daniel Balderston and Donna J. Guy (New York: New York University Press, 1997). Thanks to Brandi Townsend for initially bringing the Beattie essay to my attention.

73. For autobiographical fiction, see Ignacio Álvares, "Un puñado de pistas para entrar a *Tiempo irremediable*," in *Tiempo irremediable* (Santiago: Zig-Zag, 2015), 10–11.

74. Daniel Valenzuela Medina, "Pobres diablos: Masculinidad burladas de *Sombras contra el muro*," *Anales de literatura chilena* 22, no. 35 (June 2021): 236.

75. Rojas, *Hijo del ladrón*, 1:106–7. See also *La oscura vida radiante*, in *Tiempo irremediable* (1971; repr., Santiago: Zig-Zag, 2015), 2:326–27. Gastón Carrasco sees this scene as a marker of the narrator's "apparently discriminatory" attitude. See Carrasco, "Formas de comunidad y practices socioafectivas en *Mejor que el vino* de Manuel Rojas," *Anales de literatura chilena* 22, no. 35 (June 2021): 174n67. The best book treatment of conventillos is María Ximena Urbina Carrasco, *Los conventillos*

*de Valparaíso, 1880–1920: Fisonomía y percepción de una vivienda popular urbana* (Valparaíso: Ediciones Universitarias de Valparaíso de la Universidad Católica de Valparaíso, 2002).

76. Manuel Rojas, *Sombras contra el muro*, 1:341.

77. Manuel Rojas, *Hijo del ladrón*, 1:99.

78. Rojas, *Hijo del ladrón*, 1:171.

79. On Rojas and anarchism, see Jorge Guerra C., "Manuel Rojas, primer anarquismo: Recuerdo y relato," *Anales de literatura chilena* 22, no. 35 (June 2021): 191–201.

80. Rojas, *La oscura vida radiante*, 2:126–27.

81. Rojas, *La oscura vida radiante*, 2:323–24.

82. James N. Green and Florence E. Babb, "Introduction," *Latin American Perspectives* 29, no. 2, (Mar. 2002): 12. More broadly, see James N. Green, "'Who Is the Macho Who Wants to Kill Me?' Male Homosexuality, Revolutionary Masculinity, and the Brazilian Armed Struggle of the 1960s and 1970s," *Hispanic American Historical Review* 92, no. 3 (Aug. 2012): 437–69; Green, *Exile within Exiles: Herbert Daniel, Gay Brazilian Revolutionary* (Durham, NC: Duke University Press, 2018); and Lillian Guerra, "Gender Policing, Homosexuality and the New Patriarchy of the Cuban Revolution, 1965–70," *Social History* 35, no. 3 (Aug. 2010): 268–89.

83. Carrasco, "Formas de comunidad," 175.

84. Rojas, *La oscura vida radiante*, 2:76.

85. Rojas, *Lanchas en la bahía*, 41–51. *Compañerito* is the diminutive of *compañero*, suggesting a fondness and closeness between them.

86. Rojas, *Lanchas en la bahía*, 52–53. On miners and physical appearance, see Klubock, *Contested Communities*, 139.

87. Rojas, *Lanchas en la bahía*, 29–30.

88. González U., "Entre 'sodomitas,'" 61, 88.

89. For other takes on literature and male-male sex among maritime people in Latin America, see James N. Green, *Beyond Carnival: Male Homosexuality in Twentieth-Century Brazil* (Chicago: University of Chicago Press, 1999), 35–38; and Beattie, "Conflicting Penile Codes."

90. Antonio B. Agacio (Consulado General de Chile, Panama y Zona del Canal) to Ministro de Marina de Chile, 5 Nov. 1910, Confidencial, AMRREE-C, FH, vol. 410 A, no. 599. This case is briefly discussed in Harris Bucher and Garrido, *La gente de mar en chile y el exterior*, 66.

91. Agacio to Ministro de Marina de Chile, 5 Nov. 1910, Confidencial, AMRREE-C, FH, vol. 410 A, no. 599.

92. Magally Alegre Henderson, "Androginopolis: Dissident Masculinities and the Creation of Republican Peru (Lima, 1790–1850)" (PhD diss., Stony Brook University, 2012), esp. ch. 1. Thanks to José Ragas for calling my attention to this dissertation. See also Fernanda Molina, "Sodomy, Gender, and Identity in the Viceroyalty of Peru," in *Sexuality and the Unnatural in Colonial Latin America*, ed. Zeb Tortorici, (Oakland: University of California Press, 2016), esp. 153–54.

93. Carmen McEvoy, "Civilización, masculinidad y superioridad racial."
94. Skuban, *Lines in the Sand*, 79-80.
95. Comparatively, see Beattie, "Conflicting Penile Codes," 71.
96. The Ministry of Foreign Relations forwarded the letter to the Department of the Navy and the Ministry of the Navy in November 1910, and the Ministry of the Navy forwarded it on to the Dirección Jeneral de la Armada in December. I have yet to find any response thereafter. For the chain of letters, see Ministerio de Relaciones Exteriores to Consul Jeneral de Chile en Panama, 26 Nov. 1910, Confidencial, AMRREE-C, FH, vol. 395 A, no. 467; and Ministerio de Marina to Consul Jeneral de Chile en Panama, 5 Dec. 1910, ARNAD, MM, vol. 1768, no. 690. Two vague letters from the Chilean Ministry of Foreign Relations to the intendant of Valparaíso from December 1910, wherein they ask for the intendant to speak with the directors of the CSAV about methods to stop actions happening on their ships that might "redundan... en descrédito de nuestra bandera" (result... in discrediting our national flag), perhaps in reference to this case. See Ministerio de Relaciones Esteriores to Intendente de Valparaíso, Santiago, 14 Dec. 1910, Confidencial, ANH, IV, vol. 1252, no. 498; and Ministerio de Relaciones Esteriores to Señor Intendente de Valparaíso, Santiago, 28 Dec. 1910, ANH, IV, vol. 1251, no. 3537.
97. See McEvoy, "Civilización, masculinidad, y superioridad racial," 88. On the campaigns in the north, see González Miranda, *Chilenizando a Tunupa*; González Miranda, *El dios cautivo*; and Skuban, *Lines in the Sand*. In a revealing letter concerning the CSAV bringing workers from Panama to Chile in 1889, the Ministerio de Relaciones Exteriores asked that they bring all of the workers they wished, "con escepción de chinos i negros" (with the exception of Chinese and Blacks). See Ministerio de Relaciones Esteriores to Intendente de Valparaíso, Santiago, 7 Jan. 1889, ANH, IV, vol. 556, no. 1290.
98. For a broad take on Chile, as well as some other Latin American nations, see Karin Alejandra Rosemblatt, "Sexuality and Biopower in Chile and Latin America," *Political Power and Social Theory* 15 (2002): 229–62, esp. 238–40. See also Sarah Walsh, "'One of the Most Uniform Races of the Entire World': Creole Eugenics and the Myth of Chilean Racial Homogeneity," *Journal of the History of Biology* 48 (2015): 613–39. Literature on the "roto" is quite large. For a literary take, see Claudia Darrigrandi, "Cuerpos y trayectos urbanos: Santiago de Chile y Buenos Aires, 1880–1935" (PhD diss., University of California, Davis, 2009), ch. 4. For a view by Peruvians from Tacna living in Lima in 1920, see Skuban, *Lines in the Sand*, 80–82.
99. George Chauncey Jr., "Christian Brotherhood or Sexual Perversion? Homosexual Identities and the Construction of Sexual Boundaries in the World War One Era," *Journal of Social History* 19, no. 2 (Winter 1985): 189–211; and Dian H. Murray, *Pirates of the South China Coast, 1790–1810* (Stanford, CA: Stanford University Press, 1987). See also Clare A. Lyons, "Mapping an Atlantic Sexual Culture: Homoeroticism in Eighteenth-Century Philadelphia," *William and Mary Quarterly* 60, no. 1 (Jan. 2003): 119–54.

## CHAPTER 3. TRANSNATIONAL CHOLERA

1. "El cólera," *El Mercurio* (Valparaíso), 29 Nov. 1886, 2 (*El Mercurio* was not paginated at this point, so all references to page numbers are my own).
2. "Brasil: Medidas precauciones contra el cólera," *El Mercurio*, 1 Dec. 1886, 2; "Por correo trasandino: República Argentina; Restablecimiento de la libre comunicación en toda la república," *El Mercucio*, 30 Nov. 1886, 4; and "Por correo trasandino: República Arjentina; El cólera," *El Mercucio*, 4 Dec. 1886, 4.
3. "Proyecto de incendio de la Boca," *El Mercurio*, 29 Nov. 1886, 4.
4. "Crónica," *El Mercurio*, 30 Nov. 1886, 2.
5. Kenneth F. Kiple, "Cholera and Race in the Caribbean," *Journal of Latin American Studies* 17, no. 1 (May 1985): 157–77; Richard J. Evans, *Death in Hamburg: Society and Politics in the Cholera Years* (New York: Oxford University Press, 1987); Greg Grandin, *The Blood of Guatemala: A History of Race and Nation* (Durham, NC: Duke University Press, 2000), ch. 3; Marcos Cueto, "Stigma and Blame during an Epidemic: Cholera in Peru, 1991," in *Disease in the History of Modern Latin America: From Malaria to AIDS*, ed. Diego Armus (Durham, NC: Duke University Press, 2003); Charles L. Briggs, "Theorizing Modernity Conspiratorially: Science, Scale, and the Political Economy of Public Discourse in Explanations of a Cholera Epidemic," *American Ethnologist* 31, no. 2 (May 2004): 164–87; María Angélica Illanes Oliva, *"En el nombre del pueblo, del estado y de la ciencia (. . .)": Historia social de la salud pública, Chile 1880/1973*, seg. ed. (Santiago: Ministerio de Salud, Chile, 2010) chs. 4–5; Carlos S. Dimas, "Harvesting Cholera: Fruit, Disease and Governance in the Cholera Epidemic of Tucumán, Argentina, 1867–68," *Journal of Latin American Studies* 49, no. 1 (Feb. 2017): 115–42; Rosana Aguerregaray, "Representaciones, discursos y practices durante la epidemia de cólera (1886–1887, Mendoza, Argentina)," *História, Ciências, Saúde–Manguinhos* 26, no. 1 (Jan.–Mar. 2019): 187–207.
6. Eric Tagliacozzo, *The Longest Journey: Southeast Asians and the Pilgrimage to Mecca* (New York: Oxford University Press, 2013), ch. 6; Tagliacozzo, "Hajj in the Time of Cholera: Pilgrim Ships and Contagion from Southeast Asia to the Red Sea," in *Global Muslims in the Age of Steam and Print*, ed. James L. Gelvin and Nile Green (Berkeley: University of California Press, 2013); Valeska Huber, "The Unification of the Globe by Disease? The International Sanitary Conferences on Cholera, 1851–1894," *Historical Journal* 49, no. 2 (June 2006): 453–76; David Arnold, *Colonizing the Body: State Medicine and Epidemic Disease in Nineteenth-Century India* (Berkeley: University of California Press, 1993), ch. 4; Michael Christopher Low, "Empire and the Hajj: Pilgrims, Plagues, and Pan-Islam under British Surveillance, 1865–1908," *International Journal of Middle East Studies* 40, no. 2 (2008): 269–90; and Mark Harrison, "Quarantine, Pilgrimage, and Colonial Trade: India 1866–1900," *Indian Economic and Social History Review* 29, no. 2 (1992): 117–44.
7. Huber, "Unification of the Globe by Disease?," 454.
8. Cross-class collaboration comes out briefly in Aguerregaray, "Representaciones," 201.

9. Philip Abrams, "Notes on the Difficulty of Studying the State," *Journal of Historical Sociology* 1, no. 1 (Mar. 1988): 58–89 (quotes on 76) (this article was reprinted from a 1977 talk). For some examples of the Latin American work emphasizing the cultural and ideological, see Gilbert M. Joseph and Daniel Nugent, eds., *Everyday Forms of State Formation: Revolution and the Negotiation of Rule in Modern Mexico* (Durham, NC: Duke University Press, 1994), esp. Joseph and Nugent's theoretical essay "Popular Culture and State Formation in Revolutionary Mexico"; for prisons and ideological-political causes to the expansion of prisons in Peru, see Aguirre, *Criminals of Lima*, 20; and more recently, Christopher Krupa and David Nugent, "Off-Centered States: Rethinking State Theory through an Andean Lens," in *State Theory and Andean Politics: New Approaches to the Study of Rule*, ed. Christopher Krupa and David Nugent (Philadelphia: University of Pennsylvania Press, 2015), esp. 5.

10. Paul Gootenberg, "Seeing a State in Peru: From Nationalism of Commerce to the Nation Imagined, 1820–1880," in *Studies in the Formation of the Nation-State in Latin America*, ed. James Dunkerley (London: Institute of Latin American Studies, 2002): 254–74 (quote on 262). See also Gootenberg, "Fishing for Leviathans? Shifting Views of the Liberal State and Development in Peruvian History," *Journal of Latin American Studies* 45, no. 1 (Feb. 2013): 121–41, esp. 130–31, 140.

11. Decreto, Santiago, 4 Dec. 1886, ANH, Ministerio del Interior (hereafter cited as MI), vol. 1468. Two days later the decree was published in "Clausura de la cordillera," *El Mercurio*, 6 Dec. 1886, 2.

12. For the late eighteenth century, for instance, see Pablo Lacoste, "El arriero y el transporte terrestre en el cono sur (Mendoza, 1780–1800)," *Revista de Indias* 68, no. 244 (2008): 35–68.

13. See Kyle Harvey, "Prepositional Geographies: Rebellions, Railroads, and the Transandean, 1830s–1910s" (PhD diss., Cornell University, 2019); and Harvey, "Engineering Value: The Transandine Railway and the 'Techno-Capital' State in Chile at the End of the Nineteenth Century," *Journal of Latin American Studies* 52, no. 4 (Nov. 2020): 711–33.

14. On smallpox, see María Angélica Illanes Oliva, *"En el nombre del pueblo"*, chs. 3–4; and William F. Sater, "The Politics of Public Health: Smallpox in Chile," *Journal of Latin American Studies* 35, no. 3 (Aug. 2003): 513–43.

15. Josefina Cabrera G., "El cólera en Chile (1886–1888): Conflict politico y reacción popular," *Anales Chilenos de Historia de la Medicina* 17, no. 1 (2007): 17–23.

16. Ministerio de Marina to Comandante de Gral de Marina, Santiago, 4 Dec. 1886, ANH, IV, vol. 574. The *Theben* ship arrived and left Montevideo on 11 December and gave the Ministerio de Marina nine reasons that it should be allowed to dock at Valparaíso after eight days of quarantine and a disinfecting of the passengers, their bags, and the crew. See Ministerio de Marina to Intendente de Valparaíso, Santiago, 30 Dec. 1886, ANH, IV, vol. 574.

17. Eulojio Allende to Ministro del Interior, Talca, 6 Dec. 1886, ANH, MI, vol. 1468.

18. Acta de la sesión celebrada por el I. Municipalidad el 17 de Enero de 1887, ANH, Cabildo y Municipalidad de Valparaíso (hereafter cited as CMV), vol. 76, fol. 197–98.

19. Telegram through the Telegráfo Transandino, 31 Dec. 1886; and Decree, Santiago, 31 Dec. 1886, both in ANH, MI, vol. 1468. For a more detailed account of the path taken by cholera in Chile, see Alvaro Góngora Escobedo, "La epidemia de cólera en Santiago, 1886–1888," *Dimensión histórica de Chile* 10 (1993–1994): 108–34; and Wenceslao Díaz, *Memoria de la comisión directiva del servicio sanitario del cólera presentad al señor ministro del Interior* (Santiago de Chile: Imprenta Nacional, 1888), 294–316.

20. Uriel García Cácares, "El cólera en la historia de la medicina social peruana: Comentarios sobre un decreto precursor," *Revista Peruana de Medicina Experimental y Salud Pública* 19, no. 2 (Apr.–June 2002): 97–101.

21. Juan Corradi, "El colera morbu asiatico y la Fiebre Amarilla ¿son contagiosos?" (tesis de bachiller, Facultad de Medicina, Universidad Nacional Mayor de San Marcos, 1857), 15.

22. Lizando Maurtua, "Estudios médico-sociales del Callao" (tesis de bachiller, Facultad de Medicina, Universidad Nacional Mayor de San Marcos, 1885), 3–5 (quotes on 3).

23. Maurtua, "Estudios medico-sociales," 10, 14.

24. Maurtua, "Estudios medico-sociales," 14–15 (quote on 15). Maurtua seems to have forgotten the smallpox epidemic of the sixteenth century.

25. In an 1891 thesis, Isais Morales Pacheco centered the ocean in his analysis of yellow fever in Callao: "the ocean being the only route in, and the crew and cargo of ships the moveable focal point of infection." See Isais Morales Pacheco, "La fiebre amarilla del Callao en los años de 1888 y 1889" (tesis de bachiller, Facultad de Medicina, Universidad Mayor de San Marcos, 1891), 3.

26. Marcos Cueto y Betty Rivera, "Entre la Medicina, el comercio y la política: El cólera y el Congreso Sanitario Americano de Lima, 1888," in *El Rastro de la Salud en el Perú*, ed. Marcos Cueto, Jorge Lossio, and Carol Pasco (Lima: Instituto de Estudios Peruanos/Universidad Peruana Cayetano Heredia, 2009), 123.

27. Ministerio de Justicia, Culto, Instrucción y Beneficencia, Sección Consular y de Contabilidad to Ministro de Estado en el Despacho de Relaciones Exts., Lima, 4 Jan. 1887, fol. 1; Ministerio de Justicia, Culto, Instrucción y Beneficencia, Sección Consular y de Contabilidad, to Ministro de Estado en el Despacho de Relaciones Exteriores, Lima, 8 Jan. 1887, fol. 8; Ministerio de Justicia, Culto, Instrucción y Beneficencia, Sección Consular y de Contabilidad, to Ministro en el Despacho de Relaciones Exters., Lima, 14 Jan. 1887, fol. 24–25, all in AMRREE-P, correspondencia, caja 316, carpeta 4, código 2–4, 1887. Changes in these regulations continued throughout the outbreak. See Federico Cruzat H. (Consulado General de Chile en Callao) to Don Francisco Freire (Ministro de Relaciones Exteriores), 8 Jun. 1887; and Cruzat H. to Freire, 24 Nov. 1887, both in ANH, MRREE, vol. 370.

28. Tagliacozzo, *Longest Journey*, ch. 6; Harrison, "Quarantine, Pilgrimage, and Colonial Trade"; and for the 1890s, Myron Echenberg, *Plague Ports: The Global*

*Urban Impact of Bubonic Plague, 1894–1901* (New York: New York University Press, 2007). For a broad look at quarantines across centuries, see Alison Bashford, ed., *Quarantine: Local and Global Histories* (New York: Palgrave Macmillan, 2016). Even before steamships, diseases spread more easily in the nineteenth century due in part to faster sailing ships. See Igler, *Great Ocean*, 62–65.

29. For Brazil, see Legación de Chile to Ministro de Relaciones Esteriores, Petropolis, 19 Jan. 1887; Legación de Chile to Ministro de Relaciones Esteriores, Petropolis, 12 May 1887, both in ANH, MRREE, vol. 355. For Colombia, see Ministerio de Relaciones Esteriores to Ministerio de Marina, Santiago, 5 Nov. 1887, ANH, MM, vol. 479. For Ecuador, see Ministerio de Relaciones Esteriores to Ministerio de Marina, Santiago, 10 Dec. 1887, ANH, MM, vol. 479.

30. Ramon Freire to Capitán de Navio, Mayor de Ordenes del Departamento, al ancla, Callao, 17 Dec. 1886, fol. 48; Manuel Contreras Villanueva to Secretario de la Prefectura de la Provincia Constitucional del Callao, Callao, 23 Dec. 1886, fol. 51; Ramon Freire to Señor Capitán de Navio Mayor de Ordenes del Departamento, al ancla Callao, 20 Dec. 1886, fol. 65–66, all in AHM, Buques, Perú, vapor, 1886, caja P4, sobre P60.

31. Ministerio de Justicia, Culto, Instruccion y Beneficencia, Sección Consular y de Contabilidad, to Ministro de Estado en el Despacho de Relaciones Exteriores, Lima, 1 Mar. 1887, fol. 94; Ministerio de Justicia, Culto, Instrucción y Beneficencia, Sección Consular y de Contabilidad, to Ministro de Estado en el Despacho de Realciones Exteriores, Lima, 18 May 1887, fol. 183–184; Ministerio de Justicia, Culto, Instrucción y Beneficencia, Sección Consular y de Contabilidad, to Ministro de Estado en el Despacho de Relacs Exters., Lima, 28 May 1887, fol. 195, all in AMRREE-P, correspondencia, caja 316, carpeta 4, código 2–4, 1887.

32. See Ministerio de Justicia, Culto, Instrucción y Beneficencia, Sección Consular y de Contabilidad to Ministro de Estado en el Despacho de Relaciones Exteriores, Lima, 30 Mar. 1887, fol. 130; Zegarra to Ministro de Estado en el despacho de Relaciones Exteriores, Lima, 1 Apr. 1887, fol. 134–35, 140; Zegarra letter copied by Placido Garrido Mendivilto, Lima, 1 Apr. 1887, fol. 136; Zegarra letter copied by Plácido Garrido Mendivilto, Callao, 24 Mar. 1887, fol. 138–39; Telegrams copied by Plácido Garrido Mendivilto, Lima, 1 Apr. 1887, fol. 142–43; Palacios letter copied by Plácido Garrido Mendivilto, Lima, Apr. 1887 (original letter 25 Mar. 1887), fol. 144; Manuel Bedoya letter copied by Plácido Garrido Mendivilto, Callao, 24 Mar. 1887, fol. 145; Jesus Elias to Junta de Sanidad, Callao, 28 Mar. 1887, copied by Plácido Garrido Mendivilto, fol. 146; M. B. Rodriguez to Secretario de la Junta Suprema de Sanidad, Callao, 28 Mar. 1887, letter copied by Plácido Garrido Mendivilto, fol. 147; M. Palacios to Prefecto de la Provincia Constitucional del Callao, Callao, 28 Mar. 1887, letter copied by Plácido Garrido Mendivilto, fol. 148; Ministerio de Justicia, Culto, Instrucción y Beneficencia, Sección Consular y de Contabilidad to Ministro de Estado en el Despacho de Relaciones Exteriores, Lima, 4 Apr. 1887, fol. 150, all in AMRREE-P, correspondencia, caja 316, carpeta 4, código 2–4, 1887.

33. See letter dated 16 June 1888, fol. 5 (perhaps from the Capitanía de Pacasmayo); letter to Señor Capitan de Navio, Pacasmayo, 13 June 1888, fol. 6; C. Zachlehnen to

[Manual M. Villar], Pacasmayo, 9 June 1888, fol. 7; Manual M. Villar to C. Zachlehnen, Pacasmayo, 11 June 1888, fol. 8; 'Interrogatorio que se sirva absolver firmandolo el Capitan del vapor Trasporte Chileno 'Lautaro' segun ordenes que tengo recibidas," Pacasmayo, 12 June 1888, fol. 9, all in AHM, Capitanías, carpeta Capitanía de Puerto de Pacasmayo, 1888, caja P2, exp. P10; and Consulado General de Chile en Callao to Demetrio Lastarria, Ministro de Relaciones Exteriores, 2 June 1888, ANH, MRREE, vol. 410.

34. Lauren Benton, *A Search for Sovereignty: Law and Geography in European Empires, 1400–1900* (New York: Cambridge University Press, 2010), 112.

35. Mawani, *Across Oceans of Law*, 128.

36. *Conclusiones aprobadas por el Congreso Sanitario Americano de Lima, 1888* (Santiago de Chile: Imprenta Nacional, 1888). For the discussions in the congreso, see Andrés S. Muñoz, *Congreso Sanitario Americano de Lima reunido en el año de 1888* (Lima: Imp. de Torres Aguirre, 1889), iii–iv, 3–22. See also Cueto y Rivera, "Entre la Medicina."

37. Cesáreo Chacaltana Reyes to Ministro de Estado en el Despacho de Justicia, Lima, 23 Jun. 1887, AMRREE-P, correspondencia, caja 316, carpeta 5, código 2–4, 1887, fol. 95–96.

38. On their thoughts on sanitation in Valparaíso, see Acta de la sesión celebrada por la I. Municipalidad de Diciembre de 1886, ANH, CMV, vol. 76, 1886–88, fol. 112.

39. Acta de la sesión celebrada por la I. Municipalidad de Diciembre de 1886, ANH, CMV, vol. 76, 1886–88, fol. 113–15.

40. Charles E. Rosenberg, *The Cholera Years: The United States in 1832, 1849, and 1866* (Chicago: University of Chicago Press, 1987), 22–23.

41. For an approach to historicizing how people view the coast and ocean, see Alain Corbin, *The Lure of the Sea: The Discovery of the Seaside in the Western World, 1750–1840*, trans. Jocelyn Phelps (Cambridge, UK: Polity Press, 1994).

42. Legación de Chile to Señor Intedente de Valparaíso, Lima, 18 Dec. 1886, ANH, IV, vol. 548, no. 88.

43. Ministerio de lo Interior, 30 Dec. 1886; Intendencia de Valparaíso to Ministro de Relaciones Exteriores, 30 Dec. 1886, Valparaíso, both in ANH, MI, vol. 1454.

44. On the *Ayacucho*, see Ministro de lo Interior, Santiago, 11 Feb. 1887; Dirección del Tesoro to Ministerio de lo Interior, Santiago, 9 Feb. 1887; Intendencia de Valparaíso, 20 Jan. 1887, all in ANH, MI, vol. 1455; and Dirección del Tesoro to Ministro de lo Interior, Santiago, 11 Mar. 1887, ANH, MI, vol. 1456.

45. Ministro de lo Interior, Santiago, 24 Jan. 1887, ANH, MI, vol. 1454.

46. Ministro de lo Interior, Santiago, 4 Mar. 1887, ANH, MI, vol. 1456.

47. Dirección del Tesoro, Santiago, 15 May 1888, ANH, MI, vol. 1525, with the receipts following the letter. It is unclear who H. Gomez was, but his payments suggest he worked in transporting goods both by sea and on land.

48. Decreto, Ministerio del Interior, Santiago, 10 Dec. 1887, ANH, MI, vol. 1459; Ministerio de lo Interior, Santiago, 11 Feb. 1887, ANH, MI, vol. 1455; and Ministerio de lo Interior, Santiago, 9 May 1887, ANH, MI, vol. 1457.

49. Patricia Palma, "'Una medida violenta y perjudicial': Cuarentenas en Perú y el surgimiento de una política sanitaria panamericana (1850–1905)," *Apuntes: Revista de Ciencias Sociales* 48, no. 89 (2nd sem. 2021): 20.

50. On the lazaretto in Callao, see Ministerio de Justicia, Culto, Instrucción y Beneficencia, Sección Consular y de Contabilidad, to Ministro de Estado en el Despacho de Relaciones Exteriores, Lima, 26 Nov. 1887, AMRREE-P, correspondencia, caja 316, carpeta 5, código 2–4, 1887, fol. 169; and Ministerio de Justicia, Culto, Instrucción y Beneficencia, Sección Consular y de Contabilidad, to Ministro de Estado en el Despacho de Relaciones Exteriores, Lima, 16 Oct. 1888, AMRREE-P, correspondencia, caja 326, carpeta 10, código 2–4, 1888, fol. 60. On the lazaretto in San Lorenzo, see Federico Cruzat H. (Consulado General de Chile en Callao) to Francisco Freire (Ministro de Relaciones Exteiores), 24 Nov. 1887; Cruzat H. to Freire, 10 Dec. 1887, both in ANH, MRREE, vol. 370; and "Medidas contra el Cólera asiático," *La Crónica Médica* (Lima, Peru) 4, no. 47, 30 Nov. 1887, 409. For the *Vauban* and the lazaretto, see Zegarra to Ministro de Estado en el despacho de Relaciones Exteriores, Lima, 1 Apr. 1887, 140, AMRREE-P, correspondencia, caja 316, carpeta 4, código 2–4, 1887, fol. 134–35.

51. Ricardo Cruz-Coke Madrid, *Historia de la medicina chilena* (Santiago de Chile: Editorial Andres Bello, 1995), 413.

52. On speculation of cholera and change, see Paul S. B. Jackson, "Fearing Future Epidemics: The Cholera Crisis of 1892," *Cultural Geographies* 20, no. 1 (2012): 43–65.

53. See Illanes, *"En el nombre del pueblo"*, chs. 2–5; and Illanes, *Cuerpo y sangre de la política. La construcción histórica de las visitadoras sociales: Chile, 1887–1940* (Santiago: LOM, 2006), esp. ch. 1.

54. For various perspectives on this debate, see Scott Kirsch and Don Mitchell, "The Nature of Things: Dead Labor, Nonhuman Actors, and the Persistence of Marxism," *Antipode* 36, no. 4 (Sept. 2004): 687–705; Jane Bennet, *Vibrant Matter: A Political Ecology of Things* (Durham, NC: Duke University Press, 2010); Hylton White, "Materiality, Form, and Content: Marx contra Latour," *Victorian Studies* 55, no. 4 (Summer 2013): 667–82.

55. E. P. Thompson, "The Poverty of Theory or an Orrery of Errors," in *The Poverty of Theory and Other Essays* (New York: Monthly Review Press, 2008), 17–18 (quote on 18).

56. F. Puga Borne, "Hijiene del cólera: Instrucción popular para los chilenos," *Boletín de Medicina* (Santiago, Chile) 3, no. 29 (Nov. 1886): 194. This *Boletín* was basically republished as *Como se evita el cólera: Estudio de hijiene popular* (Santiago de Chile: Imprenta Nacional, 1886).

57. Augusto Villanueva and Carlos Killing, *Reglamento de la Junta de Salubridad de Valparaíso e informe, presentado por los señores Augusto Villanueva i Cárlos Killing relativo a la epidemia del "cólera" i algunos medios para la desinfección* (Valparaíso: Imprenta del Nuevo Mercurio, 1887), 12–13. More broadly on Koch and Virchow, see Evans, *Death in Hamburg*, 265–75.

58. Jorge Lossio, *Acequias y gallinazos: Salud ambiental en Lima del siglo XIX* (Lima: Instituto de Estudios Peruanos, 2003), 14–15, 58–60; Carlos G. Osorio,

"Sobre el origen de la Bacteriología Experimental en Chile," *Revista médica de Chile* 138, no. 7 (July 2010): 913–19, esp. 914. More broadly, see Ronn F. Pineo, "Misery and Death in the Pearl of the Pacific: Health Care in Guayaquil, Ecuador, 1870–1925," *Hispanic American Historical Review* 7, no. 4 (Nov. 1990): 609–37, esp. 620–22; Paul S. Sutter, "Nature's Agents or Agents of Empire? Entomological Workers and Environmental Change during the Construction of the Panama Canal," *Isis* 98, no. 4 (Dec. 2007): 724–54; Carlos Alcalá Ferráez, "De miasmas a mosquitos: El pensamiento médico sobre la fiebre amarilla en Yucatán, 1890–1920," *História, Ciências, Saúde–Maguinhos* 19, no. 1 (Jan.–Mar. 2012): 71–87; and Rosenberg, *Cholera Years*, 168–172, 193–200.

59. For a few of the many references to specific chemicals and/or fumigation, see Puga Borne, "Hijiene del cólera," 221; *Actas de la Junta General de Salubridad mandadas publicar por acuerdo de la misma* (Santiago de Chile: Imprenta Nacional, 1887), 12, 38–39; and "Reglamento General de Sanidad (continuación)," *La Crónica Médica* 4, 28 Feb. 1887, 45.

60. Puga Borne, "Hijiene del cólera," 207, 221. On some of the debates in Chile at the time, see Cueto y Rivera, "Entre la Medicina," esp. 129–30.

61. José Palza[?] to Decano de la Facultad de Medicina, Moquegua, 26 Feb. 1887, Achivo de la Facultad de Medicina de San Marcos, Lima, Peru (hereafter cited as AFMSM), Documentos Recibidos (hereafter cited as DR), caja no. 4, archivador no. 18, 1887–88, carpeta 1887, fol. 154.

62. Dr. Manuel Barros Borgoño to Dr. Rejes Varas, Santiago, 3 Jan. 1887, ANH, MI, vol. 1454. For similar difficulty in finding medical personnel (nurses in this case) in New York City during the 1832 cholera outbreak, see Rosenberg, *Cholera Years*, 95.

63. Puga Borne, "Hijiene del cólera," 209–13.

64. Intedencia de Valparaíso to Ministro de lo Interior, Valparaíso, 29 Jan. 1887, ANH, MI, vol. 1454. Concern over the trickle-down effect of slowing international commerce began in December. See Acta de la sesión celebrada el 30 de Diciembre de 1886, ANH, CMV, vol. 76, fol. 149.

65. "Memoria elevada por el Subprefecto de la provincia de Callao al prefecto," Callao, 1887–88, BN-P, Sala de Libros Raros y Manuscritos.

66. Ministerio de Justicia, Culto, Instrucción y Beneficencia, Sección Consular y de Contabilidad, to Sr. Ministro de Estado en el Despacho de Relaciones Extes., Lima, 1 Mar. 1887, AMRREE-P, correspondencia, caja 316, carpeta 4, código 2–4, 1887, fol. 111. For similar issues of control around cholera, see Grandin, *Blood of Guatemala*, chap. 3, esp. 93–94.

67. On Tucumán, see Dimas, "Harvesting Cholera," 124.

68. There are two letters on this, with slightly different signature counts, and neither letter is dated, but a follow-up is dated 21 Feb. 1888. Venders to Ministro del Interior[?], no date; Venders to Ministro del Interior[?], no date, both in ANH, MI, vol. 1524. Fruit had been banned twice, once in January 1887 and then again when cholera cases rose in mid-December 1887. See Intendencia de Valparaíso, 10 Jan. 1887, no. 110; Intendencia, 19 Dec. 1887, no. 3212, both in ANH, IV, vol. 581.

69. Intendencia de Valparaíso to Ministro del Interior, Valparaíso, 25 Feb. 1888, ANH, MI, vol. 1524.

70. Carlos Madrid, "Epidemia de cólera en Valparaíso: 1886–1888," *Autoctonía: Revista de Ciencias Sociales e Historia* 1, no. 1 (Jan. 2017): 136; and Cabrera G., "El cólera en Chile," 17–23.

71. Signatories to Intendente, Arica, 7 Jan. 1887, ANH, MI, vol. 1454. Still, the Chilean government acted slowly on these calls for banning ships. On March 7, ships going to the provinces of Coquimbo, Atacama, Tarapacá, and Tacna that were leaving from Valparaíso were allowed to dock "without any restrictions" if they had a patente limpia and had "no suspicious cases onboard" during the trip. See Ministerio de Marina to Intendente de Valparaíso, Santiago, 7 Mar. 1887, ANH, IV, vol. 574.

72. Grandin, *Blood of Guatemala*, 135. See also Florencia Mallon's critique of some seeing the state as only repressive for nonelite people; David Nugent's argument about many in Chachapoyas seeing the state as a "potential[ly] liberating force[] in their lives"; and Lila Caimari's point that many people in early twentieth-century Buenos Aires actively sought more police in order to secure their neighborhoods. Florencia E. Mallon, "Decoding the Parchments of the Latin American Nation-State: Peru, Mexico and Chile in Comparative Perspective," in *Studies in the Formation of the Nation-State in Latin America*, ed. James Dunkerley (London: Institute of Latin American Studies, 2002), 13–53, esp. 18, 48; David Nugent, *Modernity at the Edge of Empire: State, Individual, and Nation in the Northern Peruvian Andes, 1885–1935* (Stanford, CA: Stanford University Press, 1997), 8; and Lila Caimari, *While the City Sleeps: A History of Pistoleros, Policemen, and the Crime Beat in Buenos Aires before Perón*, trans. Lisa Ubelaker Andrade and Richard Shindell (Oakland: University of California Press, 2017), 85–95.

73. On Balmaceda and public health, see Carl J. Murdock, "Physicians, the State and Public Health in Chile, 1881–1891," *Journal of Latin American Studies* 27, no. 3 (Oct. 1995): 551–67; Illanes, *"En el nombre del pueblo"*, ch. 5; and Cabrera G., "El cólera en Chile," 17–23. On the Balmaceda era and the expansion of the state, see Maurice Zeitlin, *The Civil Wars in Chile, (or the Bourgeois Revolutions That Never Were)* (Princeton, NJ: Princeton University Press, 1984), esp. 104.

74. F. Garcia Calderon to Decano de la Facultad de Medicina, Lima, 5 Nov. 1886, AFMSM, DR, caja no. 4, archivador no. 17, 1886, fol. 240.

75. H. Concejo Provincial de Lima to Decano de la Facultad de Medicina, Lima, 14 Oct. 1886, AFMSM, DR, caja no. 4, archivador no. 17, 1886, fol. 226.

76. "La manía de lo estrangero," *Boletín de Medicina* 3, no. 25 (Sept. 1886): 97–99. During the cholera epidemic, Wagner was appointed a member of a central committee of doctors charged with proposing measures to control cholera in Valparaíso. See Intendencia de Valparaíso, 18 Jan. 1887, no. 232, ANH, IV, vol. 581.

77. The *Boletín de Medicina* is filled with European medical studies and references to European doctors. See also Osorio, "Sobre el origen de la Bacteriología Experimental en Chile"; and Marcos Cueto and Steven Palmer, *Medicine and Public Health in Latin America: A History* (New York: Cambridge University Press, 2015), 75, 81.

78. Ministerio de Relaciones Exteriores to Decano de la Facultad de Medicina, Lima, 12 Oct. 1887, AFMSM, DR, caja no. 4, archivador no. 18, 1887–88, carpeta 1887, no. 160; Sesion ordinaria del 15 de Oct. de 1887, AFMSM, Libro de Actas, Actas de Sesiones, Feb. 1884–92, vol. 4, 173; and Legación de Chile [en Lima] to Ministro de Relaciones Exteriores del Perú, don Domingo de Vivero, Lima, 12 Oct. 1887, fol. 83, AMRREE-P, correspondencia, caja 319, carpeta 10, código 6–4, 1887.

79. Ministerio de Justicia, Culto, Instruccion y Beneficencia to Decano de la Facultad de Medicina, Lima, 13 Dec. 1888, AFMSM, DR, caja no. 4, archivador no. 18, 1887–88, carpeta 1888, fol. 49.

80. Matto's biography is pulled together from "Medidas contra el cólera asiático," *La Crónica Médica* 4, no. 47, 30 Nov. 1887, 409; "Comisionado para estudiar el cólera en la República de Chile," *La Crónica Médica* 4, no. 47, 30 Nov. 1887, 435 ("study the"); and "El doctor don David Matto," *El Perú Ilustrado* (Lima, Perú) 1, sem. 2, no. 40, 11 Feb. 1888, 3. For another take on David Matto's work, see Cueto y Rivera, "Entre la Medicina," 129–34. Thanks to Patricia Palma for sending me this issue of *El Perú Ilustrado*.

81. "Comisionado para estudiar el cólera en la República de Chile," *La Crónica Médica* 4, no. 47, 30 Nov. 1887, 435.

82. Casimiro Medina, ed., *La verruga peruana y Daniel A. Carrión, estudiante de la facultad de medicina muerto el 5 de Octubre de 1885* (Lima: Imprenta del Estado, 1886), 11, 12, 59, 65.

83. See "Nuestros Grabados," *El Perú Ilustrado* 1, sem. 2, no. 40, 11 Feb. 1888, 2; and "El doctor don David Matto," *El Perú Ilustrado* 1, sem. 2, no. 40, 11 Feb. 1888, 3.

84. María Emma Mannarelli, *Limpias y modernas: Genero, hygiene y cultura en la Lima del novecientos* (Lima: Ediciones Flora Tristan, 1999), 56–58.

85. Dr. Almenara Butler, "El Cólera: Congreso Sanitario Sud Americano," *La Crónica Médica* 5, no. 49, 31 Jan. 1888, 2.

86. On the reports initially not being published, see Consulado General de Chile en Callao to Don Miguel Luis Amunátegui, Ministro de Relaciones Exteriores, 2 Jan. 1888, ANH, MRREE, vol. 410.

87. David Matto, "El Cólera en Chile: Informes oficiales," *La Crónica Médica* 5, no. 49, 31 Jan. 1888, 5–10. The letter is dated 22 Dec. 1887. See also the same article, letter dated 30 Dec. 1887, 9: "Esta visita de inspección es por supuesto insuficiente." The "imperfect" map was not reproduced in *La Crónica Médica*.

88. Matto, "El Cólera en Chile," 31 Jan. 1888, 5–10 (quotes on 6).

89. Matto, "El Cólera en Chile," 31 Jan. 1888, 7.

90. Cecilio Velazquez to Alcalde de la H. Municipalidad, Lima, 22 Jun. 1868, Archivo Histórico de la Municipalidad de Lima, Lima, Peru, Higiene y Vacunas (1857–1938), Higiene, 1857–69, caja 1.

91. Matto, "El Cólera en Chile," 31 Jan 1888, 5.

92. "Sección variedades: 'El Cólera en Chile,'" *La Crónica Médica* 5, no. 49, 31 Jan. 1888, 36–37 (quote on 37).

93. María Soledad Zárate C., "Notas preliminares sobre profesión médica y masculinidad, Chile, siglo XIX," in *Hombres: Identidad/es y violencia*, ed. José Olavarría

(Santiago: FLACSO/Universidad Academia de Humanismo Cristiano, 2001), esp. 80 (for census information), 81 (for homosocial and "men of science"); Zárate C., *Dar a luz en Chile, siglo XIX. De la "ciencia de hembre" a la ciencia obstétrica* (Santiago: Universidad Alberto Hurtado/Dirección de Bibliotecas, Archivos y Museos, 2007), 89–94.

94. Mannarelli, *Limpias y modernas*, 48–54.

95. David Matto, "El Cólera en Chile: Informes oficiales," *La Crónica Médica* 5, no. 50, 29 Feb. 1888, 69. This is a set of three letters under the same title. This particular letter is dated Valparaíso, 31 Jan. 1888.

96. Villanueva and Killing, *Reglamento de la Junta de Salubridad de Valparaíso*, 25.

97. Villanueva and Killing, *Reglamento de la Junta de Salubridad de Valparaíso*, 11.

98. Matto, "El Cólera en Chile," 29 Feb. 1888, 69. This letter is dated Valparaíso, 13 Jan. 1888. See also Cueto and Rivera, "Entre la Medicina," 131.

99. Matto, "El Cólera en Chile," 29 Feb. 1888, 71. This letter is dated Valparaíso, 27 Jan. 1888.

100. Matto, "El Cólera en Chile," 29 Feb. 1888, 71. This letter is dated Valparaíso, 21 Jan. 1888.

101. Matto, "El Cólera en Chile," *La Crónica Médica*, 29 Feb. 1888, 71. This letter is dated Valparaíso, 27 Jan. 1888.

102. Kapil Raj, *Relocating Modern Science: Circulation and the Construction of Knowledge in South Asia and Europe, 1650–1900* (New York: Palgrave Macmillan, 2007).

103. Matto, "El Cólera en Chile," 29 Feb. 1888, 71–73. This letter is dated Valparaíso, 27 Jan. 1888. Emphasis in original. Matto does not provide the first name of Salazar; it appears the Salazar was A. E. Salazar, who cowrote a book on cholera and produced photographs of his cholera research. See A. E. Salazar and C. Newman, *Notas sobre el espirilo del cólera asiático (Bacillus Coma de Koch)* (Valparaíso: Imprenta del Universo de G. Helfmann, 1888).

104. David Matto, "El Colera en Chile: Informes Oficiales," *La Crónica Médica* 5, no. 51, 31 Mar. 1888, 81. This letter is dated Santiago, 2 Mar. 1888.

105. Matto, "El Colera en Chile," 31 Mar. 1888, 81 (list of places visited), 83 (extract). This letter is dated Santiago, 2 Mar. 1888.

106. Matto, "El Colera en Chile," 31 Mar. 1888, 86 for the table. This letter is dated Santiago, 30 Mar. 1888. According to the *Anuario estadístico de la República de Chile*, total deaths recorded in hospitals in Chile due to cholera (labeled as cólera morbus and cólera nostra) reached 857 in 1887, 132 in 1888, and 25 in 1889, when the column for cólera morbus was no longer used. See *Anuario estadístico de la República de Chile correspondiente a los años 1887–1888*, tomo 26 (Valparaíso: Imprenta de "La Patria," 1892), 200–203; and *Anuario estadístico de la República de Chile correspondiente a los años 1888–1889*, tomo 27 (Valparaíso: Imprenta de "La Patria," 1894), 182–84, 636–39. These are obviously low numbers and do not account for those who died outside of hospitals, which appears to have been the vast majority

of those who lost their lives to cholera. In his report to the Ministry of the Interior, for instance, Dr. Wenceslao Díaz created a table broken down by deaths in each province, the total across the country reaching 23,686. See Díaz, *Memoria de la comisión*, 278–83. On the difficulty of collecting statistics on those who died during epidemics, see Sater, "Politics of Public Health," 518–19; and Kiple, "Cholera and Race in the Caribbean."

107. On being sent back after completing his work, see Consulado General de Chile en Callao to Demetrio Lastarria (Ministro de Relaciones Exteriores), 13 Jun. 1888, ANH, MRREE, vol. 410.

108. "Homenaje al Dr. D. David Matto," *La Crónica Médica* 5, no. 52, 30 Apr. 1888, 140–41.

109. "El Dr. David Matto," *La Crónica Médica* 5, no. 55, 31 July 1888, 241–42; "El Dr. don David Matto," *Boletín de Medicina* 4, no. 37 (July 1888): 48.

110. "El Dr. David Matto," 31 July 1888, 242.

111. David Matto, "El Cólera en Chile," *La Crónica Médica* 5, no. 55, 31 July 1888, 243–44 (quote on 243).

112. Leela Gandhi, *Affective Communities: Anticolonial Thought, Fin-de-Siècle Radicalism, and the Politics of Friendship* (Durham, NC: Duke University Press, 2005), esp. ch. 4 (on vegetarianism, anticolonialism, socialism, and anarchism).

113. For the racialized and gendered rhetoric of the War of the Pacific, see Carmen McEvoy, "Civilización, masculinidad y superioridad racial"; and Beckman, "Creolization of Imperial Reason." For anarquismo sin adjetivo, see George Richard Esenwein, *Anarchist Ideology and the Working-Class Movement in Spain, 1868–1898* (Berkeley: University of California Press, 1989), ch. 8; and Benedict Anderson, *Under Three Flags: Anarchism and the Anti-Colonial Imagination* (New York: Verso Press, 2005), 171–73.

114. Sutter, "Nature's Agents or Agents of Empire?," esp. 728–29.

115. Gandhi, *Affective Communities*, 17 ("'affective cosmopolitanism,' the ethicopolitical practice of a desiring self inexorably drawn toward difference"), 30 ("friend over country," quoting E. M. Forster).

116. Matto, "El Cólera en Chile," 31 July 1888, 243–44.

117. Putnam, "To Study the Fragments/Whole," 618. Emphasis in original.

118. Consulado del Perú [en Valparaíso] to Ministro de Relaciones Exteriores [en Lima], Valparaíso, 5 Dec. 1888, AMRREE-P, correspondencia, caja 332, carpeta 1, código 8-10-G, 1888, fol. 56.

119. Cruz-Coke, *Historia de la Medicina Chilena*, 374 (on Villanueva), 399 (on Villanueva), 439 (on Villanueva and Thiele), 545 (on Edwin Espic); and Intendencia de Valparaíso, Valparaíso, 15 Dec. 1887, ANH, IV, vol. 581, no. 3183 (Villanueva in the Junta de Salubridad).

120. Ministerio de Relaciones Esteriores to Ministro de Marina, Santiago, 3 Nov. 1890, ANH, MM, vol. 538, no. 2309. The idea of using ships as floating hospitals off the coast of small islands circulated during the cholera outbreak, but it is unclear if this occurred in any substantial way. See Joaquin Aguirre to Sr. Rector de la Universidad de Chile, Santiago, 17 Dec. 1887, ANH, MRREE, vol. 211.

121. E. Oyanguren (Consulado General del Perú [en Valparaíso]) to Ministro de Relaciones Exteriores, Valparaíso, July 1903, AMRREE-P, correspondencia, caja 523, carpeta 3, código 8-10-G, 1903, fol. 143–46.

122. Cámara de Comercio, Guayaquil, to Presidente de la Cámara de Comercio, 8 Apr. 1904, ANH, IV, vol. 1075.

123. *Report of the Delegates of the United States to the Pan-American Scientific Congress, Held at Santiago, Chile December 25, 1908, to January 5, 1909* (Washington, DC: Government Printing Office, 1909), 38.

124. Julio Etchepare, "Informes referentes a la morbosidad infecto-contagiosa—disposiciones y procedimientos adoptados por la administración sanitaria para su obtención," in *Proceedings of the Second Pan American Scientific Congress* (Washington, DC: Government Printing Office, 1917), 9:352–54.

125. Karl Marx, *Grundrisse: Foundations of the Critique of Political Economy (Rough Draft)*, trans. Martin Nicolaus (New York: Penguin Books, 1993), 543.

126. David Matto, "Bacteriologia sobre el bacilo del tetano" (tesis presentada para optar en grado de doctor de medicina) (Lima: Imprenta de Benito Gil, 1891), 3.

127. David Matto, *La Enseñanza Médica en el Perú* (Lima: Tip. El Lucero, 1908), 26.

128. Matto, *La Enseñanza Médica en el Perú*, 42. The appendix with the full agreement is "Convención entre el Perú i Chile sobre ejercicio de profesiones liberals," 65–66.

CHAPTER 4. COMPARISONS AND CONNECTIONS IN PACIFIC ANARCHISM

An earlier version of this chapter was published as Joshua Savala, "Ports of Transnational Labor Organizing: Anarchism along the Peruvian-Chilean Littoral, 1916–1928," *Hispanic American Historical Review* 99, no. 3 (August 2019): 501–31. *Hispanic American Historical Review* is published by Duke University Press. All rights reserved. Republished by permission of the publisher. www.dukeupress.edu.

1. Wooblie [sic], "La organización marítima peruana," *La Voz del Mar* (Valparaíso), 30 Nov. 1924, 3–4.

2. Wooblie [sic], "La organización marítima peruana," 3–4.

3. Blanchard, *Origins of the Peruvian Labor Movement*; Peter DeShazo, *Urban Workers and Labor Unions in Chile, 1902–1927* (Madison: University of Wisconsin Press, 1983); Peter Winn, *Weavers of Revolution: The Yarur Workers and Chile's Road to Socialism* (New York: Oxford University Press, 1986); Luis Tejada R., *La cuestión del Pan: El Anarcosindicalismo en el Perú, 1880–1919* (Lima: Instituto Nacional de Cultura/Banco Industrial del Perú, 1988); Klubock, *Contested Communities*; and Paulo Drinot, "Fighting for a Closed Shop: The 1931 Lima Bakery Workers' Strike," *Journal of Latin American Studies* 35, no. 2 (May 2003): 249–78.

4. See, for instance, parts of Sergio Grez Toso, *Los anarquistas y el movimiento obrero: La alborada de "la Idea" en Chile, 1893–1915* (Santiago: LOM, 2007).

5. For a review of some of the recent literature, see Jorell Meléndez-Badillo, "Labor History's Transnational Turn: Rethinking Latin American and Caribbean Migrant Workers," *Latin American Perspectives* 42, no. 4 (July 2015): 117–22. For an excellent example, see Lara Putnam, *Radical Moves: Caribbean Migrants and the Politics of Race in the Jazz Age* (Chapel Hill: University of North Carolina Press, 2013).

6. Braudel, preface to the English Edition, *The Mediterranean*, 1:110; and Matsuda, *Pacific Worlds*, 2. For a recent example of transnational and comparative port labor history, see Peter Cole, *Dockworker Power: Race and Activism in Durban and the San Francisco Bay Area* (Urbana: University of Illinois Press, 2018).

7. Sartorious and Seigel, "Introduction," 3; and Herod, "From a Geography of Labor."

8. Miguel Flórez Nohesell, *Historia marítima del Perú: Los puertos del Perú* (Lima: Instituto de Estudios Histórico-Marítimas del Perú, 1986), 1:209–10. For *izadores* being specific to Mollendo and the use of the term *playeros* in other ports, see El Capitán de Navío to Señor Coronel Ministro en el Despacho de Guerra y marina, Callao, 19 Mar. 1917, AHM, EA, Gremio de Trabajadores Marítimos de Mollendo, 1917–1963, caja G-3, sobre G-72 (hereafter cited as GTMM), fol. 100.

9. W. R. Grace & Co. to Capitan de Navío, Comandante Gral de las Milicias Navales, Callao, 6 May 1907, fol. 17; Foribio Raygada to Director de Marina, Callao, 6 May 1907, fol. 18–19, both in AHM, EA, Gremio de Tarjadores Marítimos del Callao, 1907–1963, caja G-2, sobre G-58; and Cayo Córdova, *Historia marítima del Perú*, 428–30.

10. Valdivieso to Comandante Principal, 20 Mar. 1918, fol. 16; Valdivieso to Capitanía del Puerto, Mollendo, 19 Mar. 1918, fol. 17; Ernesto Ruiz copy of Valdivieso to Capitan de Navío, Comandante Principal de las Milicias Navales y Capitan del Puerto del Callao, copy date 20 Mar. 1918, fol. 102; Valdivieso to Comandante Principal, 22 de Marzo [de 1918], all in AHM, EA, GTMM.

11. Thomas Joseph Hutchinson, *Two Years in Peru, with Exploration of Its Antiquities* (London: Sampson Low, Martson Low, and Searle, 1873), 1:76. Originally seen in Alberto Flores Galindo, *Arequipa y el sur andino: Ensayo de historia regional (siglos XVIII-XX)* (Lima: Editorial Horizante, 1977), 88–89.

12. Heraclio Bonilla, *Islay y la economía del sur peruano en el siglo XIX* (Lima: Instituto de Estudios Peruanos, 1973), 4; and Flórez Nohesell, *Historia marítima*, 448–49.

13. Sater, *Andean Tragedy*, 219; and Flores Galindo, *Arequipa*, 93.

14. Rosemary Thorp and Geoffrey Bertram, *Peru, 1890–1977: Growth and Policy in an Open Economy* (New York: Columbia University Press, 1978), 62, 64–66. From 1897 through 1901, exports through Mollendo remained relatively stable. During this period, though, the ratio of exports between Callao and Mollendo did increase, from Mollendo exporting 54 percent of what was exported through Callao in 1897 to 28 percent in 1901. See Rosendo Melo, *Derrotero de la costa del Perú: Guía marítimo-comercial* (Lima: C. F. Southwell, 1906), xxvii.

15. Flores Galindo, *Arequipa*, 95.

16. Acta 29, signed by Capitán de Navio y del Puerto, los Srs. J. W. Donnelly jefe de la casa Donnelly y Co., J. Rowlands C. jefe de la casa Golding y Cia. y los capataces del gremio de jornaleros D. Andrés C. Caspía y D. Alejandro Velasquez, 26 Jan. 1916, AHM, EA, GTMM, fol. 2.

17. Petition to Capitan de Corbeta y Capitán del Puerto, Mollendo, 12 Nov. 1917, AHM, EA, GTMM, fol. 3.

18. Valdivieso, Capitán de Corbeta y del Puerto, to Capitán de Navío, Comandante Principal de las Milicias Navales, Capitán de Puerto del Callao, Mollendo, 2 Dec. 1917, AHM, EA, GTMM, fol. 4.

19. Gremio de Lancheros to Capitan de Corbeta y Capitan del Puerto, Mollendo, 12 Nov. 1917, AHM, EA, GTMM, fol. 56–57.

20. Valdivieso to Señor Capitán de Navio, Comandante Pricipal de las Milicias Navales, Capitán del Puerto del Callao, Mollendo, 29 Dec. 1917, AHM, EA, GTMM, fol. 58.

21. Chambers, *From Subjects to Citizens*, esp. 101–9, 192–200; and Rosemblatt, "Sexuality and Biopower in Chile and Latin America."

22. For the historian Leon Fink, the maritime workers' close connection to family, of taking up the notion of "'provider ideal' toward his immediate dependents" developed in the early twentieth century due to the speed of steamships and the reduced time seamen spent away from their home cities. Lanchero work was different than that of a seaman, but in both cases gendered notions of the family were a part of how they conceived of themselves and their organizing. Fink, *Sweatshops at Sea*, 120. See also the discourse on the union as a family in Caruso, *Embarcados*, xxv, 42–46. The position as male head of household could also reproduce violent masculinity. For an excellent analysis of this in a later time period, see Heidi Tinsman, "More Than Victims: Women Agricultural Workers and Social Change in Rural Chile," in *Victims of the Chilean Miracle: Workers and Neoliberalism in the Pinochet Era, 1973–2002*, ed. Peter Winn (Durham, NC: Duke University Press, 2004).

23. Gremio de Izaje to Capitan de Puerto, Mollendo, 14 Apr. 1917, fol. 28; Gremio to Estibadores to Capitan de Puerto, Mollendo, 19 May 1917, fol. 29, both in AHM, EA, GTMM.

24. Acta, Mollendo, 15 Aug. 1917, fol. 37; meeting, 15 Aug. 1917, fol. 40, both in AHM, EA, GTMM. Carpio had also signed a labor agreement in Mollendo in 1913. See AHM, Capitanías, carpeta Capitanía de Puerto de Mollendo, 1913, caja M4, exp. M13 (hereafter cited as CPM), fol. 15–16, 22, 25.

25. José M. Tirado (El Capitán de Navío) to Coronel Ministro de Guerra y Marina, Callao, 6 Aug. 1917, AHM, EA, GTMM, fol. 34–35.

26. El Capitán de Navío to Coronel Ministro de Estado en el Despacho de Guerra y Marina, Callao, 17 Sept. 1917, AHM, EA, GTMM, fol. 42.

27. El Capitán de Navío to Coronel Ministro de Estado en el Despacho de Guerra y Marina, Callao, 17 Sept. 1917, AHM, EA, GTMM, fol. 43.

28. El Capitán de Navío to Señor Coronel Jefe del Gabinete Militar, Callao, 13 Nov. 1917, AHM, EA, GTMM, fol. 112–13.

29. José M. Tirado (El Capitán de Navío) to Coronel Ministro de Guerra y Marina, Callao, 6 Aug. 1917, fol. 34–35; Ernesto Ruiz to Coronal Ministro de Estado en el Despacho de Guerra y Marina, Callao, 14 Nov. de 1917, fol. 44–45, both in AHM, EA, GTMM.

30. Letter to Señor Capitan de Puerto, Mollendo, 15 June 1917, fol. 30; José M. Tirado (El Capitán de Navío) to Coronel Ministro de Guerra y Marina, Callao, 6 Aug. 1917, fol. 34–35; El Capitán de Navío to Coronel Ministro de Estado en el Despacho de Guerra y Marina, Callao, 17 Sept. 1917, fol. 42; El Capitán de Navío to Coronel Ministro de Estado en el Despacho de Guerra y Marina, Callao, 17 Sept. 1917, fol. 43; Ernesto Ruiz too Coronal Ministro de Estado en el Despacho de Guerra y Marina, Callao, 14 Nov. 1917, fol. 44–45 (44 for "patriotic obligation"); El Capitán de Navío to Coronel Jefe del Gabinete Militar, Callao, 13 Nov. 1917, fol. 113–14; El Capitán de Navío to Coronel Ministro de Estado en el Despacho de Guerra y Marina (Gabinete Militar), Callao, 21 Dec. 1917, fol. 122, all in AHM, EA, GTMM. See also "Los Obresos" [sic], *El Porteño* (Mollendo, Perú), 23 Mar. 1918, 2; "La huelga de los trabajadores de mar en Mollendo. Detalles de la solución del conflicto," *El Comercio* (Lima, Perú), 4 Apr. 1918, edición de la tarde, 3, both in *La huelga de Mollendo de 1918: Un antecedente del establecimiento de la jornada de las ocho horas en el Perú*, ed. José Coloma Gygax (Lima: Instituto Latinoamericano de Cultura y Desarrollo, 2005), 34, 57. Concern over renewed competition with Arica preceded the completion of the Arica-La Paz railroad, too. See Acta, 25 Feb. 1913, AHM, CPM, fol. 9; and Melo, *Derrotero de la costa del Perú*, 257.

31. Victor V. Valdivieso to Señor Capitán de Navío, Comandante Principal de las Milicias Navales, Capitán de Puerto del Callao, Mollendo, 2 Dec. 1917, AHM, EA, GTMM, fol. 4.

32. Gremio de Izaje, Gremio de Estivadores, Gremio lancheros de la "Grau," Gremio de lanchas de la Iglesia, Gremio de Jornaleros de abordo to Sr. Capitan de Corbeta y Capitan del Puerto, Mollendo, 16 Mar. 1918, AHM, EA, GTMM, fol. 23.

33. Petition to Señor Capitan de Corbeta y Capitan del Puerto, Mollendo, 5 Mar. 1918, AHM, EA, GTMM, fol. 75.

34. Stefan Rinke, *Latin America and the First World War* (New York: Cambridge University Press, 2017), 66–68, 71, 180–84; and Manuel Burga and Alberto Flores Galindo, *Apogeo y crisis de la República Aristocrática*, in Alberto Flores Galindo, *Obras completas* (Lima: Fundación Andina / SUR Casa de Estudios del Socialismo, 1994), 2:71, 188–89, 205–6. On a similar situation in Philadelphia, see Peter Cole, *Wobblies on the Waterfront: Interracial Unionism in Progressive-Era Philadelphia* (Urbana: University of Illinois Press, 2007), 74–92.

35. The Mollendo Agencies Company to Victor Valdivieso, Mollendo, 8 Mar. 1918, fol. 84; The Pacific Steam Navigation Comp. to Señor Capitán del Puerto, Mollendo, 8 Mar. 1918, fol. 85–86, both in AHM, EA, GTMM.

36. Victor V. Valdivieso to Señor Capitán de Navío Comandante Principal de las Milicias Navales, Capitán del Puerto del Callao, Mollendo, 16 Mar. de 1918, AHM, EA, GTMM, fol. 24.

37. See AHM, EA, GTMM, fol. 16, 17, 102, 104.

38. Ernesto Ruiz copy of Victor V. Valdivieso to Capitan de Navío, Comandante Principal de las Milicias Navales y Capitan del Puerto del Callao, copy date 20 Mar. 1918, AHM, EA, GTMM, fol. 102

39. "Noticias de Mollendo: La huelga de los trabajadores del puerto," *El Comercio*, 23 Mar. 1918, edición de la mañana, 3, in Coloma Gygax, *La huelga de Mollendo de 1918*, 36, 37.

40. "La huelga de los trabajadores de mar en Mollendo," *El Comercio*, 30 Mar. 1918, edición de la mañana, 8, in Coloma Gygax, *La huelga de Mollendo de 1918*, 43, 44.

41. Acta, 29 Mar. de 1918, Mollendo, AHM, EA, GTMM, fol. 129. Reprinted in "La huelga terminada con intervención de la Cámara de Comercio de Arequipa," *El Porteño* (Mollendo), 30 Mar. 1918, 2; "La huelga de los trabajadores de mar en Mollendo: Detalles de la solución del conflicto," *El Comercio*, 4 Apr. 1918, edición de la tarde, 3, both in Coloma Gygax, *La huelga de Mollendo de 1918*, 46–51, 52–57.

42. Fernando Ortiz Letelier, *El Movimiento Obrero en Chile (1891–1919)* (Santiago: LOM, 2005), 177–78; Eduardo Andrés Godoy Sepúlveda, *La huelga del mono: Los anarquistas y las movilizaciones contra el retrato obligatorio (Valparaíso, 1913)* (Santiago de Chile: Quimantú, 2014); Grez, *Los anarquistas*, 252–57; and DeShazo, *Urban Workers*, 137–39. On state conversations on photographing port and maritime workers, see Ministerio de Relaciones Exteriores to Señor Ministro de Marina, Stantiago, 15 May 1913, no. 1368; letter to Sr. Director del Territorio Marítimo, Valparaíso, 10 May 1913, no. 214; letter to Director Jeneral de la Armada, Valparaíso, 24 May 1913, all in ARNAD, MM, vol. 1905.

43. Mario Araya Saavedra, "Los *wobblies* criollos: Fundación e ideología en la Región chilena de la *Industrial Workers of the World*–IWW (1919–1927)" (tesis para optar al grado de Licenciado en Historia, Universidad ARCIS, 2008), 23; and DeShazo, *Urban Workers*, 151, 154.

44. Grez, *Los anarquistas*, 197n533; Araya Saavedra, "Los *wobblies* crollos," 28; Godoy Sepúlveda, *La huelga del mono*, 76; DeShazo, *Urban Workers*, 151, 166–67; Policía de Valparaíso to Intendente de Valparaíso, 2 May 1913, ANH, IV, vol. 1332, no. 299; Policía de Valparaíso to Señor Intendente [de Valparaíso], 5 Nov. 1913, ANH, IV, vol. 1333, no. 998; Policía de Valparaíso to Intendente, 24 Dec. 1913, ANH, IV, vol. 1333, no. 1275; and Prefecto, Policia de Valparaíso, to Señor Intendente, Valparaíso, 20 Apr. 1917, ANH, IV, vol. 1382, no. 474.

45. Intendencia de Valparaíso to Prefecto de Policía, 26 Dec. 1913, ANH, IV, vol. 1335, no. 5114.

46. Araya Saavedra, "Los *wobblies* criollos," 23–33; and DeShazo, *Urban Workers*, 151, 154.

47. DeShazo, *Urban Workers*, 181, 183, 189–92; and Raymond B. Craib, *The Cry of the Renegade: Politics and Poetry in Interwar Chile* (New York: Oxford University Press, 2016).

48. William Vergara (Inspección Regional del Trabajo) to Don Agustin Ortuzar E. (Director General del Trabajo), Valparaíso, 18 Jun. 1925, no. 87, ARNAD, Dirección del Trabajo (hereafter cited as DT), vol. 102, 3; and DeShazo, *Urban Workers*, 200.

49. Craib, *Cry of the Renegade*; Craib, "Students, Anarchists and Categories of Persecution in Chile, 1920," *A Contracorriente* 8, no. 1 (Fall 2010): 22–60; Maxine Molyneux, "No God, No Boss, No Husband: Anarchist Feminism in Nineteenth-Century Argentina," *Latin American Perspectives* 13, no. 1 (Winter 1986): 119–45; DeShazo, *Urban Workers*; Piedad Pareja Pflucker, *Anarquismo y sindicalismo en el Perú (1904–1929)* (Lima: Ediciones Rikchay Perú, 1978); Grez Toso, *Los anarquistas*; Alberto Flores Galindo, *La Agonía de Mariátegui*, in Flores Galindo, *Obras completes* 2:465, 563–70, 587; Anderson, *Under Three Flags*; and Rudolf Rocker, *Anarcho-Syndicalism: Theory and Practice*, trans. Ray E. Chase (Oakland, CA: AK Press, 2004).

50. For the decree abolishing the system, see Ministerio de Marina, 24 Oct. 1921, ARNAD, MM, vol. 2666. For how the redondilla worked, see Arturo Acevedo L., *El Problema de las Faenas Marítimas en la Zona Salitrera: El sistema de redondilla y la nueva reglamentación* (Talcahuano: Lib. e Imprenta "Moderna", 1923), 7–8; Victor Muñoz Cortés, *Cuando la patria mata: La historia del anarquista Julio Rebosio (1914–1920)* (Santiago: Editorial USACH, 2011), 43 and 43n37, where he points out that this system is described in Manuel Rojas's *Lanchas en la bahía*; and DeShazo, *Urban Workers*, 24. For the section on the redondilla in Rojas, see Rojas, *Lanchas en la bahía*, 44–45. For the most complete view of the redondilla, one that complicates the work of DeShazo and Muñoz Cortés, see Camilo Santibáñez Rebolledo, "Los trabajadores portuarios chilenos y la experiencia de la eventualidad: Los conflictos por la redondilla en los muelles salitreros (1916–1923)," *Historia* 50, no. 2 (July–Dec. 2017): 699–728; and Santibáñez Rebolledo, "La IWW y el movimiento obrero en Chile: El caso de los obreros portuarios nortinos (1919–1923)," *Diálogo Andino* 55 (2018): 19–28. While Santibáñez Rebolledo is critical of the historiographical emphasis on the IWW in northern ports, the case of Valparaíso is different.

51. Informe, attached to letter to Señor Director de la Oficina Internacional del Trabajo, Geneva, Santiago, 14 Nov. 1921, ARNAD, DT, vol. 76, no. 193, 20; Acevedo L., *El Problema de las Faenas Marítimas*, 3–5, 13; Alfredo Weber G. (Jefe de la Ofic. del Trabajo [en Valparaíso]) to Director de la Ofc. del Trabajo en Santiago, Valparaíso, 30 May 1921, ARNAD, DT, vol. 72, no. 210; and DeShazo, *Urban Workers*, 191.

52. Claudio Arteaga (Jefe de la Inspección del Trabajo de Valapraíso), memorandum "Desocupación y condiciones del trabajo marítimo en Valparaíso," Confidencial, Santiago 8 May 1922, ARNAD, DT, vol. 73; telegram, Jefe de la Oficina del Trabajo to Luis Rojas Ramirez (Oficina del Trabajo en Valparaíso), 21 Apr. 1922; telegram, Jefe Oficina Trabajo to Luis Rojas Ramirez (Oficina del Trabajo) and Intendencia de Valparaíso, Santiago, 11 May 1922; Claudio Arteaga (Jefe Accidental de la Inspec. del Trabajo de Valparaíso) to Moises Poblete Troncoso (Director de la Oficina del Trabajo de Chile), Valparaíso, 14 June 1922, no. 410, 4–5, these three in ARNAD, DT, vol. 83; Ministerio de Marina to Señor Director Jeneral de la Armada, Santiago, 13 Apr. 1923, ARNAD, MM, vol. 2581, no. 168; and Santibáñez Rebolledo, "Los trabajadores portuarios chilenos."

53. Ministerio de Marina, Decreto, Santiago, 20 Oct. 1923, ARNAD, MM, vol. 2563.

54. For thinking about this relationship, see Harry Cleaver, *Reading* Capital *Politically* (Oakland, CA: AK Press / Antitheses, 2000).

55. For the context of these social laws, see Juan Carlos Yáñez Andrade, *La intervención social en Chile y el nacimiento de la sociedad salarial, 1907–1932* (Santiago: RiL editores, 2008), ch. 5.

56. For the original law, see the entry at the Biblioteca del Congreso Nacional de Chile website, http://bcn.cl/1xxi7. See also DeShazo, *Urban Workers*, 219.

57. On the *Palena*, see William Vergara to Ministro de Higiene, Prevision Social y Trabajo, Santiago, 19 May 1925, ARNAD, DT, vol. 108, no. 864. On bakers refusing to pay the 2 percent, see William Vergara (Inspector Regional) to Alfredo Weber G. (Director General del Trabajo), Valparaíso, 2 Sept. 1926, ARNAD, DT, vol. 124, no. 889.

58. Intendencia de Valparaíso to Dirección General del Trabajo, Valparaíso, 24 Feb. 1926, ARNAD, DT, vol. 117, no. 557; and J. O. Chamorro I., "La organización," *La Voz del Mar* (Valparaíso), 1 May 1926, 2.

59. Intendencia de Valparaíso to Dirección General del Trabajo, Valparaíso, 24 Feb. 1926, ARNAD, DT, vol. 117, no. 557; Intendencia de Valparaíso to Dirección General del Trabajo, Valparaíso, 24 Feb. 1926, , ARNAD, DT, vol. 117, no. 558; Intendencia de Valapraíso to Dirección General del Trabajo, Valparaíso, 16 Mar. 1926, ARNAD, DT, vol. 118, no. 761; Intendencia de Valparaíso to Dirección General del Trabajo, Valparaíso, 27 Apr. 1926, ARNAD, DT, vol. 119, no. 1206; Intendencia de Valparaíso to Dirección General del Trabajo, Valparaíso, 11 Nov. 1926, ARNAD, DT, vol. 126, no. 2976; Intendencia de Valparaíso to Dirección General del Trabajo, Valparaíso, 29 Nov. 1926, ARNAD, DT, vol. 126, no. 3145; and Intendencia de Valparaíso to Dirección General del Trabajo, Valparaíso, 7 Dec. 1926, ARNAD, DT, vol. 127, no. 3234.

60. See previous two notes and "Las Leyes Sociales y la de Reserva del Cabotaje," *La Voz del Mar*, 2 Feb. 1926, 5; "El próximo movimiento y las asambleas públicas," *La Voz del Mar*, 19 Mar. 1926, 3; and Alcon, "La organización," *La Voz del Mar*, 16 Apr. 1926, 4.

61. William Vergara (Inspección Regional del Trabajo) to Agustin Ortuzar E. (Director General del Trabajo), Valparaíso, 18 Jun. 1925, ARNAD, DT, vol. 102, no. 87.

62. L. A. T., "Las leyes sociales y marítimas," *La Voz del Mar*, 1 May 1925, 4. It is possible that L. A. T. was short for Luis Toro, former secretario of the Federación de Jente de Mar in the early 1920s, active participant in the IWW, and writer for *La Voz del Mar* in the mid-1920s. For similar views from other IWW locals (and one anarchist but not explicitly IWW), as well as some reports on protests against Ley 4054 in Valparaíso, see Danto Velial, "La Ley 4054," *Adelante* (Rancagua), Dec. 1926, 1–2; "Comisio. El 22 de Febrero se efectuó en ésta el Comicio auspiciado por el Comité Pro-Abolición de la Ley 4054," *Bandera Roja* (Concepción), Mar. 1926, 3–4; "Actividades de la I. W. W.," 3–4 and "El Comité Pro-Abolición de la Ley 4054, efectúa un comicio el 23 de Marzo," *Bandera Roja*, Apr. 1926, 4; "Actividades de la I. W. W.," *Bandera Roja*, May 1926, 3–4; and "La Ley 4054," *Bandera Roja*, Aug. 1926, 1. On a similar law in Argentina, see Joel Horowitz, "Cuando las élites y los

trabajadores coincidieron: La resistencia al programa de bienestar patrocinado por el gobierno argentine, 1923–1924," *Anuario IEHS*, no. 16 (2001): 109–28.

63. *Tom Barker and the I.W.W.*, recorded, edited, and with an introduction by E. C. Fry (Canberra: Australian Society for the Study of Labour History, 1965), 34; and Araya Saavedra, "Los *wobblies* criollos," 34–39. For more on Barker, see Paula de Angelis, "Tom Barker and Revolutionary Europe," in *Wobblies of the World: A Global History of the IWW*, ed. Peter Cole, David Struthers, and Kenyon Zimmer (London: Pluto Press, 2017).

64. Araya Saavedra, "Los *wobblies* criollos," 38–39.

65. Tim Harper, *Underground Asia: Global Revolutionaries and the Assault on Empire* (Cambridge, MA: Belknap Press of Harvard University Press, 2021), 91–93.

66. "Los Mártires de Tokio," *La Voz de los Mártires* (Valparaíso), 1 May 1911, 2. On Montjuich as a central node in global anarchism and anti-colonialism, see Anderson, *Under Three Flags*, ch. 5.

67. Miguel Rodríguez Hernández, "El movimiento de confraternidad obrera peruana-chilean y el final del gobierno de Guillermo Billinghurst," in *Las historias que nos unen. 21 relatos para la integración entre Perú y Chile*, comp. Daniel Parodi Revoredo y Sergio González Miranda (Lima: Fondo Editorial de la Pontificia Universidad Católica del Perú, 2014); and Godoy Sepúlveda, *La huelga del mono*.

68. L.A.T., "Nuestra Organización en el Perú: Notas de Supe," *La Voz del Mar*, 1st quincena de Nov. 1924, p. 5.

69. On Toro at *Campana Nueva*, see Luis Toro, "Un audaz robo en nuestro local," *Campana Nueva* (Valparaíso) 1, no. 3, 1st quincena de June 1924, 4. In this article, Toro provides the address Avenida Errázuriz 414, which is also given as the address for *La Voz del Mar*, the official newpaper of the Transporte Marítimo of the IWW in Chile.

70. Wooblie [*sic*], "La organización marítima peruana," *La Voz del Mar*, 30 Nov. 1924, 3–4.

71. "El choque con los chilenos tripulantes del 'Cóndor,'" *Variedades: Revista Seminal Ilustrada* (Lima) 3, no. 201, 6 Jan. 1912, 5–6; Consulado General de Chile en Callao to Señor Ministro de Relaciones Exteriores, 5 Jan. 1912, Confidencial, no. 344, Sección D; Consulado General de Chile to Señor Ministro de Relaciones Exteriores, 5 Jan. 1912, Confidencial, no. 345, Sección D; Consulado General de Chile [en Callao] to Señor Ministro de Relaciones Exteriores, 5 Feb. 1912, Confidencial, no. 358, Sección D, all in AMRREE-C, FP, v. 347.

72. As Louise E. Walker writes of rumor in another context: "The veracity of ... rumors is uncertain; likely they mixed fact and fiction. But for rumor to spread ... it had [to] be credible to those who received and repeated, and sometimes acted upon, the information." See Louise E. Walker, *Waking from the Dream: Mexico's Middle Classes after 1968* (Stanford, CA: Stanford University Press, 2013), 52.

73. On Haya de la Torre in Chile, see also Armando Triviño, "Mensaje a los trabajadores del Perú," in *La I.W.W. en la teoria y en la práctica* (Santiago: Editorial Lux, 1925).

74. Blanchard, *Origins of the Peruvian Labor Movement*, 150–55 (153 for Haya de la Torre's involvement); Jeffrey L. Klaiber, "The Popular Universities and the Origins of Aprismo, 1921–1924," *Hispanic American Historical Review* 55, no. 4 (Nov. 1975): 696; and García-Bryce, *Haya de la Torre*.

75. Luis Toro, "Los deportados peruanos," *La Voz del Mar*, 15 Jan. 1925, 5–6; Klaiber, "Popular Universities"; Craib, *Cry of the Renegade*, 69; and DeShazo, *Urban Workers*, 158.

76. Skuban, *Lines in the Sand*, 25–27.

77. See various letters (fol. 78. 80, 84, 87–88, 89–90, 100, 102, 103, 110) in AMRREE-P, correspondencia, caja 827, carpeta 8, código 2-2, 1923.

78. There was a total of twenty-one instances of sources of money from Peruvian ports. All entries except for one included a specific location (the one exception simply notes "the coasts of Peru"), resulting in nine entries from Supe, five from Huacho, four from Pacasmayo, and one each from Salaverry and Mollendo. Of the ten people with their names listed, two bought the newspaper or donated two different times, with a possible third person, but the first name is left out of one entry. For the ledgers, see *La Voz del Mar*, Nov. 1924–Feb. 1927.

79. Prefectura del Departamento, no date, "De la 'Voz del Mar' No. 12, correspondiente al 24 de Marzo de 1925—de Valparaíso," Archivo Regional de Arequipa, Arequipa, Peru (hereafter cited as ARA), Prefectura, 1925.

80. Craib, *Cry of the Renegade*; Jeffrey L. Gould, *To Lead as Equals: Rural Protest and Political Consciousness in Chinandega, Nicaragua, 1912–1979* (Chapel Hill: University of North Carolina Press, 1990); James Brennan, *The Labor Wars in Córdoba, 1955–1976: Ideology, Work, and Labor Politics in an Argentine Industrial City* (Cambridge, MA: Harvard University Press, 1994); and Peter Winn, *Weavers of Revolution: The Yarur Workers and Chile's Road to Socialism* (New York: Oxford University Press, 1986).

81. Marriage of Benigno Quintana to Sofia Barrientos, 13 Apr. 1908, Inmaculada Concepción, Mollendo, Arequipa, Peru, found in Perú, matrimonios, 1600–1940, FamilySearch database, Genealogical Society of Utah, Salt Lake City, FHL microfilm 1,154,820, fol. 187.

82. On the police being sent to Mollendo and staying on afterward, see Dirección de Gobierno y Policía, Sección Gobierno, to Prefecto del Departamento de Arequipa, Lima, 20 Mar. 1918, ARA, Prefectura, 1918. On urban violence in other ports during protests, see Peter DeShazo, "The Valparaíso Maritime Strike of 1903 and the Development of a Revolutionary Labor Movement in Chile," *Journal of Latin American Studies* 11, no. 1 (May, 1979): 145–68.

83. Ministerio de Gobierno y Policía, Dirección y Estado Mayor de Policía, to Prefecto de Arequipa, Lima, 19 Apr. 1923, ARA, Prefectura, 1923, legajo 1.

84. Subprefectura de la Provincia de Islay, Mollendo, to Prefecto del Departamento, Mollendo, 18 Nov. 1924, ARA, Prefectura, 1924.

85. See also the discussion of Mollendo and Chilean Wobblies in Steven J. Hirsch, "Peruvian Anarcho-Syndicalism: Adapting Transnational Influences and Forging Counterhegemonic Practices, 1905–1930," in *Anarchism and Syndicalism in*

*the Colonial and Postcolonial World, 1870–1940*, ed. Steven Hirsch and Lucien van der Walt (Boston: Brill, 2010), 255–57.

86. As Daniel James remarked on Peronism: "In this sense Peronism's power ultimately lay it its capacity to give public utterance to what had until then been internalised, lived as private experience." Chileans were not Perón and Peruvians Peronist, but this exchange and connection would not have been successful if they did not speak in similar political terms and experiences. See Daniel James, *Resistance and Integration: Peronism and the Argentine Working Class, 1946–1976* (New York: Cambridge University Press, 1993), 30.

87. Anton Rosenthal has suggested that these methods "did not require years of political groundwork." See Anton Rosenthal, "Moving between the Global and the Local: The Industrial Workers of the World and Their Press in Latin America," in *In Defiance of Boundaries: Anarchism in Latin American History*, ed. Geoffroy de Laforcade and Kirwin R. Shaffer (Gainesville: University Press of Florida, 2015), 85. See also Cole's analysis of the attraction of the IWW to African American and recent immigrants in Philadelphia, in Cole, *Wobblies on the Waterfront*, ch. 3.

88. Within the pages of *La Voz del Mar*, too, port and maritime workers in Mollendo would have read numerous articles about labor organizing at the port and onboard ships. On organizing onboard, see, for instance, A. Bull, "Los que pasarían mañana: Un palo para los rehacios," *La Voz del Mar*, 2nd quincena de of July 1924, 2; "A bordo del 'Flora,'" and "Como se hace la propaganda a bordo," *La Voz del Mar*, 1st quincena of Oct. 1924, 4, 6; and "Abordo del "Huacho"" and "A bordo del "Santiago,"" *La Voz del Mar*, 30 Nov. 1924, 6.

89. C. H. Woordward, Ministerio de Marina, Estado Mayor General, to Director Gobierno, Lima, 19 Feb. 1925, AGN, Prefecturas, Ministerios, Marina, 1925, paq. 258.

90. "Nuestra propaganda en el exterior," *La Voz del Mar*, 24 Mar. 1925, 5.

91. "Nuestra propaganda en el exterior," *La Voz del Mar*, 24 Mar. 1925, 5; José Moreno to Compañero Secretario de la AIT [Asociación Internacional de Trabajadores], 4 Aug. 1925, International Institute of Social History, Amsterdam, Netherlands (hereafter cited as IISH), Diego Abad de Santillán Papers, carpeta 366 ("gesto viril"). Both letters mention the *Mapocho*, the article in *La Voz del Mar* mentions the *Cachapoal*, and Moreno mentions the *Mantaro*.

92. "Nuestra propaganda en el exterior," *La Voz del Mar*, 24 Mar. 1925, 5. For the settlement, see Prefectura del Departamento, Arequipa, to Ministro de Gobierno, Arequipa, 27 Feb. 1925, AGN, Prefecturas, Arequipa, 1925, paq. 255. This is also briefly discussed in Héctor Ballón Lozada, *Cien años de vida política de Arequipa, 1890–1990* (Arequipa: Universidad Nacional de San Agustín/Talleres Gráficos Flores, 1992), 2:31–32.

93. For the case of Colombia, see Lesley Gill, *A Century of Violence in a Red City: Popular Struggle, Counterinsurgency, and Human Rights in Colombia* (Durham, NC: Duke University Press, 2016).

94. Cuerpo de Seguridad 12a Compañía Comandancia to Señor General Prefecto, 19 May 1920, ARA, Prefectura, 1925.

95. Subprefectura de la Provincia de Islay to General Prefecto del Departamento, 1 Jun. 1925, ARA, Prefectura, 1925.

96. Ivanna Margarucci, "Apuntes sobre el movimiento anarquista en Perú y Bolivia, 1880–1930," *Nuevo Mundo Mundos Nuevos* (8 Oct. 2019), https://doi.org/10.4000/nuevomundo.77382; and Julio Portocarrero, *Sindicalismo Peruano: Primera Etapa, 1911–1930* (Lima: Editorial Gráfica Labor, 1987), 122–24.

97. Subprefectura de la Provincia de Islay to General Prefecto del Departamento, 1 Jun. 1925, ARA, Prefecutra, 1925. This is a different letter than the one cited in note 95.

98. "Deportados peruanos," *La Voz del Mar*, 6 Jun. 1925, 1.

99. Subprefectura de la Provincia de Islay, Mollendo, Perú, to Prefecto del Departamento, Mollendo, 31 Jan. 1923; Subprefectura de la Provincia de Islay, Mollendo, Peru, to Prefecto del Departamento, Mollendo, 21 Jan. 1923; Subprefectura de la Provincia de Islay, Mollendo, Peru, to Prefecto del Departamento, 5 Feb. 1923, all in ARA, Prefectura, 1923, legajo 2.

100. Subprefectura de la Provincia de Islay to General Prefecto del Departamento, 1 Jun. 1925, ARA, Prefectura, 1925; letter to Coronel Lopoldo Arias, Prefecto del Departmento, Arequipa, Mollendo, 8 Feb. 1926, ARA, Prefectura, 1926, legajo 3; Capitan del Puerto to Subprefecto de Islay, Mollendo, 2 Mar. 1926, ARA, Prefectura, 1926, legajo 3; and Capitan del Puerto to Contralmirante Jefe del Estado, Mollendo, 9 [Mar. 1926?], and "Of Reservado" to Capitan del Puerto, attached to previous letter, ARA, Prefectura, 1926, legajo 1. On Quintana's involvement in the 1922 lancheros contract, see the transcribed contract in Capitan del Puerto to Prefecto del Departamento de Arequipa, Mollendo, 21 Apr. 1926, ARA, Prefectura, 1926, legajo 1.

101. For the original Cervantes, see Miguel de Cervantes, *The History of That Ingenious Gentleman Don Quijote de la Mancha*, trans. Burton Raffel (New York: W. W. Norton, 1996), 657.

102. Letter to Coronel Lopoldo Arias, Prefecto del Departmento, Arequipa, Mollendo, 8 Feb. 1926, ARA, Prefectura, 1926, legajo 3. Everything past the second page of the letter is missing in the archive, so we do not know the author.

103. Capitan del Puerto to Subprefecto de Islay, Mollendo, 2 Mar. 1926, ARA, Prefectura, 1926, legajo 3.

104. Subprefectura de la Provincia de Islay to General Prefecto del Departamento, 1 Jun. 1925, ARA, Prefectura, 1925.

105. Ex-Prefecto General Francisco La Rosa Villanueva, 18 May 1925, attached to Prefectura del Departamento, Arequipa, to Director de Gobierno, 8 Sep. 1926, AGN, Prefecturas, Arequipa, 1926, paq. 259-A. Similar to Quintana, they floated the idea of bringing Escalona to Lima on another pretext, probably to not agitate workers in Mollendo, and then deporting him from the capital.

106. Grupo de "Jornaleros de Abordo" to Coronel Dr. Juan Manuel de la Torre, Prefecto del Departamento, Mollendo, 28 Feb. 1923, ARA, Prefectura, 1923, legajo 2.

107. Prefectura del Departamento, Arequipa, to Ministro de Gobierno, Arequipa, 27 Feb. 1925, AGN, Prefecturas, Arequipa, 1925, paq. 255.

108. Capitan del Puerto to Coronel Prefecto de Arequipa, RESERVADO, 23 Feb. 1925, part of packet beginning with Capitan del Puerto de Contralmirante Jefe del Estado, Mollendo, 9 [Mar. 1926?], ARA, Prefecturas, 1926, legajo 1.

109. Capitan del Puerto de Subprefecto de Islay, Mollendo, 2 Mar. de 1926, ARA, Prefecturas, 1926, legajo 3.

110. J. Ernesto Besnard (El Capitán de Corbeta, Capitán del Puerto) to Director Material, Mollendo, 19 Nov. 1926, no. 123, attached to A. R. Pimentel (Ministerio de Marina, Director del Material) to Director de Gobierno, Lima, 26 Nov. 1926, AGN, Prefecturas, Ministerios, Marina, 1926, paq. 261–A, oficio 109.

111. M. Benigno Valdivia to Contra Almirante Prefecto del Departamento, 17 Dec. 1927, ARA, Prefecturas, 1928, legajo 1.

112. Federación Obrera Local, Arequipa, Perú, to Presidente de la Sociedad Unión de Empleados, 8 Apr. 1926, ARA Prefectura, 1926, legajo 3; Subprefectura de Islay to Prefecto del Departamento, Mollendo, 20 May 1926; Centro Social Obrero de la Confederación Coaligada de la Provincia de Islay, Mollendo, to Subprefecto de la Provincia de Islay, 20 May 1926, these two in AGN, Prefecturas, Arequipa, 1926, paq. 259-A. Hirsh, In "Peruvian Anarcho-Syndicalism," also refers to the "Liberty and Justice" present in the Federación Obrera Local (251).

113. El vigilante de investigación to Señor Oficial 20 de Investigación de la espresada, no date; Cuerpo de Investigación, 5a Sección, to Señor Oficial 20 de la expresada, Arequipa, 21 May 1927; César Fernández Oliva to Señor Oficial Segundo de la expresada, Arequipa, 21 May 1927, these three in ARA, Prefectura, 1927, legajo 2; and Cuerpo de Seguridad, Arequipa, to Contra-Almirante Prefecto del Departamento, Arequipa, 24 Jan. 1927, ARA, Prefectura, 1927, legajo 1.

114. A. G. Howe (Contralmirante, Jefe del Estado Mayor General de Marina) to Prefecto del Departamento de Arequipa, Lima, 17 Jan. 1928, ARA, Prefectura, 1928, legajo 2.

115. Braudel, *Mediterranean*, 1:14.

116. Dening, *Beach Crossings*, 19.

117. Rojas, *Sombras contra el muro*, 353.

118. Rojas, *Sombras contra el muro*, 353.

119. Fink, *Sweatshops at Sea*, 106, 128–41 (quote on 128). On the Maritime world, see also Michael D. Thompson, *Working on the Dock: Labor and Enterprise in an Antebellum Southern Port* (Columbia: University of South Carolina Press, 2015); Rashauna Johnson, *Slavery's Metropolis: Unfree Labor in New Orleans during the Age of Revolutions* (New York: Cambridge University Press, 2016); Warren, *Sulu Zone*; Moon-Kie Jung, *Reworking Race: The Making of Hawaii's Interracial Labor Movement* (New York: Columbia University Press, 2006); and Brown, *Dropping Anchor*. For workers along the Peru-Chile border, see Skuban, *Lines in the Sand*, 167–77.

CHAPTER 5. PACIFIC POLICING

1. "Revista de la Policía de Valparaíso," *RPV* 1, no. 1, 31 Oct. 1906, 3.

2. "Revista de la Policía de Valparaíso," *RPV*, 1, no. 1, 31 Oct. 1906, 4.

3. The literature on the social question is vast. For Chile, see Mario Garcés Durán, *Crisis social y motines populares en el 1900*, 2nd ed. (Santiago: LOM, 2003); Sergio Grez Toso, *La "cuestión social" en Chile: Ideas y debates precursores (1804–1902)* (Santiago: Dirección de Bibliotecas, Archivos y Museos / Centro de Investigaciones Diego Barros Arana, 1995). For Peru, and in particular related to policing, see Aguirre, *Criminals of Lima*, chs. 1–3.

4. Doctor Pedro N. Barros Ovalle, "La filiación antropometrica en la seccion de seguridad," *RPV* 1, no. 3, 31 Dec. 1906, 83.

5. Deborah A. Poole, "Ciencia, peligrosidad y represión en la criminología indigenista peruana," in *Bandoleros, abigeos y monteneros: Criminalidad y violencia en el Perú*, ed. Carlos Aguirre and Charles Walker (Lima: La Siniestra ensayos, 2019). See also José Ragas, "Documenting Hierarchies: State Building, Identification and Citizenship in Modern Peru" (PhD diss, University of California, Davis, 2015).

6. Nathan Perl-Rosenthal, *Citizen Sailors: Becoming American in the Age of Revolution* (Cambridge, MA: Belknap Press of Harvard University Press, 2015).

7. Ricardo Cruzat E., "Algo sobre el Jiu-jitsu," *RPV* 4, no. 40, 31 Jan. 1910, 4–8.

8. *Memoria del Ministro de Gobierno, Policía, Correos y Telégrafos, 1911* (Lima: Imprenta Americana, 1911), xxii–xiii, 141–42, 154–55. Thanks to José Ragas for passing along this citation.

9. "Curso de educación física," *RPV* 2, no. 21, 30 Jun. 1908, 276–77 (quote on 276).

10. Ricardo Cruzat E., "El aprendizaje del box," *RPV* 4, no. 41, 28 Feb. 1910, 30–32.

11. Vania Cárdenas Muñoz, *El orden gañan: Historia Social de la Policía, Valparaíso, 1896–1920* (Concepción: Ediciones Escaparte, 2013), 230.

12. In early 1908, the Prefecture of Valparaíso learned that many officers had fired their guns without reason. As a result, any and all firing of guns would be investigated, and in the event that there was no "reasonable cause" for doing so, officers would be fined $5.00 for each bullet fired, which would be deducted directly from their wage. See "Ordenes del dia de character permanente," *RPV* 2, no. 17, 29 Feb. 1908, 153. Considering that a Guardian 1st's salary had recently risen to $155 a month, a Guardian 2nd's to $143 a month, and Guardian 3rd's to $121 a month, the $5 fine (if only one bullet was fired without cause) meant a 3.23 percent deduction for the month for a Guardian 1st, 3.5 percent for a Guardian 2nd, and 4.14 percent for a Guardian 3rd. For their recent raises, see "Miscelanea," *RPV* 1, no. 12, 30 Sept. 1907, 382.

13. "Reuniones públicas," *RPV* 7, no. 89, 1 Jun. 1913, 6–7.

14. "Uso del tabladillo en la Plaza de la Victoria," *RPV* 7, no. 92, 1 Sept. 1913, 11–12.

15. "Uso de kioskos y tabladillos públicos," *RPV* 7, no. 93, 1 Oct. 1913, 2–3.

16. On the strike, see Godoy Sepúplveda, *La huelga del mono*.

17. Antonio Santibáñez Rojas, "La reglamentación de las reuniones públicas," *RPV* 7, no. 95, 1 Dec. 1913, 28–33.

18. Cárdenas Muñoz, *El orden gañan*, 104, 109.

19. Prefectura de Policia to Intendente de la Provincia, Valparaíso, 24 Sep. 1907, ANH, IV, vol. 1203, no. 559; and Prefectura de Policía to Intendencia de Valparaíso, 1 Feb. 1908, ANH, IV, vol. 1225, no. 108.

20. C. A. Velarde to Subprefecto é Intendente de Policía, 15 Apr. 1910; letter to Prefecto de la Provincia, 16 Nov. 1912, both in a packet beginning with Prefectura del Callao, mesa de partes, Expediente iniciado por la Subprefectura en solicitor de la subsistencia de la Sección de Investigaciones, Identificación y Estadistica, Letra S, no. 44, fol. 410, Principiado el 18 Nov. 1912, AGN, Prefecturas, Callao, 1913.

21. On this, see Kirsten Weld, *Paper Cadavers: The Archives of Dictatorship in Guatemala* (Durham, NC: Duke University Press, 2014), esp. ch. 4.

22. See *Convenio celebrado entre las Policías de La Plata y Buenos Aires (Argentina)—de Rio de Janeiro (Brasil)—de Santiago de Chile y de Montevideo (R. O. del Uruguay)* (Buenos Aires: Imprenta y Encuadernación de la Policía de la Capital Federal, 1905), 3, 5–6, 16, 19–20. See also the discussion in Diego Galeano, "Traveling Criminals and Transnational Police Cooperation in South America, 1890–1920," in *Voices of Crime: Constructing and Contesting Social Control in Modern Latin America*, ed. Luz E. Huertas, Bonnie A. Lucero, and Gregory J. Swedberg (Tucson: University of Arizona Press, 2016).

23. *Convenio celebrado entre las Policías*, 7, 53, 58–59. The exact distance from the subject and the focal length of the camera lens are not detailed in the convenio. Distortion happens as the film or plate approaches or is set farther away from the subject. The operator could use different focal lengths to achieve the desired size of the subject's face, but if they used a wider focal length, which required setting up the camera much closer to the subject, the parts of the face closest to the camera, such as the nose, would appear larger than they are in real life—or on the street.

24. *Conferencia internacional sudámericana de policía* (Buenos Aires: Imprenta de José Tragant, 1920), 77–78.

25. The Chilean state (and the others at the conferences) recognized the power of photography in apprehending and identifying suspected criminals. Its power—in the form of cinema—also lent itself to showing the world the improvements made in Chile over the years. When a representative from the Fox Film Corporation, based in the United States, approached the Chilean consulate in Washington, D.C. with the objective of filming the "cities, industries, buildings, etc.," the Chilean consulate urged those in Chile to "offer them all of the help possible in order to best succeed in their project." On the other hand, some in Chile were cognizant of the trouble photography might cause for their own security, as well. In 1911 a local photography club member, as well as others, notified the local authorities of Germans taking pictures, paintings, or drawings of "State objects and places which could be, or are, used for military purposes." Letters went back and forth on laws prohibiting such reproductions, but in the end no such laws were found. Still, these exchanges show the power of photography. On the Fox Film venture, see Ministerio de Relaciones Exteriores to Intedentes y Gobernadores de la República, Santiago, 12 Dec. 1922, ARNAD, Ministerio de Relaciones Exteriores (hereafter cited as MRREE), vol. 2302, no. 2404. On

the Germans, see Ministerio de Relaciones Esteriores to Ministro de Marina, Santiago, 26 Jul. 1911, ARNAD, MM, vol. 1805, no. 2386; Auditor de Guerra y Marina to Director Jeneral, Valparaíso, 2 Sep. 1911, ARNAD, MM, vol. 1805; Dirección General de la Armada to Ministro de Marina, Valparaíso, 14 Sep. 1911, ARNAD, MM, vol. 1805, no. 1639; and Ministerio de Marina to Ministro de Relaciones Esteriores, Santiago, 22 Sep. 1911, ARNAD, MM, vol. 1815, no. 485.

26. Pedro N. Barros Ovalle, *Manual de antropometría criminal i jeneral, escrito segun el sistema de A. Bertillon para la identificación personal i destinado al uso de los establecimientos penitenciarios, autoridades judiciales, compañías de seguros, cuerpos, armados, etc., etc.* (Santiago de Chile: Imprenta de Enrique Blanchard-Chessi, 1900), vii.

27. Barros Ovalle, *Manual de antropometría criminal*, 114–15.

28. Barros Ovalle, *Manual de antropometría criminal*, vii–viii.

29. Barros Ovalle, *Manual de antropometría criminal*, 59.

30. Barros Ovalle, *Manual de antropometría criminal*, 48.

31. Barros Ovalle, *Manual de antropometría criminal*, 71. In Mexico, one of the early adapters of the Bertillon system decided to not place as much importance on eye color due to the general similarity of eye color in Mexico and the difficulty in differentiating. See Mercedes García Ferrari and Diego Galeano, "Cartografía del *bertillonage*: Circuitos de difusión, usos y resistencias al sistema antropométrico en América Latina," in *Delincuentes, policías y justicias: América Latina, siglos XIX y XX*, ed. Daniel Palma Alvarado (Santiago: Ediciones Universidad Alberto Hurtado, 2015), 288.

32. Barros Ovalle, *Manual de antropometría criminal*, 100.

33. Barros Ovalle, *Manual de antropometría criminal*, 111–13, 113n. Barros Ovalle had read the terms used in Argentine Spanish for the Bertillon system, and in the note on translation, argued that many of the terms were not faithful to the original French version.

34. Pedro N. Barros Ovalle, "La filiación antropometrica en la sección de seguridad," *RPV* 1, no. 3, 31 Dec. 1906, 82–89; and Barros Ovalle, "Clasificación antropométrica de las filiaciones," *RPV* 1, no. 4, 31 Jan. 1907, 110–12.

35. Barros Ovalle, *Manual de antropometría criminal*, 11–12; Barros Ovalle, "Clasificación antropométrica de las filiaciones," *RPV* 1, no. 4, 31 Jan. 1907, 111–12; and "Estudios sobre antropolojia juridica," *RPV* 7, no. 84, 1 Jan. 1913, 52–53.

36. "La dactiloscopía o sistema de identificación," *RPV* 1, no. 3, 31 Dec. 1906, 65–66. See also Pedro N. Barros Ovalle, "La filiación antropometrica en la sección de seguridad," *RPV* 1, no. 3, 31 Dec. 1906, 87.

37. "Estadistica de Policía de Lima," *Revista de Policía* (Lima) 1, no. 3 (Mar. 1910): 5.

38. Julia Rodríguez, "South Atlantic Crossings: Fingerprints, Science, and the State in Turn-of-the-Century Argentina," *American Historical Review* 109, no. 2 (Apr. 2004): 392.

39. Rodríguez, "South Atlantic Crossings," 402; García Ferrari and Galeano, "Cartografía del *Bertillonage*"; and Cristian Enrique Palacios Laval, "Entre Bertillon y Vucetich: Las tecnologías de identificación policial. Santiago de Chile, 1893–1924," *Revista Historia y Justicia* 1 (2013): 1–28.

40. "Identificación i pesquisa," *RPV* 1, no. 1, 31 Oct. 1906, 23, 24. See also Barros Valle, "Clasificación antropométrica de las filiaciones," *RPV* 1, no. 4, 31 Jan. 1907, 112n1 ("La impression dactiloscópica establece la certidumbre en úlimo término"); Julio Ovalle, "El Sistema Dactiloscópico Arjentino," *RPV* 4, no. 46, 31 July 1910, 16–20; Julio Ovalle, "El Sistema Dactiloscópico Arjentino," *RPV* 4, no. 47, 31 Aug. 1910, 27–31; "Estudios sobre antropolojia juridica," *RPV* 7, no. 84, 1 Jan. 1913, 50–55; and Cárdenas Muñoz, *El orden gañán*, 106.

41. On the Bertillon system and Vucetich system in Chile, see also Craib, *Cry of the Renegade*, 124–27.

42. Weld, *Paper Cadavers*, 14.

43. Rojas, *Hijo del ladrón*, 1:147.

44. Rojas, *La oscura vida radiante*, 2:184.

45. Craib, *Cry of the Renegade*, 122–23.

46. Julio Vicuña Cifuentes, *Coa: Jerga de los delincuentes chilenos; Estudio y vocabulario* (Santiago: Imprenta Universitaria, 1910), 56–57. See also the discussion of slang within the criminal world in Marco Antonio León León, *Construyendo un sujeto criminal: Criminología, criminalidad y sociedad en Chile, siglos XIX y XX* (Santiago: Centro de Investigaciones Diego Barros Arana / DIBAM / Editorial Universitaria, 2015), 80–81.

47. *Conferencia internacional sudámericana de policía*, 30.

48. *Conferencia internacional sudámericana de policía*, 37–38. Translation from the Portuguese is the authors'.

49. *Conferencia internacional sudámericana de policía*, 42.

50. Craib, *Cry of the Renegade*, 35.

51. *Conferencia internacional sudámericana de policía*, 81–82.

52. *Conferencia internacional sudámericana de policía*, 102–3. The delegate from Paraguay asked to add "and other documents" after "passports" since some countries did not require passports when entering or leaving (105).

53. Consulado General to Oficial Mayor de Relaciones Exteriores, Valparaíso, 30 Jan. 1903, AMRREE-P, correspondencia, caja 523, carpeta 3, código 8-10-G, 1903, fol. 13. The pamphlets were titled "Reglamento de la Policía de Seguridad de Valparaíso" and "El Guardián de Policía."

54. Consulado General to Oficial Mayor de Relaciones Exteriores, Valparaíso, 12 Mar. 1903, AMRREE-P, correspondencia, caja 523, carpeta 3, código 8-10-G, 1903, fol. 26.

55. Consulado General to Ministro de Relaciones Exteriores, Valparaíso, 20 Mar. 1903, AMRREE-P, correspondencia, caja 523, carpeta 3, código 8-10-G, 1903, fol. 37; and Consulado General to Ministro de Relaciones Exteriores, Valparaíso, 15 May 1903, AMRREE-P, correspondencia, caja 523, carpeta 3, código 8-10-G, 1903, fol. 69 (quote in this letter).

56. Consulado General del Perú en Chile to Alejandro Lira (Ministro de Relaciones Exteriores), Valparaíso, 8 Sep. 1918, no. 281; Consulado General del Perú en Chile to Lira, Valparaíso, 29 Sept. 1915, no. 294, both in ARNAD, MRREE, vol. 1930.

57. Consulado General de Chile en Callao to César A. Alguera (Oficial Mayor del Ministerio de Relaciones Exteriores del Perú), Callao, 14 Feb. 1918, AMRREE-P, correspondencia, caja 713, carpeta 27, código 9-9, 1918, fol. 8.

58. Julio Denbom (Capitan de Vaio, Director del Territorio Marítimo) to Cónsul de Francia, Valparaíso, 22 Dec. 1926, fol. 49; G. Le Lorrain (Cónsul de Francia encargado del Consulado General del Perú) to Director del Territorio Marítimo, Valparaíso, 22 Dec. 1926, fol. 50, both in AMRREE-P, correspondencia, caja 941, carpeta 26, código 8-10-G, 1926.

59. Ministerio de Relaciones Exteriores to Presidente de la exma. Corte Suprema, Santiago, 8 Sept. 1922, no. 1709; Ministerio de Relaciones Exteriores to Presidente de la exma. Corte Suprema de Justicia, Santiago, 14 Sept. 1922, no. 1748; Ministerio de Relaciones Exteriores to Presidente de la exma. Corte Suprema de Justicia, Santiago, 16 Sept. 1922, no. 1757; Ministerio de Relaciones Exteriores to Presidente de la exma. Corte Suprema de Justicia, Santiago, 28 Sept. 1922, no. 1837; Ministerio de Relaciones Exteriores to Presidente de la exma. Corte Suprema de Justicia, Santiago, 9 Oct. 1922, no. 1899, all in ARNAD, MRREE, vol. 2302.

60. "Manifestación honrosa," *RPV* 2, no. 16, 31 Jan. 1908, 118. The police declined the donation, instead offering to route the money to a local casa de beneficencia. Grace and Company in turn gave the 200 pesos to two charity organizations, Las Hermanas de la Santa Cruz and Asilo de Lourdes.

61. Antonio Santibáñez Rojas, "Aumento de personal y de atribuciones," *RPV* 4, no. 46, 31 July 1910, p. 4.

62. Rojas, *Lanchas en la bahía*, 9–14.

63. Ministerio de Guerra y Marina to Ministro de Estado en el Despacho de Relaciones Exteriores, Lima, 31 Mar. 1919, AMRREE-P, correspondencia, caja 721, carpeta 10, código 2-1, 1919, fol. 27–28.

64. See follow-up to Ministro de Relaciones Exteriores to Prefecto de la Provincia Constitucional del Callao, Lima, 19 Dec. 1874, AHM, Prefecturas, Ministerio de Gobierno, Culto y Obras Públicas, 1874, caja 24, sobre 187, fol. 186.

65. For a discussion of desertions, see chapter 1.

66. Letter to Señor Director de Gobierno, 1 July 1913, AGN, Prefecturas, Callao, 1913.

67. Francisco Aliaga (2nd Oficial del vapor Chileno "Huasco") to Cónsul Jeneral de Chile, Callao, 17 Oct. 1918, AMRREE-P, correspondencia, caja 713, carpeta 27, código 9-9, 1918, fol. 17.

68. Barros Ovalle, *Manual de antropometría criminal*, 35, 108.

69. Marino C. Alegre y Pacheco, *Los delincuentes tatuados de la penitenciaria nacional* (Lima: Tipografía y Encuadernación de la Penitenciaria, 1917), 43. On tattoos on the coast and their relation to foreign maritime workers, see Alegre y Pacheco, *Los delincuentes tatuados*, 37. On tattoos in prisons, see also Aguirre, *Criminals of Lima*, 164–67.

70. "Estracto de la memoria de la prefectura de policía de Valparaíso correspondiente al año 1906," *RPV* 1, no. 8, 31 May 1907, 233.

71. Packet beginning with Junta Departamental, Callao, to Director General de Hacienda, 18 Aug. 1891, AGN, Prefecturas, Callao, 1891; Prefectura de Callao to Director de Gobierno, 27 Jan. 1903, AGN, Prefecturas, Callao, 1903; and letter to Director de Gobierno, 1 Jul. 1913, AGN, Prefecturas, Callao, 1913. The "población flotante" is referenced in passing in a letter to the prefect of Callao in 1887. See Manuel Zedoya to Señor Prefecto de la Provincia, 7 Sept. 1887, Anexo no. 4, in "Memoria elevada por el Subprefecto de la provincia de Callao al prefecto," BN-P.

72. See Gabriel Salazar, *Labradores, peones y proletarios: Formación y crisis de la sociedad popular chilena del siglo XIX* (Santiago: LOM, 2000); José Ragas, *Lima Chola: Una historia de la Gran Migración Andina* (Lima: Taurus/Penguin Random House, forthcoming), ch. 2; and Ragas, "Documenting Hierarchies," 175.

73. "La sección de seguridad," *RPV* 1, no. 12, 30 Sept. 1907, 377.

74. Rojas, *Lanchas en la bahía*, 69.

75. "La policía de Valparaíso," *RPV* 1, no. 1, 31 Oct. 1906, 20 ("thousands and thousands of hiding places"); "Criminalidad i policía," *RPV* 1, no. 6, 31 Mar. 1907, 163 ("full of crossroads and intricate pathways"); and "Importante nota," *RPV* 1, no. 10, 31 July 1907, 291 ("twice as difficult").

76. Prefectura de Policía to Intendente de la Provinica, Valparaíso, 13 Feb. 1903, ANH, IV, vol. 1049, no. 84; and Prefectura de Policia to Intedente de la Provincia, Valparaíso, 4 Dec. 1903, ANH, IV, vol. 1056, no. 710.

77. Ministerio de Gobierno, Dirección de Policía, to Prefecto de la Provincia Constitucional del Callao, Lima, 10 Mar. 1876, AHM, Prefecturas, Ministerio de Gobierno, 1876, caja 25, sobre 191, fol. 68; and Ministerio de Gobierno, Dirección de Policía, to Prefecto de la Provincia Constitucional del Callao, Lima, 18 Mar. 1876, AHM, Prefecturas, Ministerio de Gobierno, 1876, caja 25, sobre 191, fol. 84.

78. J. Forbin, "El delincuente y el perro detective," *RPV* 6, no. 76, 1 May. 1912, 35–43; and "El perro como ajente de seguridad," *RPV* 2, no. 23, 31 Aug. 1908, 28–29.

79. See, for instance, Sara E. Johnson, *The Fear of French Negroes: Transcolonial Collaboration in the Revolutionary Americas* (Berkeley: University of California Press, 2012), ch. 1.

80. "Proyecto de organización del servicio veternario," *RPV* 2, no. 24 [*sic*, should be 25], 31 Oct. 1908, 25–28 (quote on 25); Gabriel Varela O., "Los perros policías," *RPV* 4, no. 54, 1 Mar. 1911, 16–20 (18 on dogs removing the distraction). Comparatively, while some people in Buenos Aires viewed the use of automobiles as a new technology to help officers better police the city, others saw this new method of patrolling as creating a physical distance between police officers and the community. See Caimari, *While the City Sleeps*, 116–17.

81. It is worth noting that the police, especially those lower down in the hierarchy, were entrusted with policing people who were in large part their neighbors and people possibly within their social circles. If the ever-changing population of port cities worried some within the police, the inability of the police to maintain a consistent labor force themselves also grew worrisome. Police officers received low wages—Vania Cárdenas Muñoz compares a guardián's pay in 1907 of $2 per day to a carpenter's pay of $10–12 per day, or a guardián in 1912 making $4 per day compared to a gañán

at the same pay—and were expected to cover large areas of the city. As Cárdenas Muñoz notes, "In this sense, and despite the attempts to physically and ideologically separate the guardián from workers, their material conditions of life imposed themselves on the guardianes, to the point that sometimes the higher command recognized the equivalence in life between the guardián and worker." Even though they were tasked with tracking suspected criminals and labor organizers, their own labor conditions led them to the idea of a police mutual aid society. On police pay, the comparisons, and living conditions in Valparaíso, see Cárdenas Muñoz, *El orden gañán*, 237–64 (240 and 244 for comparisons; quote on 264). On possibly creating a mutual aid society (or things of a similar nature) for police officers, see "Interesante proyecto," *RPV* 2, no. 21, 30 June 1908, 257–65; Alberto Navarrete, "Necesidad de una asociación mútua en el personal de policía," *RPV* 2, no. 21, 30 June 1908, 268–72 (with explicit references to La Protectora de Empleados and the Asociación de Artesanos as examples); and "La justicia en la cuestión social," *RPV* 4, no. 66, 1 Sept. 1911, 1–4.

82. On the strike, see Blanchard, *Origins of the Peruvian Labor Movement*, 89–90.

83. Paulo Drinot, *The Allure of Labor: Workers, Race, and the Making of the Peruvian State* (Durham, NC: Duke University Press, 2011), 19–27, 54.

84. Ragas, "Documenting Hierarchies," ch. 3.

85. Drinot, *Allure of Labor*, 54–55. On the Labor Sections, see Aguirre, *Criminals of Lima*, 73; and Blanchard, *Origins of the Peruvian Labor Movement*, 89–91.

86. Jefe de la Oficina del Trabajo to Director de la Sección Obrera, Santiago, 23 June 1913, no. 219; Pedro Saenz (jefe de la Sección Obrera) to Frias Collao (Jefe de la Oficina del Trabajo), Lima, 26 July 1913; Saenz to Collao, Lima, 5 Aug. 1913, all in ARNAD, DT, vol. 23.

87. See Consulado del Perú to Señor Ministro, Valparaíso, 24 July 1890, AMRREE-P, correspondencia, caja 352, carpeta 3, Código 8-10-G, 1890, fol. 63–65, 84; and Consulado General de la República del Perú to Ministro de Relaciones Exteriores, Valparaíso, 9 June 1903, fol. 99–102; E. Oyanguren to Ministro de Relaciones Extereiores, Valparaíso, 25 June 1903, fol. 131; Oyanguren to Ministro de Relaciones Exteriores, Valparaíso, 24 Aug. 1903, fol. 170, these last three in AMRREE-P, correspondencia, caja 523, carpeta 3, Código 8-10-G, 1903.

88. Pedro Saenz to Señor Sub-Prefecto é Intendente de Policía, 18 July 1913, AGN, Republicano, Prefecturas, Lima, 1913.

89. Police spy reports are scattered throughout the volumes of the Intendencia de Valparaíso in the ANH. Workers were cognizant of the use of spies, too. Manuel Rojas, for instance, wrote about the use of secret police agents. See Rojas, *Hijo del ladrón*, 341–42; and Cárdenas Muñoz, *El orden gañán*, 115.

90. DeShazo, *Urban Workers*, 183; and "Manifiesto de los I.W.W. contestando al manifiesto desafío y amenaza de la Asociación del Trabajo que dirige el ex-Capitán del ejército y ex-prefecto de Valapraíso Enrique Caballero," in Triviño, *La I.W.W.*, 28.

91. "La huelga del personal Astillero Las Habas," *El Obrero Metalurgico*, no. 5, 19 Nov. 1924, 1–2 (quote on 2).

92. Informe sobre visita Policia de San Antonio i desorganización de ésta, Santiago, 6 Nov. 1917, ANH, Fondo Juan Luis Sanfuentes Andonaegui, vol. 8, fol. 151–53.

93. Prefectura de Policía to Intendente de la Provincia, Valparaíso, 10 June 1903, no. 256; Prefectura de Policía to Intendente de la Provincia, Valparaíso, 10 June 1903, no. 258, both in ANH, IV, vol. 1051.

94. Prefectura de Policía to Intendente, Valparaíso, 17 July 1907, ANH, IV, vol. 1203, no. 453. See also "Importante nota," *RPV* 1, no. 10, 31 July 1907, 293.

95. Letter to Intendente, Valparaíso, 19 Mar. 1913, no. 184; letter to Intendente de Valparaíso, Valparaíso, 28 Mar. 1913, both in ANH, IV, vol. 1332.

96. C. A. Velarde (Prefectura de Callao) to Director de Gobierno, 25 Jan. 1913, AGN, Prefecturas, Callao, 1913.

97. "Memoria de la Policía de Valparaíso correspondiente a 1912," *RPV* 7, no. 88, 1 May 1923, 9–10.

98. On the strikes, see Ministerio de Marina to Ministro de Relaciones Esteriores, Santiago, 9 Jan. 1920, no. 15; Ministerio de Marina to Director Jeneral de la Armada, Santiago, 27 Jan. 1920, no. 43; Ministerio de Marina to Cap. de Navio don Agustin Dagnino, Santiago, 27 Jan. 1920, no. 45; Ministerio de Marina to Director Jral. de la Armada, Santiago, 12 July 1920, no. 299; Ministerio de Marina to Ministro del Interior, Santiago, 10 Aug. 1920, no. 399, all in ARNAD, MM, vol. 2358. On the 1920 actions against subversives, see Craib, *Cry of the Renegade*. On the radio-telegraphy equipment and installation, see Ministerio de Marina to Ministro del Interior, Santiago, 28 Aug. 1920, no. 369; Ministerio de Marina to Director Jeneral de Obras Públicas, Santiago, 2 Sept. 1920, no. 377; Ministerio de Marina to Director de Obras Públicas, Santiago, 20 Oct. 1920, no. 458 ("urgent necessity); Ministerio de Marina to Director Jral. de Obras Públicas, Santiago, 6 Dec. 1920, no. 522; Ministerio de Marina to Director Jeneral de Obras Públicas, Santiago, 31 Dec. 1920, all in ARNAD, MM, vol. 2358. Lila Caimari notes that state projects of expanding roads and maps in early twentieth-century Buenos Aires, unbeknownst to those pushing for this expansion, helped criminals to spread out geographically. Whereas this paragraph and other parts of the chapter emphasize new technology in response to crime or labor organizing, the relationship between the two should be seen as constantly in motion. See Caimari, *While the City Sleeps*, 27–28.

99. Lyle N. McAlister, *The "Fuero Militar" in New Spain, 1764–1800* (Gainesville: University of Florida Press, 1957), 15 ("class apart"). See also Leon G. Campbell, *The Military and Society in Colonial Peru* (Philadelphia: American Philosophical Society, 1978), 40, 193–94, 204–6; Mónica Ricketts, *Who Should Rule? Men of Arms, the Republic of Letters, and the Fall of the Spanish Empire* (New York: Oxford University Press, 2017), 77–80.

100. James A. Wood, "The Burdens of Citizenship: Artisans, Elections, and the Fuero Militar in Santiago de Chile, 1822–1851," *Americas* 58, no. 3 (Jan. 2002): 443–69.

101. Letter to Ministro de Guerra y Marina, Paita, 17 Aug. 1917, AHM, EA, Gremios de trabajadores marítimos de Paita, 1894–1963, caja G-4, sobre G-74 (hereafter cited as GTMP), fol. 9–10. The letter was signed by seventeen workers.

102. César A. Valdivieso, Paita, 17 June 1917, fol. 14; E. G. Cole, Capitan del V. "Chile," Paita, 17 June 1917, fol. 16, both in AHM, EA, GTMP.
103. Antecedentes de los matriculados de Paita separados del Gremio, AHM, EA, GTMP, fol. 26–28.
104. Antecedentes de los matriculados de Paita separados del Gremio, AHM, EA, GTMP, fol. 26–28. Additionally, two marineros were brought to the "Juzgado respectivo" and expelled from their gremio.
105. For a view of this process in Lima, see Aguirre, *Criminals of Lima*, chs. 1–3.
106. *Conferencia internacional sudámericana de policía*, 128.
107. *Conferencia internacional sudámericana de policía*, 140.
108. *Conferencia internacional sudámericana de policía*, 7.
109. On this in Mollendo, Peru, see chapter 4.
110. Nils G. Boklund to Capitan de Navío, Director de Capitanías, Callao, 13 Sept. 1920, fol. 52; El Capitán de Navio, Director de Capitanes, Callao, 16 Sept. 1920, fol. 52–53, both in AHM, EA, Compañía Sudamericana de Vapores, 1874–1948, caja C-4, sobre C-101.
111. Camilo Plaza Armijo y Victor Muñoz Cortés, "La ley de residencia de 1918 y la persecución a los extranjeros subversivos," *Revista de Derechos Fundamentales*, no. 10 (2013): 106–36; Verónica Valdivia Ortiz de Zárate, "'Los tengo plenamente identificados': Seguridad interna y control social en Chile, 1918–1925," *Historia* 50, no. 1 (Jan.–June 2017): 241–71; Craib, *Cry of the Renegade*; and Craib, "Students, Anarchists and Categories of Persecution in Chile, 1920."
112. Antonio Santibáñez Rojas, "La del Anarquismo," *RPV* 3, no. 39, 31 Dec. 1909, 2 ("immediately"), 1 ("horda anarquista"); Alberto Morales Munizaga, "El anarquismo," *RPV* 6, no. 80, 1 Sept. 1912, 23; and Plaza Armijo y Muñoz Cortés, "La ley de residencia," 119.
113. Antonio Santibáñez Rojas, "Aumento de personal y de atribuciones," *RPV* 4, no. 46, 31 July 1910, 1–5 (quote on 1).
114. Blanchard, *Origins of the Peruvian Labor Movement*, 62.
115. Letter to Director de Gobierno, 17 Nov. 1913, Lima, AGN, Prefecturas, Ministerios, Relaciones Exteriores, 1913. The initial idea behind this movement of people came from the Peruvian consulate in Antofagasta, Chile, and the letter was also sent to the prefectures in Piura, Tumbes, Lambayeque, Libertad, Callao, Ancash, Lima, Ica, Arequipa, and Tacna.
116. See Antonio Santibáñez Rojas, "El anarquismo, los fraudes electorales y el rejistro de habitantes," *RPV* 6, no. 75, 1 Apr. 1912, 1–9; Hugo de la Fuente Silva, "El Anarquismo," *RPV* 6, no. 80, 1 Sept. 1912, 22–29; Antonio Santibáñez Rojas, "Nuevas advertencias del anarquismo," *RPV* 6, no. 83, 1 Dec. 1912, 1–7; E. Alejandro Peralta R., "Las huelgas y la Policía," *RPV* 7, no. 91, 1 Aug. 1913, 46–50; Antonio Santibáñez Rojas, "La Patria," *RPV* 7, no. 92, 1 Sept. 1913, 17–21; and Arturo Calvo Fontecilla, "Nuestra primera victíma del anarquismo," *RPV* 8, no. 107, Dec. 1914, 43–44.
117. Hugo de la Fuente Silva, "El anarquismo," *RPV* 6, no. 80, 1 Sept. 1912, 22–29.
118. Barros Ovalle, "La filiación antropometrica en la sección de seguridad," *RPV* 1, no. 3, 31 Dec. 1906, 83.

119. Peralta R., "Las huelgas y la Policía," 49 ("gangrena social que se llama anarquismo"). Many had linked crime and disease around the turn of the century, too. For a view of this in Mexico, for instance, see Nesvig, "Lure of the Perverse," 9, 15, 18–19.

120. "El Prefecto de policía de Santiago," *RPV* 2, no. 18, 13 Mar. 1908, 185–88; "El Sarjento Pedro José Muñoz," *RPV* 2, no. 21, 30 June 1908, 10–11; Antonio Santibáñez Rojas, "Un gran ejemplo," *RPV* 7, no. 93, 1 Oct. 1913, 19–21; and Gumecindo Vallejos S., "A los héroes del 21 de Mayo de 1879," *RPV* 7, no. 100, May 1914, 70–74. On civilian-military overlap in policing in a different context, see Micol Seigel, *Violence Work: State Power and the Limits of Police* (Durham, NC: Duke University Press, 2018).

121. See, for instance, the story of Argentine Julio R. Barcos and Puerto Rican Nemecio Canales supposedly being funded by anarchists in Buenos Aires *and* the Peruvian state. Legación de Chile en Panamá to Ministro de Relaciones Exteriores, 15 Sept. 1920, AMRREE-C, FH, vol. 840, Confidencial no. 2; Legación de Chile en Panamá to Ministro de Relaciones Exteriores, 1 Sept. 1920, AMRREE-C, FH, vol. 841, no. 10; and Legación de Chile to Ministro de Relaciones Exteriores, 16 Sept. 1920, AMRREE-C, FH, vol. 841, no. 11. See also the copy sent to the Ministerio del Interior dated 28 Oct. 1920, AMRREE-C, FH, vol. 842.

122. Legación de Chile en Montevideo to Ministro de Relaciones Exteriores, 9 Feb. 1920, no. 6; Legación de Chile to Ministro de Relaciones Exteriores, 9/10 Feb. 1920, no. 7; Ministerio de Relaciones Exteriores to Legación de Chile, 13 Feb. 1920, no. 8; Legación de Chile to Ministro de Relaciones Exteriores, 14 Feb. 1920, no. 9; Ministerio de Relaciones Exteriores to Legación de Chile, 26 Feb. 1920, no. 15, all in AMRREE-C, FH, vol. 841. For the life of Rebosio, see Muñoz Cortés, *Cuando la patria mata*.

123. Seigel, *Violence Work*, 10.

EPILOGUE: OF PARALLELS

1. "Desde hoy el Perú litigará en La Haya," *El Comercio* (Lima), 16 Jan. 2008.
2. "'Será el más grande desafio professional de mi carrera,'" *El Comercio*, 21 Dec. 2007.
3. "Seis años podría durar procesos ante La Haya," *El Comercio*, 22 Dec. 2007; and "Wagner: 'No vamos a pelearnos con Chile,'" *El Comercio*, 6 Jan. 2008.
4. Cecilia Rosales Ferroyros and Rocío La Rosa, "Alan García lamenta que no se haya logrado una solución por la vía bilateral," *El Comercio*, 17 Jan. 2008.
5. "Acuerdo Nacional respalda las gestiones ante La Haya," *El Comercio*, 11 Jan. 2008; and "Respuesta de Chile no afectaría las relaciones," *El Comercio*, 9 Dec. 2007.
6. Cordelia Freeman, "Historical Everyday Geopolitics on the Chile-Peru Border," *Bulletin of Latin American Research* 39, no. 4 (Sept. 2020): 439–52; and Skuban, *Lines in the Sand*, 227n12.
7. Hugh O'Shaughnessy, *Pinochet: The Politics of Torture* (New York: New York University Press, 2000), 16.

8. Augusto Pinochet Ugarte, *Guerra del Pacífico, 1879: Primeras operaciones terrestres (antecedentes, organización de las fuerzas, desarrollo de la campaña y ocupación del departamento de Tarapacá)* (Santiago: Instituto Geográfico Militar, 1972).

9. *Memorial of the Government of Peru, Maritime Dispute (Peru v. Chile)*, International Court of Justice (hereafter cited as ICJ), 20 Mar. 2009, 5–7, 76, 118, 127, 137, 147.

10. *Memorial of the Government of Peru*, ICJ, 232.

11. *Memorial of the Government of Peru*, ICJ, 237.

12. *Counter-Memorial of the Government of Chile, Maritime Dispute (Peru v. Chile)*, ICJ, 9 Mar. 2010, 50–55 (quote on 55).

13. *Counter-Memorial of the Government of Chile*, ICJ, 16, 65–71.

14. *Counter-Memorial of the Government of Chile*, ICJ, 7, 97–105.

15. *Memorial of the Government of Peru*, ICJ, 33 ("disrupting"), 44 ("Tacna's natural harbor").

16. *Memorial of the Government of Peru*, ICJ, 22, 27.

17. *Memorial of the Government of Peru*, ICJ, 37.

18. *Counter-Memorial of the Government of Chile*, ICJ, 26.

19. *Counter-Memorial of the Government of Chile*, ICJ, 26–27.

20. *Counter-Memorial of the Government of Chile*, ICJ, 26, 26n81; and Aljovín de Losada and Cavieres Figueroa, "Reflexiones."

21. Emilio Camarcho, "La frontera que no los separa," *La República* (Lima), 2 Dec. 2012, https://larepublica.pe/archivo/677311-la-frontera-que-no-los-separa. Thank you to Tilsa Ponce Romero for calling my attention to this article in 2012.

22. Aljovín de Losada and Cavieres Figueroa, "Reflexiones," 13; and Parodi Revoredo y González Miranda, "Introducción," 12.

# BIBLIOGRAPHY

## ARCHIVES

**Amsterdam, Netherlands**
International Institute of Social History (IISH)
    Diego Abad de Santillán Papers

**Arequipa, Peru**
Archivo Regional de Arequipa (ARA)
    Prefectura

**Callao, Peru**
Archivo Histórico de Marina (AHM)
    Buques
    Capitanías
    Expedientes Administrativos (EA)
    Prefecturas

**Lima, Peru**
Archivo de la Facultad de Medicina de San Marcos (AFMSM)
    Documentos Recibidos (DR)
    Libros de Actas
Archivo del Ministerio de Relaciones Exteriores (AMRREE-P)
    Correspondencia
Archivo General de la Nación, Republicano (AGN)
    Ministerio de Fomento
    Ministerio de Justicia, Beneficencia e Instrucción (MJBI)
    Prefecturas
Archivo Histórico de la Municipalidad de Lima (AHML)
    Higiene y Vacunas
Biblioteca Nacional (BN-P)

Santiago, Chile
Archivo del Ministerio de Relaciones Exteriores (AMRREE-C)
　Fondo Histórico (FH)
　Fondo Perú (FP) (The Fondo Perú in the Archivo del Ministerio de Relaciones Exteriores contains volumes on Chilean foreign relations in and relative to Peru. Unfortunately, this collection is closed to the public. The director of the archive did let me see two volumes, though. If this collection becomes open to the public, it will undoubtedly reveal new insights into Peru-Chile relations.)
Archivo Nacional de la Administración (ARNAD)
　Dirección del Trabajo (DT)
　Ministerio del Interior (MI)
　Ministerio de Marina (MM)
　Ministerio de Relaciones Exteriores (MRREE)
Archivo Nacional Histórico (ANH)
　Cabildo y Municipalidad de Valparaíso (CMV)
　Fondo Emilio Bello Codesido
　Fondo Juan Luis Sanfuentes Andonaegui
　Intendencia de Valparaíso (IV)
　Juzgado Civil de Valparaíso
　Juzgado del Crimen de Arica
　Juzgado del Crimen de Iquique
　Juzgado del Crimen de Valparaíso
　Juzgado de Letras Civil de Valparaíso
　Ministerio del Interior (MI)
　Ministerio de Marina (MM)
　Ministerio de Relaciones Exteriores (MRREE)
Biblioteca Nacional (BN-C)

### PERIODICALS

*Adelante* (Rancagua), 1926
*Bandera Roja* (Concepción), 1926
*Boletín de Medicina* (Santiago), 1886-1888
*Campana Nueva* (Valparaíso), 1924-1925
*El Comercio* (Lima), select dates, 2007-2008
*El Hambriento* (Lima), 1905-1910
*El Mercurio* (Valparaíso), select dates
*El Obrero Metalurgico* (Valparaíso), 1924-1926
*El Perú Ilustrado* (Lima), select dates
*La Crónica Médica* (Lima), 1886-1888
*La Voz del Mar* (Valparaíso), 1924-1927
*La Voz de los Mártires* (Valparaíso), 1911

*Mar y Tierra* (Valparaíso), 1917
*Revista de Policia* (Lima), 1910
*Revista de la Policia de Valparaíso* (Valparaíso), 1906-1914, 1921-1922
*The South Pacific Mail* (select dates in 1913, 1925)

PRINTED PRIMARY SOURCES

Acevedo L., Arturo. *El Problema de las Faenas Marítimas en la Zona Salitrera: El sistema de redondilla y la nueva reglamentación*. Talcahuano: Libreria Imprenta "Moderna," 1923.
*Actas de la Junta General de Salubridad mandadas publicar por acuerdo de la misma*. Santiago de Chile: Imprenta Nacional, 1887.
Alegre y Pacheco, Marino C. *Los delincuentes tatuados de la penitenciaria nacional*. Lima: Tipografia y Encuadernación de la Penitenciaria, 1917.
*Anuario estadistico de la República de Chile correspondiente a los años 1887–1888*. Tomo 26. Valparaíso: Imprenta de "La Patria," 1892.
*Anuario estadistico de la República de Chile correspondiente a los años 1888–1889*. Tomo 27. Valparaíso: Imprenta de "La Patria," 1894.
Barros Ovalle, Pedro N. *Manual de antropometría criminal i jeneral, escrito segun el sistema de A. Bertillon para la identificación personal i destinado al uso de los establecimientos penitenciarios, autoridades judiciales, compañías de seguros, cuerpos, armadaos, etc., etc.* Santiago de Chile: Imprenta de Enrique Blanchard Chessi, 1900.
Callirgos M., Benigno A. "Algunas consideraciones sobre una estadistica venérea del Callao." Thesis, Universidad Nacional Mayor de San Marcos, Facultad de Medicina, 1933.
*Censo de la Provincia Constitucional del Callao, 20 de Junio de 1905*. Lima: Imprenta y Librería de San Pedro, 1906.
Centro Internacional Obrero de Solidaridad Latino-Americana. *Confraternidad Obrera Chileno-Peruana. Una Actuación Histórica, 1913–1917*. Lima: Imprenta "Lux" de E. L. Castro, 1928.
Coloma Gygax, José, ed. *Le huelga de Mollendo de 1918: Un antecedente del establecimiento de la jornada de las ocho horas en el Perú*. Lima: Instituto Latinoamericano de Cultura y Desarrollo, 2005.
*Conclusiones aprobadas por el Congreso Sanitario Americano de Lima, 1888*. Santiago de Chile: Imprenta Nacional, 1888.
*Conferencia internacional sudámericana de policía*. Buenos Aires: Imprenta de José Tragant, 1920.
*Convenio celebrado entre las Policías de La Plata y Buenos Aires (Argentina)—de Rio de Janeiro (Brasil)—de Santiago de Chile y de Montevideo (R. O. del Uruguay)*. Buenos Aires: Imprenta y Encuadernación de la Policía de la Capital Federal, 1905.
Corradi, Juan. "El colera morbu asiatico y la Fiebre Amarailla ¿son contagiosos?" Tesis de bachiller, Facultad de Medicina, Universidad Nacional Mayor de San Marcos, 1857.

Darío, Rubén. "The Bale." In Ilan Stavans, ed., *Selected Writings*. Translated by Andrew Hurley, Greg Simon, and Steven F. White. New York: Penguin Books, 2005.

Díaz, Wenceslao. *Memoria de la comisión directiva del servicio del cólera presentad al señor ministro del Interior*. Santiago de Chile: Imprenta Nacional, 1888.

*Documentos parlamentarios: Discursos de apertura en las sesiones del congreso i memorias ministeriales en los dos primeros años del Segundo quinquenio de la administraición Montt (1857–1858)*. Tomo 6. Santiago: Imprenta del Ferrocarril, 1859.

Etchepare, Julio. "Informes referentes a la morbosidad infecto-contagiosa—disposiciones y procedimientos adoptados por la administración sanitaria para su obtención." In *Proceedings of the Second Pan American Scientific Congress*, 9:352–54. Washington, DC: Government Printing Office, 1917.

Fry, E. C., ed. *Tom Barker and the I.W.W*. Canberra: Australian Society for the Study of Labour History, 1965.

Garces, Daniel. "La mentalidad del marinero peruano y su valoración por los test de inteligencia." Lima: Universidad Nacional Mayor de San Marcos, Facultad de Medicina, 1925.

González Prada, Manuel. *Obras*. Tomo 1, vols. 1–2. Prólogo y notas de Luis Alberto Sánchez. Lima: Ediciones COPÉ, 1985.

Hutchinson, Thomas Joseph. *Two Years in Peru, with Exploration of Its Antiquities*. 2 vols. London: Sampson Low, Martson Low, and Searle, 1873.

Levano, Delfin. *Mi palabra: La jornada de ocho horas y el boicot de la casa Duncan fox del Callao*. Segunda edición. Lima: La Protesta, 1934.

Lévano La Rosa, César, and Luis Tejada Ripalda, comps. *La Utopia libertaria en el Perú: Manuel y Delfin Lévano, obra completa*. Lima: Fondo Editorial del Congreso del Perú, 2006.

Matto, David. "Bacteriologia sobre el bacio del tetano." Tesis presentada para optar en grado de doctor de medicina. Lima: Imprenta de Benito Gil, 1891.

Matto, David. *La Enseñanza Médica en el Perú*. Lima: Tip. El Lucero, 1908.

Maurtua, Lizando. "Estudios médicos-sociales del Callao." Tesis de Bachiller, Facultad de Medicina, Universidad Nacional Mayor de San Marcos, 1885.

Medina, Casimiro, ed. *La verruga peruana y Daniel A. verruga peruana, estudiante de la facultad de medicina muerto el 5 de Octubre de 1885*. Lima: Imprenta del Estado, 1886.

*Memoria del Ministro de Gobierno, Policía, Correos y Telégrafos, 1911*. Lima: Imprenta Americana, 1911.

Morales Pacheco, Isais. "La fiebre amarilla del Callao en los años de 1888 y 1889." Tesis de bachiller, Facultad de Medicina, Universidad Mayor de San Marcos, 1891.

Muñoz, Andrés S. *Congreso Sanitario Americano de Lima reunido en el año de 1888*. Lima: Imprenta de Torres Aguirre, 1889.

Portocarrero, Julio. *Sindicalismo Peruano: Primera etapa, 1911–1930*. Lima: Editorial Gráfica Labor, 1987.

Puga Borne, F. *Como se evite el cólera: Estudio de hijiene popular*. Santiago de Chile: Imprenta Nacional, 1886.

*Reglamento del Ramo de Policía relativa a la prostitución*. Valparaíso: Imprenta del Mercurio, 1868.

Report of the Delegates of the United States to the Pan-American Scientific Congress, Held at Santiago, Chile December 25, 1908, to January 5, 1909. Washington, DC: Government Printing Office, 1909.

Resúmenes del Censo de las Provincias de Lima y Callao, leventado el 17 de Diciembre de 1920. Lima: Imprenta Torres Aguirre, 1921.

Rojas, Manuel. *Hijo del ladrón*. 1951. In *Tiempo irremediable*, vol. 1. Santiago: Zig-Zag, 2015.

———. *Lanchas en la bahía*. 1932. Santiago: Tajamar Editores, 2015.

———. *Mejor que el vino*. 1958. In *Tiempo irremediable*, vol. 2. Santiago: Zig-Zag, 2015.

———. *La oscura vida radiante*. 1971. In *Tiempo irremediable*, vol. 2. Santiago: Zig-Zag, 2015.

———. *Sombras contra el muro*. 1964. In *Tiempo irremediable*, vol. 1. Santiago: Zig-Zag, 2015.

———. "El vaso de leche." 1929. In *Cuentos*. Santiago: Ediciones Universidad Alberto Hurtado, 2016.

Salazar, A. E., and C. Newman. *Notas sobre el epirilo del cólera asiático (Bacillus Coma de Koch)*. Valparaíso: Imprenta del Universo de G. Helfmann, 1888.

Triviño, Armando. *La I.W.W. en la teoría y en la práctica*. Santiago: Editorial Lux, 1925.

Vicuña Cifuentes, Julio. *Coa. Jerga de los delincuentes chilenos: Estudio y vocabulario*. Santiago: Imprenta Universitaria, 1910.

Villanueva, Augusto, and Carlos Killing. *Reglamento de la Junta de Salubridad de Valparaíso e informe, presentado por los señores Augusto Villanueva i Cárlos Killing relativo a la epidemia del "cólera" i algunos medios para la desinfección*. Valparaíso: Imprenta del Nuevo Mercurio, 1887.

SECONDARY SOURCES

Abrams, Philip. "Notes on the Difficulty of Studying the State." *Journal of Historical Sociology* 1, no. 1 (March 1998): 58–89.

Abu-Lughod, Janet L. *Before European Hegemony: The World System, A.D. 1250–1350*. New York: Oxford University Press, 1989.

Aguerregaray, Rosana. "Representaciones, discursos y practices profilácticas durante la epidemia de cólera (1886–1887, Mendoza, Argentina)." *História, Ciências, Saúde–Manguinhos* 26, no. 1 (January–March 2019): 187–207.

Aguirre, Carlos. *The Criminals of Lima and Their Worlds: The Prison Experience, 1850–1935*. Durham, NC: Duke University Press, 2005.

Ahuja, Ravi. "Mobility and Containment: The Voyages of South Asian Seamen, c. 1900–1960." *International Review of Social History* 51, no. S14 (December 2006): 111–14.

Alcalá Ferráez, Carlos. "De miasmas a mosquitos: El pensamiento médico sobre la fiebre amarilla en Yucatán, 1890–1920." *História, Ciências, Saúde–Maguinhos* 19, no. 1 (January–March 2012): 71–87.

Alegre Henderson, Magally. "Androginopolis: Dissident Masculinities and the Creation of Republican Peru (Lima, 1790–1850)." PhD diss., Stony Brook University, 2012.
Alimahomen-Wilson, Jake, and Immanuel Ness, eds. *Choke Points: Logistics Workers Disrupting the Global Supply Chain*. London: Pluto Press, 2018.
Aljovín de Losada, Cristóbal, and Eduardo Cavieres Figueroa. "Reflexiones para un análisis histórico de Chile-Perú en el siglo XIX y la Guerra del Pacífico." In *Chile-Perú, Perú-Chile en el siglo XIX*, compiled by Cavieres Figueroa and Aljovín de Losada, 11–24. Valparaíso, Chile: Ediciones Universitarias de Valparaíso, 2005.
Álvares, Ignacio. "Un puñado de pistas para entrar a *Tiempo irremediable*." In Manuel Rojas, *Tiempo irremediable*, vol. 1. Santiago: Zig-Zag, 2015.
Amrith, Sunil. *Crossing the Bay of Bengal: The Furies of Nature and the Fortunes of Migrants*. Cambridge, MA: Harvard University Press, 2011.
Anderson, Benedict. *Imagined Communities: Reflections on the Origin and Spread of Nationalism*. Rev. ed. New York: Verso, 2006. Originally published 1983.
———. *Under Three Flags: Anarchism and the Anti-Colonial Imagination*. New York: Verso, 2005.
Araya Saavedra, Mario. "Los *wobblies* criollos: Fundación y ideología de la Región chilena de la *Industrial Workers of the World*–IWW (1919–1927)." Tesis para optar al grado de Licenciado en Historia, Universidad de Arte y Ciencias Sociales (Arcis), 2008.
Arguedas, José María. *Deep Rivers*. Translated by Frances Horning Barraclough. Austin: University of Texas Press, 1978.
Arnold, David. *Colonizing the Body: State Medicine and Epidemic Disease in Nineteenth-century India*. Berkeley: University of California Press, 1993.
Artaza Barrios, Pablo, Pedro Bravo Elizondo, Luis Castro, Luis A. Galdames Rosas, Cristián Gazmuri, Sergio González Miranda, José Antonion González Pizarro, Sergio Grez Toso, Bernardo Guerrero Jiménez, Hans Gundermann Kröll, Alberto Harambour Ross, María Angélica Illanes, Pedro Milos, Jorge Núñez Pinto, Juan Panadés Vargas, Jorge Pinto Rodríguez, Julio Pinto Vallejos, Gabriel Salazar, Rigoberto Sánchez Fuentes, Isabel Torres Dujisin, Rosa Troncoso de la Fuente, and Peter Winn. *A 90 años de los sucesos de la Escuela Santa María de Iquique*. Santiago: DIBAM / LOM ediciones, 1998.
Bakunin, Michael. *Statism and Anarchy*. Translated and edited by Marshal S. Shatz. New York: Cambridge University Press, 2002.
Ballón Lozada, Héctor. *Cien años de vida política de Arequipa, 1890–1990*. Tomo 2. Arequipa: Universidad Nacional de San Agustín / Talleres Gráficos Flores, 1992.
Bantman, Constance, and Bert Altena. "Introduction: Problematizing Scales of Analysis in Network-Based Social Movements." In *Reassessing the Transnational Turn: Scales of Analysis in Anarchist and Syndicalist Studies*, edited by Constance Bantman and Bert Altena, 3–22. Oakland, CA: AK Press, 2017.
Barragán Romano, Rossana, and Leda Papastefanaki. "Women and Gender in the Mines: Challenging Masculinity through History; An Introduction." *International Review of Social History* 65, no. 2 (August 2020): 191–230.

Bashford, Alison, ed. *Quarantine: Local and Global Histories*. New York: Palgrave Macmillan, 2016.

Bassi, Ernesto. *An Aqueous Territory: Sailor Geographies and New Granada's Transimperial Greater Caribbean World*. Durham, NC: Duke University Press, 2016.

Bauer, Arnold J. "Rural Workers in Spanish America: Problems of Peonage and Oppression." *Hispanic American Historical Review* 59, no. 1 (February 1979): 34–63.

Beattie, Peter. "Conflicting Penile Codes: Modern Masculinity and Sodomy in the Brazilian Military, 1860–1916." In *Sex and Sexuality in Latin America: An Interdisciplinary Reader*, edited by Daniel Balderston and Donna J. Guy, 65–85. New York: New York University Press, 1997.

Beckman, Ericka. "The Creolization of Imperial Reason: Chilean State Racism in the War of the Pacific." *Journal of Latin American Cultural Studies* 18, no. 1 (March 2009): 73–90.

Ben, Pablo. "Plebian Masculinity and Sexual Comedy in Buenos Aires, 1880–1930." *Journal of the History of Sexuality* 16, no. 3 (September 2007): 436–58.

Bennet, Jane. *Vibrant Matter: A Political Ecology of Things*. Durham, NC: Duke University Press, 2010.

Benton, Lauren. *A Search for Sovereignty: Law and Geography in European Empires, 1400–1900*. New York: Cambridge University Press, 2010.

Bergquist, Charles. *Labor in Latin America: Comparative Essays on Chile, Argentina, Venezuela, and Colombia*. Stanford, CA: Stanford University Press, 1986.

Blanchard, Peter. *The Origins of the Peruvian Labor Movement, 1883–1919*. Pittsburgh: University of Pittsburgh Press, 1982.

———. "The Recruitment of Workers in the Peruvian Sierra at the Turn of the Century: The Enganche System." *Inter-American Economic Affairs* 33, no. 3 (Winter 1979): 63–83.

———. *Slavery and Abolition in Early Republican Peru*. Wilmington, DE: Scholarly Resources, 1992.

Bolaño, Roberto. *Distant Star*. Translated by Chris Andrews. New York: New Directions Books, 2004.

Bonilla, Heraclio. "The Indian Peasantry and "Peru" during the War with Chile." In *Resistance, Rebellion, and Consciousness in the Andean Peasant World, 18th to 20th Centuries*, edited by Steve J. Stern, 219-31. Madison: University of Wisconsin Press, 1987

———. *Islay y la economía del sur peruano en el siglo XIX*. Lima: Instituto de Estudios Peruanos, 1973.

———. *La metamorfisis de los Andes: Guerra, economía y sociedad*. La Paz and Cochabamba: Centro de Estudios para la América Andina y Amazónica and Editorial Kipus, 2014.

———. "The War of the Pacific and the National and Colonial Problem in Peru." *Past & Present* 81 (November 1978): 92–118.

Borucki, Alex. "Shipmate Networks and Black Identities in the Marriage Files of Montevideo, 1768–1803." *Hispanic American Historical Review* 93, no. 2 (May 2013): 205–38.

Bowser, Frederick P. *The African Slave in Colonial Peru, 1524–1650*. Stanford, CA: Stanford University Press, 1974.

Braudel, Fernand. *The Mediterranean and the Mediterranean World in the Age of Philip II*. Translated by Sián Reynolds. 2 vols. New York: Harper & Row, 1972–73.

Brennan, James. *The Labor Wars in Córdoba, 1955–1976: Ideology, Work, and Labor Politics in an Argentine Industrial City*. Cambridge, MA: Harvard University Press, 1994.

Briggs, Charles L. "Theorizing Modernity Conspiratorially: Science, Scale, and the Political Economy of Public Discourse in Explanations of a Cholera Epidemic." *American Ethnologist* 31, no. 2 (May 2004): 164–87.

Brown, Jacqueline Nassy. *Dropping Anchor, Setting Sail: Geographies of Race in Black Liverpool*. Princeton, NJ: Princeton University Press, 2005.

Burga, Manuel, and Alberto Flores Galindo. *Apogeo y crisis de la República Aristocrática*. In Alberto Flores Galindo, *Obras Completas*, vol. 2. Lima: Fundación Andina/SUR Casa de Estudios del Socialismo, 1994.

Burton, Valerie. "A Seafaring Historian's Commentary on 'The Body' as a Useful Category for Working-Class History." *Labor: Studies in Working-Class History of the Americas* 4, no. 2 (2007): 55–59.

Cabrera G., Josefina. "El cólera en Chile (1886–1888): Conflicto político y reacción popular." *Anales Chilenos de Historia de la Medicina* 17, no. 1 (2007): 15–29.

Caimari, Lila. *While the City Sleeps: A History of Pistoleros, Policemen, and the Crime Beat in Buenos Aires before Perón*. Translated by Lisa Ubelaker Andrade and Richard Shindell. Oakland: University of California Press, 2017.

Campbell, Leon G. *The Military and Society in Colonial Peru*. Philadelphia: American Philosophical Society, 1978.

Candela, Ana Maria. "Nation, Migration and Governance: Cantonese Migrants to Peru and the making of Overseas Nationalism, 1849–2013." PhD diss., University of California, Santa Cruz, 2013.

Cárdenas Muñoz, Vania. *El orden gañán: Historia Social de la Policía: Valparaíso, 1896–1910*. Concepción, Chile: Ediciones Escaparte, 2013.

Carrasco, Gastón. "Formas de comunidad y prácticas socioafectivas en *Mejor que el vino* de Manuel Rojas." *Anales de literatura chilena* 22, no. 35 (June 2021): 171–78.

Caruso, Laura. *Embarcados: Los trabajadores marítimos y la vida a bordo; Sindicato, empresas y Estado en el puerto de Buenos Aires, 1889–1921*. Buenos Aires: Imago Mundi, 2016.

Cavieres Figueroa, Eduardo. *El comercio chileno en la economía mundo colonial*. Valparaíso: Ediciones Universitarias de Valparaíso de la Universidad Católica de Valparaíso, 1996.

———. "Ni vencedores ni vencidos: La Guerra del Pacifico como análisis de conflico y no del conflicto en sí mismo." In *Ni vencedores ni vencidos: La Guerra del Pacifico en perspectiva histórica*, edited by José Chaupis Torres, Juan Ortiz Benites, and Eduardo Cavieres Figueroa, 9–22. Lima: La Casa del Libro Viejo, 2016.

Cavieres Figueroa, Eduardo, and Cristóbal Aljovín, comps. *Chile-Perú, Perú-Chile en el siglo XIX: La formación del Estado, la economía y la sociedad*. Valparaíso: Ediciones Universitarias de Valparaíso, 2005.

Cayo Córdova, Percy. *Historia marítima del Perú. La República, 1906–1919*. Tomo 13. Lima: Instituto de Estudios Histórico-Marítimos del Perú, 2009.

Cervantes, Miguel de. *The History of That Ingenious Gentleman Don Quijote de la Mancha*. Translated by Burton Raffel. New York: W. W. Norton, 1996.

Chambers, Sarah C. *From Subjects to Citizens: Honor, Gender, and Politics in Arequipa, Peru, 1780–1854*. University Park: Pennsylvania State University Press, 1999.

Chang, Kornel. *Pacific Connections: The Making of the U.S.-Canadian Borderlands*. Berkeley: University of California Press, 2012.

Chappell, David A. *Double Ghosts: Oceanian Voyagers on Euroamerican Ships*. Armonk, NY: M. E. Sharpe, 1997.

———. "Shipboard Relations between Pacific Island Women and Euroamerican Men, 1767–1887." *Journal of Pacific History* 27, no. 2 (December 1992): 131–49.

Chatterjee, Partha. *The Nation and Its Fragments: Colonial and Postcolonial Histories*. Princeton, NJ: Princeton University Press, 1993.

Chaudhuri, K. N. *Trade and Civilization in the Indian Ocean: An Economic History from the Rise of Islam to 1750*. Cambridge: Cambridge University Press, 1985.

Chauncey, George, Jr. "Christian Brotherhood or Sexual Perversion? Homosexual Identities and the Construction of Sexual Boundaries in the World War One Era." *Journal of Social History* 19, no. 2 (Winter 1985): 189–211.

Cid, Gabriel. "De la Araucanía a Lima: Los usos del concepto 'civilización' en la expansión territorial del Estado Chileno, 1855–1883." *Estudios Ibero-Americanos* 38, no. 2 (July/December 2012): 265–83.

Clayton, L. A. "Trade and Navigation in the Seventeenth-Century Viceroyalty of Peru." *Journal of Latin American Studies* 7, no. 1 (May 1975): 1–21.

Cleaver, Harry. *Reading* Capital *Politically*. Oakland, CA: AK Press/Antitheses, 2000.

Cohen, Daniel A., ed. *The Female Marine and Related Works: Narratives of Cross-Dressing and Urban Vice in America's Early Republic*. Amherst: University of Massachusetts Press, 1997.

Cole, Peter. *Dockworker Power: Race and Activism in Durban and the San Francisco Bay Area*. Urbana: University of Illinois Press, 2018.

———. *Wobblies on the Waterfront: Interracial Unionism in Progressive-Era Philadelphia*. Urbana: University of Illinois Press, 2013.

Corbin, Alain. *The Lure of the Sea: The Discovery of the Seaside in the Western World, 1750–1840*. Translated by Jocelyn Phelps. Cambridge, UK: Polity Press, 1994.

Craib, Raymond B. *The Cry of the Renegade: Politics and Poetry in Interwar Chile*. New York: Oxford University Press, 2016.

———. "Students, Anarchists and Categories of Persecution in Chile, 1920." *A Contracorriente: Revista de Historia Social y Literatura en América Latina* 8, no. 1 (2010): 22–60.

Crow, Joanna. "Photographic Encounters: Martín Chambi, Indigeneity and Chile-Peru Relations in the Early Twentieth Century." *Journal of Latin American Studies* 51, no. 1 (February 2019): 31–58.

Cruz-Coke Madrid, Ricardo. *Historia de la medicina chilena*. Santiago de Chile: Editorial Andres Bello, 1995.

Cueto, Marcos. "Stigma and Blame during an Epidemic: Cholera in Peru, 1991." In *Disease in the History of Modern Latin America: From Malaria to AIDS*, edited by Diego Armus, 268–89. Durham, NC: Duke University Press, 2003.

Cueto, Marcos, Jorge Lossio, and Carol Pasco, eds. *El Rastro de la Salud en el Perú*. Lima: Instituto de Estudios Peruanos / Universidad Peruana Cayetano Heredia, 2009.

Cueto, Marcos, and Steven Palmer. *Medicine and Public Health in Latin America: A History*. New York: Cambridge University Press, 2015.

Cueto, Marcos, and Betty Rivera. "Entre la Medicina, el comercio y la política: El cólera y el Congreso Sanitario Americano de Lima, 1888." In *El Rastro de la Salud en el Perú*, edited by Marcos Cueto, Jorge Lossio, and Carol Pasco, 111–49. Lima: Instituto de Estudios Peruanos / Universidad Peruana Cayetano Heredia, 2009.

Cushman, Gregory T. *Guano and the Opening of the Pacific World: A Global Ecological History*. New York: Cambridge University Press, 2013.

Daniel, Evan Matthew. "Rolling for the Revolution: A Transnational History of Cuban Cigar Makers in Havana, Florida, and New York City, 1853–1895." PhD diss., The New School for Social Research, 2010.

Darrigrandi, Claudia. "Cuerpos y trayectos urbanos: Santiago de Chile y Buenos Aires, 1880–1935." PhD diss., University of California, Davis, 2009.

de Angelis, Paula. "Tom Barker and Revolutionary Europe." In *Wobblies of the World: A Global History of the IWW*, edited by Peter Cole, David Struthers, and Kenton Zimmer, 253–61. London: Pluto Press, 2017.

de la Fuente, Alejandro. *Havana and the Atlantic in the Sixteenth Century*. Chapel Hill: University of North Carolina Press, 2008.

Dening, Greg. *Beach Crossings: Voyaging across Times, Cultures, and Self*. Philadelphia: University of Pennsylvania Press, 2004.

———. *Islands and Beaches: Discourses on a Silent Land. Marquesas, 1774–1880*. Melbourne, Australia: Melbourne University Press, 1980.

DeShazo, Peter. *Urban Workers and Labor Unions in Chile, 1902–1927*. Madison: University of Wisconsin Press, 1983.

———. "The Valparaíso Maritime Strike of 1903 and the Development of a Revolutionary Labor Movement in Chile." *Journal of Latin American Studies* 11, no. 1 (May 1979): 145–68.

Devés, Eduardo. *Los que van a morir te saludan: Historia de una masacre; Escuela Santa María, Iquique, 1907*. Santiago: Ediciones Documentas / America Latina Libros / Nuestra America, 1989.

Dimas, Carlos S. "Harvesting Cholera: Fruit, Disease and Governance in the Cholera Epidemic of Tucumán, Argentina, 1867–68." *Journal of Latin American Studies* 49, no. 1 (February 2017): 115–42.

Drinot, Paulo. *The Allure of Labor: Workers, Race, and the Making of the Peruvian State*. Durham, NC: Duke University Press, 2011.

———. "Fighting for a Closed Shop: The 1931 Lima Bakery Workers' Strike." *Journal of Latin American Studies* 35, no. 2 (May 2003): 249–78

———. *The Sexual Question: A History of Prostitution in Peru, 1850s–1950s*. New York: Cambridge University Press, 2020.

———. "Website of Memory: The War of the Pacific (1879–84) in the Global Age of YouTube." *Memory Studies* 4, no. 4 (2011): 370–85.

Echenberg, Myron. *Plague Ports: The Global Urban Impact of Bubonic Plague, 1894–1901*. New York: New York University Press, 2007.

Esenwein, George Richard. *Anarchist Ideology and the Working-Class Movement in Spain, 1868–1898*. Berkeley: University of California Press, 1989.

Evans, Richard J. *Death in Hamburg: Society and Politics in the Cholera Years*. New York: Oxford University Press, 1987.

Fernández, Evan. "Pan-Americanism and the Definition of the Peruvian-Chilean Border, 1883-1929." *Diplomatic History*, forthcoming.

Fernández, Nona. *Space Invaders*. Translated by Natash Wimmer. Minneapolis, MN: Graywolf Press, 2019.

———. *The Twilight Zone*. Translated by Natasha Wimmer. Minneapolis, MN: Graywolf Press, 2021.

Ferraro, Joanne M. "Making a Living: The Sex Trade in Early Modern Venice." *American Historical Review* 123, no. 1 (February 2018): 30–59.

Fink, Leon. *Sweatshops at Sea: Merchant Seamen in the World's First Globalized Industry, from 1812 to the Present*. Chapel Hill: University of North Carolina Press, 2011.

Flores Galindo, Albero. *La Agonía de Mariátegui*. In Alberto Flores Galindo, *Obras Completas*, vol. 2. Lima: Fundación Andina / SUR Casa de Estudios del Socialismo, 1994.

———. *Arequipa y el sur andino: ensayo de historia regional (siglos XVIII–XX)*. Lima: Editorial Horizante, 1977.

Flórez Nohesell, Miguel. *Historia Marítima del Perú. Los Puertos del Perú*. Tomo 1. Lima: Instituto de Estudios Histórico-Marítimos del Perú, 1986.

Frazier, Lessie Jo. *Salt in the Sand: Memory, Violence, and the Nation-State in Chile, 1890 to the Present*. Durham, NC: Duke University Press, 2007.

Freeman, Cordelia. "Historical Everyday Geopolitics on the Chile-Peru Border." *Bulletin of Latin American Research* 39, no. 4 (September 2020): 439–52.

French, John D. "Another *World* History Is Possible: Reflections on the Translocal, Transnational, and Global." In *Workers across the Americas: The Transnational Turn in Labor History*, edited by Leon Fink, 3–11. New York: Oxford University Press, 2011.

Galeano, Diego. "Traveling Criminals and Transnational Police Cooperation in South America, 1890–1920." In *Voices of Crime: Constructing and Contesting Social Control in Modern Latin America*, edited by Luz E. Huertas, Bonnie A. Lucero, and Gregory J. Swedberg. Tucson: University of Arizona Press, 2016.

Gandhi, Leela. *Affective Communities: Anticolonial Thought, Fin-de-Siècle Radicalism, and the Politics of Friendship*. Durham, NC: Duke University Press, 2005.

Gänger, Stefanie. *Relics of the Past: The Collecting and Study of Pre-Columbian Antiquities in Peru and Chile, 1837–1911*. New York: Oxford University Press, 2014.

Garcés Durán, Mario. *Crisis social y motines populares en el 1900*. Segunda edición. Santiago: LOM, 2003.

García-Bryce, Iñigo. *Haya de la Torre and the Pursuit of Power in Twentieth-century Peru and Latin America*. Chapel Hill: University of North Carolina Press, 2018.

García Cáceres, Uriel. "El cólera en la historia de la medicina social peruana: Comentarios sobre un decreto precursor." *Revista Peruana de Medicina Experimental y Salud Pública* 19, no. 2 (April–June 2002): 97–101.

García Ferrari, Mercedes, and Diego Galeano. "Cartografía del *bertillonage*: Circuitos de difusión, usos y resistencias al sistema antropométrico en América Latina." In *Delincuentes, policías y justicias: América Latina, siglos XIX y XX*, edited by Daniel Palma Alvarado, 279–311. Santiago: Ediciones Universidad Alberto Hurtado, 2015.

Gellner, Ernst. *Nations and Nationalism*. Ithaca, NY: Cornell University Press, 1983.

Gill, Lesley. *A Century of Violence in a Red City: Popular Struggle, Counterinsurgency, and Human Rights in Colombia*. Durham, NC: Duke University Press, 2016.

Glasco, Jeffrey D. "'The Seaman Feels Him-self a Man.'" *International Labor and Working-Class History* 66 (Fall 2004): 40–56.

Godoy Orellana, Milton. "'Ha traído hasta nosotros desde territorio enemigo, el alud de la guerra': Confiscación de maquinarias y apropiación de bienes culturales durante la ocupación de Lima, 1881–1883." *Historia* 44, no. 2 (July–December 2011): 287–327.

———. "Los 'colonos polinesios' en Sudamérica: La variante chilena en el tráfico de rapanui a Perú, 1861–1864." In *Américan en diásporas: Esclavitudes y migraciones forzadas en Chile y otras regiones americanas (siglos XVI–XIX)*, edited by Jaime Valenzuela Márque, 469–509. Santiago: RIL editores / Instituto de Historia, Pontificia Universidad Católica de Chile, 2017.

Godoy Sepúlveda, Eduardo A. "Historia e historiografía del anarquismo en Chile (1980–2015)." *Cuadernos de historia* 44 (June 2016): 101–37.

———. *La huelga del mono: Los anarquistas y las movilizaciones contra el retrato obligatorio (Valparaíso, 1913)*. Santiago de Chile: Quimantú, 2014.

Góngora Escobedo, Alvaro. "La epidemia de cólera en Santiago, 1886–1888." *Dimensión histórica de Chile* núm. 10 (1993–94): 108–34.

———. *La prostitución en Santiago, 1813–1931: Visión de las elites*. Santiago: Dirección de Bibliotecas, Archivos y Museos / Centro de Investigaciones Diego Barros Arana, 1994.

Gonzales, Michael J. "Capitalist Agriculture and Labour Contracting in Northern Peru, 1880–1905." *Journal of Latin American Studies* 12, no. 2 (November 1980): 291–315.

———. "Chinese Plantation Workers and Social Conflict in Peru in the Late Nineteenth century." *Journal of Latin American Studies* 21, no. 3 (October 1989): 385–424.

González Miranda, Sergio. *Chilenizando a Tunupa: La escuela pública en el Tarapacá andino (1880–1990)*. Santiago: Dirección de Bibliotecas, Archivos y Museos / Universidad Arturo Prat, 2002.

———. *El dios cautivo: Las Ligas Patrióticas en la chilenización compulsiva de Tarapacá (1910–1922)*. Santiago: LOM, 2004.

———. *La llave y el candado: El conflicto entre Perú y Chile por Tacna y Arica (1883–1929)*. Santiago: LOM, 2008.

González U., Carolina. "Entre 'sodomitas' y 'hombres dignos, trabajadores y honrados': Masculinidades y sexualidades en causas criminales por sodomía (Chile a fines del siglo XIX)." Tesis para optar al grado de Magíster, Universidad de Chile, 2004.

Gootenberg, Paul. *Between Silver and Guano: Commercial Policy and the State in Postindependence Peru*. Princeton, NJ: Princeton University Press, 1989.

———. "Fishing for Leviathans? Shifting Views on the Liberal State and Development in Peruvian History." *Journal of Latin American Studies* 45, no. 1 (February 2013): 121–41.

———. *Imagining Development: Economic Ideas in Peru's "Fictitious Prosperity" of Guano, 1840–1880*. Berkeley: University of California Press, 1993.

———. "Seeing a State in Peru: From Nationalism of Commerce to the Nation Imagined, 1820–1880." In *Studies in the Formation of the Nation-State in Latin America*, edited by James Dunkerley, 254–74. London: Institute of Latin American Studies, 2002.

Gould, Jeffrey. *To Lead as Equals: Rural Protests and Political Consciousness in Chinandega, Nicaragua, 1912–1979*. Chapel Hill: University of North Carolina Press, 1990.

Grandin, Greg. *The Blood of Guatemala: A History of Race and Nation*. Durham, NC: Duke University Press, 2000.

———. *The Empire of Necessity: Slavery, Freedom, and Deception in the New World*. New York: Metropolitan Books, 2014.

Green, James N. *Beyond Carnival: Male Homosexuality in Twentieth-Century Brazil*. Chicago: University of Chicago Press, 1999.

———. *Exile within Exiles: Herbert Daniel, Gay Brazilian Revolutionary*. Durham, NC: Duke University Press, 2018.

———. "'Who Is the Macho Who Wants to Kill Me?' Male Homosexuality, Revolutionary Masculinity, and the Brazilian Armed Struggle of the 1960s and 1970s." *Hispanic American Historical Review* 92, no. 3 (August 2012): 437–69.

Green, James N., and Florence E. Babb. "Introduction." *Latin American Perspectives* 29, no. 2 (March 2002): 3–23.

Grez Toso, Sergio. *La "Cuestión social" en Chile: Ideas y debates precursores (1804–1902)*. Recopilación y estudio crítico. Santiago: Dirección de Bibliotecas, Archivos y Museos / Centro de Investigaciones Diego Barros Arana, 1995.

———. *Los anarquistas y el movimiento obrero: La alborada de "la Idea" en Chile, 1893–1915*. Santiago: LOM, 2007.

Guerra, Lillian. "Gender Policing, Homosexuality and the New Patriarchy of the Cuban Revolution, 1965–70." *Social History* 35, no. 3 (August 2010): 268–89.

Guerra C., Jorge. "Manuel Rojas, primer anarquismo: Recuerdo y relato." *Anales de literatura chilena* 22, no. 35 (June 2021): 191–201.

Gutman, Matthew C. "Introduction: Discarding Manly Dichotomies in Latin America." In *Changing Men and Masculinities in Latin America*, edited by Matthew C. Gutman, 1–26. Durham, NC: Duke University Press, 2003.

Halperin, David M. "How to Do the History of Male Homosexuality." *GLQ: A Journal of Lesbian and Gay Studies* 6, no. 1 (2000): 81–123.

Harper, Tim. *Underground Asia: Global Revolutionaries and the Assault on Empire*. Cambridge, MA: Belknap Press of Harvard University Press, 2021.

Harris Bucher, Gilberto, and Eugenia Garrido Alvarez de la Rivera. *La gente de mar en Chile y el exterior: Aspectos históricos, jurídicos y diplomáticos, 1818–1915; Violencia, expoliaciones, enganches, deserciones, abandonos, postraciones y repatriaciones de tripulaciones en las marinas mercante y de guerra en Chile y el exterior*. Valparaíso: Puntángeles Universidad de Playa Ancha Editorial, 2004.

Harrison, Mark. "Quarantine, Pilgrimage, and Colonial Trade: India 1866–1900." *Indian Economic and Social History Review* 29, no. 2 (1992): 117–44.

Harvey, Kyle. "Engineering Value: The Transandine Railway and the 'Techno-Capital' State in Chile at the End of the Nineteenth Century." *Journal of Latin American Studies* 52, no. 4 (November 2020): 711–33.

———. "Prepositional Geographies: Rebellions, Railroads, and the Transandean, 1830s–1910s." PhD diss., Cornell University, 2019.

Hau'ofa, Epeli. "Our Sea of Islands." *Contemporary Pacific* 6, no. 1 (Spring 1994): 148–61.

Herod, Andrew. "From a Geography of Labor to a Labor Geography: Labor's Spatial Fix and the Geography of Capitalism." *Antipode* 28, no. 1 (January 1997): 1–31.

Hirsch, Steven J. "Peruvian Anarcho-Syndicalism: Adapting Transnational Influences and Forging Counterhegemonic Practices, 1905–1930." In *Anarchism and Syndicalism in the Colonial and Postcolonial World, 1870–1940*, edited by Steven Hirsch and Lucien van der Walt, 227–71. Boston: Brill, 2010.

Horne, Gerald. *The White Pacific: U.S. Imperialism and Black Slavery in the South Seas after the Civil War*. Honolulu: University of Hawaii Press, 2007.

Horowitz, Joel. "Cuando las élites y los trabajadores coincidieron: La resistencia al programa de bienestar patrocinado por el gobierno argentine, 1923–24." *Anuario IEHS*, no. 16 (2001): 109–28.

Huber, Valeska, "The Unification of the Globe by Disease? The International Sanitary Conferences on Cholera, 1851–1894." *Historical Journal* 49, no. 2 (June 2006): 453–76.

Hutchison, Elizabeth Quay. "From 'La Mujer Esclava' to 'La Mujer Limón': Anarchism and the Politics of Sexuality in Early-Twentieth-Century Chile." *Hispanic American Historical Review* 81, nos. 3–4 (August–November 2001): 519–53.

———. *Labors Appropriate to Their Sex: Gender, Labor, and Politics in Urban Chile, 1900–1930*. Durham, NC: Duke University Press, 2001.

Igler, David. *The Great Ocean: Pacific Worlds from Captain Cook to the Gold Rush*. New York: Oxford University Press, 2013.

Illanes Oliva, María Angélica. *Chile des-centrado: Formación socio-cultural republicana y transición capitalista (1810–1910)*. Santiago: LOM, 2003.

———. *Cuerpo y sangre de la política: La construcción histórica de las visitadoras sociales. Chile, 1887–1940*. Santiago: LOM Ediciones, 2006.

———. 1993. *"En el nombre del pueblo, del estado y de la ciencia (...)": Historia social de la salud pública, Chile 1880/1973*. Segundo edición. Santiago: Ministerio de Salud, 2010. Originally published 1993.

Ioannidis, Alexadnder G., Javier Blanco-Portillo, Kara Sandoval, Erika Hagelberg, Juan Francisco Miquel-Poblete, J. Víctor Moreno-Mayar, Juan Esteban Rodríguez-Rodríguez, Consuelo D. Quinto-Cortés, Kathryn Auckland, Tom Parks, Kathryn Robson, Adrian V. S. Hill, María C. Avila-Arcos, Alexandra Sockell, Julian R. Homburger, Genevieve L. Wojcik, Kathleen C. Barnes, Luisa Herrera, Soledad Berríos, Mónica Acuña, Elena Llop, Celeste Eng, Scott Huntsman, Esteban G. Burchard, Christopher R. Gignoux, Lucía Cifuentes, Ricardo A. Verdugo, Mauricio Moraga, Alexander J. Mentzer, Carlos D. Bustamante, and Andrés Moreno-Estrada. "Native American Gene Flow into Polynesia Predating Easter Island Settlement." *Nature* 583 (2020): 572–77.

Jackson, Paul S. B. "Fearing Future Epidemics: The Cholera Crisis of 1892." *Cultural Geographies* 20, no. 1 (2012): 43–65.

James, Daniel. *Resistance and Integration: Peronism and the Argentine Working Class, 1946–1976*. New York: Cambridge University Press, 1993. Originally published 1988.

Johnson, Rashauna. *Slavery's Metropolis: Unfree Labor in New Orleans during the Age of Revolutions*. New York: Cambridge University Press, 2016.

Johnson, Sara E. *The Fear of French Negroes: Transcolonial Collaboration in the Revolutionary Americas*. Berkeley: University of California Press, 2012.

Joseph, Gilbert M., and Daniel Nugent, eds. *Everyday Forms of State Formation: Revolution and the Negotiation of Rule in Modern Mexico*. Durham, NC: Duke University Press, 1994.

Jung, Moon-Kie. *Reworking Race: The Making of Hawaii's Interracial Labor Movement*. New York: Columbia University Press, 2006.

Kiple, Kenneth F. "Cholera and Race in the Caribbean." *Journal of Latin American Studies* 17, no. 1 (May 1985): 157–77.

Kirsch, Scott, and Don Mitchell, "The Nature of Things: Dead Labor, Nonhuman Actors, and the Persistence of Marxism." *Antipode* 36, no. 4 (September 2004): 687–705.

Klaiber, Jeffrey L. "Los 'cholos' y los 'rotos': Actitudes raciales durante la Guerra del Pacífico." *Histórica* 2, no. 1 (July 1978): 27–37.

———. "The Popular Universities and the Origins of Aprismo, 1921–1924." *Hispanic American Historical Review* 55, no. 4 (November 1975): 693–715.

Klubock, Thomas Miller. *Contested Communities: Class, Gender, and Politics in Chile's El Teniente Copper Mine, 1904–1951*. Durham, NC: Duke University Press, 1998.

Krupa, Christopher, and David Nugent, "Off-Centered States: Rethinking State Theory through an Andean Lens." In *State Theory and Andean Politics: New*

*Approaches to the Study of Rule*, edited by Christopher Krupa and David Nugent, 1–31. Philadelphia: University of Pennsylvania Press, 2015.

Lacoste, Pablo. "El arriero y el transporte terrestre en el cono sur (Mendoza, 1780–1800)," *Revista de Indias* 68, no. 244 (2008): 35–68.

Legg, Stephen. "Stimulation, Segregation and Scandal: Geographies of Prostitution Regulation in British India, between Registration (1888) and Suppression (1923)." *Modern Asian Studies* 46, no. 2 (2012): 1459–1505.

León León, Marco Antonio. *Construyendo un sujeto criminal: Criminología, criminalidad y sociedad en Chile. Siglos XIX y XX*. Santiago: Centro de Investigaciones Diego Barros Arana / DIBAM / Editorial Universitaria, 2015.

Linebaugh, Peter, and Marcus Rediker. *The Many-Headed Hydra: Sailors, Slaves, Commoners, and the Hidden History of the Revolutionary Atlantic*. Boston: Beacon Press, 2000.

Lipman, Andrew. *The Saltwater Frontier: Indians and the Contest for the American Coast*. New Haven, CT: Yale University Press, 2015.

Llorca-Jaña, Manuel, and Juan Navarette-Montalvo. "The Chilean Economy during the 1810–1830s and Its Entry into the World Economy." *Bulletin of Latin American Research* 36, no. 3 (July 2017): 345–69.

Lossio, Jorge. *Acequias y galinazos: Salud ambiental en Lima del siglo XIX*. Lima: Instituto de Estudios Peruanos, 2003.

Low, Michael Christopher. "Empire and the Hajj: Pilgrims, Plagues, and Pan-Islam under British Surveillance, 1865–1908." *International Journal of Middle East Studies* 40, no. 2 (2008): 269–90.

Lyons, Clare A. "Mapping an Atlantic Sexual Culture: Homoeroticism in Eighteenth-Century Philadelphia." *William and Mary Quarterly* 60, no. 1 (January 2003): 119–54.

Madrid, Carlos. "Epidemia de cólera en Valparaíso: 1886–1888." *Autoctonía. Revista de Ciencias Sociales e Historia* 1, no. 2 (January 2017): 115–48.

Mallon, Florencia E. "Decoding the Parchments of the Latin American Nation-State: Peru, Mexico and Chile in Comparative Perspective." In *Studies in the Formation of the Nation-State in Latin America*, edited by James Dunkerley, 13–53. London: Institute of Latin American Studies, 2002.

———. *The Defense of Community in Peru's Central Highlands: Peasant Struggle and Capitalist Transition, 1860–1940*. Princeton, NJ: Princeton University Press, 1983.

———. "Nationalist and Antistate Coalitions in the War of the Pacific: Junín and Cajamarca, 1879–1902." In *Resistance, Rebellion, and Consciousness in the Andean Peasant World, 18th to 20th Centuries*, edited by Steve J. Stern, 232–79. Madison: University of Wisconsin Press, 1987.

———. *Peasant and Nation: The Making of Postcolonial Mexico and Peru*. Berkeley: University of California Press, 1995.

Mangan, Jane E. *Trading Roles: Gender, Ethnicity, and the Urban Economy in Colonial Potosí*. Durham, NC: Duke University Press, 2005.

Mannarelli, María Emma. *Limpias y modernas: Genero, hygiene y cultura en la Lima del novicientos*. Lima: Ediciones Flora Tristan, 1999.

Manrique, Nelson. *Campesinado y Nación: Las guerrillas indigenas en la Guerra con Chile*. Lima: Centro de Investigaciones y Capacitación, 1981.
Margarrucci, Ivanna. "Apuntes sobre el movimiento anarquista en Perú y Bolivia, 1880–1930." *Nuevo Mundo Mundos Nuevos*, October 8, 2019, https://doi.org/10.4000/nuevomundo.77382.
Margarrucci, Ivanna, and Eduardo Godoy Sepúlveda. *Anarquismos en confluencia: Chile y Bolivia durante la primera mitad del siglo XX*. Santiago: Editorial Eleutorio, 2018.
Marx, Karl. *Grundrisse: Foundations of the Critique of Political Economy (Rough Draft)*. Translated by Martin Nicolaus. New York: Penguin Books, 1993.
Massey, Doreen. *For Space*. Los Angeles: Sage, 2012.
———. "Space, Place and Gender." In *Space, Place, and Gender*. Minneapolis: University of Minnesota Press, 1994.
Matsuda, Matt K. *Pacific Worlds: A History of Seas, Peoples, and Cultures*. New York: Cambridge University Press, 2012.
Maude, H. E. *Slavers in Paradise: The Peruvian Slave Trade in Polynesia, 1862–1864*. Stanford, CA: Stanford University Press, 1981.
Mawani, Renisa. *Across Oceans of Law: The Komagara Maru and Jurisdiction in the Time of Empire*. Durham, NC: Duke University Press, 2018.
McAlister, Lyle N. *The "Fuero Militar" in New Spain, 1764–1800*. Gainesville: University of Florida Press, 1957.
McEvoy, Carmen. *Armas de persuasión masiva: Retórica y ritual en la Guerra del Pacífico*. Santiago: Ediciones Centro de Estudios Bicentenario, 2010.
———. *Chile en el Perú: La ocupación a traves de sus documentos, 1881–1884*. Lima: Fondo Editorial del Congreso del Perú, 2016.
———. "Civilización, masculinidad y superioridad racial: Una aproximación al discurso republicano chileno durante la Guerra del Pacífico (1879–1884)." *Revista de Sociologia e Política* 20, no. 42 (June 2012): 73–92.
———. *Guerreros civilizadores: Política, sociedad y cultura en Chile durante la Guerra del Pacífico*. Primera reimpresión. Santiago: Ediciones Universidad Diego Portales, 2013. Originally published 2011.
Meléndez-Badillo, Jorell. "Labor History's Transnational Turn: Rethinking Latin American and Caribbean Migrant Workers." *Latin American Perspectives* 42, no. 203 (July 2015): 117–22.
Melillo, Edward Dallam. "The First Green Revolution: Debt Peonage and the Making of the Nitrogen Fertilizer Trade, 1840–1930." *American Historical Review* 117, no. 4 (October 2012): 1028–60.
———. *Strangers on Familiar Soil: Rediscovering the Chile-California Connection*. New Haven, CT: Yale University Press, 2015.
Melo, Rosendo. *Derrotero de la costa del Perú: Guía marítimo-comercial*. Lima: C. F. Southwell, 1906.
———. *Historia de la marina del Perú*. Tomo primero. Lima: Imprenta de Carlos F. Southwell, 1907.
Méndez G., Cecilia. *Los trabajadores guaneros del Perú, 1840–1879*. Lima: Universidad Nacional Mayor de San Marcos / Seminario de Historia Rural Andina, 1987.

Molina, Fernanda. "Sodomy, Gender, and Identity in the Viceroyalty of Peru." In *Sexuality and the Unnatural in Colonial Latin America*, edited by Zeb Tortorici, 141–161. Oakland: University of California Press, 2016.

Molyneux, Maxine. "No God, No Boss, No Husband: Anarchist Feminism in Nineteenth-Century Argentina." *Latin American Perspectives* 13, no. 1 (Winter 1986): 119–45.

Monaghan, Jay. *Chile, Peru, and the California Gold Rush of 1849*. Berkeley: University of California Press, 1973.

Monteón, Michael. "The *Enganche* in the Chilean Nitrate Sector, 1880–1930." *Latin American Perspectives* 6, no. 3 (Summer 1979): 66–79.

Morgan, Zachary R. *The Legacy of the Lash: Race and Corporal Punishment in the Brazilian Navy and Atlantic World*. Bloomington: Indiana University Press, 2014.

Muñoz Cortés, Victor. *Cuando la patria mata. La historia del anarquista Julio Rebosio (1914–1920)*. Santiago: Editorial Universidad de Santiago de Chile, 2011.

Murdock, Carl J. "Physicians, the State and Public Health in Chile, 1881–1891." *Journal of Latin American Studies* 27, no. 3 (October 1995): 551–67.

Murray, Dian H. *Pirates of the South China coast, 1790–1810*. Stanford, CA: Stanford University Press, 1987.

Nash, June. *We Eat the Mines and the Mines Eat Us: Dependency and Exploitation in Bolivian Tin Mines*. New York: Columbia University Press, 1979.

Nencel, Lorraine. *Ethnography and Prostitution in Peru*. London: Pluto Press, 2001.

Nesvig, Martin. "The Complicated Terrain of Latin American Homosexuality." *Hispanic American Historical Review* 81, nos. 3–4 (August and November 2001): 689–729.

———. "The Lure of the Perverse: Moral Negotiation of Pederasty in Porfirian Mexico." *Mexican Studies/Estudios Mexicanos* 16, no. 1 (Winter 2000): 1–37.

Nugent, David. *Modernity at the Edge of Empire: State, Individual, and Nation in the Northern Peruvian Andes, 1885–1935*. Stanford, CA: Stanford University Press, 1997.

Olsson, Tore C. *Agrarian Crossings: Reformers and the Remaking of the US and Mexican Countryside*. Princeton, NJ: Princeton University Press, 2017.

O'Malley, Vincent. *The Meeting Place: Māori and Pākehā Encounters, 1642–1840*. Auckland: Auckland University Press, 2012.

Ortiz Letelier, Fernando. *El Movimiento Obrero en Chile (1891–1919)*. Santiago: LOM, 2005.

O'Shaughnessy, Hugh. *Pinochet: The Politics of Torture*. New York: New York University Press, 2000.

Osorio, Carlos G. "Sobre el origen de la Bacteriología Experimental en Chile." *Revista médica de Chile* 138, no. 7 (July 2010): 913–19.

Osterhammel, Jürgen. *The Transformation of the World: A Global History of the Nineteenth Century*. Translated by Patrick Camiller. Princeton, NJ: Princeton University Press, 2017.

Padrón, Ricardo. *The Indies of the Setting Sun: How Early Modern Spain Mapped the Far East as the Transpacific West*. Chicago: University of Chicago Press, 2020.

Palacios Laval, Cristian Enrique. "Entre Bertillon y Vucetich: Las tecnologías de identificación policial. Santiago de Chile, 1893–1924." *Revista Historia y Justicia* no. 1 (2013): 1–28.

Palma, Patricia. "Sanadores inesperados: Medicina china en la era de migración global (Lima y California, 1850–1930)." *História, Ciências, Saúde–Manguinhos* 25, no. 1 (January–March 2018): 13–31.

———. "'Una medida violenta y prejudicial': Cuarentenas en Perú y el surgimiento de una política sanitaria panamericana (1850–1905)." *Apuntes. Revista de Ciencias Sociales* 48, no. 89 (2nd semester 2021): 5–30.

Palma, Patricia, and José Ragas, "Enclaves sanitarios: Higiene, epidemias y salud en el Barrio chino de Lima, 1880–1910." *Anuario Colombiano de Historia Social y de la Cultura* 45, no. 1 (2018): 159–90.

Pareja Pflucker, Piedad. *Anarquismo y sindicalismo en el Perú (1904–1929)*. Lima: Ediciones Rikchay Perú, 1978.

———. *Aprismo y sindicalismo en el Perú, 1943–1948*. Lima: Ediciones Rikchay Perú, 1980.

Parodi Revoredo, Daniel. *Lo que dicen de nosotros: La Guerra del Pacífico en la historiografía y textos escolares chilenos*. Lima: Universidad Peruana de Ciencias Aplicadas, 2010.

Parodi Revoredo, Daniel, and Sergio González Miranda. "Introducción." In Parodi Revoredo and González Miranda, *Las historias que nos unen* 9–18. Lima: Fondo Editorial Pontificia Universidad Católica del Perú, 2014.

———, comps. *Las historias que nos unen: 21 relatos para la integración entre Perú y Chile*. Lima: Fondo Editorial Pontificia Universidad Católica del Perú, 2014.

Peloso, Vincent C. *Peasants on Plantations: Subaltern Strategies of Labor and Resistance in the Pisco Valley, Peru*. Durham, NC: Duke University Press, 1999.

Perl-Rosenthal, Nathan. *Citizen Sailors: Becoming American in the Age of Revolution*. Cambridge, MA: Belknap Press of Harvard University Press, 2015.

Pineo, Ronn F. "Misery and Death in the Pearl of the Pacific: Health Care in Guayaquil, Ecuador, 1870–1925." *Hispanic American Historical Review* 70, no. 4 (November 1990): 609–37.

Pinochet Ugarte, Augusto. *Guerra del Pacífico, 1879: Primeras operaciones terrestres (antecedentes, organización de las fuerzas, Desarrollo de la campana y ocupación del departamento de Tarapacá)*. Santiago: Instituto Geográfico Militar, 1972.

Pinto Vallejos, Julio. *Trabajos y rebeldia en la pampa salitrera: El ciclo del salitre y la reconfiguración de las clases populares (1850–1900)*. Santiago: Editorial Universidad de Santiago, 1998.

Pinto Vallejos, Julio, Verónica Valdivia Ortiz de Zárate, and Pablo Artaza Barrios. "Patria y clase en los albores de la identidad pampina (1860–1890)." *Historia* 36 (2003): 275–332.

Plaza Armijo, Camilo, and Víctor Muñoz Cortés. "La Lay de Residencia de 1918 y la persecución a los extranjeros subversivos." *Revista de Derechos Fundamentales*, no. 10 (2013): 106–36.

Poole, Deborah A. "Ciencia, peligrosidad y represión en la criminología indigenista peruana." In *Bandoleros, abigeos y montoneros: Criminalidad y violencia en el Perú, siglos XVIII–XX*, edited by Carlos Aguirre and Charles Walker, 335–66. Lima: La Siniestra ensayos, 2019.

Portocarrero, Julio. *Sindicalismo Peruano: Primera Etapa, 1911–1930*. Lima: Editorial Gráfica Labor, 1987.

Putnam, Lara. *The Company They Kept: Migrants and the Politics of Gender in Caribbean Costa Rica, 1870–1960*. Chapel Hill: University of North Carolina Press, 2002.

——. *Radical Moves: Caribbean Migrants and the Politics of Race in the Jazz Age*. Chapel Hill: University of North Carolina Press, 2013.

——. "To Study the Fragments/Whole: Microhistory and the Atlantic World." *Journal of Social History* 39, no. 3 (Spring, 2006): 615–30.

Ragas, José. "Documenting Hierarchies: State Building, Identification and Citizenship in Modern Peru." PhD diss., University of California, Davis, 2015.

——. *Lima Chola: Una historia de la Gran Migración Andina*. Lima: Taurus/Penguin Random House, forthcoming.

Raj, Kapil. *Relocating Modern Science: Circulation and the Construction of Knowledge in South Asia and Europe, 1650–1900*. New York: Palgrave Macmillan, 2007.

Rediker, Marcus. *Between the Devil and the Deep Blue Sea: Merchant Seamen, Pirates, and the Anglo-American Maritime World, 1700–1750*. New York: Cambridge University Press, 1987.

Reid, Anthony. *Southeast Asia in the Age of Commerce, 1450–1860*. 2 vols. New Haven, CT: Yale University Press, 1988.

Reid, Joshua L. *The Sea Is My Country: The Maritime World of the Makahs, an Indigenous Borderlands People*. New Haven, CT: Yale University Press, 2015.

Rénique, José Luis. *Imaginar la nación: Viajes en busca del "verdadero Perú" (1881–1932)*. 2nd ed. Lima: Instituto de Estudios Peruanos, 2016.

Ricketts, Mónica. *Who Should Rule? Men of Arms, the Republic of Letters, and the Fall of the Spanish Empire*. New York: Oxford University Press, 2017.

Rinke, Stefan. *Latin America and the First World War*. New York: Cambridge University Press, 2017.

Rocker, Rudolf. *Anarcho-Syndicalism: Theory and Practice*. Translated by Ray E. Chase. Oakland, CA: AK Press, 2004.

Rodríguez, Julia. "South Atlantic Crossings: Fingerprints, Science, and the State in Turn-of-the-Century Argentina." *American Historical Review* 109, no. 2 (April 2004): 387–416.

Rodríguez Hernández, Miguel. "El movimiento de confraternidad obrera peruana-chilena y el final del gobierno de Guillermo Billinghurst." In Parodi Revoredo and González Miranda, *Las historias que nos unen*, 133–62. Lima: Fondo Editorial Pontificia Universidad Católica del Perú, 2014.

Rodríguez Pastor, Humberto. *Herederos del dragón: Historia de la comunidad China en el Perú*. Lima: Fondo Editorial del Congreso, 2000.

Rojas Flores, Jorge. *Historia de la infancia en el Chile republican, 1810–2010*. Santiago: Ocho Libros Editores, 2010.

Rosemblatt, Karin Alejandra. "Sexuality and Biopower in Chile and Latin America." *Political Power and Social Theory* 15 (2002): 229–62.
Rosenberg, Charles E. *The Cholera Years: The United States in 1832, 1849, and 1866.* Chicago: University of Chicago Press, 1987.
Rosenthal, Anton. "Moving between the Global and the Local: The Industrial Workers of the World and Their Press in Latin America." In *In Defiance of Boundaries: Anarchism in Latin American History*, edited by Geoffroy de Laforcade and Kirwin R. Shaffer, 72–94. Gainesville: University Press of Florida, 2015.
Rosenthal, Gregory. *Beyond Hawai'i: Native Labor in the Pacific World.* Oakland: University of California Press, 2018.
———. "Life and Labor in a Seabird Colony: Hawaiian Guano Workers, 1857–70." *Environmental History* 17, no. 4 (October 2012): 744–82.
Sabato, Hilda. *Republics of the New World: The Revolutionary Political Experiment in 19th-Century Latin America.* Princeton, NJ: Princeton University Press, 2018.
Sahlins, Marshall. *How "Natives" Think: About Captain Cook, for Example.* Chicago: University of Chicago Press, 1995.
———. *Islands of History.* Chicago: University of Chicago Press, 1987.
Salazar, Gabriel. *Labradores, peones y proletarios: Formación y crisis de la sociedad popular chilena del siglo XIX.* Santiago: LOM, 2000.
———. *Mercaderes, empresarios y capitalistas (Chile, siglo XIX).* Santiago: Editorial Sudamericana, 2011.
Sánchez, Luis Alberto. "Prólogo sobre don Manuel González Prada." In Manuel González Prada, *Obras*, tomo 1, vol. 1, 9–24. Lima: Ediciones COPÉ, 1985.
Santiago, Myrna I. *The Ecology of Oil: Environment, Labor, and the Mexican Revolution, 1900–1938.* New York: Cambridge University Press, 2006.
Santibáñez Rebolledo, Camilo. "Los trabajadores portuarios chilenos y la experiencia de la eventualidad: Los conflicts por la redondilla en los muelles salitreros (1916–1923)." *Historia* 50, no. 2 (July–December 2017): 699–728.
———. "La IWW y el movimiento obrero en Chile: El caso de los obreros portuarios nortinos (1919–1923)." *Diálogo Andino*, no. 55 (2018): 19–28.
Sartorius, David, and Micol Seigel. "Introduction: Dislocations Across the Americas." *Social Text* 28, no. 3 (Fall 2010): 1–10.
Sater, William F. *Andean Tragedy: Fighting the War of the Pacific, 1879–1884.* Lincoln: University of Nebraska Press, 2007.
———. *Chile and the War of the Pacific.* Lincoln: University of Nebraska Press, 1986.
———. "The Politics of Public Health: Smallpox in Chile." *Journal of Latin American Studies* 35, no. 3 (August 2003): 513–43.
Savala, Joshua. "'Let Us Bring It with Love': Violence, Solidarity, and the Making of a Social Disaster in the Wake of the 1906 Earthquake in Valparaíso, Chile." *Journal of Social History* 51, no. 4 (Summer 2018): 928–52.
———. "Ports of Transnational Labor Organizing: Anarchism along the Peruvian-Chilean littoral, 1916–1928." *Hispanic American Historical Review* 99, no. 3 (August 2019): 501–31.

Scheinkman, Ludmila. "'¿Dónde están los machos?' Sindicalización anarquista, masculina y femenina, en la industria del dulce (Buenos Aires, 1920–1929)." *Revista Archivos de historia del movimiento obrero y la izquierda* año 4, no. 7 (Septiembre 2015): 15–36.

Schwartz, Stuart B. *All Can Be Saved: Religious Tolerance and Salvation in the Iberian Atlantic World.* New Haven, CT: Yale University Press, 2008.

———. *Sea of Storms: A History of Hurricanes in the Greater Caribbean from Columbus to Katrina.* Princeton, NJ: Princeton University Press, 2015.

Scott, Joan W. "Gender: A Useful Category of Historical Analysis." *American Historical Review* 91, no. 5 (December 1986): 1053–75.

Scott, Julius S. *The Common Wind: Afro-American Currents in the Age of the Haitian Revolution.* New York: Verso, 2018.

Seigel, Micol. "Beyond Compare: Comparative Method after the Transnational Turn." *Radical History Review*, no. 91 (Winter 2005): 62–90.

———. *Violence Work: State Power and the Limits of Police.* Durham, NC: Duke University Press, 2018.

Seoane Byrne, Glauco. *Revisando una historiografía hostil: Sobre el origen de la Guerra del Pacífico, la industria del salitre y el papel de la casa Gibbs de Londres.* Lima: Instituto Riva-Agüero / Pontificia Universidad Católica del Perú, 2013.

Sigal, Pete. "(Homo)Sexual Desire and Masculine Power in Colonial Latin America: Notes Toward an Integrated Analysis." In *The Infamous Desire: Male Homosexuality in Colonial Latin America*, edited by Pete Sigal, 1–24. Chicago: University of Chicago Press, 2003.

Sivasundaram, Suvit, Alison Bashford, and David Armitage. "Introduction: Writing World Oceanic Histories." In *Oceanic Histories*, edited by David Armitage, Alison Bashford, and Sujit Sivasundaram, 1–28. New York: Cambridge University Press, 2018.

Skuban, William E. *Lines in the Sand: Nationalism and Identity on the Peruvian-Chilean Frontier.* Albuquerque: University of New Mexico Press, 2007.

Sobrevilla, David. Introduction to *Free Pages and Other Essays: Anarchist Musings*, edited by David Sobrevilla, xxiii–lvii. New York: Oxford University Press, 2003.

Steinberg, Philip. "Of Other Seas: Metaphors and Materialities in Maritime Regions. *Atlantic Studies* 10, no. 2 (2013): 156–69.

———. *The Social Construction of the Ocean.* New York: Cambridge University Press, 2001.

Strasser, Ulrike, and Heidi Tinsman. "It's a Man's World? World History Meets the History of Masculinity, in Latin American Studies, for Instance." *Journal of World History* 21, no. 1 (March 2010): 75–96.

Subrahmanyam, Sanjay. "Connected Histories: Notes towards a Reconfiguration of Early Modern Eurasia." *Modern Asian Studies* 31, no. 3 (July 1997): 735–62.

Sutter, Paul S. "Nature's Agents or Agents of Empire? Entomological Workers and Environmental Change during the Construction of the Panama Canal." *Isis* 98, no. 4 (December 2007): 724–54.

Tagliacozzo, Eric. "Hajj in the Time of Cholera: Pilgrim Ships and Contagion from Southeast Asia to the Red Sea." In *Global Muslims in the Age of Steam and Print*, edited by James L. Gelvin and Nile Green, 103–20. Berkeley: University of California Press, 2013.

———. *The Longest Journey: Southeast Asians and the Pilgrimage to Mecca*. New York: Oxford University Press, 2013.

———. *Secret Trades, Porous Borders: Smuggling and States along a Southeast Asian Frontier, 1865–1915*. New Haven, CT: Yale University Press, 2005.

Te Punga Somerville, Alice. *Once Were Pacific: Māori Connections to Oceania*. Minneapolis: University of Minnesota Press, 2012.

Tejada R., Luis. *La Cuestión del Pan: El Anarcosindicalismo en el Perú, 1880–1919*. Lima: Instituto Nacional de Cultura/Banco Industrial del Perú, 1988.

Thompson, E. P. "The Poverty of Theory or an Orrery of Errors." In *The Poverty of Theory and Other Essays*. New York: Monthly Review Press, 2008.

Thompson, Michael D. *Working on the Dock: Labor and Enterprise in an Antebellum Southern Port*. Columbia: University of South Carolina Press, 2015.

Thorp, Rosemary, and Geoffrey Bertram. *Peru, 1890–1977: Growth and Policy in an Open Economy*. New York: Columbia University Press, 1978.

Thurner, Mark. *From Two Republics to One Divided: Contradictions of Postcolonial Nationmaking in Andean Peru*. Durham, NC: Duke University Press, 1997.

Tinsman, Heidi. "More Than Victims: Women Agricultural Workers and Social Change in Rural Chile." In *Victims of the Chilean Miracle: Workers and Neoliberalism in the Pinochet Era, 1973–2002*, edited by Peter Winn, 261–97. Durham, NC: Duke University Press, 2004.

———. "Narrating Chinese Massacre in the South American War of the Pacific." *Journal of Asian American Studies* 22, no. 3 (October 2019): 277–313.

———. "Rebel Coolies, Citizen Warriors, and Sworn Brothers: The Chinese Loyalty Oath and Alliance with Chile in the War of the Pacific." *Hispanic American Historical Review* 98, no. 3 (August 2018): 439–69.

Ugarte Díaz, Emilio José. "La Guerra del Pacífico como referente nacional y punto condicionante de las relaciones chilenos-peruanas." *Si Somos Americanos: Revista de Estudios Transfronterizos* 14, no. 2 (July–December 2014): 159–85.

Urbina Carrasco, María Ximena. *Los conventillos de Valparaíso, 1880–1920: Fisonomía y percepción de una vivienda popular urbana*. Valparaíso: Ediciones Universitarias de Valparaíso de la Universidad Católica de Valparaíso, 2002.

Valdivia Ortiz de Zárate, Verónica. "'Los tengo plenamente identificados': Seguridad interna y control social en Chile, 1918–1925." *Historia* 50, no. 1 (January–June 2017): 241–71.

Valenzuela Medina, Daniel. "Pobres diablos: Masculinidad burladas de *Sombras contra el muro*." *Anales de literatura chilena* 22, no. 35 (junio 2021): 235–42.

Valle Vera, María Lucía. "Los 'hijos de la guerra': Niños peruano-chilenos durante la ocupación de Lima (1881–1883). *Historica* 41, no. 1 (2017): 125–57.

Villalobos R., Sergio. *Chile y Perú. La historia que nos une y nos separa, 1535–1883*. Santiago: Ediciones Universitaria, 2002.

Walker, Charles F. *Smoldering Ashes: Cuzco and the Creation of Republican Peru, 1780–1840*. Durham, NC: Duke University Press, 1999.

Walker, Louise E. *Waking from the Dream: Mexico's Middle Classes after 1968*. Stanford, CA: Stanford University Press, 2013.

Walsh, Sarah. "'One of the Most Uniform Races of the Entire World': Creole Eugenics and the Myth of Chilean Racial Homogeneity." *Journal of the History of Biology* 48 (2015): 613–39.

Walker, Tamara J. "'That is How Whores Get Punished': Gender, Race, and the Culture of Honor-Based Violence in Colonial Latin America." *Journal of Women's History* 31, no. 2 (Summer 2019): 11–32.

Warren, James. *Pirates, Prostitutes and Pullers: Explorations in the Ethno- and Social History of Southeast Asia*. Crawley: University of Western Australia Press, 2008.

Warren, James Frances. *The Sulu Zone, 1768–1898: The Dynamics of External Trade, Slavery, and Ethnicity in the Transformation of a Southeast Asian Maritime State*. Kent Ridge, Singapore: Singapore University Press, 1981.

Weld, Kirsten. *Paper Cadavers: The Archives of Dictatorship in Guatemala*. Durham, NC: Duke University Press, 2014.

White, Hylton. "Materiality, Form, and Content: Marx contra Latour." *Victorian Studies* 55, no. 4 (Summer 2013): 667–82.

Winn, Peter. *Weavers of Revolution: The Yarur Workers and Chile's Road to Socialism*. New York: Oxford University Press, 1986.

Wintersteen, Kristin A. *The Fishmeal Revolution: The Industrialization of the Humboldt Current Ecosystem*. Oakland: University of California Press, 2021.

Womack, John, Jr. "Doing Labor History: Feelings, Work, Material Power." *Journal of the Historical Society* 3 (Fall 2005): 255–96.

Wood, James A. "The Burdens of Citizenship: Artisans, Elections, and the Fuero Militar in Santiago de Chile, 1822–1851." *Americas* 58, no. 3 (January 2002): 443–69.

Yáñez Andrade, Juan Carlos. *La intervención social en Chile y el nacimiento de la sociedad salarial, 1907–1932*. Santiago: RiL editores, 2008.

Yávar Meza, Aldo. "El gremio de jornaleros y lancheros de Valparaíso, 1837–1859: Etapa de formación." *Historia* 24 (1989): 319–95.

Young, Elliott. *Alien Nation: Chinese Migration in the Americas from the coolie era through World War II*. Chapel Hill: University of North Carolina Press, 2014.

Zárate C., María Soledad. *Dar a luz en Chile, siglo XIX: De la "ciencia de hembre" a la ciencia obstétrica*. Santiago: Universidad Alberto Hurtado / Dirección de Bibliotecas, Archivos y Museos, 2007

———. "Notas preliminares sobre profesión médica y masculinidad, chile, siglo XIX." In *Hombres: Identidad/es y violencia*, edited by José Olavarría, 73–84. Santiago: FLACSO/Universidad Academia de Humanismo Cristiano, 2001.

Zeitlin, Maurice. *The Civil Wars in Chile (or the Bourgeois Revolutions That Never Were)*. Princeton, NJ: Princeton University Press, 1984.

# INDEX

Note: page numbers followed by *fig.* refer to figures; those followed by *tab.* refer to tables; and those followed by *n* refer to notes, with note number.

1918 Mollendo strike, 14, 90, 92–94, 102–3

Academia Libre de Medicina (Lima), 73
adolescents. *See* teenagers
Afro-Peruvians, 56–57
Agacio, Antonio, 55–57
aguateros, 33
alcohol, 35, 37, 38, 52
Alessandri Palma, Arturo, 96
Aljovín de Losada, Cristóbal, 140
Allende, Salvador, 138
*Amazonas* (Peruvian frigate): 1863 crew of, 18–19, 19*tab.*, 20*tab.*, 42–43; discipline on, 34; journey of, 17–18; Peruvian-Chilean relations and, 9, 13; treatment on, 31–32; workers on, 24, 36
American Popular Revolutionary Alliance (APRA), 9, 137
anarcha-feminists, 95
anarchism: labor organizing and, 94–95; nationalism and, 151n42; oceans and, 109–10; Peruvian-Chilean relations and, 98–99; policing and, 133, 134–35; study of, 11–12; transnationalism and, 97–98
anarchists, 51, 53–54, 95, 106–7, 133
anarcho-syndicalism, 95, 104, 106
Andean Community, 140
anthropometry, 14, 117, 119*fig.*, 135, 136

anti-colonialism, 81
antilegalism, 97
Arguedas, José María, 8
autopsies, 78
*Azul* (1888 short story collection), 33–34

bacteriology, 84
Bakunin, Mikhail, 134
Balmaceda, José Manuel, 61, 68, 71
Barros Ovalle, Pedro N., 116–17, 119*fig.*, 124, 135, 191n33
belonging, ways of, 12, 39
Bertillon system, 112, 116, 118, 120, 191n31
Billinghurst, Guillermo, 128
*Boletín de la Policía de Santiago*, 122
*Boletín de Medicina*, 72, 80
Bolivia, 4–5, 6, 90
border disputes: Bolivia-Chile, 5; nationalism and, 141, 142; Peru-Chile, 137–39, 141, 142; Tacna-Arica, 6, 14–15, 88, 101, 139
Braudel, Fernand, 10–11, 87
British Pacific Steam Navigation Company (PSNC), 30–31, 32
brothels, 46–47, 48, 49, 58
bubonic plague, 83

Cáceres, Andrés, 5–6
Callao, Peru: policing in, 123–24, 125, 128–29; port of, 21–24, 22*tab.*, 23*tab.*;

Callao, Peru (*continued*)
    transnational labor organizing in,
    86–87; venereal infections in,
    44–45, 48
Callirgos, Benigno A., 44–45, 46
capitalism, 143
Carpio, Fermin, 91, 94
Carrión, Daniel A., 74
Carrión disease, 74
Casa Grace, 91, 93
caudillos, 2
Cavieres Figueroa, Eduardo, 140
Chamorro, Juan Onofre, 94–95, 97, 98
Chile: colonial rule by, 25–26; enganche system and, 35; male-male sex and, 55–56, 57–58; occupations by, 5; repatriation of workers to, 29–30; state formation in, 68
chileanization, 6, 141
Chilean Revolutionary Left (MIR), 54
Chinese laborers, 27–28, 70
cholera: 1880s outbreaks, 59, 60–61, 85, 175n106; economic effects of, 67–68; regulations and, 66, 67, 172–73n71; responses to, 61, 71, 79–80, 82, 83–84; spread of, 63, 69, 74–75; state formation and, 13, 60, 68–70, 75, 85; study of, 59–60, 62, 74–76, 77–78; transnational medical community and, 72, 73, 74, 75
circulation: commerce and, 84; infectious diseases and, 60, 63; oceans as sites of, 10–11; Peruvian-Chilean relations and, 3–4, 12, 13; policing and, 123; radical politics and, 87; sexual relations and, 45; sex work and, 48–49; South American Pacific world and, 11, 16–17, 27–28, 38–39; workers and, 13, 17, 39
class formation, 40–41
Comisión Directiva del Servicio Sanitario, Santiago, 78–79
communism, 95
communists, 134
Compañía Sud Americana de Vapores (CSAV; South American Steamship Company), 30, 50, 67, 68, 165n97
Concejo Provincial de Lima, 72
Consejo Superior de Higiene (Chile), 68
conventillo, 53

"coolie" trade, 24, 27–28
cooperation, 77–78, 84–85, 121–22, 140, 141
cosmopolitanism, 21, 38–39, 45, 47. *See also* multinationalism
criminology, 113, 117–18, 136
Cuba, Andrés, 106, 108

dactyloscopy, 14, 118, 120, 135, 136
Darío, Rubén, 33
Daza, Hilarión, 5
debt peonage. *See* enganche system
de la Fuente Silva, Hugo, 134
Dening, Greg, 109, 159n96
deportation, 97, 106–7, 108, 133, 136
desertion, 30–31, 35–36, 38
Dirección de Obras Públicas (Peru), 68
discipline, 34
disinfection, 75, 167n16
doctors. *See* transnational medical community
Drinot, Paulo, 46, 47, 48, 128

Easter Island, 11, 16, 25, 26–27
effeminate men, 7, 41
*El Comercio* (newspaper), 137
*El Mercurio* (newspaper), 59, 61
enganche system, 34–35, 56
enslavement, 24–25, 27
Escalona, Manuel, 107, 187n105
extradition, 122, 133, 136

family, the, 91, 105–6, 179n22
Federación de Estudiantes (Chile), 100
Federación de Jente de Mar, 96, 99
Federación Obrera de Chile (FOCH), 97
Federación Obrera Marítima de Supe, 98
Federación Obrera Regional Peruana (FORP), 98, 99–100
filiación antropométrica. *See* anthropometry
filiación descriptiva, 117–18
Fourth Latin American Scientific Congress, 84–85
Fox Film Corporation, 190n25
fuero militar, 131–32

García, Alan, 137
gay men. *See* homosexuality

gender: anarchists and, 51, 95; class formation and, 40–41; ideas about, 56; labor and, 43; labor organizing and, 50–51, 91, 105, 179n22; race and, 41; South American Pacific world and, 40, 42; transnational medical community and, 76; War of the Pacific and, 7
Góngora, Mario, 140
González Prada, Manuel, 1–2, 4, 7, 8, 108–9
Grace Company, 88, 123, 193n60
Gremio de Izaje, 91, 92
guano industry: demand and, 27; ecology of, 11; indentured labor and, 28; mining and exports of the, 5, 16, 29
Guerrero, Sergio, 141

Hague, The, 14–15, 137, 138, 142
Hawaiian diaspora, 27
Haya de la Torre, Víctor Raúl, 9, 100
hegemony, 71
heterosexuality, 53
*Hijo de ladrón* (1951 novel), 26–27, 53
hombría. *See* masculinity
homophobia, 51–52, 54
homosexuality, 53–54
homosociality, 40, 41–42, 58, 76
*Huáscar* (Peruvian ship), 11, 138

Iglesias, Miguel, 5
imprisonment, 34, 36–37, 38
indentured labor, 27–28
indigenous peoples, 7–8, 16, 25–26, 27
Industrial Workers of the World (IWW): Chilean branch of, 101; masculinity and, 50; Mollendo branch of, 104–5, 106–7; representations in fiction of, 54; Santiago branch of, 9; strikes organized by, 95–96; transnational organizing and, 14, 37–38, 86–87, 97–99, 100; Valparaíso branch of, 14, 95, 97, 130
infectious diseases, 60, 63, 66, 83–84. *See also individual diseases*
Insular Pacific. *See* Oceania
International Court of Justice (ICJ), 137
internationalism, 88, 100
International Workingmen's Association (IWA), 134
izadores, 91–92, 93

Japanese laborers, 27
jiu-jitsu, 113–14, 136
jornaleros, 103
Junta Central de Vacuna de Chile, 73
Junta de Salubridad de Valparaíso, 69, 76
Junta de Sanidad (Peru), 75
Junta Litoral (Peru), 65–66
Junta Suprema de Sanidad (Lima), 62–63, 65–66

Killing, Cárlos, 69, 76–77, 78, 82, 84–85

labor: circulation and, 13; contracted, 34–35; enslavement and, 24–25; gender and, 43; imprisonment and, 36, 37; indentured, 27–28; transnational history of, 87
Labor Office (Chile), 128
labor of policing, 112
labor organizing: anarcho-syndicalism and, 95; gender and, 105, 179n22; *La Voz del Mar* and, 186n88; masculinity and, 50–51, 91; Peruvian-Chilean relations and, 101; policing and, 112, 114–15, 127–31; repression and, 106–7, 108; South American Pacific world and, 87, 88, 104, 110; state formation and, 96; workers and, 90, 91–93, 94. *See also* transnational labor organizing
labor recruitment: coercion and, 24–25, 34–35, 36, 37, 38; transpacific ties and, 27–29
Labor Sections (Peru), 128–29
*La Crónica Médica,* 73, 76, 80–81
*Lanchas en la bahía* (1932 novel), 54–55, 123
*La oscura vida radiante* (1971 novel), 53–54
*La Unión* (newspaper), 61
*La Voz del Mar* (newspaper): circulation of, 101–2, 185n78; labor organizing and, 37, 186n88; masculinity and, 51; masthead of, 104, 105*fig*; transnationalism and, 87, 98, 99–100
Law of Obligatory Social Security (Law 4054), 96–97
leftist politics, 50, 51, 54, 95. *See also* anarchism; anarcho-syndicalism
Leguía, Augusto, 100, 106, 134
Lenin, Vladimir, 108

*Lerzundi* (Peruvian ship), 19, 21
Ley de Residencia (Chile), 133–34
*Los funerales de Atahualpa* (painting), 6
*Los ríos profundos* (1958 novel), 8

male-male sex: in fiction, 53, 54–55; maritime workers and, 51–52, 55–56; masculinity and, 41; racial anxieties and, 13, 56–58; War of the Pacific and, 56, 57–58
manliness. *See* masculinity
*Manual de antropometría criminal i jeneral*, 116, 119*fig.*
Māori people, 39
*Mapocho* (steamship), 30–31
maricón, 53, 56, 57
maritime workers: the family and, 179n22; male-male sex and, 51–52, 55–56; masculinity and, 40–42, 49–50, 54–55; nationalities of, 18–19; policing and, 123, 125; sexual lives of, 40, 52, 58; tattoos and, 124; teenage, 36–37; venereal infections and, 43–44; working conditions and, 30–31, 32–34, 35–36. *See also* workers
Martí, José, 108
masculinity: conceptions of, 13; heterosexuality and, 53; labor organizing and, 50–51, 91; *La Voz del Mar* (newspaper) and, 51; maritime workers and, 40–42, 49–50, 54–55
materiality of cholera, 69, 71
materiality of the state, 60, 68–69, 71, 96, 136
Matto, David: career of, 73–74, 84–85; Cárlos Killing and, 76–77, 78; Dr. Patiño Luna and, 78–80; portrait of, 73*fig.*; study of cholera by, 74–76; transnational work by, 13–14, 81–82
Maurtua, Lizando, 62
maximalism, 133
medical community. *See* transnational medical community
medicolegal regulations, 66
*Mejor que el vino* (1958 novel), 53
micrography, 77
migration, 47
militarization of policing, 131–32
Ministerio de Beneficencia (Peru), 74

Ministerio de Marina (Chile), 61
Ministry of Foreign Relations (Chile), 24, 83
Ministry of Foreign Relations (Peru), 123
Ministry of the Interior (Chile), 60–61, 68, 70, 75
Mollendo, Peru, 89–90, 89*fig. See also* 1918 Mollendo strike
Mollendo Agencies Company, The, 91, 93
Montero, Luis, 6
multinationalism, 18–19, 21–24, 23*tab.*, 39

nationalism: anarchism and, 151n42; border disputes and, 141, 142; nonelites and, 2; peasants and, 7–8; policing and, 135; scholarship on, 11–12; transnational medical community and, 72, 74, 80–81, 82; War of the Pacific and, 1–2
Neira, Eugenio, 107, 108
nitrate industry: forced labor recruitment and, 35; gender and, 41; mining and exports of the, 5, 16, 29–30; Peruvian loss of, 7
nonelites, 2, 11–12

ocean, the: anarchism and, 109–10; crime and, 125–26; disease spread and, 63, 66–67, 75, 168n25; labor organizing and, 109; Manuel Rojas on, 17, 38, 109; as sites of circulation, 10–11
Oceania, 11, 16, 25–27, 159n96
Oficina del Trabajo (Chile), 128
O'Higgins, Bernardo, 140

Pacific Steam Navigation, 93
Partido Comunista (PC; Communist Party), 99
patente de sanidad, 64*fig.*, 65*fig.*, 66
patente limpia, 64–65, 172–73n71
patente sucia, 64
Patiño Luna, Dr., 68, 78–80
patria, 2, 106
patriarchy, 45–46, 47, 49–50, 51–52
patriotism, 2
peasants, 7–8
pederasty, 52
Perl-Rosenthal, Nathan, 113
Peru: anarchism and, 98; Chilean workers in, 29; nationalism and, 7–8; nitrate

industry in, 7; patria and, 2; state formation in, 68, 75; venereal infections in, 44
*Peru* (steamship), 63, 65*fig.*
Peru-Bolivia Confederation, 139, 140
Peruvian-Chilean Pacific. *See* South American Pacific world
Peruvian-Chilean relations: *Amazonas* (Peruvian frigate) and, 9, 13; anarchism and, 98–99; children and, 43; circulation and, 3–4, 12, 13; cooperation and, 9; labor organizing and, 101; maritime border and, 139–41; scholarship on, 2–3; solidarities and, 8–9, 140; South American Pacific world and, 3–4; War of the Pacific and, 8
"peruvianization," 57–58
photography, 115–17, 136, 190nn23,25
Pinochet, Augusto, 138
piracy, 123
población flotante, 14, 123–25, 126, 128
police spies, 129–30, 134, 195n89
policing: anarchism and, 133, 134–35; dactyloscopy and, 118; data collection and, 120, 129*fig.*; labor organizing and, 112, 114–15, 127–30; maritime workers and, 123, 125; methods of, 113–14, 130, 131–32; nationalism and, 135; photography and, 115–17, 190nn23,25; port cities and, 112, 124–25, 126, 135; repression and, 111; resources for, 130–31, 189n12, 194–95n81; sex work and, 46–47; South American Pacific World and, 14, 124; state power and, 136; strikes and, 130, 131; transnational, 120–23, 133, 135–36
Portales, Diego, 139
port cities: infectious diseases and, 83–84; multinationalism and, 21–24, 23*tab.*; policing in, 112, 124–25, 126, 135; sanitation and, 62, 67
portrait law, 94, 95
portraits. *See* photography
port workers, 33, 93–94. *See also* workers
prisoner labor, 36
prisoners, 124, 125*fig.*
prostitution. *See* sex work
protests, 114–15

Puga Borne, Federico, 69, 70

quarantines: lazarettos and, 62, 68–69, 70, 75; maritime, 59, 61, 63, 65–66, 176n120
Quintana, Benigno, 94, 102–3, 107, 108

rabona, 43
race, 13, 41, 55–57, 58, 113
racial anxieties, 13, 56–58
radiotelegraphy, 131
railroad workers, 94, 105, 106, 115
Rapa Nui, 11, 16, 25, 26–27
redondilla system, 96
Reglamento del Ramo de Policia relativa a la prostitución (1868), 46–47
repatriation, 29–30
*Revista de la Policía de Valparaíso* (newspaper), 111, 117
Rodríguez, Luis Manuel, 121, 133
Rojas, Manuel: the ocean and, 17, 38, 109; writings of, 26–27, 45, 53–54, 123
roto, 58

Sánchez, Luis Alberto, 1
sanitary cordons, 61, 70, 71
sanitation: cholera and, 69, 70–71, 75, 83–84; port cities and, 62, 67
Sanitation Conference (Lima, 1888), 66, 69
San Lorenzo Island, 68
San Martín, José de, 140
Santa Cruz, Andrés de, 140
Santiago Declaration of 1952, 139
School of Medicine, National University of San Marcos, 70, 72–73
Sección de Investigaciones, identificación i estadística (Peru), 124, 125
Secciones Obreras. *See* Labor Sections
Servicio Nacional de Pesca de Chile, 141
sex trafficking, 47, 56
sexual abuse, 56
sexuality, 40, 51–52, 53–54
sexual relations, 45, 58
sex work, 26, 45–47, 48–49
sex workers, 40, 45–46, 47–49
shipping, 66–67, 178n14
Sindicato de Pescadores Artesanales de Arica, 141
slavery, 24–25, 27

smallpox, 27, 61, 62, 82
Sociedad de Estibadores y Gente de Mar (Chile), 95
Sociedad Médica (Santiago), 70, 80
Sociedad Médica "Unión Fernandina" (Peru), 73
sodomy, 52, 55, 56
solidarities: history of, 143; Peruvian-Chilean, 8–9, 140; transnational labor organizing and, 8–9, 25, 87, 88, 98–99; War of the Pacific and, 110; workers and, 94
*Sombras contra el muro* (1964 novel), 53, 109
South American Pacific world: borders and, 142; circulation and, 11, 16–17, 27–28, 38–39; conceptualization of, 3–4, 10; gender and, 40, 42; labor organizing in, 87, 88, 104, 110; Peruvian-Chilean relations and, 3–4; policing and, 14, 124; sex work and, 48–49
*South Pacific Mail* (newspaper), 7
Spain, 4, 16
Special Guards of the Bay, 123
state expansion, 69–71
state formation: cholera and, 13, 60, 68–70, 75, 85; labor organizing and, 96; in Peru and Chile, 68, 75
state power, 136
state responses, 79–80
state-scientific power, 84
stevedores, 91–92, 93, 94
strikebreakers, 50–51, 93, 106
strikes: 1907 Tarapacá, 8–9; 1913 Callao, 128; 1913 Valparaíso, 94; 1917 Valparaíso, 94–95; 1918 Mollendo, 90, 92, 93, 103–4; Lima-Callao general strike, 100; policing and, 130, 131; railroad workers and, 105; working conditions and, 95–96
student protests, 100–101
subversives, 134
suicide, 34
surveillance, 111, 116, 125, 136
syndicalism, 102–3

Tacna-Arica region: border dispute regarding, 6, 14–15, 88, 101, 139; scholarship on, 7

tattoos, 124, 125*fig.*, 136
teenagers, 36–37
telephone lines, 68, 131
tetanus, 84
Toro, Luis, 86, 96, 99, 100
transnationalism, 10, 14, 87, 98, 99–100
transnational labor organizing: anarchism and, 97–98; Industrial Workers of the World (IWW) and, 14, 37–38, 86–87, 97–99, 100; scholarship on, 109–10; solidarities and, 8–9, 25, 87, 88, 98–99
transnational medical community: cholera and, 72, 73, 74, 75; cooperation within, 84–85; David Matto and, 13–14, 81–82; gender and, 76; nationalism and, 72, 74, 80–81, 82; research by, 77–78, 80, 85; War of the Pacific and, 71–72, 84–85
transnational policing, 120–22, 123, 133, 135–36
Treaty for the Settlement of the Dispute regarding Tacna and Arica. *See* Treaty of Lima (1929)
Treaty of Ancón (1883), 5–6, 72
Treaty of Lima (1929), 6, 138, 139, 140

Unión Marítima y Terrestre de la Compañía Peruana de Vapores y Dique del Callao (UMT), 86, 99
United States of America, 101, 138
USSR (Union of Soviet Socialist Republics), 138

Valcárcel, Luis, 108
Valdivieso, Victor V., 88, 92, 93
Valparaíso, Chile, 14, 127*fig.*
Vargas, Juan, 91, 94
Vasconcelos, José, 108
Velasco Alvarado, Juan, 138
venereal infections, 43–44, 45–46, 48, 160n27
verruga peruana, 74
Villanueva G., Augusto, 77
Vucetich, Juan, 118
Vucetich system, 118, 120

Wagner, Allan, 137
War of the Pacific: Battle of Angamos, 11; contemporary significance of, 141, 142;

gender and, 7; history of, 4–5, 6, 139–40; male-male sex and, 56, 57–58; nationalism and, 1–2, 82; Peruvian-Chilean relations and, 8; pillage of Mollendo during, 90; scholarship on, 2–3, 7; sex work and, 48; solidarities and, 110; transnational medical community and, 71–72, 84–85
West Coast Telephone company, 68
whiteness, 58
Wobblies. *See* Industrial Workers of the World (IWW)
women, 40, 42–43, 46–47, 91

wool exports, 92–93
workers: circulation and, 10–11, 17, 39; transnational labor organizing and, 87–88, 100–101
working-class identity, 41–42, 50–51, 53
working conditions: maritime workers and, 30–31, 32–34, 35–36; strikes and, 90, 95–96, 103
workplace injuries, 33–34
World War I, 92–93
W. R. Grace & Co., 88, 123, 193n60

yellow fever, 62, 69, 75, 168n25

Founded in 1893,
UNIVERSITY OF CALIFORNIA PRESS
publishes bold, progressive books and journals
on topics in the arts, humanities, social sciences,
and natural sciences—with a focus on social
justice issues—that inspire thought and action
among readers worldwide.

The UC PRESS FOUNDATION
raises funds to uphold the press's vital role
as an independent, nonprofit publisher, and
receives philanthropic support from a wide
range of individuals and institutions—and from
committed readers like you. To learn more, visit
ucpress.edu/supportus.